FROMMER'S
EasyGuide
To
IRELAND

By
Jack Jewers

Easy Guides are ✦ Quick To Read ✦ Light To Carry
✦ For Expert Advice ✦ In All Price Ranges

FrommerMedia LLC

Published by
FROMMER MEDIA LLC

Copyright © 2015 by Frommer Media LLC. All rights reserved. No part of this publication may be repro-
duced, stored in a retrieval system, or transmitted in any form or by any means, electronic, mechanical,
photocopying, recording, scanning, or otherwise, except as permitted under Sections 107 or 108 of the
1976 United States Copyright Act, without the prior written permission of the Publisher. Requests to the
Publisher for permission should be addressed to support@frommermedia.com.

Frommer's is a registered trademark of Arthur Frommer. Frommer Media LLC is not associated with
any product or vendor mentioned in this book.

ISBN 978-1-62887-106-7 (paper), 978-1-62887-107-4 (e-book)

Editorial Director: Pauline Frommer
Production Editor: Lynn Northrup
Cartographer: Roberta Stockwell
Indexer: Maro Riofrancos
Front cover photo: Kylemore Abbey, Ireland © NCG

For information on our other products or services, see www.frommers.com.

Frommer Media LLC also publishes its books in a variety of electronic formats. Some content that
appears in print may not be available in electronic formats.

Manufactured in the United States of America

5 4 3 2 1

AN IMPORTANT NOTE

The world is a dynamic place. Hotels change ownership, restaurants hike their prices, museums
alter their opening hours, and busses and trains change their routings. And all of this can occur
in the several months after our authors have visited, inspected, and written about these hotels,
restaurants, museums, and transportation services. Though we have made valiant efforts to keep
all our information fresh and up-to-date, some few changes can inevitably occur in the periods
before a revised edition of this guidebook is published. So please bear with us if a tiny number
of the details in this book have changed. Please also note that we have no responsibility or liabil-
ity for any inaccuracy or errors or omissions, or for inconvenience, loss, damage, or expenses suffered by anyone as a result of assertions in this guide.

CONTENTS

ABOUT THE AUTHOR

Jack Jewers has written about Ireland for Frommer's since 2006. Born and raised in England, he loved listening to his great aunt's tales about life in Dublin during the civil war. Jack proposed to his Irish-American wife at a spa on the Ring of Kerry. It gets a great review in this book.

ABOUT THE FROMMER TRAVEL GUIDES

For most of the past 50 years, Frommer's has been the leading series of travel guides in North America, accounting for as many as 24% of all guidebooks sold. I think I know why.

Though we hope our books are entertaining, we nevertheless deal with travel in a serious fashion. Our guidebooks have never looked on such journeys as a mere recreation, but as a far more important human function, a time of learning and introspection, an essential part of a civilized life. We stress the culture, lifestyle, history, and beliefs of the destinations we cover, and urge our readers to seek out people and new ideas as the chief rewards of travel.

We have never shied from controversy. We have, from the beginning, encouraged our authors to be intensely judgmental, critical—both pro and con—in their comments, and wholly independent. Our only clients are our readers, and we have triggered the ire of countless prominent sorts, from a tourist newspaper we called "practically worthless" (it unsuccessfully sued us) to the many rip-offs we've condemned.

And because we believe that travel should be available to everyone regardless of their incomes, we have always been cost-conscious at every level of expenditure. Though we have broadened our recommendations beyond the budget category, we insist that every lodging we include be sensibly priced. We use every form of media to assist our readers, and are particularly proud of our feisty daily website, the award-winning Frommers.com.

I have high hopes for the future of Frommer's. May these guidebooks, in all the years ahead, continue to reflect the joy of travel and the freedom that travel represents. May they always pursue a cost-conscious path, so that people of all incomes can enjoy the rewards of travel. And may they create, for both the traveler and the persons among whom we travel, a community of friends, where all human beings live in harmony and peace.

Arthur Frommer

THE BEST OF IRELAND

Tiny, and with ever-changing scenery, Ireland is an addictive place to explore. Within a few miles you can travel from plunging cliffs and flat pastureland to towering mountains and gloomy peat bogs. You can spend the night in ancient castles or state-of-the-art spa hotels, dine on fine Irish cuisine or snack on crispy fish and chips served in a paper bag. The sheer number of sights, little villages, charming pubs, and adorable restaurants and shops is overwhelming—you always feel that you might be missing something. So it's nice to have somebody to help you focus, and that's why we've put together this list of some of our favorite places and things to do in Ireland. We hope that while you're exploring this magical country, you'll find a few of your own.

THE best AUTHENTIC EXPERIENCES

o **Seeing a traditional music session at a proper Irish pub:** It's not hard to track down live music in Irish pubs, and while there are plenty of shows for the tourist crowd, nothing beats the energy, atmosphere, and authenticity of a genuine small-town traditional music session. We've listed some of the best places in this book, including pubs such as the Long Valley in Cork or Gus O'Connor's and McGann's in little Doolin, County Clare. The instructions for getting the most out of a session are simple: Buy a pint, grab a seat (preferably one near a smoldering peat fire), and wait for the action to begin. See p. 161.

o **Getting lost down the back roads of County Kerry:** This is Ireland's most visited county by far, and it's impossible to escape the tourist throngs in the summer, especially if you stick to the beaten path. When it all gets too much, you can just veer off onto the winding back roads and allow yourself to get gloriously, hopelessly lost. Forget the clock and embrace a sense of fatalism. There are always new discoveries to be made down its breathtaking byways. See chapter 7.

o **Touching the bullet holes in the walls of the General Post Office** (Dublin, County Dublin): It's hard to overstate what a potent national symbol this humble mail hub is. Patrick Pearse read his independence proclamation from its front steps in 1916, and the original document is now displayed inside. The post office was also the scene of fierce fighting during the civil war of 1922, which left the bullet scars that pock the facade. See p. 75.

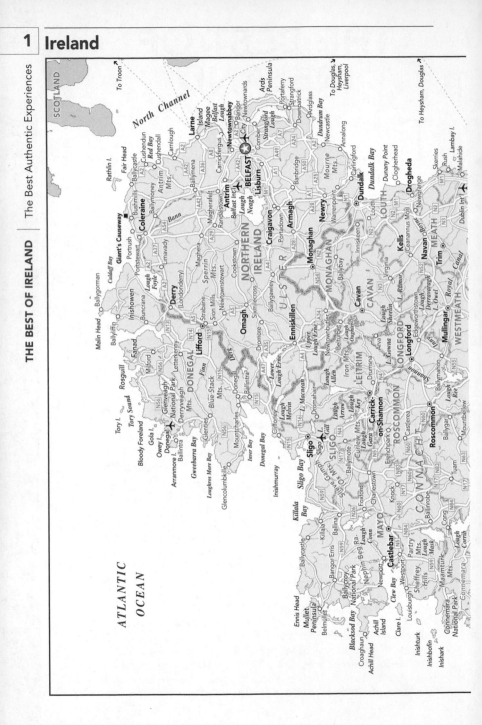

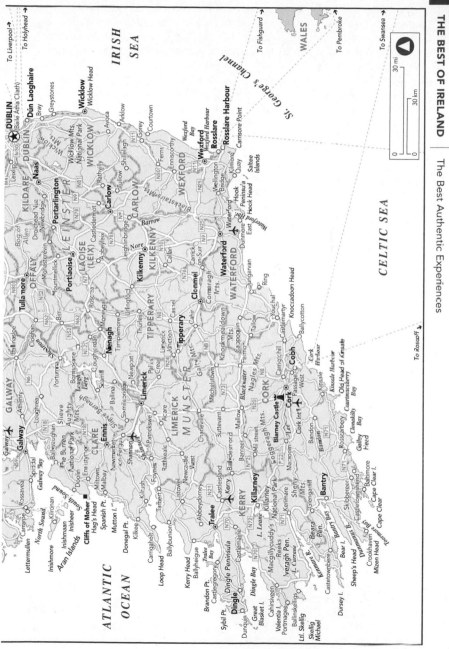

ATLANTIC OCEAN

IRISH SEA

CELTIC SEA

St. George's Channel

WALES

To Liverpool→
To Holyhead→
To Fishguard→
To Pembroke→
To Swansea→
To Rosscoff→

DUBLIN (Baile Átha Cliath)
Dún Laoghaire
Wicklow
Wicklow Head

KILDARE
WICKLOW
LEINSTER
OFFALY
LAOISE (LEIX)
CARLOW
KILKENNY
WEXFORD
TIPPERARY
WATERFORD
LIMERICK
MUNSTER
CLARE
GALWAY
KERRY
CORK

Galway
Ennis
Limerick
Tralee
Killarney
Bantry
Cork
Cobh
Clonmel
Waterford
Wexford
Rosslare
Rosslare Harbour
Carlow
Portlaoise
Portarlington
Naas
Nenagh
Tullamore

Cliffs of Moher
Aran Islands
Dingle Peninsula
Macgillycuddy's Reeks
Iveragh Pen.
Beara Pen.
Blarney Castle

30 mi
30 km

- **Poking around the shops in Temple Bar** (Dublin, County Dublin): Modern Dublin is a cosmopolitan place, and nowhere is this more so than its trendiest neighborhood, Temple Bar. The name actually has a rather obscure, 17th-century origin, although it's curiously appropriate today given the preponderance of hip watering holes full of beautiful, style-worshipping young things. There's always something to discover here during the day too; seemingly around every corner is another trendy boutique, funky store, or art gallery to discover. See p. 72.

- **Checking out what's new in Kinsale's restaurant scene** (County Cork): Kinsale has gone from sleepy fishing port to the food capital of Ireland. On every return trip there's almost inevitably a hot new, must-try place to sample. They don't all last forever, but those that do are in themselves worth the trip to County Cork. See chapter 6.

- **Driving through the Burren** (County Clare): Ireland is full of memorable landscapes, but none of them quite as unique as this one. The countryside has a haunting, alien feel, although it's strikingly beautiful, too, especially as the sun goes down and the craggy limestone planes turn an evening shade of red. See chapter 8.

- **Taking afternoon tea at the Shelbourne Hotel** (Dublin, County Dublin): It's easy to feel like an overgrown kid in the fanciest candy store at the Shelbourne as you sink into a huge leather armchair while demolishing a tower of cakes and daintily cut sandwiches. If you're in the mood for a history fix afterward, sneak upstairs to find room no. 112. This is where the Irish Constitution was written in 1922. If nobody's staying there—and the concierge is in a good mood—you might even get to look inside. See p. 53.

- **Photographing the murals in Belfast and Derry** (County Antrim/County Derry, Northern Ireland): Half a generation has grown up in Northern Ireland without knowing full-on sectarian bloodshed firsthand. Yet the long, ugly "peace wall" dividing Catholic neighborhoods from near-identical Protestant streets in Belfast is still covered in political street art, much of it preaching nonviolence. Likewise, the so-called "People's Gallery" in Derry will guarantee some of the most striking photos of your trip. See chapter 12.

- **Walking the path down to the Giant's Causeway** (County Antrim): It's like hiking through a fantasy landscape to take the half-mile walk down to this extraordinary natural wonder—37,000 columns of basalt sitting at the base of cliffs along the Antrim Coast. Geologists claim these mystical rocks were formed millions of years ago by cooling volcanoes. But don't you prefer to believe they were really made by giants, as the ancient belief would hold? See chapter 12, p. 224.

THE best HOTELS

- **Monart Spa** (Enniscorthy, County Wexford): A sumptuous countryside retreat, this pampering paradise is consistently rated among the top spas in Ireland. It's a serene, adults-only zone located in a beautiful setting. See p. 93.

- **Lawcus Farm Guesthouse** (Stonyford, County Kilkenny): You can help out with feeding the animals at this idyllic B&B in Kilkenny before relaxing in the beautifully converted farmhouse. See p. 91.

- **Aghadoe Heights** (Killarney, County Kerry): Another of Ireland's top spas, this one overlooks the Lakes of Killarney from a high vantage point just north of the town. See p. 126.

- **Ashford Castle** (Cong, County Mayo): Live like royalty for a night at this fairytale castle in County Mayo. The great and the good have been coming here for decades to see what the fuss is about. The fuss, it turns out, is justified. See p. 178.

- **Temple House** (Ballymote, County Sligo): Proving that not all the best overnight stays are to be found in luxury hotels, Temple House is an historic countryside B&B that feels like it's in a world of its own. See p. 180.

- **The Bervie** (Keel, County Mayo): Overlooking the Atlantic Ocean on an island off the Mayo coast, the Bervie is a haven of magnificent views and gourmet food. See p. 179.

- **Two Rooms in Dublin** (County Dublin): This exceptionally welcoming townhouse B&B in Dublin has just two rooms, but try as hard as you can to get one. You'll feel better taken care of here than in many of the capital's most upscale hotels. See p. 53.

- **Dolphin Beach House** (Clifden, County Galway): This incredibly special B&B on the Galway coast is a converted, early-20th-century homestead. It adds up to amazing views, gorgeous food, and gregarious hosts. See p. 165.

- **Gregan's Castle Hotel** (Ballyvaughn, County Clare): J. R. R. Tolkein took inspiration for *The Lord of the Rings* while staying at this elegant country house surrounded by the lunar landscape of Burren. See p. 152.

- **Rathmullan House** (Rathmullan, County Donegal): Remote and windswept, County Donegal attracts a fraction of the visitors of Dublin or Kerry. That's good news for those that make the journey to enjoy a night at this incredible 18th-century mansion. See p. 194.

- **Dunnanelly Country House** (Downpatrick, County Down, Northern Ireland): A Regency mansion surrounded by 80 rolling acres of countryside, Dunnanelly is a captivating hideaway just 18 miles away from Belfast. See p. 207.

- **The Merchant Hotel** (Belfast, Northern Ireland): Once a Victorian bank, this trendy hotel in Belfast has been utterly transformed into one of Ireland's most handsome city retreats. See p. 209.

THE best RESTAURANTS

- **Chapter One** (Dublin, County Dublin): In the vaulted basement of the Dublin Writers Museum, this is one of the capital's very best restaurants. It's quite a splurge, but come at lunchtime to experience the same wonderful food at almost half the price. See p. 61.

- **Sabor Brazil** (Dublin, County Dublin): We've deliberately kept the restaurant choices for this book focused on unique, local Irish experiences. But this tiny place in Dublin makes the cut, because where else would you find such an extraordinary fusion of Brazilian and Irish flavors? See p. 63.

- **Gallagher's Boxty House** (Dublin, County Dublin): Think again if you assume that the best meals always require the deepest pockets. A local man who wanted to preserve the culinary traditions of his childhood started this hugely popular restaurant in Dublin's Temple Bar. The result is captivating. See p. 57.

- **Fishy Fishy Café** (Kinsale, County Cork): Kinsale is Ireland's unofficial gourmet capital, and the delightful Fishy Fishy is among its best restaurants. The seafood is so local that the menu tells you who caught it—and we're talking dish by dish, name by name. See p. 112.

o **Crackpots** (Kinsale, County Cork): Another Kinsale favorite, Crackpots is a charming combination of designer pottery shop and outstandingly good restaurant. It's one of the very best places to eat in a town where the competition is stiff. See p. 111.

o **Aniar** (Galway, County Galway): Galway City's most sought-after table has a tiny but impeccably judged menu of innovative, modern Irish cuisine. Aniar is one of just a handful of Michelin-starred restaurants in Ireland. See p. 166.

o **The Lodge at Ashford Castle** (Cong, County Mayo): On the grounds of Ashford Castle, this wonderful restaurant has a superlative view over the glassy waters of Lough Corrib. See p. 181.

o **Richmond House** (Cappoquin, County Waterford): One of the real destination restaurants of the southeast, the Richmond House is a converted 18th-century mansion. They serve exquisite, seasonal meals, and many of the ingredients come from their own garden. See p. 94.

o **The Lime Tree** (Kenmare, County Kerry): This has long been one of the most respected restaurants in County Kerry, and with good reason—the sophisticated modern Irish menu, full of local flavors, is impressive but still surprisingly affordable. See p. 133.

o **Doyle's Seafood Bar** (Dingle, County Kerry): Dingle isn't short of places offering super-fresh, local seafood, and it's hard to pick between them, but this is probably the best. What you find on the menu will depend on the catch of the day, and it's all impeccably done. See p. 134.

o **Deane's Seafood Bar** (Belfast, County Antrim, Northern Ireland): The flagship restaurant in Belfast, Chef Michael Deane's eponymous mini-chain, Deane's, serves outstanding Irish-French cuisine. The attached seafood bar is just as good—and much cheaper. See p. 211.

THE best PICTURE-POSTCARD TOWNS

o **Dalkey** (County Dublin): The cutest of a string of upscale seaside towns in suburban Dublin, this spot is nicknamed "Bel Eire" (pronounced "Bellaire," get it?) for its wealth, beauty, and density of celebrity residents. Dalkey is both a short drive and a million miles away from the busy city. With a castle, a mountaintop folly, lovely beaches, and some fine restaurants, this is a town that tempts you to settle into its comfortable affluence. See chapter 4.

o **Kinsale** (County Cork): Kinsale's narrow streets all lead to the sea, dropping steeply from the hills around the harbor, although the crowds of visitors teeming on the sidewalks every summer attest to the fact that the Kinsale secret is out. The walk from Kinsale through Scilly to Charles Fort and Frower Point is breathtaking. Kinsale has the added benefit of being a foodie town, and there's no shortage of good restaurants. See chapter 6.

o **Kenmare** (County Kerry): It's easy to fall in love with Kenmare, with its stone cottages, colorful gardens, and flowers overflowing from window boxes. It's also home to several elegant hotels, so it makes an enchanting base when exploring the Ring of Kerry. See chapter 7.

o **Dingle/An Daingean** (County Kerry): Dingle is a charming hilltop medieval town. Stone buildings ramble up and down hills, and the small population is relaxed about visitors. It has lots of little diners and picturesque pubs, plus a lovely, historic church. See chapter 7.

o **Ardara** (County Donegal): On the southwest coast of County Donegal, the tiny town of Ardara looks as if it were carved out of a solid block of granite. Its streets undulate up and down the rocky hills and are lined with little boutiques and charming arts shops, many selling clothes made of the famed Donegal wool. You can wander its entirety in a few minutes. It's a bite-sized place. See chapter 11.

THE best NATURAL WONDERS

o **MacGillycuddy's Reeks** (County Kerry): A mountain range on the Iveragh Peninsula, MacGillycuddy's Reeks not only has the best name of any mountain range in Ireland, it also has the highest mountain on the island, Carrantuohill (1,041m/3,414 ft.). The Reeks are among Ireland's greatest spectacles. See p. 138.

o **The Burren** (County Clare): We can guarantee this: The Burren is one of the strangest landscapes you're likely to see anywhere in the world. Its vast limestone grassland is spread with a quilt of wildflowers from as far afield as the Alps, all softening the stark stones jutting out of the ground. Its inhabitants include nearly every species of butterfly found in Ireland. See p. 160.

o **Cliffs of Moher** (County Clare): Rising from Hag's Head to the south, these magnificent sea cliffs reach their full height of 214m (702 ft.) just north of O'Brien's Tower. The views of the open sea, of the Aran Islands, and of the Twelve Bens mountains of Connemara (see below) are spectacular. A walk south along the cliff edge at sunset makes a perfect end to any day. See p. 160.

o **The Twelve Bens** (County Galway): Amid Connemara's central mountains, bogs, and lakes, the rugged Twelve Bens range crowns a spectacular landscape. Some of the peaks are bare and rocky, others clothed in peat. The loftiest, Benbaun in Connemara National Park, reaches a height of 729m (2,392 ft.). See p. 175.

o **Slieve League** (County Donegal): The Slieve League peninsula stretches for 48km (30 miles) into the Atlantic. Its pigmented bluffs rise to startlingly high sea cliffs. They can also be walked along, if you dare. See p. 198.

o **Giant's Causeway** (County Antrim): At the foot of a cliff by the sea, this mysterious mass of tightly packed, naturally occurring hexagonal basalt columns is nothing short of astonishing. This volcanic wonder, formed 60 million years ago, looks marvelous from above, and even better when negotiated (cautiously) on foot. See p. 224.

THE best CASTLES

o **Kilkenny Castle** (County Kilkenny): Although parts of the castle date from the 13th century, the existing structure has the feel of an 18th-century palace. There have been many modifications since medieval times, including the addition of colorful landscaping, and the old stables now hold numerous art galleries and shops. See p. 102.

o **Blarney Castle** (County Cork): Despite the mobs of tourists who besiege it daily, this majestic tower house is worth a visit. While you're there, check out the Badger Cave and dungeons at the tower's base, as well as the serpentine paths that wind through the castle gardens. Need we mention the Blarney Stone? You sidle in under the upper wall with your head hanging over a 10-story drop. You kiss it. It's a thing people do. See p. 118.

o **Bunratty Castle and Folk Park** (County Clare): This grand old castle has been well restored and filled with a curious assortment of medieval furnishings, offering a glimpse into the life of its past inhabitants. This is the first stop for many arrivals from Shannon, so expect crowds. See p. 158.

o **Carrickfergus Castle** (County Antrim): This well-preserved Norman fortress on the bank of Belfast Lough is huge and impressive, complete with an imposing tower house and a high wall punctuated by corner towers. See p. 219.

o **Dunluce Castle** (County Antrim): These castle ruins surmount a razor-sharp promontory jutting into the sea. This was a highly defensible setting, and the castle wasn't abandoned until a large section collapsed and fell into the breakers. See p. 224.

THE best PREHISTORIC SITES

o **Hill of Tara** (County Meath): Of ritual significance from the Stone Age to the early Christian period, Tara has seen it all and kept it a secret. This was the traditional center and seat of Ireland's high kings. Although the hill is only 154m (512 ft.) above sea level, from here you can see each of Ireland's four Celtic provinces on a clear day. The site is mostly unexcavated and tells its story in whispers. It's a place to be walked slowly. See p. 86.

o **Newgrange** (County Meath): One of the archaeological wonders of Western Europe, Newgrange is the centerpiece of a megalithic cemetery dating back 5,000 years—that's older than the Egyptian pyramids or Stonehenge. Walking down the long, atmospheric central tunnel, trying to visualize just how many generations have passed since it was built, is mind-blowing. A bit of perspective: The dawn of the Roman Empire is closer in time to us today than the building of Newgrange was to the dawn of the Roman Empire. But the question remains: What was it all for? See p. 87.

o **Knowth** (County Meath): Another great passage tomb, Knowth's awesome presence is matched only by its inscrutability. Hundreds of prehistoric carvings were discovered here when the site was first excavated, in the 1960s. And yet, nobody seems to quite understand it to this day. See p. 86.

o **Dún Aengus** (County Galway): No one knows who built this massive stone fort or what year it was constructed. The eminent archaeologist George Petrie called Dún Aengus "the most magnificent barbaric monument in Europe." Facing the sea, where its three stone rings meet steep 90m (295-ft.) cliffs, Dún Aengus still stands guard today over the southern coast of the island of Inishmore, the largest of the Aran Islands. See p. 170.

o **Carrowmore and Carrowkeel** (County Sligo): These two megalithic cities of the dead (Europe's largest) may have once contained more than 200 passage tombs. The two together—one in the valley and the other atop a nearby mountain—convey an unequaled sense of the scale and wonder of the ancient peoples' reverence for the dead. Carrowmore is well presented and interpreted, while Carrowkeel is left to itself for those who seek it out. See p. 187.

THE best EARLY CHRISTIAN RUINS

o **Glendalough** (County Wicklow): Nestled in "the glen of the two lakes," this atmospheric monastic settlement was founded in the 6th century by St. Kevin, who was looking for seclusion and certainly found it here. The setting is endlessly scenic with lakes and forests surrounding it. Although quite remote, Glendalough suffered assaults from the Vikings and English forces and eventually faded away. Today its stone ruins collude with the countryside to create one of the loveliest spots in Ireland. See p. 98.

o **The Rock of Cashel** (County Tipperary): In name and appearance, "the Rock" suggests a citadel, a place designed more for power than prayer. In fact, Cashel (or *Caiseal*) means "fortress." The rock is a huge outcropping—or an *up*cropping—of limestone topped with spectacularly beautiful ruins, including what was formerly the country's finest Romanesque chapel. This was the seat of clerics and kings, a power center to rival Tara. Now, however, the two sites vie only for the attention of tourists. See p. 219.

o **Jerpoint Abbey** (County Kilkenny): Jerpoint is the finest representative of the many Cistercian abbeys whose ruins dot the Irish landscape. Somehow, hundreds of years of rain and wind have failed to completely wipe away medieval carvings, leaving us a rare chance for a glimpse of how magnificent these abbeys once were. The splendid, richly carved cloister is the best place to spot the engravings, particularly at the top of the columns. See p. 101.

o **Skellig Michael** (County Kerry): Thirteen kilometers (8 miles) offshore of the Iveragh Peninsula, rising sharply 214m (702 ft.) out of the Atlantic, this is a remote, rocky crag dedicated to the archangel Michael. In flight from the world, early Irish monks in pursuit of "white martyrdom" (meaning martyrdom without bloodshed) chose this spot to build their austere hermitage. Today the journey to Skellig across choppy seas, and the arduous climb to its summit, are challenging and unforgettable. See p. 144.

o **Inishmurray** (County Sligo): This uninhabited island off the Sligo coast holds another striking monastic ruin, this one surrounded by what appears to be the walls of an even more ancient stone fort. Despite its remoteness, the Vikings sought out this outpost of peace-seeking monks for destruction in A.D. 807. Today its circular walls and the surrounding sea create a stunning view, well worth the effort required to reach it. See chapter 10.

THE best LITERARY SPOTS

o **Dublin Writers Museum** (Dublin, County Dublin): Filled with letters, personal possessions, and other eclectic ephemera, this great museum in Dublin is a pilgrimage for lovers of Irish literature. Bibliophiles of all kinds will learn more about Ireland's masters of the printed word than they ever imagined while basking in their collective glow. See p. 68.

o **Davy Byrnes Pub** (Dublin, County Dublin): This place crops up in *Ulysses* when the hero, Leopold Bloom, famously orders a lunch of burgundy and a Gorgonzola sandwich here. The pub is acutely aware of its heritage, but happily knows better than to ruin the appeal by being too touristy. See p. 83.

o **St. Patrick's Cathedral** (Dublin, County Dublin): Jonathan Swift tickled and horrified the world with his vicious wit. He shook up political establishments with his sarcasm and nauseated the English-speaking world with his suggestion that people should dine on Irish babies. While kicking up such a stir, he was dean of St. Patrick's Cathedral, which sponsored and supported him through it all. He is buried here alongside his longtime companion, Stella Johnson. See p. 72.

o **County Sligo:** With its many connections to the beloved poet W. B. Yeats, this county is a pilgrimage destination for true fans. The poet's writing was shaped by the landscape, and many of the monuments—Lough Gill, Glencar Lake, Ben Bulben Mountain, and Maeve's tomb—appear in his words. There are also several museums housing first editions, photographs, and other memorabilia, and Yeats's dark and somber grave is in Drumcliff. See chapter 10.

THE best FAMILY ACTIVITIES

o **Dublin Zoo in the Phoenix Park** (Dublin): Kids love this sympathetically designed zoo featuring wild creatures, animal-petting corners, and a train ride. The surrounding park has room to run, picnic, and explore. See p. 74.

o **Irish National Heritage Park** (County Wexford): Millennia of history are made painlessly educational for children and adults at this engaging "living history" museum. It's a fascinating, informative way to while away a couple of hours or more. See p. 100.

o **Fota Island & Wildlife Park** (County Cork): In this wildlife park, rare and endangered animals roam freely. You'll see everything from giraffes and zebras to kangaroos, flamingos, penguins, and monkeys wandering the grassland. Add in a small amusement park for toddlers, a tour train, picnic tables, and a gift shop, and you have the makings of a wonderful family outing. See p. 121.

o **Muckross House & Gardens** (Killarney, County Kerry): This impressive mansion acts as the gateway to Killarney National Park today, but the interior has been preserved in all its Victorian splendor. Nearby, people on the Muckross Historic Farms engage in traditional farm activities while dressed in authentic period clothes. See p. 139.

o **Dingle Dolphin Boat Tours** (Dingle, County Kerry): Every day, fishing boats ferry visitors out into the nearby waters to see Fungie, the friendliest dolphin you're ever likely to meet. Fungie swims right up to the boat, and the boatmen stay out long enough for ample sightings. You can also arrange an early-morning dolphin swim. See p. 146.

o **The Giant's Causeway** (County Antrim): About as alien-looking as natural wonders come, the seemingly endless basalt pillars of the Giant's Causeway are like a super-size jungle gym. Little ones will have their imaginations run riot as they try to figure out just how this incredible landscape came to look this way. See p. 224.

o **Bunratty Castle and Folk Park** (County Clare): Kids love Bunratty, which looks every bit as satisfyingly medieval as an old castle should. The grounds have been turned over to a replica 19th-century village—complete with actors playing Victorian residents going about their daily lives. It's great fun to walk through. See p. 158.

THE best DRIVING TOURS

o **Antrim Coast:** The Antrim Coast is 97km (60 miles) long, stretching north of Larne and west past Bushmills and the Giant's Causeway to Portrush. If you start in gorgeous Glenarm with its castle walls and barbican gate, then head north along the coast from there, the route takes in sweeping views of midnight-blue sea against gray unforgiving cliffs and deep green hillsides. You often have the road mostly to yourself. See chapter 12.

o **Slea Head Drive** (Dingle Peninsula): This drive, starting from Dingle Town and heading down the Ventry road, follows the sea past a series of ancient ruins such as the Dunbeg Fort. Taking in deep blue ocean views along the way, it brings you to Dunquin, where you can embark on boats to the Blasket Islands, famous for their ancient remains. From there you continue on to Gallarus Oratory and then back to Dingle Town. See chapter 7.

o **Inishowen Peninsula** (County Donegal): This far-flung promontory in the northern outreaches of Ireland stretches out from Lough Foyle to the east and Lough Swilly to the west toward Malin Head, its farthest point. Around the edges are ancient sites, charming villages, and beautiful beaches surrounded by intimidating rocky coves attacked by crashing waves. At its center are gorgeous views, mountains, and quiet, vivid green pastures. If you are looking to get lost, this is a great place to do it. See chapter 11.

o **The Ring of Kerry** (County Kerry): It's by far the most well-travelled of Ireland's great routes, but there's no denying the Ring of Kerry's appeal—it's a seductive combination of beautiful countryside, gorgeous villages, and enticing historical sites. The road gets quite busy in summer, but come in the spring or autumn, and it's a much more peaceful experience. See chapter 7.

SUGGESTED ITINERARIES

reland is such a small island that you can cover a lot of ground in a week and feel quite at home within two. But even with the best of intentions and all the energy in the world, you'll never see it all on a short visit. However, with a few long days and a savvy attitude, it is possible to see a sizable chunk of the island in just a week. The suggested itineraries over the next few pages will help you get the most out of this extraordinary and varied country—no matter how long you have to see it.

If you've only got a week to spend here, the southern regions probably have more to offer. They're generally easier to get around, and the major sights are somewhat closer together. If you're travelling with kids, Dublin and County Kerry have particularly rich pickings when it comes to kid-friendly attractions. However, those in search of the road less travelled will be drawn northwards, especially to places such as Mayo, Sligo, and the wilds of Donegal beyond.

THE REGIONS IN BRIEF

The island of Ireland is divided into two political units: the **Republic of Ireland,** which makes up the vast majority of the country, and **Northern Ireland,** which along with England, Scotland, and Wales is part of the United Kingdom. Of Ireland's 32 counties, all but 6 are in the Republic.

The ancient Gaelic regions that once divided Ireland are still used in conversation and directions: Ulster is north, Munster is south, Leinster is east, and Connaught is west. Each region is divided into counties:

○ **In Ulster** (to the north): Cavan, Donegal, and Monaghan in the Republic; Antrim, Armagh, Derry, Down, Fermanagh, and Tyrone in Northern Ireland.

○ **In Munster** (to the south): Clare, Cork, Kerry, Limerick, Tipperary, and Waterford.

○ **In Leinster** (to the east): Dublin, Carlow, Kildare, Kilkenny, Laois, Longford, Louth, Meath, Offaly, Westmeath, Wexford, and Wicklow.

○ **In Connaught** (to the west): Sligo, Mayo, Galway, Roscommon, and Leitrim.

DUBLIN & ENVIRONS With 40 percent of the Republic's population living within 97km (60 miles) of Dublin, the capital is the center of the profound, high-speed changes that have transformed Ireland into a prosperous and increasingly European country. Within an hour's drive of Dublin are Dalkey, Dún Laoghaire, and many more engaging coastal towns, as well as the rural beauty of the Wicklow Mountains and the prehistoric ruins in County Meath.

THE SOUTHEAST The southeast offers sandy beaches, Wexford's lush and mountainous countryside, Waterford's famous Crystal Factory, Kilkenny and Cahir's ancient castles, the Rock of Cashel, and the Irish National Heritage Park at Ferrycarrig.

CORK & ENVIRONS Cork, Ireland's second-largest city, feels like a buzzy university town and provides a congenial gateway to the south and west of the island. Within arm's reach are Blarney Castle (and its famous stone), the culinary and scenic delights of Kinsale, the Dromberg Stone Circle, Cape Clear Island, and Mizen Head. Also in this region is the dazzling landscape of West Cork.

THE SOUTHWEST The once remote splendor of County Kerry has long ceased to be a secret, so at least during the high season, be prepared to share the view in this gorgeous section. The Ring of Kerry (less glamorously known as hwys. N70 and N71) encircling the Iveragh Peninsula is the most visited attraction in Ireland after the Book of Kells. That's both a recommendation and a warning. Killarney National Park provides a stunning haven from buses. Killarney is surrounded by natural beauty but is filled with souvenir shops and tour groups. Marginally less visited highlights include the rugged Dingle Peninsula and two sets of islands with rich histories: the Skelligs and the Blaskets.

THE WEST The west of Ireland offers a first taste of Ireland's wild beauty and striking diversity for those who fly into Shannon Airport. County Limerick has an array of impressive castles: Knappogue, Bunratty, and (just over the county line in Galway) Dunguaire. County Clare's natural offerings—particularly the unique landscapes of the Burren—are unforgettable. Farther up the coast to the north, past Galway, County Mayo is the home of the sweet town of Westport on Clew Bay. Achill Island (accessible by car) has beaches and stunning cliff views.

GALWAY & ENVIRONS Galway Town is busy, colorful, and funky—a youthful, prospering port and university city and the self-proclaimed arts capital of Ireland with theater, music, dance, and an exciting street life. County Galway is the gateway to Connemara's moody, magical landscapes. Here are the Twelve Bens Mountains, Kylemore Abbey, and the charming seaside town of Clifden. Offshore lie the mysterious Aran Islands—Inishmore, Inishmaan, and Inisheer—with their irresistible desolation.

THE NORTHWEST In Ireland it's easy to become convinced that isolated austerity is beautiful, and nowhere is this more evident than Donegal, with its jagged, desolate coastline that, if you don't mind the cold, offers some fine surfing. Inland, Glenveagh National Park has as much wilderness as you could want. County Sligo inspired the poetry of W. B. Yeats with its dense collection of megalithic sites such as the stone circles, passage tombs, dolmens, and cairns at Carrowmore, Knocknarea, and Carrowkeel.

NORTHERN IRELAND Across the border, Northern Ireland's six counties are a decade-and-a-half into a period of intense change. Still one of the most underrated parts of Ireland, the stunning Antrim Coast (particularly Ballycastle and Cushendun), the extraordinary, octagonal basalt columns of the Giant's Causeway, and the Glens of Antrim are unforgettable. The old city walls of Derry, the past glory of Carrickfergus Castle, and Belfast's elaborate political murals make a trip across the border worthwhile.

HOW TO SEE IRELAND
To Drive or Not to Drive?

To get the most out of Ireland, you need to know at least in part what you want to see. You don't *have* to rent a car. However, if your ideal Ireland involves wandering through the countryside, visiting small villages, climbing castle walls, hailing history from a ruined abbey, or finding yourself alone on a rocky beach—you simply cannot do those things without one.

Out of the main towns, public transportation exists, but it's slow and limiting. Every major town has car-rental agencies, so give strong consideration to renting a car. (Just remember: They drive on the *left*.)

Be Smart Where You Start

The next step is deciding where to start. That decision can be made for you by where your flight terminates. If you're flying into Shannon Airport, then it makes good geographic sense to start out on the west coast. If you're flying into Dublin, you might as well explore that city first, then either head up to the North and the ruggedly beautiful Antrim Coast, or south down to the Wicklow Mountains, Kilkenny, and the rolling green hills of Wexford and Waterford.

Still, if you fly into Dublin but your heart is in Galway, no worries. You can traverse the width of the country in a few hours (once you get out of Dublin's stultifying sprawl), so if you start early enough, it's doable. Just bear in mind that rural roads are not well lighted or well signposted, so driving at night should be avoided. It's too stressful, and being lost in unfamiliar territory (where it can be many miles between villages) is no fun at all. This is more of an issue in the winter, when it can get dark as early as 4pm. During summer time, the driving is a little easier, as it often stays light until after 10pm.

So . . . Where to Go?

So taking all of these factors into consideration, the question remains: *Where do you want to go?* We can't answer that question for you, but we can give you some itineraries that we have used ourselves. They might help you focus on ways in which you can orchestrate your journey so that you can get the most out of it with the fewest scheduling worries—the last thing you want to do on vacation is to spend the whole time looking at your watch.

If you've never visited Ireland, Dublin is a great place to start, and the surrounding area holds plenty to keep you busy. If you have been here before, and Dublin and Galway are old hat, you might consider heading north through County Mayo, County Sligo, and on to the exotic wilds of Donegal and the Antrim Coast.

All of these tours (bar one) assume you have a week to see the country. Where there's potential for a longer trip, we've given some alternatives for an extended version. Pick and choose the parts that appeal to you, add in your own favorite shopping or scenic drives, and turn it all into a custom-made holiday for yourself.

THE BEST OF IRELAND IN 1 WEEK

There's something terribly romantic about flying into Dublin. The compact, laid-back city awaits a few miles down the road, packed with old-fashioned pubs, modern restaurants, and absorbing sights all laid out for walking. If you've never been here, a couple of days in Dublin make for a quick primer on Ireland. It's just enough time to do some shopping on **Grafton Street,** head up O'Connell Street to the **General Post Office,** and discover the Georgian beauty of **St. Stephen's Green** and **Merrion Square.** It's not nearly enough time, but you can give the surface of the city a good brush in a couple of days, and then head south to **Kilkenny** and **Wicklow,** on to **Waterford, Cork,** and **Kerry,** and up to **Clare** for a quick glance before the clock runs out. It is only hitting the high points but, as high points go, they're hard to beat.

Days 1 & 2: Arrive in Dublin

If it happens that you're arriving from North America, you start with an advantage: Most flights arrive early in the morning, which effectively gives you an extra day's sightseeing. Check into your hotel, say yes to any tea and scones offered, take a minute to relax, and then head out on foot. Get a map from your concierge and then just start walking.

Stay south of the River Liffey and head down Dame Street to **Dublin Castle** (p. 68), home of the magical **Chester Beatty Library** (p. 65) with its vast collection of gorgeous illuminated manuscripts. Later, take in **St. Patrick's Cathedral** (p. 72) and the vibrant green quadrangles of **Trinity College** (p. 72), before heading down to Merrion Square, with its impressive granite architecture and two of the main sites of Ireland's **National Museum** (the third is on the west side of the city; the final one is in County Mayo—see p. 184). **Archaeology** has an extraordinary hoard of ancient gold, while the recently refurbished **Natural History** building contains an array of objects from the ancient past. It's a short stroll from here down to **St. Stephen's Green.** Rest your weary toes and soak up the floral view here, before strolling up **Grafton Street** for a last bit of shopping before collapsing in your hotel.

On **Day 2,** have a hearty breakfast in your hotel before striking out for the trendy cultural hub of **Temple Bar.** Stroll down Parliament Street to the river, then take a right, and walk along the noisy, vibrant waterfront to the effervescent arc of the **Ha'penny Bridge.** Head across and down to O'Connell Street and walk on up past its many statues to the bullet-ridden columns of the **General Post Office** (p. 75). This is where the 1916 Easter Rising was based. After exploring its displays, head farther up O'Connell Street to the **Dublin Writers Museum** (p. 68), which bookish types love for its extensive display of memorabilia. Let someone else do the work in the evening, either on a walking tour—such as the **Irish Music Pub Crawl,** perhaps (p. 75)—or some good-natured scares aboard the **Dublin Ghost Bus** (p. 79). However, those in search of something a little less like organized fun will fall in love with the simple, atmospheric pleasure of **An Evening of Food, Folklore and Fairies** (p. 84).

Day 3: South to Wicklow & Kilkenny

It takes less than 2 hours to drive from the hustle and traffic of Dublin to the peace and quiet of the **Wicklow Mountains.** Drive through the town of Enniskerry to the great estate of **Powerscourt** (p. 87) on the south end of the village. After lunching in its Avoca Café, head on to **Glendalough** (p. 98) and feel your soul relax in the pastoral mountain setting of this ancient monastic retreat. From there drive on to the colorful village of **Kilkenny** where you can spend the rest of the day shopping in its pottery and crafts shops and exploring noble **Kilkenny Castle** (p. 102). This is a good place to spend your first night outside of Dublin.

Day 4: West to Waterford & Cork

Waterford, Ireland's oldest city, is less than an hour south of Kilkenny, so you'll be able to get there with plenty of time to fit in a half day's sightseeing. Have a quick look around some or all of the **Waterford Treasures** museums (p. 96), before dropping in for a tour of the **House of Waterford Crystal.** After lunch, you have a choice—either head to **Cork,** Ireland's busy second city, or **Kinsale,** a smaller, quieter harbor town (see chapter 6). Both have plenty to keep you busy for the rest of the day and make a good base for the night. But they're very different places, so it depends if you want a bustling or peaceful experience.

Days 5 & 6: The Ring of Kerry

If you're not allergic to touristy things, you could stop at **Blarney Castle** (p. 118) on your way out of Cork in the morning; otherwise, on to County Kerry at the southwest tip of the island. Here the most popular place to explore—and one of the busiest tourist spots in Ireland—is the **Ring of Kerry** (see "The Ring of Kerry" in chapter 7). It is a beautiful drive, but because of the frequency of tourist buses, not everybody will want to make it. Others will brave the masses to see extraordinary countryside filled with historic sites and tiny villages. If you have the stamina, the entire Ring is doable at a reasonable pace over 2 days, although you'd have to skip pretty much everything else around it to make that goal.

If it's quiet you're after, you could instead take the short section of the Ring that runs from lovely **Kenmare** (see chapter 8) to the bucolic peace of **Killarney National Park** (p. 137). Here you can indulge in a buggy ride around the lake and leave only your footsteps.

Day 7: County Clare

Time is short now, so you won't be able to see as much of Clare as it deserves. But make a promise to yourself to come back someday and head for the perilously tall **Cliffs of Moher** (p. 160) where the view seems to stretch all the way to America (although the price to park will make you shiver). Then you've another choice: Spend the rest of the day exploring **Bunratty Castle** (p. 158)—where medieval fortress meets historical theme park—or marveling at the other-worldly landscape of the **Burren** (see chapter 8). If it's the latter, strike out for the R480 road that offers the best immediate gratification, as it winds its way through the extraordinary limestone landscape. What a way to end your trip!

THE BEST OF IRELAND IN 2 WEEKS

With 2 weeks, your visit to Ireland will be much more relaxed. You can stretch out a bit more in your travels, heading to less crowded counties with more time to meet the locals. In your second week, head up to Galway, Mayo, and Donegal, taking time to smell the heather along the way.

Days 1 through 7

Follow "The Best of Ireland in 1 Week" itinerary, as outlined above.

Day 8

After spending Day 7 exploring Clare, you'll discover that you need more time to really get the most out of this big, varied place. If you didn't make it to the Burren, spend most of your day here. Otherwise, you could visit another of the county's great medieval buildings such as **Knappogue Castle** (p. 161) or the exquisite ruins of **Corcomroe Abbey** (p. 161). In a different vein, lovers of live music will want to spend the evening in **Doolin** (p. 161). It's one of the very best places in the country to catch proper, traditional music.

Days 9 & 10: County Galway

Start the day with a drive up from Clare to Galway City (it will take around an hour). You could spend a relaxing day walking the delightful streets of this artsy, vibrant town, take a cruise out to the misty **Aran Islands** (see "The Aran Islands" in chapter 9), or, if you've got kids to keep amused, take them to the fabulous **Galway Atlantaquaria** (p. 171). Use the following day to explore **Connemara National Park** (p. 175). If it's time to get out from behind the wheel, you can see this lovely park by horseback (see chapter 9). You could either head back to Galway City for a second night or pick a B&B in the countryside.

Day 11: County Mayo

Driving up from Galway, the scenery is also spectacular in Mayo. Here the rocky shoreline plunges into the cobalt sea in glorious fashion. Head to the south Mayo town of **Westport.** It sits at the edge of a picturesque river and is a delightful, peaceful place to wander. Probably depending on whether or not you've got a family to entertain, you could either spend a couple of hours at **Westport House and Pirate Adventure Park** (p. 185) or visit the **National Museum of Ireland: Country Life** (p. 184) near Castlebar. Ancient history buffs will probably want to press right ahead to County Sligo at this point (see below), but if it's quiet retreat you're after, drive across the strangely empty flatlands to **Achill Island** (p. 186). The route along the coast and out across the bridge to the island is slow and windy, but the views are fantastic. If you do make it out to Achill, consider an overnight stay at the **Bervie** (p. 179), where the sea is right outside the door.

Day 12: County Sligo

Depending on where you based yourself for the night, you may be in for a long drive, so start early. **Sligo Town** (p. 187) has a few worthwhile attractions, but mostly it will be useful as a stop for lunch. The real reason to come this far lies in the surrounding countryside. There is an astonishing concentration of ancient burial sites here, including **Carrowkeel** and **Carrowmore** that contain the world's oldest piece of freestanding architecture. Our favorite place to stay the night in these parts is the extraordinary **Temple House** (p. 180).

Day 13: North to Donegal

You're really entering the wilds of Ireland now. Head up the coast past Donegal Town until you catch the N15 road. Then follow it around the breathtaking coastline to the busy hill town of **Ballyshannon,** an excellent spot for crafts shops and glorious views from the top of the hill. The adventurous can explore the **Catsby Cave,** a picturesque grotto at the edge of the Abbey River. But here the drive is really the thing, so head on to the darling town of **Glencolumbkille** (p. 198). There's an excellent folk park here that's well worth an hour of your time before you head on to the stone-cut town of Ardara at the foot of a steep hill—it's wall-to-wall arts-and-crafts shops and is a pleasure to explore. Art lovers won't want to miss the revelatory gallery at **Glebe House** (p. 199). You've spent a lot of time in the car today, but if you can face another 40 minutes or so to the wonderful **Rathmullan House** (p. 194), you'll find a beautiful, elegant seaside retreat waiting for you on your last night.

Day 14: Heading Home

If your flight leaves late, you could rise early and spend the morning driving up to **Malin Head** (p. 200), the northernmost tip of Ireland. It's a wild and woolly place just a couple of hours' drive from Rathmullan. From there, expect the journey to the airport to take at least 4 hours, but allow plenty of time in case of traffic backups around Dublin—they're virtually constant.

IRELAND FOR FREE OR DIRT CHEAP

Ireland is no longer a cheap country to visit—and hasn't been for some time. The economic crash of the late 2000s drove prices down a bit, but hotels and restaurants are still pricey, and in recent years the euro/dollar exchange rate has not been favorable to travelers from the U.S. And that's not even taking into account the global economic conditions that make these uncertain financial times. But here's the good news: There are a lot of great sites you can visit for free in Ireland, including some of the biggest tourist attractions in the country. You can also save a lot of money by sticking mainly to places that can be reached by public transport, rather than hiring a car (every place we list is easily accessible by train or bus). You'd be surprised how much of Ireland you can see without blowing the budget. We're starting this tour in Northern Ireland (maybe you got a great deal on a flight to Belfast!), because it's one of the more budget-friendly regions. For more information on train and bus timetables, see **www.irishrail.ie** and **www.buseireann.ie**.

Day 1: Belfast

Belfast is rich with free attractions. The excellent **Ulster Museum** (p. 217) displays artifacts from across 9,000 years of Irish history. Exhibitions also explore Belfast and the capital's more recent industrial past. Right next door is the **Belfast Botanic Gardens & Palm House** (p. 214) that's also a short walk from the campus of **Queen's University** (p. 216). Belfast **City Hall** (p. 215) runs free guided tours. Another exceptional Victorian landmark, **Belfast Cathedral** (p. 212), is also free, and **Cave Hill Country Park** (p. 214) is a tranquil place with good walking trails and incredible views of the city. Last but not least, Belfast is still most famous for the violence and hardship it endured in the mid- to late-20th century. The epicenter of the conflict was the **Falls and Shankill roads area** (p. 213). Political murals are still a salient feature of these neighborhoods, though they are now safe for visitors to explore. To get the most out of them, you may want to spend some of that cash you've saved on a **Black Taxi Tour** (p. 213).

Catch a train from Belfast to Dublin (Connolly Station). Time: 2 hr. 10 min. Fares start at about €22 for adults.

SAVING MONEY ON trains & buses

The cost of rail travel can quickly mount up, but there are ways to save money. Whenever you can, *book in advance*. The example fares listed in this itinerary are all pre-booked; walk-up fares can be higher. The downside for booking that way is that you have to specify times of travel—but Irish Rail has a handy policy of letting you upgrade a pre-booked ticket into something more flexible for just €10.

If you're going to be spending a lot of time on public transportation, you should also strongly consider buying a money-saving pass. In the Irish Republic, the **Eurail Pass** is good for travel on trains, Expressway coaches, and the Irish Continental Lines ferries between France and Ireland. They cost around €155 for a 3-day pass and €235 for a 5-day pass. Youth passes (ages 16–25), family, and first-class passes are also available. For further details, or for purchase, visit www.eurail.com.

BritRail Pass + Ireland: Includes all rail travel throughout the United Kingdom and Ireland, including a round-trip ferry crossing on Stena Line. Available from **BritRail** (℃ 866/938-RAIL in the U.S. and Canada; www.britrail. com). Prices for a 5-day pass start at £389 adults, £289 children. The BritRail pass is not available to British citizens.

Either of these can add up to significant savings, but there are a couple bits of small print to be aware of. First, it's still advisable to make seat reservations to guarantee a space—this may cost a few extra euro or pounds each time in booking fees. Also, not everybody can buy a pass. E.U. citizens aren't allowed to buy Eurail passes, and likewise, British citizens can't buy BritRail passes.

Both passes can also be purchased from **Railpass** (www.railpass.com), **STA Travel** (℃ 800/781-4040 in the U.S.; www.sta.com) and other travel agents.

Days 2 & 3: Dublin

Ireland's capital is also the number one destination in the country for free sites. The **Chester Beatty Library** (p. 65) is, for our money, one of the best museums in Europe. The collection of illuminated gospels and early copies of the Bible, Torah, and Koran would justify a steep entrance fee, but it won't cost you a cent. Three of the four separate museums constituting the **National Museum of Ireland** are in Dublin— **Archaeology**, **Natural History** and **Decorative Arts and History**—and all are free. Each contains some incredible treasures, and collectively there's enough to keep you occupied for a day or more. All of Dublin's best major art galleries are free. The collection at the **National Gallery of Ireland,** though relatively small, includes works by Titian, Vermeer, Monet, and Picasso. Also complimentary are the **Irish Museum of Modern Art** (p. 76)**,** the **Temple Bar Gallery** (p. 81), and the excellent **Hugh Lane Gallery** (p. 69). Many of Dublin's most historic public buildings don't charge admission. **Áras an Uachtaráin** (the Irish President's House, p. 69) is accessible only by tour on a first-come, first-served basis; the queue forms at the visitor center in Phoenix Park. The **Bank of Ireland/Parliament House** (p. 78) and the **Four Courts** (p. 75) are also free. The **General Post Office** on O'Connell Street (p. 75) is still a working post office but has a small number of exhibits devoted to the Easter Rising, including the original Declaration of Independence. Add to this the great public spaces such as **Phoenix Park** (p. 79), **St. Stephen's Green** (p. 72), and

Trinity College (p. 72), and you'll see it's possible to spend a full 2 days here without spending a penny on sightseeing.

Catch a train from Dublin (Heuston Station) to Galway. Time: 2 hr. 40 min. Fares start at about €33 for adults.

Day 4: Galway

Ireland's artsy, seductive west coast city offers plenty of free pursuits. The **Galway Arts Centre** (p. 171) usually has good exhibitions, and you can often score cheap tickets for performances. The **Galway City Museum** (p. 172) makes for a stellar introduction to the region, with its fine collection of artifacts from the medieval period onward. **St. Nicholas' Collegiate Church** (p. 174), the oldest church in the city, contains a 12th-century crusader's tomb and other extraordinary historic pieces. Make sure you devote some time to just wandering the streets of this eminently walkable town too; Its central medieval district is a tiny, tangled area featuring plenty of interesting shops. Getting lost is half the fun.

Catch a bus from Galway Bus Station to Cork (Parnell Place Bus Station). Time: 3½ hrs. with one change or 4 hr. 20 min. direct. Fares start at about €27 for adults.

Day 5: Galway to Cork

This busy, youthful city doesn't have a great deal of free attractions, but if you're up for a large dose of culture, you'll find plenty to do without paying a cent. There's enough here to keep you busy for the day if you hit the ground running. Start with a trip to the **Old English Market** (p. 115) for a browse and a cheap lunch. Afterward, head to the **Crawford Art Gallery** (p. 114)—it's one of the very best in Ireland and completely free. More excellent free art is to be found at the **Lewis Glucksman Gallery** (p. 116) on the campus of **University College Cork**. In the evening, check out a few of Cork's exceptional pubs. They have a reputation for being among the best in the country for traditional music (see "A Tuneful Pint" on p. 110).

Catch a train from Cork to Killarney. Most change at Mallow. Time: 1 hr. 20 min. direct, or 2 hr. with change. Fares start at about €29 for adults.

Day 6: Cork to Killarney

It's not exactly difficult to reach **Killarney National Park** (p. 137) from Killarney town; you just walk toward the cathedral and turn left. This 65sq. km (25-sq. mile) expanse of forest, lakes, and mountains is crisscrossed with several well-conceived nature trails, plus more challenging routes for serious hikers. Formerly the grounds of a great mansion, the **Knockreer Estate** (p. 139) still has lovely gardens and beautiful views. Free sites in Killarney Town itself include the rather grand neo-Gothic **St. Mary's Cathedral.** For dinner, the frugal traveler will be drawn to **Pay as You Please**—a solid restaurant with no prices on the menu. You pay what you feel the food is worth.

Catch a train from Killarney to Dublin—again, nearly all change at Mallow. Time: 3½ hrs. Fares start at about €44 for adults.

Day 7: Homeward Bound...

Assuming your airline will let you fly out of Dublin, an early-ish train back to the capital should allow you some time to pick up any of the free sites you didn't manage to cover earlier in the tour. Otherwise, you'll have to catch a train straight on to Belfast for your flight home (about 7½ hrs. with up to three changes; fares from Killarney start at about €38 adults). And that's it! You've done a fair bit of Ireland without breaking the bank. Pick your accommodations early and wisely to save the most. There are plenty of inexpensive B&Bs listed in this book for all of these cities. Your other main expense on this itinerary will be rail fares, but there are ways to save money on those too (see "Saving Money on Trains & Buses" on p. 19).

IRELAND FOR FAMILIES

Traveling with children is always a bit of an adventure, and you'll want all the help you can get. Luckily Ireland—with its vast open countryside, farm hotels, and castles—is a fairy-tale playground for kids. You may have trouble finding babysitters outside major towns, so just take the kids with you. Most restaurants, sights, and even pubs (during the day) welcome children. The best part of the country for those traveling with kids is arguably Cork and Kerry, where everything seems to be set up for families. Here's a sample itinerary to give you some ideas.

Days 1 & 2: Dublin

The sprawling greens of **Phoenix Park** (p. 79) are a great place for little ones to let off steam (it's the best place in the city for a picnic too, if the weather's good). Within the park, **Dublin Zoo** (p. 74) is thoughtfully designed to cater to the younger ones (you can take a train ride around the zoo, for instance). Inquisitive young minds will be inspired by the cabinets of curiosity at the **National Museum of Ireland: Natural History** (p. 71), and have their interest piqued by **Number Twenty-Nine: Georgian House Museum** (p. 78), a house which has been kept exactly as it would have been at the turn of the 19th century. The guides at another museum, the **Little Museum of Dublin** (p. 77), do a great job of putting the ordinary lives of Dubliners in the last hundred years into context for younger visitors. But if their attention spans demand something a little flashier, try a **Viking Splash Tour** (p. 79), a historical whirl around the city in a World War II amphibious vehicle, complete with headlong splash into the River Liffey. Parents who don't mind indulging a junior fascination with all the ghoulish may want to take their kids to see the creepy crypts at **St. Michan's Church** (p. 80); but if that's too much like real scares, kids with a teen in their age are all but guaranteed to love an evening aboard the **Dublin Ghost Bus** (p. 79).

Day 2: County Cork

Okay, so it's not exactly untouched by the tourism fairy, but kids find plenty to love about **Blarney Castle** (p. 118), just outside Cork City. They can kiss the famous stone if they don't mind an attendant holding them upside down. A few miles away, the **Fota Island & Wildlife Park** is a well-designed zoo where the docile animals (those that don't bite, kick, or stomp) roam among the visitors.

Days 3 & 4: County Kerry

Kerry is probably Ireland's most kid-friendly county, so there's enough to keep you busy here for at least a couple of days. Fungie, star of the **Dingle Dolphin Boat Tours** (p. 146) has been entertaining kids and grown-ups alike for the last

30 years. In Kenmare, **Seafari** cruises and seal-watching trips (p. 141) teach kids about conservation issues by putting them in touch with the underwater residents of Kenmare Bay. **Blueberry Hill Farm** (p. 143), in Sneem, is a working, old-fashioned farmstead where kids can help milk cows, make butter, and take part in a treasure hunt. Meanwhile, an underground tour of the atmospheric **Crag Cave** (p. 143) is a surefire winner—as is a stop for high-energy playtime at the **Crazy Cave** (p. 145) adventure playground. And don't overlook what **Killarney National Park** (p. 137) has to offer little ones. A ride around the park in a horse-drawn "jarvey" is bound to meet with their approval.

Day 6: Bunratty Folk Park

You could spend most of the day at **Bunratty Castle and Folk Park** (p. 158), an attraction that combines one of Ireland's best medieval castles with a living history museum. It's a brilliant recreation of a 19th-century village, complete with costumed actors strolling down the street, chatting to passers-by, and even working in the shops. Bunratty is also the setting for a lively (and hugely popular) **Medieval Banquet**. It's raucous, but surprisingly good fun; book an early evening sitting to suit young bedtimes.

Day 7: Heading Home

If you have time before the drive back to the airport, head into the **Burren** (see chapter 8). Young imaginations will be fired up by the dolmens and other ancient sites that litter the otherworldly landscape. It's also where you'll find the **Burren Birds of Prey Centre** at Aillwee Cave (p. 158); you can see buzzards, falcons, eagles, and owls in flight at this working aviary.

Beyond a Week...

If your trip extends beyond a week, there are plenty of standout attractions for kids to be found further north.

The **Atlantaquaria** (p. 171), just outside Galway City, is a new, state-of-the-art aquarium, while pony trekking across **Connemara National Park** (p. 175) is a unique way to see this beautiful, windswept landscape.

In Mayo, **Westport House and Pirate Adventure Park** (p. 185) has all the components necessary for high-activity fun, and young ones are bound to enjoy learning all about the region's real-life pirate hero, **Grace O'Malley** (see box p. 185).

If you're going as far as Belfast, the attractions around the new Titanic Quarter hold plenty of kid-friendly appeal. Try the hands-on science center, **W5** (p. 217), and the state-of-the-art **Titanic Belfast** museum (p. 216).

And the **Antrim Coast Drive** (see box p. 223) has two key highlights that children will adore: the perilous (but fun) **Carrick-a-Rede Rope Bridge** (p. 222) and the awe-inspiring alien shapes of the **Giant's Causeway** (p. 224).

EXPLORING ANCIENT IRELAND

Ireland has treasured and protected its ancient past, and its mysterious stone circles, cairns, and huge stone tables called *dolmens* can still be found perfectly preserved in pastures and on hillsides all over the island. These are precious connections to our own long-lost pasts, as they provide a window through which we can catch a hazy glimpse of what life was like very long ago. You'll need to be intrepid and cover a lot of ground

HIGH CROSSES: icons of ireland

You see them all over Ireland, often in the most picturesque rural surroundings, standing alone like sentries; high Celtic crosses with faded stories carved into every inch of space. They are extraordinary, mournful, and unforgettable, but when they were created, they served a useful purpose: They were books, of sorts, in the days when the written word was rare and precious. Think of the carvings as illustrations acting like cartoons, explaining the Bible to the uneducated population. When they were created, the crosses were probably brightly painted as well, but the color has long been lost to the wind and rain.

One of the most famous examples of a high cross is at **Monasterboice ★**, a group of early Christian ruins near Drogheda, about 53km (33 mi) north of Dublin. The **Muiredach Cross**, as it's known, has carvings telling the stories of Adam and Eve, Cain and Abel, David and Goliath, and Moses, as well as the wise men bringing gifts to the baby Jesus. At the center of the old cross, the carving is thought to be of Revelation, while, at the top, St. Paul stands alone in the desert. The western side of the cross tells the stories of the New Testament, with, from the top down, a figure praying, the Crucifixion, St. Peter, Doubting Thomas, and, below that, Jesus' arrest. On the base of the cross is an inscription found often carved on stones in ancient Irish monasteries. It reads in Gaelic, "A prayer for Muiredach for whom the cross was made." Muiredach was the abbot at Monasterboice until 922, so the cross was probably made as a memorial shortly after his death.

Monasterboice is on the M1 motorway, about 8km (5½ mi) north of Drogheda, Co. Louth. Admission is free.

in the car, but it'll be worth it. Some of the oldest tombs predate the Egyptian pyramids by centuries, and, in many cases, the sites are preserved but their meaning has long since disappeared, making them intriguing and elusive in equal measures. Exploring these rocky symbols can be the most memorable part of any trip to Ireland.

Day 1: Knowth & the Boyne Valley

After an early breakfast, head north to the rich rolling Boyne Valley (about an hour's drive north of Dublin off the N2) to the Brú na Bóinne Visitor Centre and this extensive Neolithic burial ground. This huge necropolis holds numerous sites, with three open to visitors—**Newgrange** (p. 87), **Knowth** (p. 86), and **Dowth**. Register at the center to tour Newgrange first. A tour here, early in the day before it gets crowded, is spectacular. Next tour the burial ground at Knowth with its extensive collection of passage-grave art. In the afternoon, head down the N3 to the **Hill of Tara** (p. 86). Here mounds and passage graves date from the Bronze Age.

Day 2: Céide Fields

It will take a couple of hours to drive to the remote location in north County Mayo, but your efforts will be rewarded. This extraordinary ancient site (p. 184) holds the stony remains of an entire prehistoric farming village on top of a cliff and boasts breathtaking views of the sea and surrounding countryside. Spend the day exploring the 5,000-year-old site, and lunch in the excellent visitor center.

Day 3: County Sligo

In the morning, drive east to County Sligo. On the N4, south of Sligo Town, visit the **Carrowkeel Passage Tomb Cemetery** (p. 187) perched on a hilltop overlooking Lough Arrow. It has wide, sweeping views, and the 14 cairns and dolmens are often very quiet early in the day—with luck you might have them all to yourself. Then head on to Sligo Town and follow signs to **Carrowmore Megalithic Cemetery** (p. 187). This extraordinary site has 60 stone circles, passage tombs, and dolmens scattered across acres of green pastures. They are believed to predate Newgrange by nearly a millennium. In the afternoon, if you're feeling energetic, climb to the hilltop cairn of **Knocknarea** located nearby—it's believed to be the grave of folklore fairy Queen Maeve.

Day 4: Inishmurray Island

After a relaxing morning, travel by boat to the island of **Inishmurray** off the coast of Sligo. There you can spend the day wandering the impressively complete remains of the early monastic settlement founded in the 6th century. You can still make out its ancient chapels, beehive cells, and altars. If the weather is fine, pack a picnic lunch and eat on the sunny beach. Return to Sligo for the night.

Day 5: The Burren

Today begins with another long drive, but you'll pass through some of the most beautiful parts of Galway and Mayo along the way. **The Burren**, in County Clare, is one of the richest areas of the country for ancient remains from the Neolithic period through medieval times. There are around 120 dolmens and wedge tombs—including the impressive **Poulnabrone Dolmen** (p. 162)—and as many as 500 ring forts. For more on this extraordinary region, see chapter 8.

Day 6: Skellig Michael

Right after breakfast, head south to County Kerry, where this starkly beautiful island sits 13km (8 miles) offshore, standing sternly as a kind of memorial to the hardy souls who once eked out a living amid its formidable cliffs and stony mountains (see "The Ring of Kerry" in chapter 7). Deeply observant early Christian monks punished their bodies by living here in miserable conditions and spent their days carving 600 steps into the unyielding stone, so their walk up to the beehive huts and icy chapels could be made somewhat safer. Today it is an unforgettable landscape, and the ruins of their homes are evocative and profoundly moving. A trip out here by boat and an afternoon's exploration will take up much of the day. Once you return to the mainland, reward yourself with a relaxing evening in Kenmare.

Day 7: Glendalough

Drive east today to County Wicklow, where the evocative ruins of the monastery at **Glendalough** (p. 98) are sprawled around two peaceful lakes nestled on the side of a mountain. Get a map from the visitor center before beginning your exploration of the round towers, chapels, and huts dotted around the wooded site. Don't miss the ancient chapel known as **St. Kevin's Kitchen.** If the weather is warm, bring your lunch and picnic by the lake. You can easily spend a day here.

IRELAND OFF THE BEATEN PATH

We start this tour in Belfast, a city in the midst of an immense transformation since the 1998 Good Friday Agreement that finally established a detente in Northern Ireland. Tourism has steadily increased in this region over the last decade, but the crowds still have yet to arrive en masse. If the best sites of the Antrim Coast were in County Cork or Kerry, they'd be overrun with tourists; as it is, one can still visit a spectacular setting such as the Giant's Causeway and find oneself alone with nature. This tour then heads west to take a couple of Sligo's prehistoric sites and continues south for a visit to Achill Island, a peaceful retreat off the coast of County Mayo.

Days 1 & 2: Belfast

Northern Ireland's capital—and the island of Ireland's second largest city —is a historic, vibrant town. Start with a visit to the **Ulster Museum** (p. 217) and experience some of the city's more recent past firsthand with a **Black Taxi Tour** (p. 213). The new museums in the Titanic Quarter, such as the immense **Titanic Belfast** (p. 216), provide a more high-tech dose of history; alternatively, you could immerse yourself in the city's present by exploring its busy shopping districts. The **Belfast Botanic Gardens & Palm House** (p. 214) and **Queen's University** (p. 216) are also worth a look. Round off the day with a pint at one of Belfast's extraordinarily pretty pubs like the **Crown Liquor Saloon** (p. 215) and a meal at one of the small but growing number of world-class restaurants.

Day 3: County Antrim

One of the North's loveliest counties, Antrim is home to two gorgeous parks: the **Castlewellan Forest Park** (p. 219) with formal gardens and gorgeous woodland walks, and the **Silent Valley Mountain Park** (p. 221) with beautiful walks and even more incredible views.

Alternatively, the Antrim coast road is one of Ireland's great coastal drives—and one of the least spoiled. Few tourists ever venture this far north; those who do will reap spectacular rewards. Start in **Carrickfergus,** with a brief stop to look around its medieval castle (p. 219), before heading north along the coast road. For the best views take the **Torr Head Scenic Road** (p. 225) located just after the village of **Cushendun** (p. 224). It's an alternative, signposted road running parallel to the main route, ideal for those with a good head for heights. From up here on a clear day, you can see all the way to the Mull of Kintyre in Scotland. The Antrim coast's most remarkable asset is the **Giant's Causeway** (p. 224), an uncanny natural rock formation comprised of thousands of tightly packed basalt columns. You could do the drive in about 2 hours, but you'll want to allow considerably longer than that to give yourself time to stop along the way. There are places along the coast to spend the night, or you could go straight on into **Derry.** It's about another hour on from the Giant's Causeway.

Day 4: Derry to Sligo

Straddling the border between Northern Ireland and the Republic, this vibrant town was synonymous with political strife. Though it's peaceful these days, it's still a divided place—the residents can't even agree on what to call it. Road signs from the Republic point to Derry; those in the North point to Londonderry. How can a place like that not be full of character and history? Check out the award-winning **Tower Museum** (p. 231) and the Gothic, 17th-century **Cathedral of St. Columb** (p. 230) before recharging for a long drive to County Sligo in the afternoon.

Day 5: County Sligo

Nestled within the gentle, verdant hills of this underrated county are some dramatic archaeological sites. Within a short drive from Sligo Town are two of the most incredible: **Carrowkeel Passage Tomb Cemetery** (p. 187) packed with 14 cairns, dolmens, and stone circles, and the impossibly ancient **Carrowmore Megalithic Cemetery** (p. 187). Here's a thought to ponder while clambering around the latter: The innocuously named tomb 52A is thought to be 7,400 years old, making it the earliest known piece of free-standing stone architecture in the world.

Day 6: Sligo to Achill Island

This is a wild and beautiful place of unspoiled beaches and spectacular scenery. But you'll also find a handful of excellent little hotels and B&Bs, mostly in the vicinity of **Keel,** the island's most attractive village. This is also major outdoor sports territory, as the constant wind off the Atlantic Ocean is ideal for windsurfing, hang gliding, and any other sport that depends on a breeze. One of the best (and least known) discoveries on Achill Island is a deserted village on the slopes of Mount Slievemore (p. 186). Not too many people venture up there, making it an even more extraordinary and moving place to visit.

Day 7: Achill Island to Shannon

It's a long drive to whichever airport you're flying home from, but a flight out of Shannon will give you the most spectacular route. If you can extend your trip a little, **Clare Island** (p. 184) is a lovely place to spend a day. Even more peaceful and isolated than its near neighbor, Achill, Clare's permanent population amounts to just 150 people, and you can go a long way without bumping into any of them.

IRELAND IN CONTEXT

A BRIEF HISTORY

THE FIRST SETTLERS With some degree of confidence, we can place the date of the first human habitation of the island somewhere after the end of the last ice age, around the late 8000s B.C. Ireland's first colonizers, Mesolithic Homo sapiens, walked, waded, or floated across the narrow strait from what is now Britain in search of flint and, of course, food.

The next momentous prehistoric event was the arrival of Neolithic farmers and herders, sometime around 3500 B.C. Unlike Ireland's Mesolithic hunters, who barely left a trace, this second wave of colonizers began to transform the island at once.

They came with stone axes that could fell a good-sized elm in less than an hour. Ireland's hardwood forests receded to make room for tilled fields and pastureland. Villages sprang up, and more permanent homes, planked with split oak, appeared at this time.

Far more striking, though, was the appearance of massive megalithic monuments, including court cairns, dolmens (stone tables), round subterranean passage tombs, and wedge tombs. There are thousands of these scattered around Ireland, and to this day only a small percentage of them have been excavated. These megalithic monuments speak volumes about the early Irish. To visit **Newgrange** (p. 87) and **Knowth** (p. 86) in the Boyne Valley and **Carrowmore** (p. 187) in County Sligo is to marvel at the mystical practices of the early Irish. Even today little is known about the meaning of these mysterious stone remnants of their lives.

Early Celtic inhabitants of the island assumed that the tremendous stones and mounds were raised by giants. They called them the people of the sí, who eventually became the *Tuatha Dé Danann*, and, finally, *fairies*. Over many generations of oral tradition, the mythical people were downsized into "little people," who were believed to have led a magical life, mostly underground, in the thousands of raths (earthwork structures) coursing the island like giant mole tunnels. All of these sites were believed to be protected by fairies. To tamper with them was believed to bring great bad luck, so nobody ever touched them. Thus, they have lasted to this day—ungraffitied, undamaged, unprotected by any visible fences or wires, but utterly safe.

THE CELTS Of all the successive waves of outsiders who have, over the years, shaped, cajoled, and pockmarked the timeline of Irish history, none have made quite such a deep-seated impact as that of the Celts. They came in waves, the first perhaps as early as the 6th century B.C. and continuing until the end of the first millennium. They fled from the Roman invasion and clung to the edge of Europe—Ireland being, at the time, about as far as you could go to elude a Roman force. In time, they controlled the island and absorbed into their culture everyone they found there.

Despite their cultural potency, however, the Celts developed little in the way of centralized government, existing instead in a near-perpetual state of division and conflict with one another. The island was divided among as many as 150 tribes, grouped under alliances to five provincial kings. The provinces of Munster, Leinster, Ulster, and Connaught date from this period. They fought fiercely among themselves over cattle (their "currency" and standard of wealth), land, and women. None among them ever ruled the entire island, though not for lack of trying. One of the most impressive monuments from the time of the warring Celts is the stone fortress of **Dún Aengus,** on the windswept hills of the Aran Islands (p. 170).

THE COMING OF CHRISTIANITY   The Celtic chiefs neither warmly welcomed nor violently resisted the Christians who came ashore beginning in the 5th century A.D. Although threatened, the pagan Celts settled for a bloodless rivalry with this new religion. In retrospect, this may have been a mistake.

The most famous of these Christian newcomers was a man called Maewyn Succat, a young Roman citizen torn from his Welsh homeland in a Celtic raid and brought to Ireland as a slave, where he was forced to work in a place called the Forest of Foclut (thought to be around modern County Antrim). He escaped on a ship bound for France, where he spent several years as a priest before returning to Ireland as a missionary. He began preaching at sacred Celtic festivals, a tactic that frequently led to confrontations with religious and political leaders, but eventually he became such a popular figure that after his death in 461, a dozen clan chiefs fought over the right to bury him. His lasting legacy was the establishment in Ireland of one of the strongest Christian orthodoxies in Europe—an achievement for which he was later beatified as St. Patrick.

Ireland's conversion to Christianity was a somewhat negotiated process. The church at the time of St. Patrick was, like the man who brought it, Roman. To Ireland, an island then still without a single proper town, the Roman system of dioceses and archdioceses didn't apply to the way they lived. So the Irish adapted the church. They built isolated monasteries with extended monastic "families," each more or less autonomous. The pope, like an Irish high king, was to them like an ordained prizefighter—he was expected to defend his title, one challenge after another, or lose it.

Ireland flourished in this fashion for several centuries, and became a center of monastic learning and culture. Monks and scholars were drawn to it in droves, and they were sent out in great numbers as well, to Britain and the Continent as emissaries for the island's way of thinking and praying.

Like their megalithic ancestors, these monks left traces of their lives behind, and these have become enduring monuments to their spirituality. Early monastic sites such as **Glendalough** in County Wicklow (p. 98), windswept **Clonmacnoise** in County Offaly (p. 176), and isolated **Skellig Michael** off the Kerry coast (p. 144) give you an idea of how they lived, while striking examples of their work can be seen at Trinity College (which houses the Book of Kells) and at the Chester Beatty museum.

THE VIKING INVASIONS   The monastic city-states of early medieval Ireland might have continued to lead the world's intellectual development, but the Vikings came along and ruined everything. After centuries of relative peace, the first wave of Viking invaders arrived in A.D. 795. The wealthy nonviolent Irish monasteries were among their first targets. Unprepared and unprotected, the monasteries, which had amassed collections of gold, jewels, and art from followers and thinkers around the world, were decimated. The round towers to which the monks retreated were neither high enough nor strong enough to protect them and their treasures from the onslaught.

Once word spread of the wealth to be had on the small island, the Scandinavian invaders just kept on coming, but much as they were experts in the arts of pillage and plunder, one thing of which they had no knowledge was literature. They didn't know how to read. Therefore, they paid scant attention to the magnificent books they came across, passing them over for more obvious riches. This fortunate quirk of history allowed the monks some means of preserving their dying culture—and their immeasurably valuable work—for the benefit of future generations.

After the Vikings left, Ireland enjoyed something of a renewal in the 11th and 12th centuries. Its towns grew, its regional kings made successive unsuccessful bids to unite the country under a single high kingship, and its church came under increased pressure to conform to the Vatican's rules. All of these factors would play a part in ripening Ireland for the next invasion.

The Vikings may have been gone, but prosperous and factionalized Ireland made attractive prey to other nations, and it was, tragically, an Irish king who opened the door to the next predator. Diarmait Mac Murchada, king of Leinster, whose ambition was to be king of all of Ireland, decided he could do it, with a little help. So he called on Henry II, the Norman king of England. Diarmait offered Henry a series of incentives in return for military aid: Not only did he bequeath his eldest daughter to whoever led the army, but he also offered them overlordship of the Kingdom of Leinster. To put it bluntly, he made Henry an offer he couldn't refuse. So it was that an expeditionary force, led by the Earl of Pembroke, Richard de Clare—better known as Strongbow—was sent to Diarmait's aid. After the successful invasion and subsequent battles in which Strongbow emerged victorious, he remained in Ireland as governor, and thus gave the English their first foothold in Ireland. What Diarmait did not realize, of course, was that they would never leave.

THE NORMAN INVASION In successive expeditions from 1167 to 1169, the Normans, who had already conquered England, crossed the Irish Sea with crushing force. During the next century, the Norman-English settled in, consolidating their power in new towns and cities. Indeed, many settlers grew attached to the island, and did their best to integrate with the local culture. Marriages between the native Irish and the invaders became commonplace. Over the next couple of centuries, they became more Irish and less English in their loyalties.

Over the next 2 centuries, attempts to rid Ireland of its English overlords fell short. Independent Gaelic lords in the North and West continued to maintain their territories. By the close of the 15th century, English control of the island was effectively limited to the Pale, a walled and fortified cordon around what is now greater Dublin. (The phrase "beyond the pale" comes from this—meaning anything that is uncontrollable or unacceptable.)

ENGLISH POWER & THE FLIGHT OF THE EARLS During the reign of the Tudor monarchs in England (1485–1603), the brutal reconquest of Ireland was set in motion. Henry VIII was the first to proclaim himself king of all Ireland—something even his warlike ancestors had stopped short of doing—but it wasn't until later that century that the claim was backed up by force. Elizabeth I, Henry's daughter, declared that all Gaelic lords in Ireland must surrender their lands to her, with the dubious promise that she would immediately grant them all back again—unsurprisingly, the proposition was hardly welcomed in Ireland, and a rebel army was raised by Hugh O'Neill and "Red" Hugh O'Donnell, two Irish chieftains. Despite significant victories early on in their decade-long campaign, most notably over a force led by the Earl of Essex, whom Elizabeth had personally sent to subdue them, by 1603 O'Neill was left with few allies and no option but to surrender, which he did on March 23rd, the day before Elizabeth died.

THE COMING OF CROMWELL   By the 1640s, Ireland was effectively an English plantation. Family estates had been seized and foreign (Scottish) labor brought in to work them. A systematic persecution of Catholics, which began with Henry VIII's split from Rome but did not die with him, barred Catholics from practicing their faith. Resentment against the English and their punitive laws led to fierce uprisings in Ulster and Leinster in 1641, and by early 1642 most of Ireland was again under Irish control. Unfortunately for the rebels, any hope of extending the victories was destroyed by internal disunion and by the eventual decision to support the Royalist side in the English civil war. In 1648 King Charles I of England was beheaded, and the victorious commander of the parliamentary forces, Oliver Cromwell, was installed as ruler. Soon his supporters were taking on his enemies in Ireland. A year later, the Royalists' stand collapsed in defeat at Rathmines, just south of Dublin.

Defeat for the Royalist cause did not, however, mean the end of the war. Cromwell became paranoid that Ireland would be used to launch a French-backed insurgency if it was not brought to heel, and he detested the country's Catholic beliefs. So in 1649, Cromwell set sail for Dublin, bringing with him an army of 12,000 men, and a battle plan so ruthless that it remains notorious to this day.

In the town of Drogheda, more than 3,552 Irish soldiers were slaughtered in a single night. When a group of men sought sanctuary in the local church, Cromwell ordered the church burned down with them locked inside—an act of such monstrosity that some of his own men risked a charge of mutiny and refused the order. On another day, in Wexford, more than 2,000 were murdered, many of them civilians. The trail of destruction rolled on, devastating counties Galway and Waterford. When asked where the Irish citizens could go to be safe from him, Cromwell famously suggested they could go "to hell or Connaught"—the latter being the most far-flung, rocky, and unfarmable part of Ireland.

After a rampage that lasted 7 months, killing thousands and leaving churches, monasteries, and castles in ruins, Cromwell finally left Ireland in the care of his lieutenants and returned to England. Hundreds of years later, the memory and lore of his extraordinary violence lingers painfully in Ireland. In certain parts of the country, people still spit at the mention of his name.

THE ANTI-CATHOLIC LAWS   Cromwell died in 1658, and 2 years later the English monarchy was restored, but the anti-Catholic oppression continued. In 1685, though, something quite remarkable happened. Contrary to the efforts of the English establishment, the new king, James II, refused to relinquish his Catholic faith after ascending to the throne. It looked for a while as if things could change in Ireland, and that the Catholics might have found a new ally in the unlikeliest of quarters. However, such hopes were dashed 3 years later, when James was ousted from power, and the Protestant William of Orange installed in his place.

James fled to France to raise support for a rebellion, and then sailed to Ireland to launch his attack. He struck first at Derry, to which he laid siege for 15 weeks before finally being defeated by William's forces at the Battle of the Boyne. The battle effectively ended James's cause, and with it, the hopes of Catholic Ireland for the best part of a century.

After James's defeat, English power was once more consolidated across Ireland. Protestant landowners were granted full political power, while laws were enacted to effectively immobilize the Catholic population. Being a Catholic in late-17th-century Ireland was not exactly illegal per se, but in practice life was all but impossible for those who refused to convert to Protestantism. Catholics could not purchase land, and existing landholdings were split up unless the families who owned them became Protestants; Catholic schools were banned, as were priests and all forms of public worship. Catholics were barred from holding any office of state, practicing law, or joining the army. Those who still refused to relinquish their faith were forced to pay a tax to the Anglican Church. And by virtue of not being able to own land, the few who previously had been allowed to vote were not allowed to anymore.

The new British landlords settled in, planted crops, made laws, and sowed their own seeds. Inevitably, over time, the "Anglos" became the Anglo-Irish. Hyphenated or not, they were Irish, and their loyalties were increasingly unpredictable. After all, an immigrant is only an immigrant for a generation; whatever the birthright of the colonists, their children would be Irish-born and bred. And so it was that an uncomfortable sort of stability set in for a generation or three, albeit of a kind that was very much separate and unequal. There were the haves, the wealthy Protestants, and the have-nots, the deprived and disenfranchised Catholics.

A kind of unhappy peace held for some time. But by the end of the 18th century, the appetite for rebellion was whetted again. To understand why, one need look no further than the intellectual hotbed that flourished among the coffee shops and lecture halls of Europe's newest boomtown: Dublin.

THE UNITED IRISHMEN & THE 1798 REBELLION By the 1770s, Dublin was thriving as never before. As a center for culture and learning, it was rivaled only by Paris and London; thanks to the work of such architects as Henry Gratton (who designed Custom House, the Kings Inns, and the Four Courts), its very streets were being remodeled in a grand, neoclassical style that was more akin to the great cities of southern Italy than that of southern Ireland.

However, while the urban classes reveled in their newfound wealth, the stringent Penal Laws that had effectively cut off the Catholic workers from their own countryside forced many of them to turn to the city for work. In Dublin's buzzing intellectual scene political dissent soon brewed, and even after a campaign by Irish politicians led to many of the Penal Laws being repealed in 1783, Dublin was a breeding ground for radicals and political activists. The results were explosive.

When war broke out between Britain and France in the 1790s, the United Irishmen—a nonviolent society formed to lobby for admission of Catholic Irishmen to the Irish Parliament—sent a secret delegation to persuade the French to intervene on Ireland's behalf against the British. Their emissary, Dublin lawyer Wolfe Tone, sailed with a French force bound for Ireland in 1796. Determined to defeat forces loyal to the English crown, they were turned back by storms.

In 1798, though, full-scale insurrection led by the United Irishmen did spread across much of Ireland, particularly the southwestern counties of Kilkenny and Wexford, where a tiny republic was briefly declared in June. But it was crushed by Loyalist forces, which then went on a murderous spree, killing tens of thousands and burning towns to the ground. The nadir of the rebellion came when Wolfe Tone, having raised another French invasion force, sailed into Lough Swilley in Donegal, but was promptly captured by the British. At his trial, wearing a French uniform, Tone requested that he be shot, in accordance with the rights of a foreign soldier, but when the request was refused, he suffered a more gruesome end. While waiting for the gallows, he slit his own throat in jail; however, he missed the jugular vein, instead severing his windpipe, leading to a slow and painful death 8 days later. His last words were reputed to have been: "It appears, sir, that I am but a bad anatomist."

The rebellion was over. In the space of 3 weeks, more than 30,000 Irish had been killed. As a final indignity in what became known as "The Year of the French," the British tricked the Irish Parliament into dissolving itself, and Ireland reverted to strict British rule.

A CONFLICT OF CONFLICTS In 1828 a Catholic lawyer named Daniel O'Connell, who had earlier formed the Catholic Association to represent the interests of tenant farmers, was elected to the British Parliament as Member of Parliament for Dublin. Public opinion was so solidly behind him that he was able to persuade the British prime minister that the only way to avoid a civil war in Ireland was to force the Catholic Emancipation Act through Parliament. He remained an MP until 1841, when he was elected Lord Mayor of Dublin, a platform he used to push for repeal of the direct rule imposed from London after the 1798 rebellion.

O'Connell organized massive rallies (nicknamed "monster meetings") attended by hundreds of thousands, and provoked the conservative government to such an extent that it eventually arrested him on charges of seditious conspiracy. The charges were dropped, but the incident—coupled with growing impatience toward his nonviolent approach of protest and reform—led to the breakdown of his power base. "The Liberator," as he'd been known, faded, his health failed, and he died on a trip to Rome.

THE GREAT FAMINE Even after the anti-Catholic legislation began to recede, the vast majority of farmland available to the poor, mostly Catholic population of the countryside was harsh and difficult to cultivate. One of the few crops that could be grown reliably was the potato, which effectively became the staple diet of the rural poor. So when, in 1845, a fungus destroyed much of the potato crop of Ireland, it is not difficult to understand the scale of the devastation this caused. However, to label the Great Irish Famine of the 1840s and 1850s as merely a "tragedy" would be an incomplete description. It was, of course, tragic—but at the same time, the word implies a randomness to the whole sorry, sickening affair that fails to capture its true awfulness. The fact is that what started out as a disaster was turned into a devastating crisis by the callous response of an uninterested British establishment.

As the potato blight worsened, it became apparent to many landlords that their farm tenants would be unable to pay rent. In order to offset their financial losses, they continued to ship grain overseas, in lieu of rent from their now-starving tenants. The British Parliament, meanwhile, was reluctant to send aid, putting the reports of a crisis down to, in the words of Prime Minister Robert Peel, "the Irish tendency to exaggerate."

Of course, as people started to die by the thousands, it became clear to the government that something had to be done, and emergency relief was sent to Ireland in the form of cheap, imported Indian cornmeal. However, this contained virtually no nutrients, and ultimately contributed to the spread of such diseases as typhus and cholera, which were to claim more victims than starvation itself.

To make matters worse, the cornmeal was not simply given to those in need of it. Fearful that handouts would encourage laziness among a population they viewed as prone to that malaise, the British government forced people to work for their food. Entirely pointless make-work projects were initiated, just to give the starving men something to do for their cornmeal; roads were built that led nowhere, for instance, and elaborate follies constructed that served no discernible purpose, some of which still litter the countryside today, memorials to cruelty and ignorance.

One of the most difficult things to comprehend, more than a century and a half later, is the sheer futility of it all. For behind the statistics, the memorials, and the endless personal anguish, lies perhaps the most painful truth of all: that the famine was easily preventable. Enormous cargoes of imported corn sat in Irish ports for months, until the British government felt that releasing them to the people would not adversely affect market rates. Meanwhile, huge quantities of meat and grain were exported from Ireland. (Indeed, in 1847, cattle exports went up 33% from the previous year.)

Given the circumstances, it is easy to understand why so many chose to leave Ireland. More than a million emigrated over the next decade, about three-quarters of them to America, the rest to Britain or Europe. They drained the country. In 1841, Ireland's population was 8 million; by 1851 it was 6.5 million.

THE STRUGGLE FOR HOME RULE   As the famine waned and life returned to something like normality, the Irish independence movement gained new momentum. New fronts opened up in the struggle for Home Rule, both violent and nonviolent, and, significantly, the Republicans now drew considerable support from overseas— particularly from America. There, groups such as the Fenians fundraised and published newspapers in support of the Irish cause, while more audacious schemes, such as an 1866 "invasion" of Canada with fewer than 100 men, amounted to little more than publicity stunts, designed to raise awareness for the cause.

Back home in Ireland, partial concessions were won in Parliament, and by the 1880s, nationalists such as the MP for Meath, Charles Stewart Parnell, were able to unite various factions of Irish nationalists (including the Fenian Brotherhood in America) to fight for Home Rule. In a tumultuous decade of legislation, he came close, but revelations about his long affair with Kitty O'Shea, the wife of a supporter, brought about his downfall as a politician.

By 1912, a bill to give Ireland Home Rule was passed through the British House of Commons, but was defeated in the House of Lords. Many felt that the political process was still all but unstoppable, and that it was only a matter of time before the bill passed fully into law and effective political independence for Ireland would be secured. However, when the onset of World War I in 1914 forced the issue onto the back burner once again, many in the Home Rule movement grew tired of the political process.

THE EASTER REBELLION   On Easter Monday 1916, a group of nationalists occupied the **General Post Office** (see p. 75) in the heart of Dublin, from which they

DATELINE

proclaimed the foundation of an Irish Republic. Inside were 1,500 fighters, led by schoolteacher and Gaelic League member Patrick Pearse and Socialist leader James Connolly. The British, nervous at an armed uprising on its doorstep while it fought a massive war in Europe, responded with overwhelming force. Soldiers were sent in, and a battle raged in the streets of Dublin for 6 days before the leaders of the rebellion were captured and imprisoned. There are still bullet holes in the walls of the post office and the buildings and statues up and down O'Connell Street. Pearse, Connolly, and 13 other leaders were imprisoned, secretly tried, and speedily executed.

Ultimately, though, the British reaction was as counterproductive as it was harsh. The totality with which those involved in organizing the rebellion were pursued and dispatched acted as a lightning rod for many of those who had been undecided about the effectiveness of a purely political struggle. Indeed, a fact that has become somewhat lost in the ensuing hundred or so years since Patrick Pearse stood on the steps of the post office early on that cold Monday morning, reading a treatise on Irish independence, is that a great many Irish didn't support the rebellion at the time. Many either believed that the best course of action was to lay low until the war had ended, when concessions would be won as a result, or that it was simply the wrong thing to do, as long as sons of Ireland were sacrificing their lives in the trenches of Europe.

The aftermath of 1916 all but guaranteed, for better or for worse, that Ireland's future would be decided by the gun.

REBELLION A power vacuum was left at the heart of the nationalist movement after the Easter Rising, and it was filled by two men: Michael Collins and Eamon de Valera. On the surface, both men had much in common; Collins was a Cork man who had returned from Britain in order to join the Irish Volunteers (later to become the Irish Republican Army, or IRA), while de Valera was an Irish-American math teacher who came back to Ireland to set up a new political party, *Sinn Féin*.

When de Valera's party won a landslide victory in the general election of 1918, its MPs refused to sit in London, instead proclaiming the first Dáil, or independent parliament, in Dublin. De Valera went to rally support for the cause in America, while Collins stayed to concentrate on his work as head of the Irish Volunteers. Tensions

1500s	English rule consolidated across Ireland. Henry VIII proclaims himself king of Ireland.	1607	The flight of the Irish earls marks the demise of the old Gaelic order.
1534–52	Henry VIII begins suppression of the Catholic Church in Ireland.	1641	Irish Catholic revolt in Ulster led by Sir Phelim O'Neill ends in defeat.
1558–1603	Reign of Elizabeth I. Ireland proclaimed an Anglican country. The "plantation" of Munster divides Ireland into counties.	1649	Oliver Cromwell invades and begins the reconquest of Ireland.
1591	Trinity College founded.	1690	The forces of King James II, a Catholic, are defeated at the Battle of the Boyne, consolidating Protestant order in England.
1601–02	Spanish forces, in consort with Irish rebels, attempt to stage an invasion of Ireland. They are defeated by the English after a 3-month siege.	1704	Enactment of first anti-Catholic "Penal Laws." Apartheid comes to Ireland.

escalated into violence, and for the next 2 years, Irish nationalists fought a tit-for-tat military campaign against the British in Ireland.

The low point of the struggle came in 1920, when Collins ordered 14 British operatives to be murdered in their beds, in response to which British troops opened fire on the audience at a football game at Croke Park in Dublin, randomly killing 12 innocent people. A truce was eventually declared on July 9, 1921, and 6 months later, the Anglo-Irish treaty was signed in London, granting legislative independence to 26 Irish counties (known together as the Irish Free State). The compromise through which that freedom was won, though, was that six counties in the north would remain part of the United Kingdom. Collins knew that compromise would not be accepted by the more strident members of his rebel group. He also knew they would blame him for agreeing to it in the first place. When he signed the treaty he told the people present, "I am signing my own death warrant."

As he feared, nationalists were split between those who accepted the treaty as a platform on which to build, and those, led by the nationalist de Valera, who saw it as a betrayal, and would accept nothing less than immediate and full independence at any cost. Even the withdrawal of British troops from Dublin for the first time in nearly 800 years did not quell their anger. The result was an inexorable slide into civil war. The flashpoint came in April 1922, when violence erupted around the streets of the capital, and rolled on for eight days until de Valera's supporters were forced to surrender.

The government of the fledgling free state ordered that Republicans be shot on sight, leading to the deaths of 77 people. And Collins had been right about his own fate: Four months later he was assassinated while on a visit to his childhood home.

The fallout from the civil war dominated Irish politics for the next decade. De Valera split from the Republicans to form another party, Fianna Fáil ("the Warriors of Ireland"), which won the election of 1932 and governed for 17 years. Despite his continuing dedication to the Republican ideal, however, de Valera was not to be the one who finally declared Ireland a republic, in 1948; ironically, that distinction went to a coalition led by de Valera's opponent, Douglas Hyde, whose victory in the election of 1947 was attributed to the fact that de Valera had become too obsessed with abstract Republican ideals to govern effectively.

1778	The Penal Laws are progressively repealed.	1803	Twenty-five-year-old Robert Emmet is hanged after his uprising of fewer than 100 men is a tragic failure.
1782	The Irish Parliament is granted independence.		
1791	Wolfe Tone founds the Society of the United Irishmen.	1829	Daniel O'Connell secures passage of the Catholic Emancipation Act. He is later named lord mayor of Dublin.
1796–97	Wolfe Tone launches an invasion from France, fails, is taken captive, and commits suicide.	1845–ca. 52	The Great Famine. An estimated two million Irish either die or emigrate, mostly to the U.S.
1798	"The Year of the French." A French invasion force is defeated at Killala Bay. General Humbert surrenders to Cornwallis.	1858	The Irish Republican Brotherhood, a secret society known as the Fenians, is founded in New York.
1801	The Irish Parliament is induced to dissolve itself. Ireland becomes part of the United Kingdom.		

continues

STUCK IN NEUTRAL   One of the more controversial, not to say morally ambiguous, decisions that Eamon de Valera made while in office was to stay neutral during World War II, despite the best efforts of Winston Churchill and Franklin Roosevelt to persuade him otherwise. The basis for his decision—a combination of Ireland's size and economic weakness, and the British presence in Northern Ireland—may have made sense to some extent, but it left Ireland in the peculiar position of tacitly favoring one side in the war, but refusing to help it. After the death of Adolf Hitler in April 1945, de Valera alienated the Allies further by sending his personal sympathies to the German ambassador.

His reticence didn't find much favor among the Irish population, either. During the war, as many as 300,000 Irish men enlisted in the British or U.S. armies. In the end, more than 50,000 Irish soldiers perished in a war their country had refused to join.

TROUBLE ON THE WAY   After the war, 2 decades passed without violence in Ireland, until the late 1960s, when the outbreak of sectarian conflict in the North erupted. What started out as a civil rights movement to demand greater equality for Catholics within Northern Ireland soon escalated into a cycle of violence that lasted for 30 years.

It would be a terrible oversimplification to say that the Troubles were merely a clearcut struggle between those who wanted to complete the process of Irish unification and those who wanted to remain part of the United Kingdom—although that was, of course, the crux of the conflict. Factors such as organized crime and terrorism, together with centuries-old conflicts over religious, land, and social issues, make the conflict even harder for outsiders to understand.

The worst of the Troubles came in the 1970s. In 1972, British troops inexplicably opened fire on a peaceful demonstration in Derry, killing 12 people—many of whom were shot while they tended to the wounds of the first people injured. The IRA took advantage of the mood of public outrage to begin a civilian bombing campaign on the British mainland. The cycle of violence continued for 20 years, during which time none of the myriad sides in the conflict would talk to each other. Finally, in the early 1990s, secret talks were opened between the British and the IRA, leading to an IRA cease-fire in 1994 (although the cease-fire held only shakily—an IRA bomb in Omagh 4 years later killed 29, the most to die in any single incident of the Troubles).

1866	In an imaginative publicity stunt, a minuscule army of Fenians attempts to invade Canada.	1905–08	Founding of *Sinn Féin* ("We Ourselves") with close links to the Irish Republican Brotherhood.
1879	Michael Davitt founds the National Land League to support the claims of tenant farmers.	1912	Third Home Rule bill passes in the House of Commons and is defeated by the House of Lords.
1879–82	The "land war" forces the enactment of reform. The tenant system unravels; land returns to those who work it.	1916	Patrick Pearse and James Connolly lead an armed uprising on Easter Monday to proclaim the Irish Republic. Defeat is followed by the execution of 15 leaders of the revolt.
1886 & 1894	Bills for Home Rule are defeated in Parliament.		
1893	The Gaelic League is founded to revive the Irish language.	1919	Sinn Féin, led by Eamon de Valera, constitutes itself as the first Irish Dáil and declares independence.

The peace process continued throughout the 1990s, helped significantly by the mediation efforts of U.S. President Bill Clinton, who arguably became more involved in Irish affairs than any president before him until, eventually, on Good Friday 1998, a peace accord was finally signed in Belfast. The agreement committed all sides to a peaceful resolution of the conflict in Northern Ireland, and included the reinstatement of full self-government for the region in a power-sharing administration. It stopped short of resolving the territorial issue once and for all—in other words, Northern Ireland is still part of the U.K., and will be for the foreseeable future. On the contrary, to some extent the conflicts rage more bitterly and more divisively than ever before, the difference being that, with notable exceptions, they are fought through the ballot box, rather than the barrel of a gun. In 2005 the IRA fully decommissioned its weapons, and officially dissolved itself as a paramilitary unit.

REBIRTH While Northern Ireland still struggled to find peace, the Republic of Ireland flourished. The 1990s brought unprecedented wealth and prosperity to the country, thanks in part to European Union subsidies, and partly to a thriving economy, which acquired the nickname "the Celtic Tiger" for its new global strength. Ireland became a rich country, widely seen as one of the best places in the world to live and work.

However, that boom came crashing down after the banking crisis of 2008. The Irish government was forced to seek financial aid from the European Union, worth more than 50% of the whole economy, to save the country from bankruptcy. The op-ed pages of any Irish newspaper were filled with real feelings of betrayal and a deep sense of opportunity lost.

Since then, things have once more begun to look up for the Irish economy—although the recovery will be a slow one. And there is something to be said for the Irish spirit and the ability to find humor in the darkest of places. Every new crisis brings fresh jokes alongside the rage. Every new leader is a target for general hilarity. And while nobody in the country would tell you there is not work to be done, you get the distinct impression that the people—if not the politicians and the bankers who got them into this mess—are ready to do that work.

1919–21 The Irish War of Independence. Michael Collins commands the Irish forces.	**1932** Eamon de Valera leads Fianna Fáil to victory and becomes head of government.
1921 Anglo-Irish Treaty. Ireland is partitioned. Twenty-six counties form the Free State; the other six remain a part of the U.K. The Free State adopts its first constitution a year later.	**1937** The Free State adopts a new constitution, abandoning membership of the British Commonwealth and changing the country's official name to Eire.
1922–23 The Irish civil war, between the government of the Free State and those who opposed the Anglo-Irish treaty. Michael Collins is assassinated by the IRA, who saw the treaty as a sellout.	**1939** Dublin is bombed by Germany at start of World War II, but Ireland remains neutral.
	1948 The Republic of Ireland Act. Ireland severs its last constitutional links with Britain.

continues

IRELAND IN CULTURE

LITERATURE For more than 100 years, Ireland has had a place in literature disproportionate to its small size and modest population. Four writers from this tiny country have won the Nobel Prize for literature. Inspired by the country's unique beauty, the unfairness they perceived in its political system, and its cruel legacy of poverty and struggle, the country's authors, poets, and playwrights wrote about the Irish for the Irish, and to raise awareness in the rest of the world. No matter where you live, you've probably been reading about Ireland all your life.

One of the country's best-known early writers was satirist **Jonathan Swift,** who was born in Dublin in 1667. Educated at Trinity College, he left Ireland for England in 1688 to avoid the Glorious Revolution. He spent much of his adult life in London, returning to Ireland when he was over 50 years old, at which point he began to write his most famous works. The suffering of the poor in Ireland greatly affected him, but he translated his anger into dark, vicious humor. His tract *A Modest Proposal* is widely credited with inventing satire as we now know it. His best-known works have political undertones—even *Gulliver's Travels* is a political allegory.

Best known for his novel *Dracula*, the novelist and theatre promoter **Bram Stoker** was born in Clontarf, a coastal suburb of Dublin, in 1847. He spent most of his life in England, which largely inspired his work, although it is said that **St. Michan's Church** in Dublin (see p. 80), with its ghostly crypt, and St. Mary's in Killarney (p. 140) helped to contribute to *Dracula*'s creepy feel.

Born in Dublin in 1854, **Oscar Wilde** was a popular and successful student at Trinity College, winning a scholarship to continue his studies in England at Oxford. After a flamboyant time there, he graduated with top honors and returned to Ireland, only to lose his girlfriend to Bram Stoker in 1878, after which he left Ireland forever. His writing—including the novel *The Picture of Dorian Gray,* plays including *The Importance of Being Earnest,* and books of poetry—were forever overshadowed by his personal life. While there is a statue of him in Dublin, his works were largely inspired by British and French writers, and he spent the majority of his life abroad.

1955 Ireland is admitted into the United Nations.

1963 U.S. President John F. Kennedy visits Ireland.

1969 Violence breaks out in Northern Ireland. British troops are called in.

1972 In Derry a peaceful rally turns into "Bloody Sunday." The Northern Irish Parliament is dissolved, and direct rule is imposed from Britain.

1973 Ireland joins the European Community.

1986 The Anglo-Irish Agreement gives the Republic a say in the government of Northern Ireland.

1990 Mary Robinson is elected Ireland's first female president.

1994 The IRA announces a cease-fire, and the Protestant paramilitaries follow suit. Commencement of peace talks.

1995 Unprecedented economic growth in Ireland hails the start of the so-called "Celtic Tiger." The boom years would last for over a decade.

1995 U.S. President Bill Clinton makes an historic visit to Ireland, speaking to large crowds in

George Bernard Shaw was born in Dublin in 1856 and attended school in the city, but never went to college, as he came to loathe the organized education system. He moved to England as a young man and lived much of his life in a village in Hertfordshire in England. As a result, many of his works have a distinctly English feel. His plays are known both for their sharp wit and for their sense of outrage over unfairness in society and the absurdity of the British class system. He is the only person ever to have won both the Nobel Prize and an Oscar (for *Pygmalion*).

William Butler Yeats was born in Sandy Mount outside Dublin in 1865, and attended the Metropolitan School of Art in Dublin, but his poetry and prose were heavily inspired by County Sligo, where he spent much of his time, and where he is buried. One of the leading figures of the Irish literary revival in the early 20th century, he won the Nobel Prize in 1923.

James Joyce was born in the Dublin suburb of Rathgar in 1882 and educated at Jesuit boarding schools, and later at Trinity College. He wrote vividly—and sometimes impenetrably—about Dublin, despite spending much of his life as an expat living nomadically in Europe. His controversial and hugely complex novels *Ulysses* and *Finnegan's Wake* are his most celebrated (and least understood) works. They and his collection of short stories, *Dubliners*, are seen as touching deeply on the character of the people of Dublin.

The poet and playwright **Samuel Beckett** was born in 1906 in the Dublin suburb of Foxrock and educated at Trinity College. His work, however, was heavily influenced by German and French postmodernists, and he spent much of his life abroad, even serving with the Resistance in France during World War II. Best known for his complex absurdist play *Waiting for Godot,* he won the Nobel Prize in 1969.

Among modern Irish writers, the best known is arguably the poet **Seamus Heaney.** He was born in 1939 near a small town called Castledawson in Northern Ireland, where as a child he won scholarships to boarding school in Derry and later to Queen's University in Belfast. His years studying classic ancient Greek and Latin literature and Anglo-Saxon writing heavily influenced his poetry, but all of his writing is marked by his life in the troubled region where he grew up. His works, including *The Cure at Troy*

Belfast and Derry, and becoming directly involved with the peace process. He is received with enthusiasm in the Republic.

1996 The IRA breaks its cease-fire. An IRA bomb in Omagh kills 29. The North sees the worst rioting in 15 years.

1997 The IRA breaks its cease-fire. The IRA declares a new cease-fire. Sinn Féin enters inclusive all-party peace talks designed to bring about a comprehensive settlement.

1998 The talks conclude with the so-called Good Friday Agreement, later strongly supported in referendums held on the same day in the Republic and the North. The agreement establishes self-government in Northern Ireland.

2001 After 3 further years of political wrangling over the terms of power sharing, the IRA finally begins to decommission its weapons. It officially ceases to exist as a paramilitary organization 4 years later—though splinter groups persist to this day.

2004 The Irish government bans smoking in public places.

continues

(based on the works of Sophocles), *The Haw Lantern,* and *The Government of the Tongue,* ultimately earned him the Nobel Prize in 1995. Heaney's death in the summer of 2013 brought an outpouring of affection from fans across the world.

Other Irish writers who have been burning up the book charts in recent years include **Marian Keyes** (whose hugely popular novels include *Lucy Sullivan is Getting Married* and *This Charming Man*); **Roddy Doyle** (*The Commitments, Paddy Clarke Ha Ha Ha*), and the late **Maeve Binchy** (*A Week in Winter, Circle of Friends*).

NONFICTION   If you want to know about Ireland and the Irish, there are plenty of talented writers in and out of the country who are willing to tell you.

Jonathan Bardon's *A History of Ireland in 250 Episodes* is a good general introduction to Irish history. The book is broken up into 250 short chapters—learned without being too dense, and a very useful primer.

To understand more about the famine, try the British author **Cecil Woodham-Smith's** *The Great Hunger.* Written in 1962, it's still viewed as the definitive, dispassionate examination of this dark period in Irish history.

The author **Tim Pat Coogan** is the son of an IRA volunteer, and he has written two excellent books, *The Irish Civil War* (2001) and *The Troubles: Ireland's Ordeal 1966–1996* (1997), both of which are essential reading for anyone wanting to understand the complexities of 21st-century Ireland. He also wrote a controversial biography, *Eamon de Valera,* criticizing the former Irish president's actions and legacy.

For a look at Ireland in recent history, try **John Ardagh's** *Ireland and the Irish* (1995) or **F. S. Lyons's** *Ireland Since the Famine* (1973).

The late Irish-born American writer **Frank McCourt** earned acclaim and won the Pulitzer Prize for *Angela's Ashes* (1996), his grim memoir of a childhood spent partly in Limerick and partly in Brooklyn. But it has been bitterly disputed by many in Limerick who claim it is not an accurate representation of the city during that time, and the book is very controversial in Ireland.

FILM   Many complex and difficult Irish subjects have been tackled by an international array of directors and actors. Here are a few of the better known ones—and a few obscure gems worth seeking out.

2007   A new power-sharing executive is put into place in Northern Ireland, bringing together lifelong enemies DUP leader Ian Paisley and Sinn Féin leader Gerry Adams.

2008   Ireland's economy begins to crash as the country becomes the first in the European Union to officially enter recession.

2009   The Irish government issues a damning report into child sex abuse in the Catholic Church—part of the wide-ranging scandal that eventually leads to the resignation of Pope Benedict XVI in 2012.

2010   British Prime Minister David Cameron apologizes for "Bloody Sunday," when British soldiers killed 14 Irish protesters in Bogside, a Catholic neighborhood in Derry, Northern Ireland, in 1972.

2011   Longtime ruling party Fianna Fáil is swept out of office on a wave of voter anger, replaced by Fine Gael. New *Taoiseach* (Prime Minister) Enda Kenny vows to restore Irish economic stability.

2011   Queen Elizabeth II becomes the first British monarch to visit the Republic of Ireland. The following year, in Belfast, she

Virtually unknown today, *Maeve* (directed by John Davis/Pat Murphy, 1982) is a fascinating piece of Irish independent film from the early 1980s. Starring the American actress Mary Jackson, it follows an Irish expat in England who decides to return to strife-torn Northern Ireland.

The Commitments (directed by Alan Parker, 1991) may be the most famous Irish musical ever made. With its cast of young, largely inexperienced Irish actors playing musicians dedicated to American soul music, it's a delightful piece of filmmaking.

Michael Collins (directed by Neil Jordan, 1996) is a fine biopic about the Irish rebel, filmed largely on location and starring the Irish actor Liam Neeson.

The Wind That Shakes the Barley (directed by Ken Loach, 2006), with a mostly Irish cast and English director, won the Palme d'Or at Cannes for its depiction of Ireland's early-20th-century fight for independence.

Shadow Dancer (directed by James Marsh, 2012) is an exciting spy thriller set in early-1990s Belfast. The film, which was a hit at the Sundance Film Festival, pulls off the rare trick of being about the Troubles without getting bogged down in politics.

MUSIC   Music is inescapable in Ireland, and if you hear a band play in a bar and you like them, we strongly advise you to buy a CD from them. In the days of Internet radio, the best way to discover new sounds is to tune in to Irish radio stations online. An excellent list of stations that stream live (including links) can be found at **www.radio feeds.co.uk/irish.asp.** Good places to start are the stations run by RTÉ, the national broadcaster, particularly the music and entertainment-oriented 2FM (www.rte.ie/2fm); and **TXFM** (www.txfm.ie), a Dublin-based station that specializes in the latest indie and alternative sounds.

Obviously, traditional music is still alive and well in Ireland, particularly in close association with Irish step dancing. The folk culture is primarily found outside of Dublin, although some pubs in the city do still showcase traditional music. There's also **Cultúr-lann na hÉireann,** which offers much in the way of traditional Irish performances. In County Kerry, **Siamsa Tí** offers a mixture of Irish music, dance, and mime. For a less formal atmosphere, check out local pubs in small towns, which almost always can be counted on to host Irish music, and sometimes dancing, too.

shakes hands with Sinn Féin's Martin McGuinness—a former IRA commander, now deputy First Minister of Northern Ireland.

2011 Michael Higgins, who was once a professor at the University of Southern Illinois, is elected the 9th president of the Republic of Ireland.

2012 The death of Savita Halappanavar, an Indian national who was working as a dentist in Galway, sparks renewed debate about the country's abortion laws. Halappanavar died after being admitted to the hospital while suffering a miscarriage, only to have doctors refuse her a life-saving abortion.

2013 Enda Kenny issues an emotional public apology for the so-called "Magdalene Laundries"—government-backed religious workhouses that effectively kept women in slave labor until as recently as the 1990s.

2013 Seamus Heaney, widely acclaimed as one of the greatest poets of the modern age, dies in Dublin at the age of 74.

DUBLIN

For such an ancient town, Dublin is doing a pretty good job of not showing its age. Despite its stony gray appearance, the Irish capital is actually one of Europe's most youthful cities. Around half of its residents are under the age of 28—and almost a full third of Ireland's entire population live in the greater Dublin area. Dublin's oldest landmarks are still among its most interesting, but they're enlivened now by a new wealth of modern attractions: Edgy bars and cafes buzz alongside old pubs that have stood for centuries, while chic boutiques are snuggled into the medieval precincts of Cow's Lane. It's yours to discover afresh—and even if you think you know what to expect, you're almost certain to be surprised by what you find.

ESSENTIALS

Arriving

BY PLANE **Aer Lingus** (www.aerlingus.com; ℂ **081/836-5000**), Ireland's national airline, operates regular, direct scheduled flights between Dublin International Airport and numerous cities worldwide. From the U.S., direct routes are Boston, Chicago (O'Hare), New York (J.F.K), and San Francisco. **American Airlines** (www.aa.com; ℂ **800/433-7300**), **Delta** (www.delta.com; ℂ **800/221-1212**), and **United** (www.united.com; ℂ **800/864-8331**) all fly direct to Dublin from at least one of those same cities. From Canada, direct flights are operated by **Air Canada** (www.aircanada.com; ℂ **888/247-2262**). Most of the big European airlines have direct flights to Dublin.

   Dublin International Airport (www.dublinairport.com; ℂ **01/814-1111**) is 11km (6¾ miles) north of the city center. A travel information desk in the arrivals concourse provides information on public bus and rail services throughout the country.

   An excellent airport-to-city shuttle bus service called **AirCoach** operates 24 hours a day, making runs at 15-minute intervals. Its buses go direct from the airport to Dublin's city center and south side. Not all the major stops are covered on every service, so do check that you've got the right one before you board. City center fares are €6–€7 one-way, depending on where you are going; and to Ballsbridge, Dún Laoghaire, or Dalkey, around €10. Children aged 5 to 12 are €2–€5; children 13 and over are counted as adults. You buy your ticket from the driver. Although AirCoach is slightly more expensive than the Dublin Bus (see below), it makes fewer stops, so it is faster (the journey to the city center takes about 45 min.), and it brings you into the hotel districts. To confirm AirCoach departures and arrivals, find it online at www.aircoach.ie or call ℂ **01/844-7118.**

4

If you need to connect with the Irish bus or rail service, Dublin Bus's route 747, otherwise known as the **Airlink** (www.dublinbus.ie; ✆ **01/844-4265**), provides express coach services from the airport into central Dublin and beyond. Buses go to the city's central bus station, **Busáras**, on Store Street and on to **Connolly** and **Heuston** railway stations. Service runs daily from 6am until 11:30pm (Sun 7am–11:20pm), with departures every 15 to 20 minutes. One-way fare is €6 for adults and €3 for children 11 and under.

Finally, **Dublin Bus** (www.dublinbus.ie; ✆ **01/873-4222**) has regular daily connections between the airport and the city center from 6am to 11:30pm. The one-way trip takes about 30 minutes, and the fare is €6 adults, €3 children. Consult the travel information desk in the arrivals concourse to figure out which bus takes you closest to your hotel.

For speed and ease—especially if you have a lot of luggage—a **taxi** is the best way to get directly to your hotel or guesthouse. Depending on your destination, fares average between €20 and €35. A tip of a couple of euro is standard. Taxis are lined up at a first-come, first-served taxi stand outside the arrivals terminal.

Major international and local car-rental companies operate desks at Dublin Airport.

BY FERRY   Passenger and car ferries from Britain arrive at the Dublin Ferryport, on the eastern end of the North Docks, and at the Dún Laoghaire Ferryport, in the city's southeastern suburbs. Call **Irish Ferries** (www.irishferries.ie; ✆ **0818/300-400**), **P&O Irish Sea** (www.poirishsea.com; ✆ **01/407-3434**), or **Stena Line** (www.stenaline. com, ✆ **01/204-7777**) for bookings and information. Buses and taxis service both ports.

BY TRAIN   **Irish Rail** (www.irishrail.ie; ✆ **1850/366-222**), Iarnród Éireann in Gaelic, operates daily train service to Dublin from Belfast, Northern Ireland, and all major cities in the Irish Republic, including Cork, Galway, Limerick, Killarney, Sligo, Wexford, and Waterford. Trains from the south, west, and southwest arrive at **Heuston Station, Kingsbridge, off St. John's Road; from the north and northwest at **Connolly Station,** Amiens Street; and from the southeast at **Pearse Station,** Westland Row, Tara Street.

BY BUS   **Bus Éireann** (www.buseireann.ie; ✆ **01/836-6111**) operates daily express coach and local bus service from all major cities and towns in Ireland into Dublin's central bus station, **Busáras,** Store Street.

BY CAR   If you are arriving by car from other parts of Ireland or on a car ferry from Britain, all main roads lead into the heart of Dublin and are well signposted to **An Lar** (City Centre). To bypass the city center, the East Link (toll bridge, €2) and West Link are signposted, and M50 circuits the city on three sides. From Wexford Town, Galway, or Belfast, the drive takes around 2 hours; from Cork, 2½ hours.

Getting Around

If your stay in Dublin is short, geography is on your side. The vast majority of the capital's best sites are concentrated in the city center, an area of no more than a few square kilometers. This points to your first and most important decision: If you have a car, leave it behind at your hotel (or as close as you can get—parking is notoriously difficult). Dublin's roads are crowded and confusing. Baffling one-way streets, bad signage, and terrible traffic are all common problems.

However, cars aside, Dublin is a very easy and convenient city to get around. Public transportation is good and getting better, taxis are plentiful and reasonably

leap CARDS

If you're likely to use public transport a lot while in Dublin, consider getting a **Leap Card**. They allow you to prepay for reduced-cost travel on all Dublin buses (including Airlink and Nightlink), DART, Luas, and commuter trains. You can buy them at around 400 shops in and around the city—look out for the distinctive green logo depicting a rather overexcited-looking frog in mid-leap—including the small **Easons, Kiosk,** and **Spa** shops at Dublin Airport. You can also get them from ticket machines in some city center DART and railway stations, or order them online at **www.leapcard.ie.** They're free, but you have to pay a refundable deposit of €5 adults, €3 children, and buy at least €5 worth of credit up-front.

---

priced, and your own two feet can easily carry you from one end of town to the other. In fact, with its perennial traffic and parking problems, it's a city where the foot is mightier than the wheel.

BY BUS   After walking, buses are the most convenient and practical way to get between the city center sights. Dublin Bus operates a fleet of double-deckers, single-deckers, and minibuses (the latter charmingly called "imps"). Most originate on or near O'Connell Street, Abbey Street, and Eden Quay on the Northside, and at Aston Quay, College Street, and Fleet Street on the south side. Bus stops resembling big blue or green lollipops are located every few blocks on main thoroughfares. To tell where the bus is going, look at the destination street and bus number above its front window; those heading for the city center indicate that with an odd mix of Latin and Gaelic: VIA AN LAR.

Bus service runs daily throughout the city, starting at 6am (10am on Sunday), with the last bus at about 11:30pm. On Friday and Saturday nights, **Nitelink** service runs from the city center to the suburbs from midnight to 4am. Buses operate every 30 minutes for most runs; schedules are posted on revolving notice boards at bus stops.

Inner-city fares are based on distances traveled. Daytime journeys that take place entirely within the designated "City Centre Zone" cost €0.65. This stretches from Parnell Square in the north, Connolly Station and Merrion Square in the east, St. Stephen's Green in the south, and Ormond Quay in the west. Longer journeys cost up to €4.50 if you're going as far as the outer suburbs.

You pay on board the bus, using an automatic fare machine located in front of the driver. **No Dublin bus accepts notes or gives change.** If you don't have the exact money in coins, the driver will issue you with a "change receipt." You must then take this to the Dublin Bus headquarters on O'Connell Street to collect your change (a process not designed to encourage refunds). The sole exception to this rule is route 747 ("Airlink"), which runs between the airport and the city center. It accepts notes and gives change normally.

BY DART   An acronym for Dublin Area Rapid Transit, the electric DART trains travel aboveground, linking the city center stations at **Connolly Station, Tara Street,** and **Pearse Street** with suburbs and seaside communities as far as Malahide to the north and Greystones to the south. Service operates roughly every 10 to 20 minutes Monday to Saturday from around 6am to midnight and Sunday from 9:30am to 11pm. For further information, contact DART, Dublin Pearse Station (www.dart.ie; ✆ **01/703-3592**).

BY TRAM The sleek, modern, and wheelchair-accessible light-rail tram system known as **Luas** runs from around 5:30am to 12:30am Monday to Friday, 6:30am to 12:30am Saturday, and 7am to 11:30pm on Sunday. (The last trams to certain stations are earlier—be sure to check the timetable.) There are two lines, Red and Green: The Green Line links St. Stephen's Green with Sandyford in the south; the Red Line runs between the Point, near the O2 in Dublin Docklands, and Connolly Railway Station, down to the southwestern suburbs of Saggart and Tallaght. For further information, contact Luas (www.luas.ie; ☎ **01/800-300-604** or 01/461-4910).

ON FOOT Marvelously compact, Dublin is ideal for walking. Just remember to look right and then left (and in the direction opposite your instincts if you're from North America) before crossing the street. Pedestrians have the right of way at specially marked, zebra-striped crossings (these intersections usually have two flashing lights).

BY TAXI It's very difficult to hail a taxi on the street; instead, they line up at taxi stands (called "ranks") outside major hotels, at bus and train stations, and on prime thoroughfares such as Upper O'Connell Street, College Green, and the north side of St. Stephen's Green. You can also phone for a taxi; see the numbers listed in the "Fast Facts" section on p. 46.

[Fast FACTS] DUBLIN

ATMs/Banks Nearly all banks are open Monday to Friday 10am to 4pm (to 5pm Thursday). Convenient locations include the **Bank of Ireland**, at 2 College Green, Dublin 2, 88 Camden St. Lower, Dublin 1, and at Trinity College; and the **Allied Irish Bank (AIB)**, at 100 Grafton St., Dublin 2, and 37 O'Connell St., Dublin 1.

Currency Exchange Currency-exchange services, signposted as **Bureau de Change**, are in most Dublin banks and at many branches of the Irish post office system, known as **An Post**. A bureau de change operates daily during flight arrival and departure times at Dublin Airport. Some hotels and travel agencies offer bureau de change services. *Tip:* The best rate of exchange is almost always when you use your bank card at an ATM.

Dentists For dental emergencies, your hotel will usually contact a dentist for you; otherwise, try **Smiles Dental,** 28 O'Connell St. (☎ **1850/323-323**); or **Molesworth Dental Surgery,** 2 Molesworth Place (☎ **01/661-5544**).

Doctors & Hospitals For emergencies, dial ☎ **999.** If you need a doctor, your hotel should be able to contact one for you. Otherwise you could try **Dame Street Medical Center,** 16 Dame St. (☎ **01/679-0754**), or the **Suffolk Street Surgery,** 107 Grafton St. (☎ **01/679-8181**).

Emergencies For police, fire, or other emergencies, dial ☎ **999.**

Luggage Storage If check-out at your hotel is in the morning and your flight is in the evening (or you arrive too early to check in), many hotels will look after your

baggage. Alternatively, **Global Internet Café,** 8 Lower O'Connell St. (☎ **01/878-0295**) can store bags securely. There's also a "Left Luggage" facility at the Terminal 1 parking lot at Dublin Airport.

Pharmacies City Pharmacy, 14 Dame St. (☎ **01/670-4523**) stays open until 10pm weekdays, 9pm Saturday; **Boots the Chemist,** 20 Henry St. (☎ **01/873-0209**) or 12 Grafton St. (☎ **01/677-3000**), stays open until 9pm Thursday and Friday, 7pm Saturday and Sunday, and 8pm Monday to Wednesday. Dublin does not have 24-hour pharmacies.

Mail & Postage General Post Office, O'Connell St. (☎ **01/705-8833**) is open Monday through Saturday, 8:30am–6pm. Postage for a letter or postcard costs €0.65 within Ireland and Northern

Ireland; €0.90 to the rest of the world.

Newspapers & Magazines Look out for **Totally Dublin,** a free monthly entertainment guide, at tourism offices. One of the best online magazines is **In Dublin** (www.indublin.ie), which has comprehensive event listings. The monthly **Gay Community News** (www. gcn.ie), another free magazine, is also full of entertainment listings; there's a print edition, but the online version is completely free.

Taxis Taxi ranks are outside major hotels, at bus and train stations, and on Upper O'Connell St., College Green, and the north side of St. Stephen's Green. To call a cab, try **Co-Op** (℡ **01/677-7777**), **Trinity** (℡ **01/708-2222**), or **VIP/ACE Taxis** (℡ **01/478-3333**).

City Layout

Dublin is divided down the middle by the curves of the River Liffey, which empties into the sea at the city's farthest edge. To the north and south, the city center is encircled by canals: The Royal Canal arcs across the north and the Grand Canal through the south. Traditionally, the area south of the river has been Dublin's buzzing, prosperous hub. It still holds most of the best hotels, restaurants, shops, and sights, but the Northside is on the upswing, and hip new bars and hotels give it a trendy edge. Dublin is compact and easily walked in an hour. In fact, a 45-minute walk from the bucolic peace of St. Stephen's Green, up Grafton Street, and across the Liffey to the top of O'Connell Street offers a good overview of the city's prosperous present and troubled past.

MAIN STREETS & SQUARES In the town center just south of the river, **Dame Street,** which changes its name to College Green, Westmoreland Street, and Lord Edward Street at various points, is the main east-west artery connecting **Trinity College** with **Dublin Castle** and **Christ Church Cathedral.** On one side of Dame Street are the winding medieval lanes of **Temple Bar,** Dublin's party central (plenty of pubs). On the other side of Dame Street are tributary streets lined with shops and cafes. Where Dame Street turns into College Green, the sturdy gray stone walls of Trinity College make an excellent landmark to get your bearings. At the southwest corner is the top of **Grafton Street**—a lively pedestrianized shopping lane crowded with tourists, musicians, and artists, which leads to the bucolic, statue-filled peace of **St. Stephen's Green.** From there, heading back up via **Kildare Street** will take you past **Leinster House,** where the Irish Parliament meets, and a turn to the right brings you to **Merrion Square,** another of Dublin's well-preserved Georgian squares.

To get to the Northside, most visitors choose to walk across the photogenic arch of the **Ha'penny Bridge** (see p. 76), but most locals take the less attractive **O'Connell Bridge** nearby. You can be different and cross via the Ha'penny's sleekly modern neighbor, the **Millennium Bridge,** which is beautifully illuminated after dark. The O'Connell Bridge leads directly onto **O'Connell Street,** a wide, statue-lined boulevard that is the north's main thoroughfare. O'Connell Street runs north to **Parnell Square,** which holds a couple of marvelous museums and marks the edge of central Dublin. From the bottom to the top, O'Connell Street is lined with statues, starting with an absurdly ornate representation of the titular politician Daniel O'Connell surrounded by angels (which still have bullet holes left from the Easter Rising). The street running along the Liffey's embankment is called the **North Quays** by all, though its name changes on virtually every block, reflecting the long-gone docks that once lined it.

In the older section of the city, **High Street** is the gateway to medieval and Viking Dublin, from the city's two medieval cathedrals to the old city walls and Dublin Castle.

MURKY origins

For most visitors, the very word "Dublin" may bring to mind a heady, romantic mix of history and good times to come, but it actually has a more prosaic origin. The name comes from the ancient Celtic words *dubh linn*, meaning "the black pool." Specifically, it refers to a natural inlet where the River Liffey met the River Poddle, and the waters were dark and murky. Long since buried, the inlet is thought to be somewhere around Dublin Castle.

However, an allusion to these watery origins still survives in the city's Gaelic name, *Baile Átha Cliath*. It means "the town of the hurdled ford"—a ford being a point where a stream or river crosses a road. When fords were "hurdled" in medieval times, it meant that they were covered at low tide with woven sheets of willow, making them easier to cross.

Dublin Neighborhoods in Brief

Trinity College Area   On the south side of the River Liffey, Trinity College is an Ivy League–style university with shady quadrangles and atmospheric stone buildings. It's virtually the dead center of the city and is surrounded by bookstores, shops, and noisy traffic. This area lies in the Dublin 2 postal code.

Temple Bar   Wedged between Trinity College and the Old City, this is Dublin's party hub, and it's packed with bars, discos, and pubs. During the day, it's quieter and more refined thanks to good shops, two worthwhile art galleries, recording studios, and theaters. But at night, this is largely the stomping ground of young tourists looking for lots of alcohol, and it's easy to feel over the hill here if you're over 25. This area lies in the Dublin 2 and Dublin 8 postal codes.

Old City   Dating from Viking and medieval times, the cobblestone enclave of the historic Old City includes Dublin Castle, the remnants of the city's original walls, and Christ Church and St. Patrick's cathedrals. It encompasses the Dublin 8 and 2 zones.

Liberties   Adjacent to Old City, the Liberties district takes its name from the fact that it was once just outside the city walls, and therefore, exempt from Dublin's jurisdiction. Although it prospered in its early days, Liberties fell on hard times in the 17th

and 18th centuries and has only felt the touch of urban renewal in the last decade or so. Its main claim to fame is the Guinness Brewery. Most of this area is in the Dublin 8 zone.

St. Stephen's Green/Grafton Street Area   The biggest tourist draw in town, this district is home to Dublin's finest hotels, restaurants, and shops. The neighborhood is filled with impressive Georgian architecture and is primarily a business and shopping zone. It is part of the Dublin 2 zone.

Fitzwilliam & Merrion Squares   These two little square parks between Trinity College and St. Stephen's Green are surrounded by grand Georgian town houses. Some of Dublin's most famous citizens once lived here; today, many of the houses are offices for doctors, lawyers, and government agencies. This area is part of the Dublin 2 zone.

O'Connell Street (North of the Liffey)   The epicenter of Dublin's stormy political struggles, the north was once a fashionable area, but it lost much of its charm as it declined in the 20th century. It has experienced something of a resurgence in recent years, and now is home to some high-profile hotels, shops, and restaurants. But it still feels a little more down-at-heel than the Southside. With four theaters within walking distance of O'Connell Street, this is also

learning the lingo: "BANK HOLIDAYS"

No, they don't give banks extra vacation in Ireland. Though you can expect to see this phrase a lot, especially on lists of opening times, it simply means a public holiday. Many shops are either closed or run on reduced hours on Bank Holidays.

There are currently nine regular Bank Holidays in Ireland: New Year's Day (January 1); St. Patrick's Day (March 17); Easter Monday; the first Monday in every month from May to August, except July; the final Monday in in October; Christmas Day (December 25); and St. Stephen's Day (December 26).

Dublin's theater district. It is mostly in the Dublin 1 zone.

North Quays (Liffey Riverbanks on the Northside) Once the center of Dublin's shipping industry, this is now a trendy address for hotels, bars, and clubs. The quays are actually a series of streets named after the wharves that once stood at water's edge. The quays start near the mouth of the Liffey and end in the green peace of Phoenix Park. This area is mostly in the Dublin 1 zone.

Ballsbridge/Embassy Row Immediately south of the Grand Canal, this upscale suburb is just barely within walking distance of the city center. Primarily a prestigious residential area, it is also home to hotels, restaurants, and embassies. This area is part of the Dublin 4 zone.

WHERE TO STAY IN DUBLIN

With a healthy mix of plush hotels and grand old guesthouses, Dublin excels in providing a place to rest your head at the end of a day. Unfortunately, finding a really great, *affordable* place to stay is a tougher prospect. In this book we have tried to list as many of these "finds" as we can. However, if you're prepared to stay slightly outside of the city center, your options open up quite a bit (remember that public transportation, including taxis, is relatively cheap). This is particularly true in the leafy suburb of Ballsbridge (just south of the city center) that is fast becoming a center for affordable accommodations.

Wherever you're staying, try to book as far in advance as possible. The most sought-after places fill up fast. Always try to book online. Many hotels offer Web-only specials—sometimes through such third-party sites as Booking.com or Trivago.com—deals that can amount to massive savings on the rack rate. Remember, the fact that times are tough in the global economy right now cuts both ways: Hotels are at greater risk of closure, but they are also more eager to secure your business.

If you arrive in Ireland without a reservation, don't despair. The app **HotelTonight** can often net discounts of up to 70% off (but for one night only). However, don't forget that you will have trouble at immigration if you arrive in Ireland without a place to stay at least for your first night.

Historic Old City & Temple Bar/Trinity College Area

Temple Bar is the youngest, most vibrant niche in a young, vibrant town. Stay here and you'll be on the doorstep of practically anywhere you'd want to go. That said, it can get *very* noisy at night, so request a room on a top floor or at the rear of the establishment if you want some shut-eye.

EXPENSIVE

The Clarence ★★   Back in the 1990s, when the Celtic Tiger was starting to roar, the Clarence became something of a symbol of the "new" Dublin. Chic, fashionable, and with megastar owners to boot (Bono and the Edge from U2, who can still occasionally be spotted here), it spoke of Dublin's revival as a modern and cultured capital city. These days the Clarence has lost some of its original luster (a refurbishment is overdue in places); however, it remains a quintessential part of on-trend Temple Bar. The decent-sized guest rooms are done in contemporary tones (chocolate and cream, or white with accents of scarlet and black). Most of the furniture is the work of Irish designers, and beds are luxuriously comfortable. The Tea Room restaurant serves ultra-contemporary Irish cuisine, and dropping in at the Octagon Bar for a pint of Guinness is a must, even if you're not staying here.

6-8 Wellington Quay, Dublin 2. www.theclarence.ie. (℃ **01/407-0800.** 49 units. €165–€325. Breakfast €18–€24. Dinner, bed and breakfast packages available. Valet parking €5 per hour. **Amenities:** Wi-Fi, bar, restaurant, a/c, gym, room service, spa. Bus: 26, 66, 66A, 66B, 66D, 67, 67A.

MODERATE

Buswells ★★   There's a pleasing air of the gentleman's club in this midprice hotel in central Dublin. Decor in the public areas remains traditional, from the original, intricately detailed cornices of the 19th-century plasterwork to the polished marble fireplaces and heavy curtains. However, the small but decently furnished guest rooms are wholly contemporary in style (rather bland, even, after the lovely Georgian spaces one walks through to get to them). Visitors with mobility problems should be certain to ask for a room on a lower floor, as the old building (actually three town houses merged together), is full of stairs to climb. Pleasant though it is, Buswell's real selling point is the location—just a few minutes' walk to Trinity College in one direction and St. Stephen's Green in the other. You're in the very heart of the action here.

23-25 Molesworth St., Dublin 2. www.buswells.ie. (℃ **01/614-6500.** 69 units. €121–€285. Hotel covers cost of parking at nearby lot (overnight only). Cheaper rates do not include breakfast. **Amenities:** Wi-Fi (free), restaurant, bar, room service. DART: Pearse. Bus: 7B, 7D, 10, 10A, 11, 11A, 11B, 13, 14, 14A, 15, 15A, 15B, 15C, 15X, 20B, 25X, 32X, 27C, 33X, 39B, 40A, 40C, 41X, 46A, 46B, 46C, 51D, 51X, 58X, 67X, 84X, 92.

Eliza Lodge ★   Right in the middle of Temple Bar, above a popular Italian restaurant and overlooking the River Liffey, this smart hotel is smack-dab in the thick of the action. Guest rooms are simple and compact, with large windows letting in plenty of natural light, although the modern bathrooms can verge on shoebox size. The only real drawback to this place is the flipside of its greatest asset: the location. Eliza Lodge is on a major traffic intersection that can get loud. Even without the enticement of a better view of the river, that's good enough reason to fork over extra for an upper-floor room. One useful tip for travelers arriving on the red-eye: You can check in (very) early for just €20 extra, although this must be prebooked.

23-24 Wellington Quay, Dublin 2. www.elizalodge.com. (℃ **01/671-8044.** 18 units. €95–€179. Discount parking at nearby lot (€7 overnight, €14 for 24 hrs). Rates include breakfast. Dinner, bed and breakfast packages available. **Amenities:** Wi-Fi (free), restaurant, a/c. Bus: 26, 39B, 51, 51B, 51C, 51D, 51X, 66, 66A, 66B, 66D, 67, 67A, 68, 69, 69X, 78, 78A, 79, 79A, 90, 92, 206, 748.

Harding Hotel ★★   Just central enough not to feel like a trek to the main tourist sites, but just far enough to escape the inevitable nighttime crowds that descend on

Dublin Hotels

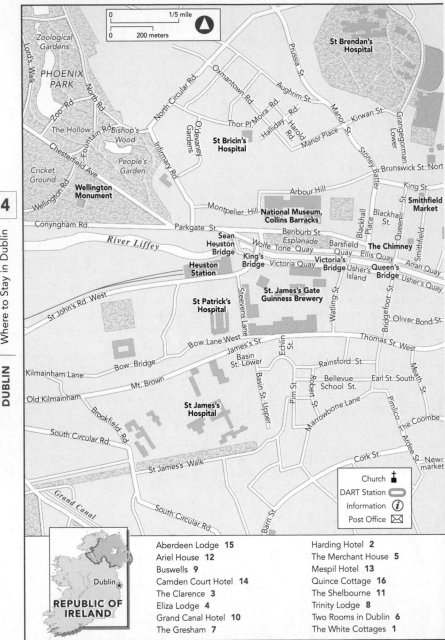

Map legend:

Church ✝
DART Station ⬭
Information ⓘ
Post Office ✉

REPUBLIC OF IRELAND

Dublin ★

Aberdeen Lodge **15**
Ariel House **12**
Buswells **9**
Camden Court Hotel **14**
The Clarence **3**
Eliza Lodge **4**
Grand Canal Hotel **10**
The Gresham **7**

Harding Hotel **2**
The Merchant House **5**
Mespil Hotel **13**
Quince Cottage **16**
The Shelbourne **11**
Trinity Lodge **8**
Two Rooms in Dublin **6**
The White Cottages **1**

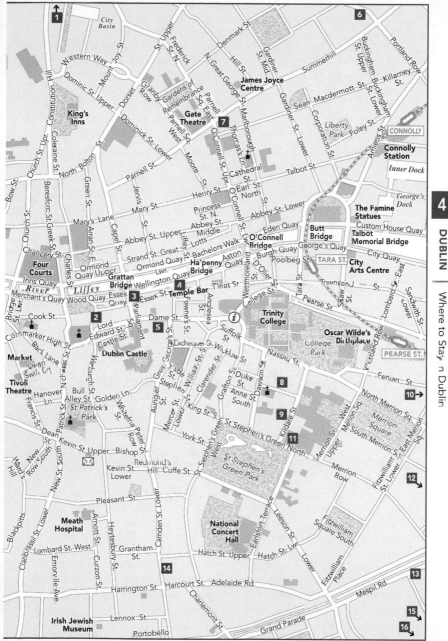

nearby Temple Bar, this is an excellent, low-cost option on the western edge of the city center. The polished wood and bright, floor-to-ceiling windows of the cheerful lobby give off a pleasantly old-fashioned vibe, even though most of the hotel is quite modern. The comfortable guest rooms are a terrific value. Even in high season, you can usually find a double room for well under €100, and triple rooms typically cost just a little bit more than standard doubles. This makes the Harding a particularly standout option for families. It's not overly fancy, but it's pleasant, clean, and has everything you need. All in all, this is one of the best finds for budget travelers the city has to offer.

Copper Alley, Fishamble St., Dublin 2. www.hardinghotel.ie. ⓒ **01/679-6500.** 52 units. €85–€102. No parking. Breakfast not included in lower rates. **Amenities:** Wi-Fi (free), restaurant, bar, accessible rooms. Bus: 37, 39, 39A, 39B, 39C, 39X, 49, 49A, 49X, 50, 50X, 56A, 70, 70A, 70X.

The Merchant House ★　One of a relatively new breed of accommodations geared toward business travelers and couples, the concept here is different from a conventional guesthouse. The Merchant House is a series of swanky guest suites, with various services attached but no dedicated reception area. The upside to this is a greater degree of privacy and freedom. The downside is that, while the entrance is secure and private, the building isn't staffed all the time. (Travelers who prefer their local color not too, well, colorful, should also be warned that it's next door to a fetish shop—albeit a discreet one.) The suites themselves are extremely well designed; features of the original 18th-century building were retained when the place was renovated in 2006. Nicely modern touches include flatscreen TVs and elegant contemporary furnishings, and fancy optional extras include a dedicated chauffeur. The bed-and-breakfast rate includes daily housekeeping service and breakfast at a nearby cafe.

8 Eustace St., Dublin 2. www.themerchanthouse.eu. ⓒ **01/633-4447.** 4 units. €113–€152. No children. No parking. Breakfast not included in lower rates. **Amenities:** Wi-Fi (free), a/c. Bus: 39B, 49X, 50X, 65X, 77X.

O'Connell Street Area/North of the Liffey

The Northside has some good offerings in the way of hotels. Though in some respects a less sought-after area, it's still very central and within walking distance of all the major sights and shops. Hotel rates tend to be lower than they are just across the bridge.

MODERATE

The Gresham ★★　The Gresham is one of Dublin's oldest hotels—it opened in 1817, and was almost destroyed during the Easter Rising of 1916. Most of the current building dates from the 1920s; the public areas retain a wonderfully glamorous Art Deco feel. Alas, guest rooms can be a little bland (in the cheaper rooms at least; the suites are nothing short of opulent), but they're comfortable, well equipped, and most importantly, surprisingly affordable for a hotel with this kind of pedigree. The Writer's Lounge, a handsome remnant of its Jazz Age heyday, is a popular spot for afternoon tea. Overlooking both the hotel lobby and busy O'Connell Street, it's also one of the best perches in the city for some unashamed people-watching.

23 Upper O'Connell St., Dublin 1. www.gresham-hotels.com. ⓒ **01/874-6881.** 298 units. €85–€200. No children under 3. Discount parking at nearby lot (€15 overnight). Breakfast not included in lower rates. Dinner, bed and breakfast packages available. **Amenities:** Wi-Fi (free), restaurants (2), bars (2), room service, discounted use of nearby gym and swimming pool (€10). Luas: Abbey St. Bus: 2, 3, 4, 5, 7, 7A, 7B, 7D, 8, 10, 10A, 11, 11A, 11B, 13.

INEXPENSIVE

Two Rooms in Dublin ★★★ This exceptionally welcoming little B&B on the Northside of Dublin is run by two of the most cultured and well-travelled hoteliers you're likely to meet. Kevin, a filmmaker, and Garvan, a photographer, always seem to be campaigning to preserve some part or other of historic Dublin. That love for heritage shines through in the chic and savvy restoration of their 1834 town house. The eponymous two guest rooms are spacious and filled with light, featuring touches like antique brass beds and sunken baths. The Garden Room opens out onto a private patio, where breakfast can be taken if the sun's out; or, in gloomier weather, you can light a fire in the original Victorian grate. TVs are banished to preserve the peaceful atmosphere, but each bedroom does have its own antique radio set. Delicious, home-cooked breakfasts make excellent use of seasonal produce and ethically sourced ingredients. This is simply one of the most charming and intimate B&Bs in Dublin.

18 Summer St. North, Dublin 1. www.tworoomsindublin.com. *C* **086/822-5572**. 2 units. €100. Two-night minimum. On-street parking nearby. Rates include breakfast. **Amenities:** Wi-Fi (free). Bus: 7, 8, 14, 15 51A, 123. Rail: Connolly (10-min. walk).

St. Stephen's Green/Grafton Street Area

St. Stephen's Green may be only a 10-minute walk from the hustle and bustle of Temple Bar and Trinity College, but it's infinitely calmer and less harried. This is a good area if you're looking for a little peace and quiet.

EXPENSIVE

The Shelbourne ★★★ Dublin hotels simply don't come with a better historic pedigree than this—the Irish constitution was written in this very building (room 112, to be precise). The Shelbourne was acquired by the Marriott group a few years ago, but traditionalists need not fear: The hotel is still its grand old self. A feeling of *fin de siècle* elegance pervades throughout the public areas, with high plaster ceilings, crystal chandeliers, and a winding iron staircase. Guest rooms have a much more discreet, contemporary elegance, with extremely luxurious beds and a host of modern extras. There's also an excellent spa, and you can even book a session with a Genealogy Butler if you need a little expert help in tracing your Irish roots. Afternoon tea at the Shelbourne is a true Dublin institution and open to nonguests.

27 St. Stephen's Green, Dublin 2. www.marriott.com. *C* **01/663-4500**. 190 units. €259–€680. Valet parking €25 per day. Breakfast €21–€29. Dinner, bed and breakfast packages available. **Amenities:** Wi-Fi (free), restaurants (3), bars (3), afternoon tea, gym, spa, a/c; accessible rooms. Luas: St. Stephen's Green. Bus: 7B, 7D, 10, 10A, 11, 11A, 11B, 14, 14A, 15, 15A, 15B, 15C, 15X, 20B, 25X, 32X, 39X, 40A, 40C, 41X, 51X, 70B, 84X.

MODERATE

Camden Court Hotel ★ Although not quite "budget," this large hotel just south of St. Stephen's Green is still a great value for what you get. A "practical base" kind of hotel, rather than one overflowing with character and charm, the Camden Court is nonetheless well equipped, with good-size and modern guest rooms (especially the family rooms), a pool, and a massage salon to soothe away those sightseeing aches and pains. You'd probably pay significantly more if this place was just a few blocks further to the north; as it is, the only real drawback is that you're a 10- to 20-minute walk away from the center.

Camden St. Lower (near jcn. With Charlotte Way), Dublin 2. www.camdencourthotel.com. *C* **01/475-9666**. 246 units. €100–€135. Parking (free). Breakfast not included in lower rates. **Amenities:** Wi-Fi (free), bar, restaurant, gym, swimming pool, beauty salon, room service, accessible rooms. Luas: Harcourt St. Bus: 15X, 16, 16A, 19, 19A, 65, 65B, 65X, 83, 122.

Trinity Lodge ★ This small hotel is full of quirks—not all of them convenient (there's no elevator and plenty of stairs, for instance), but the bedrooms are comfortable, contemporary, and surprisingly large for a place in this price range. A converted town house, the hotel was built in 1785, and some of the bedrooms retain a historic feel in their design. Quadruple rooms offer outstanding value for families. South Frederick Street is little more than a stone's throw from Trinity College, and it's also a comparative rarity in the city center—it's generally quite peaceful at night. Breakfast is basic, but there are plenty of other options in the neighborhood.

12 South Frederick St., Dublin 2. www.trinitylodge.com. ℂ **01/617-0900.** 16 units. €130–€170. Two-night minimum on some summer weekends. Discount parking at nearby lot (€3 overnight, €12.50 24 hrs.). Continental breakfast included in rates; 10% discount on cooked breakfasts at nearby cafes. **Amenities:** Wi-Fi, restaurant, a/c, room service (7am–11pm). Rail: Connolly. Luas: St. Stephen's Green. DART: Pearse. Bus: 7B, 7D, 10, 10A, 11, 11A, 11B, 14, 14A, 15, 15A, 15B, 15C, 15X, 20B, 25X, 27C, 32X, 33X, 39B, 41X, 46B, 46C, 51D, 51X, 58X, 67X, 84X, 92.

Ballsbridge & the Southern Suburbs

This district includes a prestigious Dublin residential neighborhood, south of the canal. Half the foreign embassies in Dublin are located here, coveted for its leafy streets and historic buildings. It's also growing as a hotel quarter—the distance from the city center means you'll get so much more for your money by staying here.

MODERATE

Aberdeen Lodge ★★ Drive up to this elegant Regency building in the springtime, and its front can be so covered in ivy as to resemble a vertical lawn with spaces cut for the windows. Inside, the decor is endearingly old-fashioned; the neat-as-a-pin public spaces are decorated in heritage tones, and the heavy, antique-style furnishings are scattered with embroidered pillows. Guest rooms are comfortable and quiet, albeit somewhat plain, but modern bathrooms are a big plus. Some have views of the large garden, where guests can take tea—often in the company of the hotel's friendly cat. Aberdeen Lodge is a short walk to the nearest DART station, and from there it's a short hop to the city center. Alternatively, a 5-minute stroll takes you to a pleasant walking path through a park beside the coast. If you do come this way, look out for the gray stone tower, now stuck rather ignominiously between a public toilet and a pay phone—it's an example of a Martello Tower, a small defensive fortification that was built by the British to ward off a feared invasion from France in the early 19th century.

53-55 Park Avenue, Ballsbridge, Dublin 4. www.aberdeen-lodge.com. ℂ **01/283-8155.** 11 units. €119–€169. Parking (free). Rates include breakfast. **Amenities:** Wi-Fi, restaurant, bar, use of nearby spa. DART: Sydney Parade, Sandymount. Bus: 2, 3, 18, 84N.

Ariel House ★★★ This charming guesthouse in Ballsbridge has won several plaudits over the last few years. And rightly so—it's a smoothly run, good-value-for-the-money operation. Situated on a quiet Victorian street, the most obvious landmark is, depending on your point of view, either a hideous blot on a heritage landscape or just a great day out. The Aviva Stadium, one of Ireland's major sports grounds, is literally a block away. Inside the hotel, the vibe is decidedly old school, with a subtle contemporary flourish. The small, simple guest rooms are tastefully decorated in earthy oatmeal or cream with brocade-pattern bedspreads. The lounge is a pleasant space with an honesty bar; musically inclined guests are even free to tickle the ivories of the lovely old piano. The breakfast menu doesn't veer too far from the traditional

Irish staples, but it's exceptionally well done. As long as you're not staying on a match day, the neighborhood is quiet enough to make you feel cosseted

50-54 Lansdowne Rd., Ballsbridge, Dublin 4. www.ariel-house.net. ⓒ **01/668-5512.** 37 units. €90–€190. Parking (free). Rates include breakfast. **Amenities:** Wi-Fi (free), honesty bar, afternoon tea, room service. DART: Lansdowne Road. Bus: 4, 7, 8, 84.

Grand Canal Hotel ★ Overlooking the 18th-century Grand Canal—a major part of Dublin's industrial heritage, long since abandoned as anything but a picturesque waterway—this large hotel is a strikingly modern place. The Aviva Stadium is a stone's throw away, making this a popular choice for people in town for a game, as well as business travelers and tourists looking for a no-frills place to stay. Usually rooms go for under €100 per night. It wins no awards for style, but it's cheerful, spotlessly clean, and the bedrooms are huge by Dublin standards. The neighborhood is nothing too exciting, but the center is just a short journey by public transport. You could even walk if you wanted to work off one of the hearty hotel breakfasts—Trinity College is about 25 minutes on foot.

Grand Canal St. Upper, Ballsbridge, Dublin 4. www.grandcanalhotel.ie. ⓒ **01/646-1000.** 142 units. €64–€154. Theatre and O2 Arena packages available. Parking (free). Breakfast not included in lower rates. **Amenities:** Wi-Fi (free), restaurant, bar, room service, accessible rooms. DART: Grand Canal Dock. Bus: 4, 5, 7, 7A, 8, 45, 63, 84.

Mespil Hotel ★ Another good budget option in Ballsbridge, the Mespil is within walking distance of the city center—St. Stephen's Green is about a 15-minute stroll. And the accommodations here are certainly of a higher standard than what you're likely to find uptown for the same price. The guest rooms are spacious and feature modern decor and comfortable beds. In common with most hotels of this type, breakfast is served buffet-style—tasty and excellent fuel, although you may want a break from all that fried meat and eggs after a couple of days. One nice little bonus: Although not run by the hotel, there's an excellent gourmet food market held alongside the canal, just outside, every Thursday from 11am to 2pm. See www.irishvillagemarkets.com for more details.

50-60 Mespil Rd., Dublin 4. www.mespilhotel.com. ⓒ **01/448-4600.** 255 units. €85–€136. Parking (limited). Breakfast €12. **Amenities:** Wi-Fi (free), restaurant, bar, gym, room service, accessible rooms. Bus: 10, 10A, 15X, 49X, 50X, 66D, 92.

INEXPENSIVE

Quince Cottage ★★ This place isn't the most convenient location—it's in Sandyford, a southern suburb about 20 minutes by Luas (tram) from central Dublin—but what Quince Cottage lacks in convenience, it more than makes up for in comfort. Owners Paula and Brandon have converted their century-old suburban home into a bright and modern B&B. Bedrooms are pleasant, albeit basic, with modern furnishings and decent-size beds. Breakfasts are hearty (think American-style pancakes served with fresh fruit). The spacious, buttercream-colored guest lounge adds to the feeling that you're a guest in a pleasant Dublin home, rather than a number in an impersonal hotel. For those seeking even more privacy, there's a two-room apartment (the oldest part of the house) that can be rented on a self-catering basis or with breakfast included. Sandyford is about 12km (7½ miles) south of the city center.

Kilgobbin Rd., Sandyford, Dublin 18. www.quincecottage.ie. ⓒ **01/295-8488.** 4 units. €90; €80 for 2 or more nights. Parking (free). Rates include breakfast. **Amenities:** Wi-Fi (free). Luas: Glencairn. Bus: 44.

North of Dublin

INEXPENSIVE

The White Cottages ★★★   The sea is an ever-present feature at this pleasant, whitewashed little B&B in Skerries, a pleasant seaside commuter town with good rail links, about 30km (18½ miles) from Temple Bar. The coastline is literally feet away from the wooden terrace at the back, and the sound of the waves can help soothe you to a restful sleep at night. Guest rooms are decorated in summery tones of white and blue with jaunty, candy-striped motifs. The owners are welcoming and extremely helpful—Joe, the co-owner, is a mine of information about the local area, and his wife Jackie displays some of her art around the house. Breakfasts are good, but you have to fend for yourself at dinnertime (Joe is always on hand with an exhaustive list of places to eat nearby.) The only major snag is that Skerries is far outside of the city; the train journey to the center takes about 40 minutes, and the bus over an hour. Still, it's nothing more than local commuters do every day, and you'll be hard-pressed to find a more tranquil and welcoming retreat after a long day's sightseeing.

Balbriggan Rd., Skerries, Co. Dublin. www.thewhitecottages.com. (✆ **01/849-2231.** 4 units. €80. Parking (free). Rates include breakfast. **Amenities:** Wi-Fi, picnic lunches. Rail: Skerries. Bus: 33.

WHERE TO EAT IN DUBLIN

The economic boom years of the early 2000s in Dublin brought with it a new generation of international, sophisticated restaurants. Ireland embraced a foodie culture in a way that it never really had before. However, as the economy crashed, so too came a minor resurgence in the popularity of traditional Irish fare, even in expensive restaurants. That's not to say that the food in Dublin is on the downswing—far from it—it's just become easier to find traditional-style Irish food in the city than it was a decade ago. In other words, Ireland is both re-embracing and re-inventing its food heritage.

However, Dublin is still a notoriously expensive city in which to eat out. Prices have certainly come down in recent years, but you're still likely to pay much more for a meal here than in a comparable U.S. city; maybe about the same as you'd expect to pay in Paris or London. But when the food here is good, it's very good, so if you can afford to splurge once or twice while you're in town, do so—you're in for a treat.

Temple Bar/Trinity College Area

Avoca Café ★★ CAFE   So much better than just another department store cafe, this is a great place for breakfast, lunch, or a mid-shopping snack. The morning menu is more varied and interesting than at most hotels; free-range scrambled eggs with arugula salad, several types of pancakes, French toast, and even the ubiquitous "full Irish" with (rarely found in Ireland) American-style bacon. Lunches are healthy and delicious—think crab salad with home-baked bread or a plate of Middle Eastern–style mezze made with Wicklow lamb and served with baba ghanouj and hummus. The delicious soups are famous with the locals. Or you could just drop in for a tempting slice of cake and a restorative cup of tea.

11-13 Suffolk St., Dublin 2. www.avoca.ie. (✆ **01/677-4215.** Breakfast €3–€12. Lunch €13–€20. Mon–Wed 9:30am–4:30pm; Thurs–Sat 9:30am–5:30pm; Sun 11am–4:30pm. Bus: 15X, 32X, 33X, 39X, 41X, 51D, 51X, 58X, 70X, 84X.

The Bank on College Green ★ PUB   Undoubtedly one of Dublin's most jaw-droppingly handsome interiors, this place would be worth visiting even if it didn't serve great pub food. Built in 1892 at the height of Victorian opulence, several remnants of the original bank building were kept when it was converted into a pub (including the wonderful old-style safes that you can still see downstairs). A small and fairly traditional lunch menu of burgers, fish and chips, sandwiches, and salads gives way to a more extensive selection in the evening, including steaks, pasta, and a handy sharing plate. It's all very informal but hugely satisfying. Come on Sunday for a leisurely brunch (11am–5pm) or a traditional roast at lunchtime.

20 College Green, Dublin 2. www.bankoncollegegreen.com. ⓒ 01/677-0677. Main courses €13–€31. Weekdays noon–4pm and 6–10pm; Sat and Sun noon–5pm and 6–10pm. Bus: 15X, 32X, 33X, 39B, 39X, 41X, 49X, 50X, 51X, 58X, 65X, 70X, 77X, 84X.

Brasserie Sixty6 ★★ IRISH/INTERNATIONAL This cheerful, well-run bistro near Trinity College is a popular choice with locals for special occasions. Roast meats cooked rotisserie-style are a specialty. Try the garlic and lemon chicken served with herb stuffing and a bunch of sides, or dig into citrus-glazed duck with duck fat–roasted potatoes and salad. The rest of the menu is made up of modern bistro fare like roast monkfish with artichokes or a simple, juicy steak with fondant potatoes and peppercorn sauce. Vegetarians are well catered to also, with choices such as vegetable tagine and haloumi Caesar salad. Service is stellar and the portions generous. It's not cheap, although the pre-theater menu is an excellent value (€22 for 2 courses, served until 7pm/6:30pm on Fridays and Saturdays). There's also a popular brunch served from 10am to 4pm on weekends, accompanied by a live jazz band on Sundays.

66 South Great Georges St., Dublin 2. www.brasseriesixty6.com. ⓒ 01/400-5078. Main courses €24–€33. Mon–Thurs noon–10pm; Fri noon–11pm; Sat 10am–11pm; Sun 10am–10pm. Bus: 15E, 15F, 16, 16A, 19, 19A, 65, 65B, 65X, 83, 122.

Fallon & Byrne ★★★ MODERN EUROPEAN A top-floor adjunct to the wonderful food and wine store, Fallon & Byrne, this food hall serves delicious, seasonal Irish fare sourced from artisan producers. Nothing seems to have come very far—crab from the tiny port of Castletownbere, County Cork; lamb from Lough Erne; or oysters from Carlingford. The menu strikes a nice balance between ambitious dishes and more down-to-earth options, so while you may find turbot served with pink grapefruit and crushed new potatoes, you could just as easily opt for a simple burger topped with Cashel blue cheese and smoked bacon. And if you prefer to fend for yourself, there's always the enormous selection of deli items downstairs, available to go.

11-17 Exchequer St., Dublin 2. www.fallonandbyrne.com. ⓒ 01/472-1010. Main courses €11–€33. Wed–Thurs noon–3pm and 6–10pm; Fri–Sat noon–3pm and 6–11pm; Sun noon–4pm and 6–9pm; Mon–Tues 12–3pm and 6–9pm. Bus: 15E, 15F, 16, 16A, 19, 19A, 65, 65B, 65X, 83, 122.

Gallagher's Boxty House ★★★ IRISH There's a great story behind this captivating and hugely popular restaurant in Temple Bar. While living in Venezuela as a young man, the owner was struck by the pride his fellow workers took in simple, traditional home cooking. He came home and founded a restaurant to preserve and update some of the Irish traditions in his own style. Boxty—which comes from an old Gaelic term meaning "poor bread"—is a distinctive kind of potato pancake. It's the house signature dish, served with a variety of delicious meat and fish fillings. Also on the menu are steaks, seafood, and a range of Irish stews (try the Spicy Dublin Coddle, a modern variant on an old recipe, made with chorizo and served with soda bread). Modern restaurants don't come with a greater appreciation for culinary heritage than this one.

20-21 Temple Bar, Dublin 2. www.boxtyhouse.ie. ⓒ 01/677-2762. Main courses €16–€23. Daily noon–10:30pm. Luas: Jervis. Bus: 22, 39B, 49X, 50X, 65X, 66, 66A, 66B, 66D, 67, 67A, 69X, 77X.

Dublin Restaurants

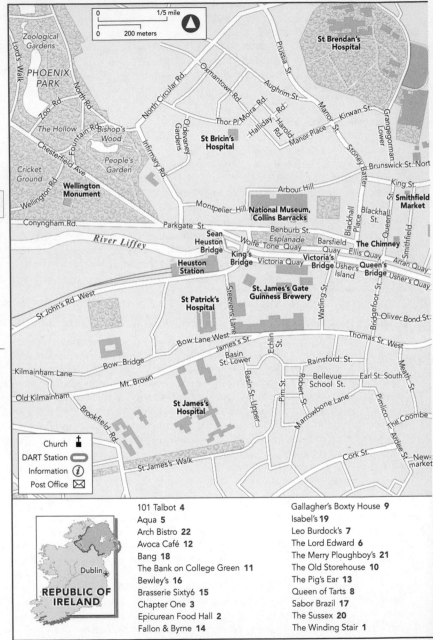

101 Talbot **4**
Aqua **5**
Arch Bistro **22**
Avoca Café **12**
Bang **18**
The Bank on College Green **11**
Bewley's **16**
Brasserie Sixty6 **15**
Chapter One **3**
Epicurean Food Hall **2**
Fallon & Byrne **14**

Gallagher's Boxty House **9**
Isabel's **19**
Leo Burdock's **7**
The Lord Edward **6**
The Merry Ploughboy's **21**
The Old Storehouse **10**
The Pig's Ear **13**
Queen of Tarts **8**
Sabor Brazil **17**
The Sussex **20**
The Winding Stair **1**

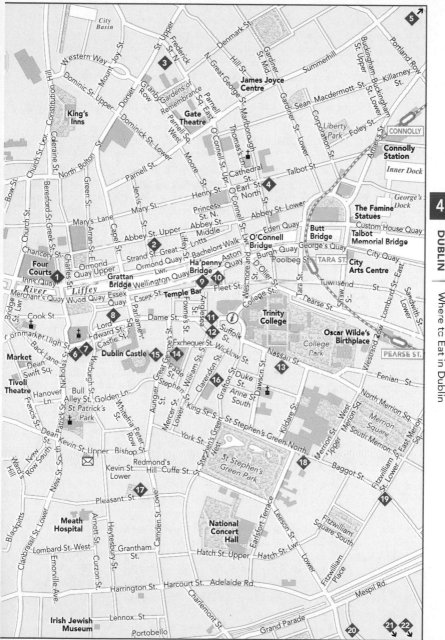

City Basin

Western Way

Dominic St. Upper

King's Inns

St. Upper Frederick St. N.

Denmark St.

Hill St.

N. Great George's St.

Gardiner St. Mid.

Summerhill

Buckingham St. Upper

Buckingham St. Lower

Portland Row

Killarney St.

3

Gate Theatre

James Joyce Centre

Sean Macdermott St. Upper

CONNOLLY

Connolly Station

Parnell St.

Gate Theatre

O'Connell St. Upr.

Marlborough St.

Corporation St.

Liberty Park

Foley St.

Amiens St.

Mary's Lane

Abbey St. Upper

Princess St. N.

Abbey St. Middle

O'Connell Bridge

Eden Quay

Butt Bridge

The Famine Statues

Inner Dock

George's Dock

Talbot Memorial Bridge

Custom House Quay

City Quay

Four Courts

1

Grattan Bridge

River Liffey

Ha'penny Bridge

9

10

Wellington Quay

Fleet St.

Temple Bar

TARA ST.

City Arts Centre

Townsend St.

Trinity College

Oscar Wilde's Birthplace

PEARSE ST.

8

Dublin Castle

15

14

11

12

13

6 **7**

Market

Tivoli Theatre

St. Patrick's Park

16

Meath Hospital

St Stephen's Green Park

18

19

17

National Concert Hall

Irish Jewish Museum

20

21 **22**

5

4

2

59

The Old Storehouse ★★ IRISH/PUB   There isn't much in the way of risk or innovation on the menu of hearty Irish classics at this popular pub in Temple Bar—and that's precisely why it's so popular. What you get is delicious, traditional pub food. Think a fat, juicy burger served with vine tomatoes and cocktail sauce; bangers and mash (sausages and mashed potatoes) with ale gravy; or perhaps some steamed mussels with garlic bread. There's a small wine list, but the beer selection is better. As much of a draw as the food is the nightly live music; all traditional and all free, they have up to 20 acts a week in the summer. The Old Storehouse doesn't accept reservations, so be prepared to wait for a table when it's busy.

Crown Alley, off Cope St., Dublin 2. www.theoldstorehouse.ie. ℂ **01/607-4003.** Main courses €11–€16. Daily noon–10pm. Bus: 39B, 49X, 50X, 65X, 77X.

The Pig's Ear ★★★ MODERN IRISH   A deliciously inventive approach to traditional Irish tastes pervades this super-cool restaurant overlooking Trinity College. However, this isn't one of those trendy eateries in which the menu is too concerned with being clever to be satisfying. Classic ingredients are offered with modern flair: pan-fried cod served with tiny garlic micro potatoes and golden raisins, for example, or pig belly with salted celeriac, burnt pear, and barley. Desserts have a playfully retro edge: guinness and date pudding (a sweet steamed cake) with vanilla ice cream and candied pecan, or cheesecake served with Hob Nobs, a brand of cookie liable to give local diners a flush of nostalgia. You certainly won't be able to miss this place from the outside; just look for the shocking-pink door with a candy-striped awning.

4 Nassau St., Dublin 2. www.thepigsear.ie. ℂ **01/670-3865.** Main courses €18–€28. Mon–Sat noon–2:45pm and 5:30–10pm. Closed Sun. DART: Pearse St. Bus: 25X, 32X, 33X, 41X, 51D, 51X, 58X, 67X, 84X, 92.

Queen of Tarts ★★ CAFE   This cheerful little tearoom in the heart of Temple Bar is a delightful pit stop for a pot of tea and some form of sweet, diet-busting snack. Cakes and tarts are the specialty; it's all good, but try the lemon meringue or the old-fashioned Victoria sponge (white cake with a jam filling and a dusting of sugar on top). They also serve breakfast until noon during the week, 1pm on Saturday, and a decadent 2pm on Sunday. At lunchtime you can order soups or sandwiches, but it's the cakes that keep us coming back.

Cows Lane, Dame St., Dublin 2. www.queenoftarts.ie. ℂ **01/633-4681.** Breakfast €4.50–€10. Lunch €6–€10. Mon–Fri 8am–7pm; Sat 9am–7pm; Sun 10am–6pm. Bus: 37, 39, 39A, 39C, 70, 70A.

Historic Old City

Leo Burdock's ★★ FISH & CHIPS   Proof that not all great food experiences come with a hefty price tag, Leo Burdock's is probably the most famous fish-and-chip shop in Ireland. In fact, it's virtually de rigueur for passing celebrities to pop in; the photographic "wall of fame" includes Sandra Bullock, Russell Crowe, and Tom Cruise. But don't come expecting cutting-edge cuisine; Leo Burdock's still trades on the same simple, winning formula that it has since 1913: battered fresh fish (cod, sole, ray, or scampi) and thick chips (like very fat fries), all cooked the old-fashioned way, in beef drippings. There are other options on the menu, including hamburgers, but frankly, what's the point of coming to a place like this if you don't order the one thing for which it's world-famous?

2 Werburgh St., Dublin 8. www.leoburdock.com. ℂ**01/454-0306.** Main courses €2.50–€7.50. Daily noon–midnight. Bus: 49X, 50X, 54A, 50X, 56A, 77, 77A, 77X, 78A, 150, 151.

The Lord Edward ★★ SEAFOOD With a believable claim to be the oldest seafood restaurant in Dublin, the Lord Edward has been a city staple since 1890. The rather unreconstructed menu contains a huge range of seafood such as sole, prawns, scallops, lobster, and various other fruits of the sea, all served every traditional way you can think of and a few you probably can't. The dining room is avowedly old-fashioned. This is certainly not the place to come if you're seeking out what's new and what's hot in the Irish culinary scene. But fans of the Lord Edward (and there are plenty of them) adore coming here for the sense of continuity and old-school charm.

23 Christchurch Place, Dublin 8. www.lordedward.ie. ℂ **01/454-2420.** Main courses €19–€39. Wed–Fri 12:30–2:30pm and 6–10:45pm; Sat 6–10:45pm. No lunch Sat. Closed Mon and Tues. Bus: 50X, 56A, 77, 77A, 77X, 150, 151.

O'Connell Street Area/North of the Liffey

101 Talbot ★★ INTERNATIONAL This cheery and informal spot, a 3-minute walk from the G.P.O. on O'Connell Street, is strong on delicious Irish cuisine with global influences and a healthy twist. The bright, airy dining room, lined with modern art, is an appealingly contemporary space. Specials may include roast salmon with asparagus and champ (mashed potatoes with spring onion and buttermilk), or steamed mussels in white wine, garlic, and cream sauce. The early-bird menu (2 courses for €20) is a particularly good deal and popular with pre-theater diners attending the Abbey Theatre located just around the corner.

101-102 Talbot St , Dublin 1. www.101talbot.ie. ℂ **01/874-5011.** Main courses €16–€18. Tues–Sat noon–3pm and 5–11pm. Closed Sun and Mon. Luas: Abbey St. Bus: 20D, 32X, 33X, 41, 41A, 41B, 41C, 42, 42A, 42B, 43, 51A, 130, 142.

Chapter One ★★★ MODERN IRISH The vaulted basement of the excellent Dublin Writers Museum (see p. 68) houses one of the city's most feted restaurants. The menus—which are all prix fixe—make excellent use of local flavors and organic ingredients. Feast on gourmet dishes like poached lobster with smoked haddock mousse or lamb served with fried sweetbreads and garlic sauce. The separate set menu for vegetarians has dishes such as aged Parmesan ravioli with asparagus and wild garlic. Adventurous diners will relish the chef's table: Seated in a little booth right inside the kitchen, guests are served a special 6-course menu (€80 per person) while the culinary theater happens before your eyes. The wine list is excellent; consider splurging on a Meerlust Rubicon 2005, an outstanding and little-seen South African vintage with a sublime, smoky flavor. *Tip:* The lunch menu is nearly half the price of dinner.

19 Parnell Sq. North, Dublin 1. www.chapteronerestaurant.com. ℂ **01/873-2266.** 4-course fixed-price menu €70. Tues–Fri 12:30–2pm and 5:30–10:30pm; Sat 6–10:30pm. No lunch Sat. Luas: Abbey St. DART: Connolly St. Bus: 1, 2, 14, 14A, 16, 16A, 19, 19A, 33X, 39X, 41X, 48A, 58X, 70B, 70X.

Epicurean Food Hall ★ MEDITERRANEAN An energetic coming together of flavors from disparate corners of the global village, this delightful food hall is a voyage of discovery for the epi-curious. The selection of lunch options changes quite regularly, but long-standing kitchens include **Istanbul,** specializing in Mediterranean dishes and Turkish kebabs; **Saburritos,** which serves a combination of authentic and California-style Mexican street food; **Rafa's Temaki,** which claims to be the first place in Ireland to sell Temaki—a healthful, fast food–style combination of Japanese sushi and sashimi; and a branch of the famous Dublin fish and chip takeaway, **Leo Burdock's** (see listing above). The various stalls share a common seating area, or you can get it to go.

1 Liffey St. Lower, Dublin 1. www.epicureanfoodhall.com. © **01/283-6077.** Main courses €4–€13. Mon–Wed 9am–7pm; Thurs—Sat 9am—8pm; Sun 11am–7pm. Luas: Jervis. Bus: 39B, 69X.

The Winding Stair ★★ MODERN IRISH   A sweet old bookstore downstairs and a chic restaurant upstairs, the Winding Stair is situated a stone's throw from the Ha'Penny Bridge. The views of the Liffey are romantic, but of course it's the inventive modern Irish cooking that pulls in the crowds. After a starter of Dingle Bay crab or Connemara ham with Irish mozzarella and rocket (arugula), you could opt for milk-poached smoked haddock with cheddar-cheese mash, or perhaps spring lamb with minted courgettes (zucchini). Desserts include pear and ginger cake topped with ice cream from Gathabawn, a small village near Kilkenny. The enormous wine list, which is helpfully arranged by character rather than region, features several decently priced options. Two- and three-course pre-theater menus are a great value at €25–€30. Just note: You must be finished by 8:15pm.

40 Lower Ormond Quay, Dublin 1. www.winding-stair.com. © **01/872-7320.** Main courses €22–€27. Daily noon–10:30pm. Luas: Jervis. Bus: 39B, 51, 51B, 51C, 51D, 51X, 68, 69, 69X, 78, 78A, 79, 79A, 90, 92, 206.

Fitzwilliam Square/Merrion Square Area

Isabel's ★★★ MODERN IRISH   The dining room of this in-vogue modern Irish restaurant, just east of St. Stephen's Green, is arrestingly well designed; expanses of ancient, exposed brickwork give way to (literally) stacks of wine in open crates. The menu infuses modern bistro cuisine with local and seasonal produce. Scallops come with Wicklow nettle risotto and sea vegetables, for example, while the slow-cooked lamb is served with samphire (a little-used vegetable found only in coastal areas that resembles seaweed and has a piquant, salty flavor). Typical desserts include chocolate mousse served with peanut panna cotta and honeycomb. If dinner here is too expensive for you, come for a simpler, cheaper lunch. They also do a small and reasonably priced breakfast menu.

112 Baggot St. Lower, Dublin 2. www.isabels.ie. © **01/661-9000.** Main courses €18–€24. Mon–Fri 11am–1pm; Sat 4–11:30. No lunch Sat. Closed Mon. Bus: 10, 10A, 15X, 49X, 50X, 66D.

The Sussex ★★ IRISH   The gastropub reinvention of traditional Irish cooking into something chic and fashionable finds one of its best proponents at this rather refined pub (above another popular bar), a 10 minutes' walk south of St. Stephen's Green. The menu takes classic pub fare, prepares it beautifully, and adds an oh-so-subtle twist—fish and chips with pea and mint puree, perhaps, or linguine served with Dingle Bay prawns, garlic, and lemon. For dessert, try the posset (a syllabub-like concoction containing cream and lemon) served with spiced shortbread. As you'd expect, all the ingredients are sourced as locally as possible, with plenty of attention to what's in season. The wine list is well judged, with plenty of reasonably priced options. *Tip:* The lunch menu is an edited version of what's for dinner—but significantly cheaper.

9 Sussex Terrace (at jcn. of Sussex Road, Dublin 4 (above M. O'Briens Pub). www.thesussex.ie. © **01/676-2851.** Main courses €16–€25. Mon noon–3; Tues noon–11pm; Sun 5–11pm. No dinner Mon. Bus: 7B, 7D, 11, 11A, 11B, 27C, 39B, 39X, 46B, 46C, 46D, 46E, 58C, 58X, 70B, 70X, 116.

St. Stephen's Green/Grafton Street Area

Bang ★★ MODERN IRISH   The presence of so many place names on the menu indicates how much this place has embraced the slow food ethos. The vast majority of ingredients are regionally sourced from specialist Irish producers. You may find Clare Island salmon served with local radishes and pickled cucumber; John Dory from Kilkeel; or perhaps a rib-eye steak from County Fermanagh. If it all seems too hard to choose from, you could opt for one of the tasting menus (€69–€79, depending on the number of courses). The wine list is expertly chosen, and there's also a small but delightfully put together cocktail menu—try the vodka martini made with sweet County Wexford strawberries.

11 Merrion Row, Dublin 2. www.bangrestaurant.com. ⓒ **01/400-4229.** Main courses €22–€33. Mon–Tues 5:30–10pm; Wed 12:30–10pm; Thurs–Sat 12:30–11pm. Closed Sun. Luas: St. Stephen's Green. Bus: 25X, 51D, 51X, 65X, 66X, 67X, 77X.

Bewley's ★ CAFE   A Dublin landmark since 1927, Bewley's has a literary pedigree as well as an historic one. James Joyce was a regular (it makes an appearance in his book *Dubliners*), and a host of subsequent literary greats made this their regular stop-off for a cup of joe and a slice of cake. It's still hugely popular, and not just for coffee; you can get a pretty good pizza, salad, or burger here at lunch or dinnertime, in addition to a more modest menu of light snacks. Fun fact: The distinctive, ornate faux-Egyptian facade (incongruously framing the rarely used full name, "Bewley's Oriental Café") owes its existence to the fact that, when the place opened, Europe was still in the grip of a craze for all things ancient Egyptian, following the discovery of Tutankhamen's tomb just 5 years before.

78-79 Grafton St., Dublin 2. www.bewleys.com. ⓒ**01/672-7720.** Breakfast €3–€12. Lunch & dinner €8–€15. Mon–Wed 8am–10pm; Thurs–Sat 8am–11pm; Sun 9am–10pm. Bus: 11, 11A, 11B, 14, 14A, 15A, 15C, 15X, 20B, 27C, 33X, 39B, 41X, 46D, 46C.

Sabor Brazil ★★★ BRAZILIAN   A good Brazilian restaurant isn't high on the list of things one expects to find in Dublin; even less so, an innovative and wildly fashionable spot in a slightly dicey neighborhood south of the center. And yet, Sabor Brazil not only serves outstanding food, but visiting here is half of the fun for a unique and memorable experience. The tiny dining room is decorated in a wry combination of Regency Baroque and Latinate flourishes. The menu (€100 per person for 7 courses, no a la carte) fuses contemporary Brazilian flavors with an Irish inflection; rock salt–coated steak filet, pan-fried in garlic with apricot and walnut sauce, for instance, or a pastel (kind of like South American dim sum) filled with whatever the chef decides is best that day. A vegetarian alternative is always available. Reservations are essential (with a booking deposit, credited to your bill on the night), and the restaurant will generally cater to couples only.

50 Pleasants St., Off Camden St., Dublin 8. www.saborbrazil.ie. ⓒ **01/475-0304.** Tasting menu only €100. Tues–Sun 6–11pm (last reservation 8:30pm). Bus: 65, 65X.

Ballsbridge & the Southern Suburbs

Arch Bistro ★★★ MODERN EUROPEAN   One of those places that even locals talk about as a "find," the Arch is an adorable little pub bistro in Churchtown, one of Dublin's southern suburbs. The lovingly crafted vintage vibe of the exterior—all thatched roofs and antique Guinness signs—shines above the urban blandness of the neighborhood. Inside, the space is elegant and cozy. The menu takes contemporary bistro classics and shakes them up with flashes of individuality; pan-seared sea bass is served with a fennel and citrus salad, and the potato gnocchi comes with aubergine (eggplant) caviar. Even the fish and chips come with a subtle twist—the batter is Japanese tempura style, and the fries are served with mango salsa. The three-course set menu is particularly good discount at just €25.

Landscape Rd., Churchtown, Dublin 14. www.thearchbistro.com. © **01/296-6340.** 2-course fixed-price menu €28. Tues–Fri 12:30–2:30 and 5:30–10pm; Sat 5–10pm; Sun noon–3pm and 5–8pm. No lunch Sat. Bus: 14.

North of Dublin

Aqua ★★★ SEAFOOD   With a jaw-dropping view of Dublin Bay, this has to be one of the most romantic dining spots in the region. Service is excellent—attentive without being overbearing—and the seafood is delicious and fresh as can be. You can start with a half-dozen oysters from Carlingford Lough, before moving on to John Dory filet with sweet potato and celeriac puree, or try the sea bass in a Chinese-style dressing. There's also a small range of tasty meat options for those who aren't wowed by the bounty of the sea. Howth is a small commuter suburb of Dublin, about 16km (10 miles) northeast of the city center. The restaurant is about a 10-minute walk from the Howth DART station, while a cab out here from the city should run you about €30. Definitely worth the splurge.

1 West Pier, Howth, Co. Dublin. www.aqua.ie. © **01/832-0690.** Main courses €17–€36. Tues–Sat 12:30–3:30pm and 5:30–10pm; Sun noon–5pm and 5:30–8:30pm; Mon 12:30–9pm (a la carte and specials only). DART: Howth. Bus: 31.

The Merry Ploughboy ★ IRISH/PUB   An exuberant live show of traditional music and dancing accompanies dinner at this hugely popular pub in Rathfarnham, one of Dublin's further-flung southern suburbs. Admittedly it's all very touristy, but you certainly get your money's worth—the show runs for 2 hours, and the food, while limited, is actually pretty good. Expect beef braised in Guinness served with root vegetables and rosemary jus or trout in a dill and lemon crust. The only real drawback is the time it takes to get here (Rathfarnham is about 6km/3¾ miles) from the center), although a dedicated minibus will pick you up and take you back at the end of the night for the bargain price of €5.50 round-trip.

Edmondstown Rd., Rockbrook, Rathfarnham, Dublin 16. www.mpbpub.com. © **01/493-1495.** Dinner and show €49.50. Bar menu €9–€21. Show: daily, dinner 7:30pm sharp; show 8:30–10:30pm. Bar food: Mon–Fri 4:30–9:30pm; Sat 12:30–9:30pm; Sun 12:30–8pm. Special bus leaves from and returns to six locations in central Dublin (€5.50 per person; must be prebooked).

EXPLORING DUBLIN

Wandering Dublin—just walking down its Georgian streets with a map only in case you get *really* lost—is one of the great pleasures of a visit here. The city center, where the vast majority of the sights are to be found, is small enough that there's almost no way you can go wrong. One minute you're walking along a quiet leafy street, and suddenly the Irish Parliament appears before you. A few minutes later, it's gorgeous Merrion Square. Then, you're upon the granite buildings of Trinity College—and on and on. So get a sturdy pair of shoes, have your umbrella at the ready, and head out to discover how rewarding this wonderful old town can be.

Tourism Offices

Dublin Tourism operates several walk-in visitor centers in greater Dublin that are open every day except Christmas. The principal center is on Suffolk Street, Dublin 2, open from Monday to Saturday from 9am to 8:30pm, Sunday and bank holidays 10:30am to 3pm. The Suffolk Street office has a currency exchange counter, a car-rental counter, an accommodations-reservations service, bus and rail information desks, a gift shop, and a cafe. For accommodation reservations throughout Ireland by credit card (including some good last-minute deals on Dublin hotels), contact Dublin Tourism at ℂ 1890/324-583 or **www.visitdublin.com.** There is also a tourism center in the arrivals concourse at Dublin Airport.

Top Attractions

Book of Kells and Old Library ★ HISTORIC SITE
This hand-drawn manu-script of the four gospels, dating to the year 800, is one of Ireland's national treasures. The elaborate scripting and colorful illumination drawn by Irish monks is undeniably magnificent. Unfortunately, you'll find it hard to see past the hordes of onlookers into the dim glass box where it is kept, and you're handsomely charged for the privilege. However, the library's **Long Room** goes a long way toward making up for that. The grand, chained library holds many rare works on Irish history and presents frequently changing displays of classic works. The Book of Kells is located in the Old Library building, on the south side of Library Square, inside the main campus.

The Library Building, Trinity College, College Green, Dublin 2. www.tcd.ie/Library/bookofkells. ℂ **01/896-2320.** Admission €10; €11 including campus tour. May–Sept Mon–Sat 9:30am–5pm, Sun 9:30am–4:30pm. Oct–Apr Mon–Sat 9:30am–5pm; Sun noon–4:30pm. DART: Pearse St., Con-nolly St. Luas: Lower Abbey St., St. Stephen's Green. Bus: College Green entrance: 7N, 15N, 15X, 44N, 46N, 48N, 49N, 51D, 51X, 54N, 56A, 70B, 70X, 77A, 77N, 92. Nassau St. entrance (for Old Library/Book of Kells): 25X, 32X, 33X, 41X, 51D, 51X, 58X, 67X, 84X, 92.

Chester Beatty Library ★★★ LIBRARY
This dazzling collection of early religious texts and other priceless artifacts is named in honor of Sir Alfred Chester Beatty, an Anglo-American industrialist who bequeathed his unique private collection to the Irish nation when he died in 1968. And what a collection it is! Beatty was one of the great 20th-century adventurer-collectors, of the kind that simply could not exist today. Highlights of the bequest include breathtaking illuminated gospels; 8th- and 9th-century Qurans; sacred Buddhist texts from Burma and Tibet; nearly 1,000 Japa-nese prints from the Edo era; jade and snuff bottles from China; and cuneiform writing tablets dating back nearly 5,000 years. If there's a better museum of this size in Ireland, we have yet to find it. Why queue and pay €10 to see two pages from the Book of Kells when you can lose yourself in this wonderful place for free?

On the grounds of Dublin Castle, Dame St., Dublin 2. www.cbl.ie. ℂ **01/407-0750.** Free admis-sion. May–Sept Mon–Fri 10am–5pm; Sat 11am–5pm; Sun 1pm–5pm. Oct–Apr Tues–Fri 10am–5pm; Sat 11am–5pm; Sun 1pm–5pm. Luas: Jervis. Bus: 37, 39, 39A, 39B, 39C, 49, 49A, 49X, 50, 50X, 56A, 65X, 70, 70A, 70X, 77, 77A, 77X, 123.

Christ Church Cathedral ★★ CHURCH
This magnificent cathedral was designed to be seen from the river, so walk to it from the riverside in order to truly appreciate its size. It dates from 1038, when Sitric, Danish king of Dublin, built the first wooden Christ Church here. In 1171, the original foundation was extended into a cruciform and rebuilt in stone by the Norman warrior Strongbow. The present structure dates mainly from 1871 to 1878, when a huge restoration took place—the work done then remains controversial to this day, as much of the building's old detail was destroyed in the process. Still, magnificent stonework and graceful pointed arches survive. (There's also a statue of Strongbow inside, and some believe his tomb is here as well, although historians are not convinced.) The best way to get a glimpse of what

Dublin Attractions

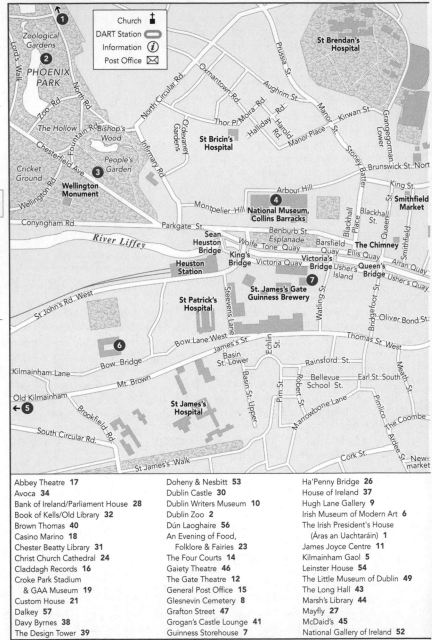

4

DUBLIN | Exploring Dublin

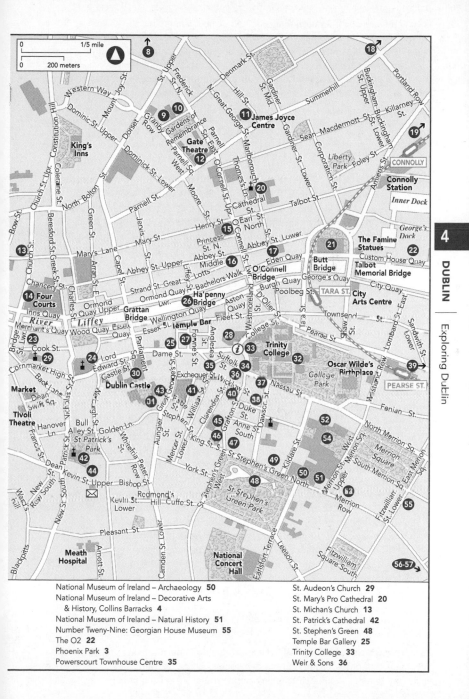

Map labels:

0 — 1/5 mile
0 — 200 meters

King's Inns

James Joyce Centre

Gate Theatre

Gardens of Remembrance

Parnell Sq. East

CONNOLLY

Connolly Station

Inner Dock

Liberty Park

The Famine Statues

Custom House Quay

George's Dock

St. Mary's Pro Cathedral

Butt Bridge

Talbot Memorial Bridge

City Quay

City Arts Centre

Four Courts

River Liffey

Ha'penny Bridge

Grattan Bridge

Temple Bar

TARA ST.

Trinity College

Oscar Wilde's Birthplace

College Park

PEARSE ST.

Dublin Castle

Market

Tivoli Theatre

St Patrick's Park

Meath Hospital

St Stephen's Green Park

National Concert Hall

Merrion Square

56-57

the original building must have been like is to visit the 12th-century crypt, which has been kept untouched. An intriguing side note: Christ Church once displayed what was believed to be the preserved heart of St. Laurence O'Toole (1128–1180). However, in early 2012, the holy relic was stolen in an audacious nighttime raid. Nothing else was taken, including items of much higher value. Other, similar thefts have taken place across Ireland in recent years, leading police to surmise that a collector may be having relics stolen to order. As of this writing, the heart is still missing.

Christchurch Place, Dublin 8. www.christchurchdublin.ie. © **01/677-8099.** Admission €6 adults, €4.50 seniors and students, €2 children (15 and under), €15 families. Mar–May Mon–Sat 9am–6pm; Sun 12:30–2:30pm and 4:30–6pm. June–Sept Mon–Sat 9am–7pm; Sun 12:30–2:30pm and 4:30–7pm. Oct–Feb Mon–Sat 9am–5pm; Sun 12:30–2:30pm. Last admission 45 min. before closing (Mon–Sat). Bus: 37, 39, 39A, 39B, 39C, 39X, 49, 49A, 49X, 50X, 54A, 56A, 70, 70A, 70X, 78A.

Dublin Castle ★ CASTLE This 13th-century structure was the center of British power in Ireland for more than 700 years, until the new Irish government took it over in 1922. You can wander the grounds for free, but they're disappointingly plain; the official tour takes in the much more impressive State Apartments, the early-18th-century Treasury, and the Gothic-style Chapel Royal chapel building that boasts fine plaster decoration and a carved-oak gallery. The castle's only extant tower now holds a small museum dedicated to the Garda (Irish police). The 13th-century structure was once used as a dungeon for those suspected of treason. The castle's Upper Yard is dominated by an impressive Georgian structure called the Bedford Tower, which used to contain the Irish crown jewels. The treasures were stolen in 1907 and have never been found. The yard was also the scene of the last trial by mortal combat to take place in Ireland in 1583. If it's open, check out the Medieval Undercroft, an excavated site on the grounds where an early Viking fortress once stood. *Note:* This is a government building, so areas may be closed for state events.

Dame St., Dublin 2. www.dublincastle.ie © **01/645-8813.** Admission €4.50 adults, €3.50 seniors and students, €2 children 11 and under. Mon–Sat 10am–4:45pm; Sun and public holidays noon–4:45pm. Luas: Jervis. Bus: 37, 39, 39A, 39B, 39C, 49, 49A, 49X, 50, 50X, 56A, 65X, 70, 70A, 70X, 77, 77A, 77X, 123.

Dublin Writers Museum ★★ MUSEUM Manuscripts, early editions, personal possessions, and other pieces of ephemera relating to Ireland's most famous writers are on display at this great museum in Parnell Square. The exhibits are laid out across two rooms, tracing the development of Irish literature up to the present day. Fans of Behan, Joyce, Shaw, Stoker, Wilde, Yeats, and the other greats of the canon will find plenty to love here—from the trivial (knickknacks such as Brendan Behan's postcard from Los Angeles extolling its virtues as a place to get drunk) to the profound (a first edition of Patrick Kavanagh's *The Great Hunger,* complete with a handwritten extra section that his publisher refused to publish, fearing it too controversial). You can take a self-guided audio tour, and there's a suitably excellent bookshop. Talks, readings, and other special events are occasionally held; check the website for details.

18 Parnell Sq., Dublin 1. www.writersmuseum.com. © **01/872-2077.** Admission €7.50 adults, €6.50 seniors and students, €5 children, €18 families. Mon–Sat 10am–5pm; Sun and public holidays 11am–5pm. Last admission 45 min. before closing. Bus: 1, 2, 8, 14, 14A, 16, 16A, 19, 19A, 33X, 39X, 40, 40A, 40B, 40C, 41X, 48A, 58X, 70B, 70X, 116, 120, 123, 145.

Grafton Street ★ NEIGHBORHOOD Dublin's most famous shopping street is a combination of big chains, chi-chi department stores, and little shops. It's as pricey as in any big city—although bargains can be found. It's also a popular site for street

monumental **WIT**

Few cities have such a love-hate relationship with their statues as Dublin. Locals have an acerbic nickname for each one, many of them unprintable. The statue of Molly Malone on Grafton Street is, variously, "the Tart with the Cart," "the Trollope with the Scallop," or "the Flirt in the Skirt"; the James Joyce statue on O'Connell Street is "the Prick with a Stick"; the statue of Anna Livia (a character in *Finnegan's Wake* who symbolized the Liffey), rising from an ornamental pond in Croppies Park, is "the Floozie in the Jacuzzi"; and, depending on who you talk to, the Spire of Dublin on O'Connell Street is either "the Stiletto in the Ghetto," "the Skewer in the Sewer," "the Stiffy by the Liffey," or "the Nail in the Pale."

performers, so you're almost guaranteed an impromptu show on a sunny day. There's an irresistible photo op to be found at the junction with Sloane Street, in the form of a life-sized bronze statue of poor, doomed Molly Malone. Unveiled in 1987, it raised a few eyebrows due to Molly's somewhat revealing décolletage. With typical dryness, locals swiftly nicknamed it "the Tart with the Cart."

Dublin 2. Bus: 11, 11A, 11B, 14, 14A, 15A, 15C, 15X, 20B, 27C, 32X, 33X, 39B, 41X, 46B, 46C, 51X, 58X, 70X, 84X.

Guinness Storehouse ★ FACTORY TOUR Opened in 1759, the Guinness Storehouse is one of the world's most famous breweries, producing the distinctive dark stout known and loved the world over. You can explore the Guinness Hopstore, tour a converted 19th-century building housing the World of Guinness Exhibition, and view a film showing how the stout is made; then move on to the Gilroy Gallery that's dedicated to the graphic design work of John Gilroy (whose work you will have seen if you've ever been in an Irish pub in your life), and last but not least, stop in at the breathtaking Gravity Bar. Here you can sample a glass of the famous brew in the glass-enclosed bar 61m (200 ft.) above the ground, complete with 360-degree views of the city.

St. James's Gate, off Robert St., Dublin 8. www.guinness-storehouse.com. ℂ **01/408-4800.** Admission €16.50 adults, €13 seniors and students over 18 €10.50 students under 18, €6.50 children, €40 families. Sept–May daily 9:30am–5pm; July–Aug daily 9:30am–7pm. Bus: 123.

Hugh Lane Gallery ★★ MUSEUM This small art gallery punches above its weight with a strong collection of Impressionist works. Highlights of the collection include Degas's *Sur la Plage* and Manet's *La Musique aux Tuileries*. There are also sculptures by Rodin, a marvelous collection of Harry Clarke stained glass, and numerous works by modern Irish artists. One room holds the maddeningly cluttered studio of the Irish painter Francis Bacon that the gallery purchased from London and moved to Dublin, where it has been reconstructed behind glass. They moved everything—right down to the dust. It's an excellent, compact art museum, and a great place to spend an afternoon.

Parnell Sq. North, Dublin 1. www.hughlane.ie. ℂ **01/222-5550.** Free admission. Tues–Thurs 10am–6pm; Fri–Sat 10am–5pm; Sun 11am–5pm. Closed Mon. Bus: 1, 2, 8, 10A, 14, 14A, 16, 16A, 19, 19A, 33X, 39X, 40, 41X, 46A, 46B, 46X, 48A, 58C, 58X, 70B, 70X, 116, 145.

The Irish President's House (Áras an Uachtaráin) ★★ HISTORIC SITE
Áras an Uachtaráin was once the Viceregal Lodge, the summer retreat of the British

viceroy, whose main digs were in Dublin Castle. From what were never humble beginnings, the original 1751 country house was expanded several times, gradually accumulating splendor. Guided tours leave from the Phoenix Park Visitor Centre every Saturday. After an introductory historical film, a bus brings visitors to and from the house. The focus of the tour is the state reception rooms. The entire tour lasts about 1 hour (a little longer in summer, when the gardens are included on the itinerary, weather permitting). A strictly limited number of tickets are given out, on a first-come, first-served basis. The house may occasionally be closed for state events, so it's wise to call ahead. *Note:* For security reasons, no backpacks, travel bags, strollers, buggies, cameras, or mobile phones are allowed on the tour.

Tour departs from Phoenix Park Visitor Centre, Dublin 8. www.president.ie. ℭ **01/677-0095** (Phoenix Park Visitor Centre). Free admission. Sat 10:30am–3:30pm. Bus: 37.

Kilmainham Gaol ★★★ HISTORIC SITE This is a key sight for anyone interested in Ireland's struggle for independence from British rule. Within these walls, political prisoners were incarcerated, tortured, and killed from 1796 until 1924. The leaders of the 1916 Easter Uprising were executed here, along with many others. Future president Eamon de Valera was its final prisoner. There is an exhibition devoted to the brutal history of the Irish penal system and a historical film. It's extremely well presented, even if it is hard not to feel overwhelmed at times by the awfulness of it all. To walk along these corridors through the grim exercise yard or into the walled compound is a moving experience that will linger in your memory.

Inchicore Rd., Kilmainham, Dublin 8. www.heritageireland.ie/en/Dublin/KilmainhamGaol. ℭ **01/453-5984.** Admission €6 adults, €4 seniors, €2 students and children, €14 families. Apr–Sept daily 9:30am–6pm; Oct–Mar Mon–Sat 9:30am–5:30pm; Sun 10am–6pm. Last admission 1 hr. before closing. Bus: 51B, 51C, 63, 69, 78A, 123, 206.

National Gallery of Ireland ★★ MUSEUM George Bernard Shaw loved this place so much that he left it a sizeable chunk of his royalties after he died. He saw it as paying a debt, so important was the gallery to his education. It is still a place to wander, wonder, and just be in thrall of so much world-class art. Highlights of the permanent collection include paintings by Caravaggio, Gainsborough, Rubens, Goya, Rembrandt, Monet, and Picasso. The Irish national portrait collection is housed in one wing, while another area is devoted to the career of Jack B. Yeats (brother of W. B. Yeats), an Irish painter of some note. Major exhibitions change regularly, and the subjects are often more imaginative than just the usual run of retrospectives and national landscapes (although those appear too); recent shows have included an exhibition devoted to painting without color. In keeping with the "art for all" ethos that so enamored Bernard Shaw, entry to the permanent collection and many of the temporary shows are free.

Merrion Sq. West, Dublin 2. www.nationalgallery.ie. ℭ **01/661-5133.** Free admission. Mon–Wed, Fri–Sat 9:30am–5:30pm; Thurs 9:30am–8:30pm; Sun noon–5:30pm; public holidays 10am–5:30pm. DART: Pearse. Luas: St. Stephen's Green, Grafton St. Bus: 4, 5, 7, 7A, 8, 13, 13A, 39, 39A, 44, 45, 46A, 48A.

National Museum of Ireland: Archaeology ★★★ MUSEUM The most impressive of the four sites that collectively make up the National Museum of Ireland, this excellent museum is devoted to the ancient history of Ireland and beyond. There are collections covering the Stone Age up to the Early Modern period. Highlights include a stunning collection of Viking artifacts from the archaeological digs that took place in Dublin from the 1960s to the early 1980s—a haul so important that in one fell swoop they rewrote the history of Viking settlement in Ireland. There is also an enormous range of Bronze Age gold and metalwork and iconic Christian treasures from the Dark Ages and early medieval periods, including the Ardagh Chalice, the Molylough Belt Shrine, and the Tara Brooch. Smaller galleries cover artifacts from the Classical world, including 2nd-century Roman figurines and homewares, and an extraordinary granite table made in Egypt circa 1870 B.C. The other sites of the NMI are the Natural History Museum on nearby Kildare Street; Decorative Arts and History, Collins Barracks, in Benburb, just west of the city center; and Country Life in Castlebar, County Mayo (p. 184).

Kildare St., Dublin 2. www.museum.ie. ✆ **01/677-7444.** Free admission. Tues–Sat 10am–5pm; Sun 2–5pm. Closed Mon. Bus: 7B, 7D, 10, 10A, 11, 11A, 11B, 14, 14A, 15, 15A, 15B, 15C, 20B, 25X, 32X.

National Museum of Ireland: Decorative Arts & History, Collins Barracks ★★ MUSEUM

As the name of this branch of the National Museum of Ireland suggests, this museum is unusually located in a converted 18th-century army building. Also unusual is the way it's curated: The collection tells the story of Irish history through fashion, jewelry, furniture, and other decorative arts, with the bulk of the exhibits spanning the 1760s to the 1960s. One gallery is devoted to the work of Eileen Gray (1878–1976), an Irish architect and furniture designer who became one of the most important figures of the Modernist movement; another showcases the extraordinary collection of Asian art bequeathed to the Irish nation in the 1930s by Irish-American philanthropist Albert Bender. This branch of the National Museum isn't entirely devoted to the arts, however; eight galleries focus on Irish military history from the 16th century to the present day, including a fascinating section about the Easter Rising of 1916.

Collins Barracks, Benburb St., Dublin 7. www.museum.ie. ✆ **01/677-7444.** Free admission. Tues–Sat 10am–5pm; Sun 2–5pm. Closed Mon. Luas: Museum. Rail: Heuston. Bus: 39B, 70N.

National Museum of Ireland: Natural History ★★ MUSEUM

Before it underwent a huge renovation in the late 2000s, this vast museum was a venerable but rather moth-eaten institution. Today the building has never looked better—right down to the grand Victorian staircase, closed for years, that takes visitors to the upper floors. The core collection itself has changed little since the museum was founded in the mid–19th century—from small stuffed native Irish animals and primates to the skeletons of enormous sea creatures. Recent additions include the new Discovery Zone, in which visitors can open a series of drawers, like cabinets of curiosity, to discover the unusual specimens within. Sadly, however, the much-trumpeted restoration was barely over when new problems were identified with safety on the balcony levels, which, at this writing, were closed pending a review. This means that some of the most unique parts of the collection are temporarily inaccessible. These include the avian galleries, and the "crystal jellies" collection—oversize glass models of microscopic sea creatures, made in the 19th century by the eccentric and brilliant Blaschka brothers of Dresden, whose work is now highly prized by collectors.

Merrion St., Dublin 2. www.museum.ie. ✆ **01/677-7444.** Free admission. Tues–Sat 10am–5pm; Sun 2–5pm. Closed Mon. Bus: 4, 5, 7A, 8, 15X, 44, 44B, 44C, 48A, 49X, 50X, 51X, 63, 65X, 77X, 84.

St. Patrick's Cathedral ★★ CHURCH   The largest church in Ireland and one of the most beloved places of worship in the world, St. Patrick's is one of two Anglican cathedrals in Dublin. Most of what you can see dates from the 14th century, but religious buildings stood here nearly a thousand years before that. It is mainly early English in style, with a square medieval tower that houses the largest ringing peal bells in Ireland, and an 18th-century spire. A moving collection of war memorials is tucked away at the very back of the cavernous nave, including a very low-key tribute to the Irish dead of World War II. (Ireland was neutral in that war, but around 300,000 men volunteered to fight with the Allies.) Admission includes an irregular program of lunchtime classical music recitals at the Cathedral. Dates vary; call or check the website for details.

St. Patrick's Close, Dublin 8. www.stpatrickscathedral.ie. ✆ **01/453-9472.** Admission €5.50 adults, €4.50 seniors and students, €15 families. Mar–Oct Mon–Fri 9am (9:20 in school term time)–5pm; Sat 9am–6pm; Sun 9–10:30am, 12:30–2:30pm and 4:30–6pm. Nov–Feb Mon–Fri 9am (9:20am in school term time)–5pm; Sat 9am–5pm; Sun 9am–10:30am and 12:30–2:30pm. Last admission 30 min. before closing. Bus: 49, 49A, 49X, 50X, 54A, 56A, 77, 77A, 77X, 150, 151.

St. Stephen's Green ★ PARK   This lovely urban park is filled with public art, and there always seems to be something new and imaginative hidden amid its leafy walkways. Among them is an impressive statue commemorating the Irish rebel Wolfe Tone (beside an affecting monument to the Great Famine) and a garden of scented plants for blind visitors. This is a great place for a summer picnic. If the weather's fine, you can take a buggy ride through the park; rides leave from the Grafton Street side and cost around €20 to €50 for one to four passengers.

Dublin 2. Luas: St. Stephen's Green. Bus: 20B, 32X, 33X, 39X, 40A, 40C, 41X, 46B, 46N, 46X, 51X, 58X, 70B, 70X, 84X, 92.

Temple Bar ★★ NEIGHBORHOOD   There are really two Temple Bars, depending on when you visit. During the day, Temple Bar is an artsy, cultured district full of trendy shops and modern art galleries, such as the excellent **Temple Bar Gallery** (p. 81). But such refinement gives way to an altogether more raucous atmosphere at night, when things can get pretty lively. With its myriad selection of pubs, bars, and hip clubs, this is definitely where it's at in Dublin after dark.

Dublin 2. DART: Tara St. Luas: Jervis. Bus: 37, 39, 39A, 39B, 39C, 49X, 50X, 51, 51B, 51C, 51D, 51X, 65X, 68, 69, 69X, 70, 70A, 77X, 78, 78A, 79, 79A, 90, 92, 206.

Trinity College ★★★ HISTORIC SITE   The oldest university in Ireland, Trinity was founded in 1592 by Queen Elizabeth I to offer an education to the children of the upper classes and protect them from the "malign" Catholic influences elsewhere in Europe. Now it is simply the most well-respected university in Ireland. Among its alumni are Bram Stoker, Jonathan Swift, Oscar Wilde, and Samuel Beckett, as well as an array of rebels and revolutionaries who helped create the Republic of Ireland. The campus spreads across central Dublin just south of the River Liffey, with cobbled squares, gardens, a picturesque quadrangle, and buildings dating from the 17th to the 20th centuries. You can wander the campus for free; alternatively, between May and September, tours take in all of the main sights, plus a ticket for the Book of Kells (p. 65) and the Old Library included in the price. You can wander the campus alone, but the guided tours are worthwhile. They operate on a first-come, first-served basis and leave from the front gate.

College Green, Dublin 2. www.tcd.ie. ✆ **01/896-1000.** Campus tours €5; including Old Library €10 (half-price for students, Oct–Mar), Library and Book of Kells only €9. Campus tours: Late

A TOUR OF trinity college

The Trinity campus is open to the public year-round, although there might be some access restrictions during the exam periods. It's a grand, romantic place to wander around—and free.

The most striking and famous monument inside the Trinity grounds, the white **Campanile,** or bell tower, grabs your attention as soon as you enter through the main archway. Dating from the mid–19th century, it stands on the site of the college's original foundations from 300 years earlier.

The **Old Library Building** is the only section of the campus that you have to pay to see. It's where you'll find the **Book of Kells,** although the library's magnificent **Long Room** is almost as great an attraction (see p. 65).

Part of the 1970s **Arts Building,** the **Douglas Hyde Gallery** displays a regularly changing program of modern art. Exhibitions switch out about every 3 months and admission is always free.

Home to the geography and geology departments, the **Museum Building** is one of Trinity's hidden gems. It was built in the mid–19th century with a combination of Byzantine and Moorish influences. Walk through and look up to the domed ceiling and the green marbled banisters.

One of the more benign remnants of English rule, the **College Park Cricket**

Pitch is a small park where you'll often find a cricket match in progress on summer weekends. The rules are notoriously arcane for the uninitiated, so instead just enjoy the uniquely picturesque sight of the players in their white uniforms and move on.

The **Berkley Library** sharply divides opinion for its austere modernism. The library's position between two architectural masterpieces—the Museum Building and Thomas Burgh's Library—caused controversy from the start. Designer Paul Koralek's library honors Bishop George Berkeley, famed for his philosophical theory of "immaterialism" (things that can't be proved cannot exist), which went against the theories of both Isaac Newton and the Catholic Church. The gleaming sculpture outside the library is *Sphere with Sphere* by Arnaldo Pomodoro (1983). Others in the same series can be found at the Vatican and the United Nations building in New York.

Tucked away in the far northeastern corner of the campus is the excellent **Science Gallery.** A combination of art space, science museum, and debating forum, it has fun and thought-provoking exhibitions, workshops, public lectures, and even shows. Entry is free, except to certain special events. See **www.science gallery.com** for more details.

Apr–mid-May Tues–Sun 10, 10:15, 10:40, 11:05, 11:35am and 12:10, 12:45, 1:35, 2:15, 3, and 3:40pm; (no 3:40pm tour Sun and public holidays); mid-late May Mon–Fri 10:15, 10:40, 11:05, 11:35am and 12:10, 12:45, 1:25, 2, 2:25, 2:50, 3:15, and 3:40pm (no 3:40pm tour Sun and public holidays); June–mid-Sept daily 10:15, 10:35, 10:55, 11:20, 11:45am and 12:10, 12:40, 1:05, 1:30, 2, 2:25, 2:50, 3:15, and 3:40pm (no 3:40pm tour Sun and public holidays); mid-late Sept Mon, Fri, Sat, and Sun 10:15, 10:35, 10:55, 11:20, 11:45am and 12:10, 12:40, 1:05, 1:30, 2, 2:25, 2:50, 3:15, and 3:40pm (no 3:40pm tour Sun and public holidays), Tues–Thurs 10:15, 10:40, 11:05, 11:35am and 12:10, 12:45, 1:35, 2:15, 3, and 3:40pm; Oct–Nov Fri–Mon 10:15, 10:40, 11:05, 11:35am and 12:10, 12:45, 1:35, 2:15, 3, and 3:40pm (no 3:40pm tour Sun and public holidays), 11:35am and 12:10, 12:45, 1:25, 2, 2:25, 2:50, and 3:15pm, Tues–Thurs according to demand (schedule posted weekly). DART: Pearse St., Connolly St. Luas: Lower Abbey St., St. Stephen's Green. Bus: College Green entrance (for tours): 7N, 15N, 15X, 44N, 46N, 48N, 49N, 51D, 51X, 54N, 56A, 70B, 70X, 77A, 77N, 92. Nassau St. entrance (for Old Library/Book of Kells). 25X, 32X, 33X, 41X, 51D, 51X, 58X, 67X, 84X, 92.

More Attractions

Croke Park Stadium & GAA Museum ★ MUSEUM   Croke Park is the headquarters and main sports ground of the Gaelic Athletic Association (GAA), which oversees most of the traditional Irish sports—including hurling, rounders, and Gaelic football. The on-site museum does a good job of covering the history of these games and putting them into a wider historical context. The interactive exhibits include a large video archive, and you can take a tour of the stadium, too. But the most excitement is, of course, to be had on match days—check the website for fixtures if you want to come and hear the roar of the crowd for real.

Jones Rd., Dublin 3. www.crokepark.ie. ⓒ **01/819-2300.** Tour and museum: €12 adults, €9 seniors and students, €8 children 11 and under; €32 families. Museum only: €6 adults, €5 seniors and students, €4 children 11 and under; €16 families. Jan–May and Sept–Dec Mon–Sat 9:30am–5pm; Sun and public holidays 10:30am–5pm. June–Aug Mon–Sat 9:30am–6pm; Sun and public holidays 10:30am–5pm. Closed on match days (unless you have a ticket to the game). Tours: Jan–May and Sept–Dec, Mon–Fri 11am, 1, and 3pm; Sat 10 and 11am, noon, 1, 2, and 3pm; Sun and public holidays 11am, noon, 1, 2, and 3pm. June Mon–Fri 11am, 1, 3, and 4pm; Sat 10 and 11am, noon, 1, 2, 3, and 4pm; Sun and public holidays 11am, noon, 1, 2, and 3pm. July–Aug Mon–Sat 10 and 11am, noon, 1, 2, 3, and 4pm; Sun and public holidays 11am, noon, 1, 2, and 3pm. No tours on match days. Bus: 1, 11, 13, 16, 33, 41, 41B, 41C, 44.

Custom House ★ HISTORIC SITE   Completed in 1791, this perfectly proportioned Georgian building has a long classical facade of graceful pavilions, arcades, and a central dome topped by a statue of Commerce. The 14 keystones over the doors and windows are known as the Riverine Heads because they represent the Atlantic Ocean and the 13 principal rivers of Ireland. Although it burned to a shell in 1921, the building has been masterfully restored. The exterior is the main attraction here and most of the interior is closed to the public, but in case you're keen on learning more, the visitor center has exhibitions and an audiovisual presentation telling the story of its reconstruction.

Custom House Quay, Dublin 1. ⓒ **01/888-2000.** Admission €1 adults, €3 families, students free. Visitor center: mid-Mar–Oct weekdays 10am–12:30pm and 2–5pm; Sat, Sun, and public holidays 2–5pm. Nov–mid-Mar Wed–Fri 10am–12:30pm and 2–5pm; Sun 2–5pm. Luas: Busaras. Bus: 27C, 41X, 90, 92, 151, 747, 748.

Dublin Zoo ★★ ZOO   If you've got kids and they're in need of a change from castles, churches, and history, here's the antidote. This modern, humane zoo provides a naturally landscaped habitat for more than 235 species of wild animals and tropical birds. The animals live inside a series of realistically created habitats such as "African Savanna," home to giraffes, rhinos, and ostriches; "Gorilla Rainforest," a 12,000-square-meter (7½-sq.-mile) enclosure that currently houses five lowland gorillas; "Asian Forest," home to Sumatran tigers and a growing pack of lions, thanks to the recent arrival of two female cubs; and the "the South American House," with an eclectic range of almost unbearably cute species, including golden lion tamarins, tiny pygmy marmosets, and two-toed sloths. Further amusements for youngsters include a train ride around the zoo and the unfailingly cute Children's Pets Corner. There are playgrounds and gift shops scattered throughout. Feeding times and scheduled talks are posted on the zoo's website. A restaurant is on-site, as well as plenty of picnic areas for those who prefer to bring their own meals.

Phoenix Park, Dublin 8. www.dublinzoo.ie. ⓒ **01/474-8900.** Admission €16.50 adults, €12.80 seniors and students, €11.80 children 3–15, €5.70 special-needs children, €9 special-needs adults, €46.50–€55 families. Mar–Sept daily 9:30am–6pm; Oct 9:30am–5:30pm; Nov–Dec 9:30am–4pm; Jan 9:30am–4:30pm; Feb 9:30am–5pm. Last admission to zoo 1 hr. before closing; last admission to African Plains 30 min. before closing. Luas: Heuston (15-min. walk). Bus: 25, 26, 46A, 66, 66A, 66B, 67, 69.

DUBLIN walking tours

Small and compact, Dublin was made for walking. Some of the best experiences the city has to offer involve taking it at your own pace, with a map and an open mind. However, if you'd like more guidance, historical background, or just some company, you might want to consider one of the following.

You could hardly be in better or more learned hands than the **Historical Walking Tours of Dublin** (www.historical tours.ie; $\textcircled{C}$ **087/688-9412**), whose guides are all post-grad students at Trinity College, Dublin. Established for nearly 30 years, the tours are engaging and peerless in their historical insight. In addition to the general tour, you can choose from a variety of intriguing themes, from Medieval and Revolutionary Dublin to Irish Food and even a Running Tour for those who like their history combined with a workout. Meet outside the front gates to Trinity College, College Green, Dublin 2. The cost is €12 adults, €10 seniors and students.

If you prefer to take in the sights at a more leisurely pace, with a bit of liquid refreshment to keep things lively, try the **Literary Pub Crawl** (www.dublin pubcrawl.com; $\textcircled{C}$ **01/670-5602**). Walking in the footsteps of Joyce, Behan, Beckett, Shaw, Kavanagh, and other Irish literary greats, this tour visits Dublin's most famous pubs and explores their deep literary connections. Actors provide humorous performances and commentary between stops. Tickets cost €12 adults, €10 students. No children are allowed, for obvious reasons.

Another fine example of sightseeing for the thirsty is the **Traditional Irish Music Pub Crawl** (www.discoverdublin. ie/musical-pub-crawl; $\textcircled{C}$ **01/475-3313**). Two professional musicians, who sing as you make your way from one famous musical pub to another in Temple Bar, lead the tour. The evening is touristy, but the music is good. The cost is €12 adults, €10 students. Again, no children.

Dublin was profoundly changed by the rebellion early in the 20th century that became known as the Easter Rising. The **1916 Rebellion Walking Tour** (www.1916rising.com; $\textcircled{C}$ **086/858-3847**) takes you into the heat of the action at the General Post Office, explaining how the anger rose until the rebellion exploded on Easter Sunday in 1916. The tour is well thought out and run by local historians who wrote a book on the events of that year. Tickets cost €12.

The Four Courts ★ HISTORIC SITE   Home to the Irish legal courts since 1796, this fine 18th-century building was designed by James Gandon (who also designed the Custom House; p. 74). It's distinguished by its graceful Corinthian columns, massive dome, and exterior statues of Justice, Mercy, Wisdom, and Moses. The building was at the center of the fighting during the civil war of 1922 and was badly damaged in the battle. It was later artfully restored, although some details, such as the statues of famous Irish lawyers that used to adorn the niches of the Round Hall, were lost. Tours are available, but frustratingly, only for law students. The only way to see the interior is usually to watch a trial in progress.

Inns Quay, Dublin 8. www.courts.ie. $\textcircled{C}$ **01/888-6000.** Luas: Four Courts. Bus: 25, 25A, 51D, 51X, 68, 69, 78, 79, 79A, 83, 151, 172.

General Post Office ★ HISTORIC SITE   Don't be fooled by the nondescript name: With a facade of Ionic columns and Greco-Roman pilasters 60m (197 ft.) long and 17m (56 ft.) high, this is more than a post office—it is the symbol of Irish freedom.

Built between 1815 and 1818, it was the main stronghold of the Irish Volunteers during the Easter Rising. On Easter Sunday, 1916, Patrick Pearse stood on its steps and read a proclamation declaring a free Irish Republic. It began, "In every generation the Irish people have asserted their right to national freedom and sovereignty." Then he and an army of supporters barricaded themselves inside. A siege ensued that ultimately involved much of the north of the city, and before it was over, the building was all but destroyed. It had barely been restored before the civil war broke out in 1922, and it was heavily damaged again. It's still a working post office today, although it does house a few exhibits, including the original Declaration of Independence. That's all very much a secondary attraction, though; touching the bullet holes in the walls out front is a far more powerful way to experience a sense of this building's history.

O'Connell St., Dublin 1. www.anpost.ie. ✆ **01/705-8833.** Free admission (museum €2). Post Office building: Mon–Sat 8:30am–6:00pm. Closed Sun and public holidays. Museum: Mon–Sat 10am–5pm. Luas: Abbey St. Bus: 10, 10A, 32X, 33X, 39X, 40A, 40C, 41X, 46A, 46B, 46C, 46D, 46E, 116, 123, 145, 747.

Glasnevin Cemetery & Museum ★ CEMETERY   North of the city center, the Irish national cemetery was founded in 1832 and covers more than 50 hectares (124 acres). Most people buried here were ordinary citizens, but there are also many famous names on the headstones, ranging from former Irish Taoiseach (prime minister) Eamon de Valera to other political heroes and rebels including Michael Collins, Daniel O'Connell, Countess Constance Markievicz, and Charles Stewart Parnell. Literary figures also have their place, and you can find writers Christy Brown (immortalized in the film *My Left Foot*) and Brendan Behan. There's a small museum devoted to the cemetery and its famous occupants. Guided tours run daily, or you can download a self-guided tour app for your smartphone for €10 via the cemetery's website. Maps showing who is buried where are also for sale in the flower shop at the entrance.

Finglas Rd., Glasnevin, Dublin 11. www.glasnevintrust.ie. ✆ **01/882-6550.** Museum and tour €12 adults; €8 seniors, students, and children; €25 families; museum only €6 adults; €4 seniors, students, and children; €15 families; self-guided audio tour €10. Weekdays 10am–5pm; Sat, Sun, and public holidays 11am–5pm. Tours: Sept–June daily 11:30am and 2:30pm; early- to mid-July daily 11:30am, 1, and 2:30pm; mid-July–Aug Mon–Wed 11:30am, 1, and 2:30pm, Thurs–Sun daily 11:30 and 2:30pm. Bus: 4, 9, 83, 140.

Ha'penny Bridge ★ ARCHITECTURE   Built in 1816 and one of the earliest cast-iron bridges in Europe, the graceful, pedestrians-only Ha'penny (pronounced Hay-penny) Bridge is still the most attractive of Dublin's bridges. Officially named the Liffey Bridge, it's universally known by the toll it once charged to cross it: half a penny. The turnstiles were removed in 1919 when passage was made free. The bridge is at its prettiest after sundown, when the old lamps atop its three filigreed arches are lit, and the underside at each end is illuminated in green. During the 2000s it became traditional for couples to leave padlocks latched onto the bridge with their names inscribed before throwing the keys into the water. Dublin's city government now forbids the practice, seeing them more as an eyesore than a symbol of eternal love.

Connects Wellington and Lower Ormond quays, Dublin 2. Luas: Jervis. Bus: 39B, 51, 51B, 51C, 51D, 51X, 68, 69, 69X, 78, 78A, 79, 79A, 90, 92, 206.

Irish Museum of Modern Art ★ MUSEUM   This small but handsome museum, located in a 17th-century former hospital building, has a strong collection of modern art dating from the 1940s to the present day. Highlights include a striking series of mid-1970s photographs by Serbian conceptual artist Marina Abramovic;

etchings and lithographs by Alice Maher, Louis le Brocquy, and Marcel Duchamp; and the Madden Arnholz Collection that's made up of around 2,000 old master prints, including works by Hogarth and Rembrandt. The masterfully restored grounds are also used as an exhibition space, with a number of changing pieces set among the formal lawns and clipped box hedges.

Royal Hospital, Military Rd., Kilmainham, Dublin 8. www.imma.ie. *C* **01/612-9900.** Free admission. Thurs–Fri and Mon–Tues 10am–5:30pm; Wed 10:30am–5:30pm; Sun and public holidays noon–5:30pm. Last admission 45 min. before closing. Closed Sun. Luas: Heuston. Bus: 26, 51, 51B, 78A, 79, 90, 123.

The James Joyce Centre ★ MUSEUM This idiosyncratic museum is set in a handsome Georgian house that once belonged to the Earl of Kenmare. Joyce himself never lived here; however, he was rather taken with a former owner of the house called Denis Maginni. An eccentric man, who was Irish but added the "i" to give himself an air of Italian sophistication, Maginni appears as a character in *Ulysses*. Today, the center functions as both a small museum and a cultural center devoted to Joyce and his work. Actual exhibits are a little thin on the ground, but they hold interesting (at least for Joyce fans) lectures and special events, and also organize a Joyce-themed walking tour of Dublin. Unsurprisingly, this place becomes an explosion of activity around Bloomsday (June 16th); unlike the rest of Dublin, which makes do with a single day of celebrating its most famous 20th-century literary hero, the James Joyce Centre turns it into a week-long festival.

35 North Great George's St., Dublin 1. www.jamesjoyce.ie. *C* **01/878-8547.** Admission €5 adults, €4 seniors and students Mon–Sat 10am–5pm, Sun noon–5pm. Bus: 1, 2, 8, 14, 14A, 16, 16A, 19, 19A, 33X, 39X, 41X, 48A, 58X, 70B, 70X, 116, 145

Leinster House ★ HISTORIC SITE The home of the Dáil (Irish House of Representatives) and Seanad (Irish Senate), this is the modern center of Irish government. Dating from 1745, it was originally known as Kildare House and was the seat of the Dukes of Leinster. Like the Parliament House building (p. 70), it is said to have been a major influence on the architects of Washington, D.C.; the resemblance to Irish-born James Hoban's design for the White House, built 78 years later, is certainly clear enough. Tickets are available for guided tours 2 to 4 days per week. When the Dáil is in session you may also be able to watch part of a debate in the public gallery. For tickets, call the events desk (*C* **01/618-3271** or 3781; event.desk@oireachtas.ie), or contact your country's embassy in Dublin and they can arrange a tour on your behalf. *Note:* You need to bring I.D. (such as a driver's license, bank card, or passport) to gain admission.

Kildare St. and Merrion Sq., Dublin 2. www.oireachtas.ie. *C* **01/618-3271** or 3781. Free admission. Entry by tour only, Mon and Fri, 10:30am, 2:30, and 3:30pm. (Additional tours when Dáil and Seanad in session, Tues and Wed, 7 and 8pm). Bus: 4, 5, 7A, 8, 7B, 7D, 10, 10A, 11, 11A, 11B, 14, 14A, 15, 15A, 15B, 15C, 15X, 20B, 25X, 32X, 44, 44B, 44C, 48A, 49X, 50X, 51X, 63, 65X, 77X, 84.

The Little Museum of Dublin ★★ MUSEUM Stuffed full of ephemera relating to the lives of ordinary Dubliners—art, toys, photographs, newspapers, prints, and other artifacts of the everyday—this delightful little museum forms a remarkably absorbing chronicle of what it was like to live in the city during the 20th century. Thoughtfully laid out inside a preserved Georgian town house, the vast majority of the items on display were donated by the people of Dublin, and the collection is being added to all the time. Among the curios are genuine documents of social history, including items relating to the World War I, the struggle for independence, and the suffrage movement. Several of the objects on display have little tales of their own—such as the music stand that, in June 1963, was hurriedly borrowed from the home of a local antique dealer by visiting U.S. President John F. Kennedy when he realized he had nowhere to put his papers during a speech. Tours are lively and informative, and guides are good at engaging younger visitors in what all this really means.

15 St. Stephen's Green, Dublin 2. www.littlemuseum.ie. ⓒ **01/661-1000.** Admission €6 adults, €5 seniors, €4 students and children, €13 families. Deluxe ticket (includes private guided tour) €10. Fri–Wed 9:30am–5pm; Thurs 9:30am–8pm. Luas: St. Stephen's Green. Bus: 15X, 32X, 39X, 41X, 46X, 51X, 58X, 66X, 67X, 70X, 84X, 92.

Marsh's Library ★★ LIBRARY   This caged library was founded by Narcissus Marsh, the Archbishop of Dublin, in 1701. Unlike Trinity College's Long Room, which is largely for show these days, Marsh's Library is still functioning. The walls are lined with scholarly volumes, chiefly focused on theology, medicine, ancient history, and maps, along with Hebrew, Greek, Latin, and French literature. Wire cages, in which readers would be locked in with the more valuable tomes, still stand anachronistically. The interior—a magnificent example of a 17th-century scholar's library—has remained much the same for 3 centuries. The excellent collection of books by and about Jonathan Swift includes volumes with his editing comments in the margins—ironically, perhaps, given that Swift himself said of Archbishop Marsh, "He is the first of human race, that with great advantages of learning, piety, and station ever escaped being a great man."

St Patrick's Close, Dublin 8. www.marshlibrary.ie. ⓒ **01/454-3511.** Admission €2.50 adults, €1.50 seniors and students, children 15 and under free. Wed–Sat and Mon, 9:30am–1pm and 2–5pm; Sat 10am–1pm. Closed Tues, Sun, public holidays, and last week in Dec. Bus: 49, 49A, 50X, 54A, 56A, 77A, 77X, 150, 151.

Number Twenty-Nine: Georgian House Museum ★★ MUSEUM   A little time capsule of family life in Georgian Dublin, Number 29 is a fascinating curiosity. Rooms are kept as close as possible to how they would have looked in the period from 1790 to about 1820. The differences between family living spaces and the basement servants' quarters are, unsurprisingly, stark. The two elegant drawing rooms, richly carpeted with expensive blue wallpaper and crystal chandeliers, stand in sharp relief to the sparse housekeeper's bedroom or the simple, homely kitchen. At the same time, however, the industriousness of the kitchen is quite a revelation—medicines and cosmetics were made here from scratch by the servants, in addition to all the family's meals. The self-guided audio tour is informative, or if you can't bear to be in a place like this without being able to ask questions, there's a full tour daily at 3pm.

Corner of Fitzwilliam St. Lower and Mount St. Upper, Dublin 2. www.esb.ie/no29. ⓒ **01/702-6165.** Admission €6 adults, €3 seniors and students, children 15 and under free. Tues–Sat 10am–5pm. Last admission 30 min. before closing. Closed mid-Dec to mid-Feb. Tours: 3pm. DART: Pearse. Bus: 15X, 49X, 50X, 65X, 77X.

Parliament House ★ HISTORIC SITE   The impressive, colonnaded facade of this building was allegedly the model for the Capitol building in Washington, D.C.—with one key difference: It's completely devoid of windows. When Parliament House was built in the 1730s, a vicious window tax was in force, so not having any was a neat way to save money. The Irish Parliament met here until 1801, when, by an extraordinary quirk of history, it voted for its own abolition. William Pitt the Younger, then Prime Minister of Britain, had promised sweeping reform of the anti-Catholic laws if Ireland agreed to a formal union with Britain. They did so, but Pitt was deposed by

DUBLIN bus tours

Convenient, comfortable, and—remember this when the heavens open in June—relatively immune to inclement weather, bus tours are a great way to pack a lot of sightseeing into a little time. And while Dublin has more than its fair share of standard tourist buses, a few are slightly more original.

For a lively tour of Dublin's Viking history, the **Viking Splash Tour** (*C* **01/707-6000;** www.vikingsplash.ie) in a reconditioned World War II amphibious "duck" vehicle starts on land and eventually splashes into the Grand Canal. Viking helmets, though supplied, are optional. Tickets are €22 adults, €18 seniors and students, €16 teenagers, and €12 children.

Of the many "hop on, hop off" style bus tours of the city, one of the best is the **Dublin Sightseeing** tour, run by **Dublin Bus** (*C* **01/703-3028;** www.dublinsightseeing.ie) The 24-stop tour takes you all around the city center and out as far as Kilmainham Gaol (p. 70). You can leave and rejoin the tours as many times as you like in a day. Buses run all day, every 10 minutes from 9am to 3.30pm, every 15 minutes until 5:30pm, and every 30 minutes until the last bus at around 6:30pm. Tickets cost €19 adults, €17 seniors and students, and €8 children.

The **North Coast and Castle Tour** and the **South Coast and Gardens Tour,** also run by Dublin Bus, take you on all-day excursions to the picturesque coastal regions on the far fringes of Dublin. Tickets for both tours include entry to a separate attraction, the medieval Malahide Castle and its landscaped park to the north and **Powerscourt House & Gardens** (p. 87) to the south. The cost is €24 adults and €12 children.

A spooky evening tour in a bus decked out in, um . . . spooky wallpaper, **Dublin Ghost Bus** (*C* **01/703-3028;** www.dublinsightseeing.ie/ghostbus) addresses Dublin's history of felons, fiends, and phantoms. You'll see haunted houses, learn of Dracula's Dublin origins, and even get a crash course in body snatching. It's all ghoulish fun but actually quite scary in places, so it's not recommended for preteens Tickets cost €28.

Likewise, the entertaining **Gravediggers Tour** (*C* **086/411-3326;** www.thegravedigger.ie) takes you in pursuit of a few ghoulish and well-intentioned scares. Just when it all seems like too much for the faint-hearted, the bus stops at the Gravediggers Pub by Glasnevin Cemetery (p. 76) for a fortifying drink—included in the ticket price of €25. Live actors and 4-D technology help bring the whole experience to life. Or should that be . . .

King George III, the reforms never happened, and the Irish lost what little self-government they had. Today the building is owned by the Bank of Ireland, but you can see parts of the magnificent interior featuring oak woodwork, 18th-century tapestries, and a sparkling crystal chandelier. Friendly porters are on hand to fill you in on the history and are known to give informal tours of rooms you can't normally see, if you ask nicely.

2 College Green, Dublin 2. *C* **01/661-5933.** Free admission. Mon, Tues, and Fri 10am–4pm; Wed 10:30am–4pm; Thurs 10am–5pm. Bus: 7N, 15N, 15X, 44N, 46N, 48N, 49N, 51D, 51X, 54N, 56A, 70B, 70X, 77A, 77N, 92.

Phoenix Park ★ PARK   The vast green expanses of Phoenix Park are Dublin's playground, and it's easy to see why. This well-designed, user-friendly park is criss-crossed by a network of roads and quiet pedestrian walkways that make its 688 hectares (1,700 acres) easily accessible. It's a restful place to spend an hour or two, but there's plenty to do here should you feel active. The home of the Irish president (see p. 69) is in the park, as is the Dublin Zoo (p. 74). The visitor center dispenses helpful maps and information.

Phoenix Park, Dublin 8. www.phoenixpark.ie. (*) **01/677-0095.** Free admission. Park: 24 hrs. Visitor center: Apr–Dec daily 10am–6pm; Jan–Mar Wed–Sun 9:30am–5:30pm (closed Mon and Tues). Last admission 45 min. before closing. Bus: Castleknock Road entrance: 37. Navan Road entrance: 37, 38, 39, 70. North Circular Road entrance: 46A.

St. Audeon's Church ★ CHURCH   Near the only remaining gate of the Old City walls (dating from 1214), this church is said to be the only surviving medieval parish in Dublin. Although it is partly in ruins, significant parts have survived, including the west doorway, which dates from 1190, and the 13th-century nave. It's a Church of Ireland property, but nearby is another St. Audeon's Church, this one Catholic and dating from 1846. It was in the latter church that Father "Flash" Kavanagh used to say the world's fastest Mass so that his congregation was out in time for the football matches. Entrance to the ancient church is through a visitor center. The center's exhibition, relating the history of St. Audeon's, is self-guided; visits to the church itself are by guided tour, and it is only open in high season.

14 High St., Dublin 8. www.heritageireland.ie. (*) **01/677-0088.** Free admission. Daily 9:30am– 5:30pm. Bus: 49X, 50X, 51B, 51C, 51N, 54A, 78A, 206.

St. Mary's Pro Cathedral ★ CHURCH   No, there's no pro and amateur league for Cathedrals in Ireland—"pro" simply means "temporary." And therein lies a fascinating piece of historical trivia. Contrary to popular belief, Dublin has no Roman Catholic cathedral (St. Patrick's and Christ Church have been part of the Anglican Church of Ireland since the 16th century). But the Vatican views Christ Church as Dublin's "true" Catholic cathedral. Therefore, St. Mary's has been designated the "temporary" official Catholic cathedral in Dublin since 1820. It's tucked away on a rather unimpressive back street, but it's nonetheless the heart of the city's Northside. It was built between 1815 and 1825 in Greek Revival Doric style. The exterior portico is modeled on the Temple of Theseus in Athens, with six Doric columns, while the Renaissance-style interior is patterned after the Church of Saint-Philippe du Roule of Paris. The church is noted for its awe-inspiring Palestrina Choir, which sings a Latin Mass every Sunday at 11am (during term times).

83 Marlborough St., Dublin 1. www.procathedral.ie. (*) **01/874-5441.** Free admission. Mon–Fri 7:30am–6:45pm; Sat 7:30am–7:15pm; Sun 9am–1:45pm and 5:30–7:45pm; public holidays 10am– 1:30pm. DART: Connolly, Tara St. Luas: Abbey St. Bus: 2, 3, 4, 5, 7, 7A, 7B, 7D, 8, 10, 10A, 11, 11A, 11B, 13, 20B, 27, 32X, 33X, 39X, 40A, 40C, 41, 41A, 41B, 41C, 41X, 42, 42A, 42B, 43, 51A, 116, 123, 130, 142, 747.

St. Michan's Church ★★ CHURCH   Built on the site of an early Danish chapel (1095), this 17th-century edifice has fine interior woodwork and an organ (dated 1724) on which Handel is said to have played his *Messiah.* A unique (and, let it be noted, macabre) feature of this church is the underground burial vault. Because of the dry atmosphere, mummified bodies have lain for centuries in an extraordinary state of preservation. A few still have their hair and fingernails; on others you can see desiccated internal organs under the skin. The tallest mummy is known as "the Crusader"; his legs were broken in order to fit him into the coffin. Others in residence include "the Nun" and "the Thief"—although their true identities were lost when the church records were destroyed during the civil war in 1922. It is said that Bram Stoker was inspired to write *Dracula* in part by having visited the vaults as a child. *Note:* The church is wheelchair-accessible, but the vaults are not.

Church St., Dublin 7. www.stmichans.com. (©) **01/872-4154.** Admission €5 adults, €4 seniors and students, €3.50 children, €15 families. Crypt: Mid-Mar–Oct Mon–Fri 10am–12:45pm and 2–4:45pm; Sat 10am–12:45pm. Nov–mid-Mar Mon–Fri 12:30–3:30pm, Sat 10am–12:45pm. No crypt tours Sun. Luas: Four Courts, Smithfield. Bus: 51D, 51X.

Temple Bar Gallery ★★ ARTS COMPLEX   This big, rambling art gallery sums up all that is good about Temple Bar. Founded in 1983 in the heart of Dublin's "Left Bank," this is one of the largest studio and gallery complexes of its kind in Europe. It's filled with innovative work by contemporary Irish artists—more than 30 of them, in a variety of disciplines, including sculpture, painting, printing, and photography. The colors and creativity are dazzling, and it's run by helpful, friendly people. Only the gallery section is open to the public, but you can make an appointment to view individual artists at work. The Studios hosts free talks and discussion panels, featuring the great and the good of the Irish arts scene. Call or go online for details.

5-9 Temple Bar, Dublin 2. www.templebargallery.com. (©) **01/671-0073.** Free admission. Tues–Sat 11am–6pm. Bus: 26, 37, 39, 39A, 39B, 39C, 49X, 50X, 65X, 66, 66A, 66B, 66D, 67, 67A, 69X, 70, 70A, 77X.

Shopping

Avoca ★★ CLOTHING/HOUSEWARES   A wonderland of vivid colors, soft, intricately woven fabrics, blankets, light woolen sweaters, children's clothes, and toys, all set in a delightful store spread over three floors near Trinity College. All the fabrics are woven in the Vale of Avoca in the Wicklow Mountains. The shop also sells pottery, jewelry, vintage and antique clothing, food, and adorable little things you really don't need, but can't live without. Hands down, this is one of the best stores in Dublin. The top-floor **cafe** is a great place for lunch (see p. 56).

11-13 Suffolk St., Dublin 2. www.avoca.ie. (©) **01/677-4215.** Mon–Wed 9.30am–6pm; Thurs–Sat 9:30am–7pm; Sun 11am–6pm. Bus: 15X, 32X, 33X, 39X, 41X, 51D, 51X, 58X, 70X, 84X.

Brown Thomas ★★ DEPARTMENT STORE   The top-hatted doorman out front sets a deceptively formal tone for this great old Dublin institution; we've always found it a relaxed and friendly place, even if the credit card seems to take a bit of a beating. Stop by for most of the major fashion labels before getting your nails done, having a one-to-one at the cosmetics counters, and indulging yourself at the bar and cafe or the elegant new restaurant.

88-95 Grafton St., Dublin 2. www.brownthomas.com. (©) **01/605-6666.** Mon, Wed, and Fri 9:30am–8pm; Tues 10am–8pm; Thurs 9:30am–9pm; Sat 9am–8pm; Sun 11am–7pm. Luas: St. Stephen's Green. Bus: 11, 11A, 11B, 14, 14A, 15A, 15C, 15X, 20B, 27C, 32X, 33X, 39B, 39X, 41X, 46B, 46C, 51X, 58X, 70X, 84X.

Claddagh Records ★★ MUSIC   Renowned among insiders in traditional Irish music circles, this is where to find "the genuine article" in traditional music and perhaps discover a new favorite. Not only is the staff knowledgeable and enthusiastic about new artists, but they're able to tell you which venues and pubs are hosting the best music sessions that week.

65 Middle Abbey St., Dublin 1. www.claddaghrecords.com. (©) **01/872-0075.** Mon–Fri 10:30am–5:30pm; Sat noon–5:30pm. Luas: Jervis. Bus: 4, 5, 7, 7A, 7B, 7D, 8, 39B, 70B, 70X, 116.

The Design Tower ★★ MARKET/ GIFTS   A cutting-edge convocation of hot designers and craftspeople work at this former sugar refinery at the Grand Canal Quay

TEMPLE BAR street markets

Not all the best shopping in Temple Bar is to be found indoors: It's also home to three of Dublin's finest street markets.

The **Designer Mart** is a great showcase for fashion designers and craftspeople from all over Ireland. It takes place in uber-trendy Cow's Lane every Saturday from 10am until 5pm.

The **Book Market** takes over Temple Bar Square all weekend, from 10am to 6pm. It's relatively small, but there's always some piece of printed treasure or other to be unearthed among its secondhand book stalls.

A must for foodies, the **Food Market** makes its presence felt most of all, through the wafts of tempting aromas that hang around Meeting House Square from 10am to 4:30pm on Saturday. Should the weather take a turn for the worse, there's even a fancy retractable roof to keep you dry while you deliberate over which Irish farmhouse cheese to take away, before waiting in line for a freshly cooked snack.

on the eastern side of the city. Occupants include Seamus Gill, who makes extraordinary, almost organic-seeming silverware; conceptual artist and fashion designer Roisin Gartland; and jewelry designer Brenda Haugh, whose work includes interesting modern interpretations of Celtic motifs. Some designers here have walk-in shops, but most prefer appointments, so call ahead if you want to see someone specific. The Design Tower is near Grand Canal Dock DART station, or about a 20-minute walk from Grafton Street.

Trinity Centre, Grand Canal Quay, Dublin 2. www.thedesigntower.com. ℂ **01/677-0107.** Mon–Fri 10am–5pm. DART: Grand Canal Dock. Bus: 1, 2, 3, 50, 56A, 77A.

House of Ireland ★ IRISH GIFTS An excellent "one-stop shop" for quality Irish souvenirs, this is the place to come for Waterford and Galway crystal, Belleek china, jewelry, linens, and clothing by big-name Irish designers such as Eugene and Anke McKernan, John Rocha, and Louise Kennedy. Just one trip here and nobody back home needs to know that you didn't really scour the country for that perfect knickknack or gift. If you've really left your souvenir shopping until the last minute, two smaller outlet branches are at Dublin Airport.

37-38 Nassau St., Dublin 2. www.houseofireland.com. ℂ **01/671-1111.** Mon–Wed 9am–6pm; Thurs 9am–8pm; Fri–Sat 9am–6pm; Sun 10:30am–6pm. Bus: 15X, 25X, 32X, 33X, 39X, 41X, 51D, 51X, 58X, 67X, 70X, 84X, 92.

Mayfly ★★ CRAFTS/ GIFTS You know you're visiting somewhere that's quintessentially Temple Bar when the directions on the website tell you to look out for the cow in the buggy out front. This is a treasure trove for deliciously creative, artsy gifts, jewelry, clothing, and other doodads that are impossible to resist. Artists whose work is for sale include Courtney Tyler, who turns old watch faces into interesting jewelry, and embroiderer Victoria White, who makes misfit toys by hand.

11 Fownes St., Dublin 2. www.mayfly.ie. ℂ **086/376-4189.** Sat–Wed 10:30am–7pm; Thurs–Fri 10:30am–8pm. Bus: 39B, 49X, 50X, 65X, 77X.

Powerscourt Townhouse Centre ★★ MARKETPLACE In a restored 1774 town house, this four-story complex consists of a central sky-lit courtyard and more than 60 boutiques, craft shops, art galleries, snack bars, wine bars, and restaurants. The wares include all kinds of crafts, antiques, paintings, prints, ceramics, leatherwork, jewelry, clothing, chocolates, and farmhouse cheeses. You can also book a behind-the-scenes tour to learn more about the history of the house. You can see the old kitchen and cellars, the former lord and lady's bedrooms and dressing rooms, the music room, ballroom, and dining room. For details and booking, contact Shireen Gail at shireengail@gmail.com or ℂ **086/806-5505.**

59 South William St., Dublin 2. www.powerscourtcentre.com. ℂ **01/679-4144.** Mon–Wed and Fri 10am–6pm; Thurs 10am–8pm; Sat 9am–6pm; Sun noon–6pm. Luas: St. Stephen's Green. Bus: 11, 11A, 11B, 14, 14A, 15A, 15C, 15X, 20B, 27C, 32X, 33X, 39B, 39X, 41X, 46B, 46C, 46N, 46X, 51X, 58X, 65X, 70X, 84X.

Weir & Sons ★ JEWELRY   Established in 1869, this is the granddaddy of Dublin's fine jewelry shops. It sells new and antique jewelry, as well as silver, china, and crystal. The ground floor of the main branch on Grafton Street also has a section devoted to 17th-, 18th-, and 19th-century antique silver from Ireland and Britain. The shop is located on the corner of Grafton and Wicklow streets. A second branch can be found in Dundrum, about 7km (4⅓ miles) south of the city center.

96-99 Grafton and 1-3 Wicklow sts., Dublin 2. www.weirandsons.ie. ℂ **01/677-9678.** Mon–Wed and Fri–Sat 9:30am–6pm; Thurs 9:30am–8pm. Closed Sun. Bus: 15X, 32X, 33X, 39X, 41X, 51X, 58X, 70X, 84X.

Nightlife

Abbey Theatre ★ THEATER   Since 1903, the Abbey has been the national theater of Ireland. The original theater, destroyed by fire in 1951, was replaced in 1966 by the current functional, although uninspired, 492-seat house. It remains one of the most respected and prestigious theaters in the country. In addition to its main stage, the theater has a 127-seat basement studio, the **Peacock,** where it presents newer and more experimental work.

26 Lower Abbey St., Dublin 1. www.abbeytheatre.ie. ℂ **01/878-7222.** Ticket prices vary; generally between €13 and €40. Event times vary; call ahead. Rail: Tara St., Connolly. Luas: Abbey St. Bus: 2, 3, 4, 5, 7, 7A, 7B, 7D, 8, 10, 10A, 15, 15A, 15B, 15C, 15E, 15F, 20B, 27B, 27C, 29A, 31, 31B, 32, 32A, 32B, 32X, 33, 33X, 38, 38A, 38C, 41, 41A, 41B, 41C, 41X, 42, 42A, 42B, 43, 45, 46A, 46B, 46C, 46E, 51A, 70B, 70X, 121, 122, 130, 142, 145.

Davy Byrnes ★ PUB   "He entered Davy Byrnes," wrote Joyce of Leopold Bloom, the hero of *Ulysses.* "Moral pub. He doesn't chat. Stands a drink now and then. But in a leap year once in four. Cashed a cheque for me once." For a place with such impeccable literary connections as this, it's unsurprising that so many writers make this something of a pilgrimage spot when they're in town. Joyce himself was a regular, although the food has certainly improved since his day—the menu of pub classics and sandwiches is actually pretty good, and well priced. *Ulysses* fans will be delighted to hear that you can still order a gorgonzola sandwich—Bloom's snack of choice.

21 Duke St., off Grafton St., Dublin 2. www.davybyrnes.com. ℂ **01/677-5217.** Mon–Wed 11am–11:30pm; Thurs–Fri 11am–12:30am; Sat 10:30am–12:30am; Sun 12:30–11pm. Bus: 11, 11A, 11B, 14, 14A, 15A, 15C, 15X, 20B, 27C, 33X, 39B, 41X, 46B, 46C.

Doheny and Nesbitt ★ PUB   From the outside this pub brings to mind a Victorian medicine cabinet, all polished wood with a rich blue-and-gold sign. Its proximity to the political and economic heart of the capital makes it a perennial hangout for politicos, lawyers, economists, and those who write about them—which can make for some spectacularly good eavesdropping. (Indeed, the name spawned a whole political shorthand, "the Doheny and Nesbitt School of Economics," to describe the great and the good who used to shoot the breeze here during Ireland's boom years of the 1990s and 2000s.) If you want to spend time admiring the cozy interior, a midweek daytime visit is best—this place gets packed in the evenings (especially on summer weekends), and even more so when a big sports match is on.

5 Baggot St. Lower, Dublin 2. www.dohenyandnesbitts.ie. ℂ **01/676-2945.** Wed–Thurs 10am–12:30am; Fri–Sat 10am–2am; Sun noon–11pm; Mon 10am–11:30pm; Tues 10am–midnight. Bus: 10, 10A, 25X, 51D, 51X, 65X, 66D, 66X, 67X, 77X.

An Evening of Food, Folklore & Fairies ★★★ DINNER THEATER   The concept of this wonderful evening is timeless, yet brilliant in its simplicity. No high-tech smoke and mirrors; just compelling tales from Irish folklore, passionately told by masters of the storytelling craft. The whole thing takes place in an atmospherically lit room inside the Brazen Head, one of the oldest pubs in Dublin. During dinner, the storytellers spin their yarns—not all of them fantastical in nature, but each one hugely absorbing. The meal, included in the price, is suitably traditional: beef and Guinness stew or bacon and cabbage with mashed potatoes. If you haven't had your fill of tradition by the end of it all, you can go downstairs and hear some live music in the bar.

The Brazen Head Pub, 20 Bridge St. Lower, Dublin 8. www.irishfolktours.com. ℂ **01/218-8555.** Tickets €46 adults, €42 seniors and students, €29 children. Mar–Dec nightly 7pm. Jan–Feb Thurs and Sat 7pm. Bus: 25, 25A, 37, 51C, 51D, 51X, 66, 66D, 69X, 70, 70A, 78A, 79, 79A, 90, 92.

Gaiety Theatre ★ PERFORMING ARTS   The elegant little Gaiety, opened in 1871, hosts a varied array of performances, including everything from opera to classical Irish plays and Broadway-style musicals. And when the thespians leave, the partygoers arrive. On Friday and Saturday from midnight on, the place turns into a nightclub, with four bars hosting live bands and DJs, spinning R&B, indie, blues, or hip-hop. There are even occasional cult movie showings. Don't forget to check out the ornate decor before you get too tipsy.

The Gaiety Theatre, South King St., Dublin 2. www.gaietytheatre.ie. ℂ **081/871-9388.** Ticket prices vary; generally between €15 and €50. Event times vary; call ahead. Luas: St. Stephen's Green. Bus: 11, 11A, 11B, 14, 14A, 15A, 15C, 15X, 20B, 27C, 33X, 39B, 40A, 40C, 41X, 46B, 46C, 46N, 46X, 51X, 58X, 67X, 70X, 84X.

The Gate Theatre ★ THEATER   Just north of O'Connell Street off Parnell Square, this recently restored 370-seat theater was founded in 1928 by Irish actors Hilton Edwards and Michael MacLiammoir to provide a venue for a broad range of plays. That policy prevails today, thanks to a program that includes a blend of modern works and the classics. Although less known by visitors, the Gate is easily as distinguished as the Abbey.

Cavendish Row, Parnell Sq., Dublin 1. www.gatetheatre.ie. ℂ **01/874-4045.** Ticket prices vary; generally between about €20 and €30. Event times vary; call ahead. Bus: 1, 2, 14, 14A, 16, 16A, 19, 19A, 33X, 39X, 40, 40A, 40B, 40C, 41X, 48A, 58X, 70B, 70X, 120. 123.

Grogan's Castle Lounge ★ PUB   There's a friendly, chatty vibe at this satisfyingly old-fashioned place, considered one of Dublin's "quintessential" pubs. There's nothing modern or polished about the dimly lit, atmospheric interior, save for the slightly incongruous art collection on the walls (most of it is for sale). Grogan's reputation rests mostly on its mixed clientele, ranging from grizzled old folks who have been coming here for years to hipster-ish, artsy types in search of a low-fi hangout.

15 South William St., Dublin 2. www.groganspub.ie. ℂ **01/677-9320.** Mon–Thurs 10:30am–11:30pm; Fri–Sat 10:30am–12:30am; Sun 12:30pm–11pm. Bus: 15, 32X, 33X, 39X, 41X, 51X, 58X, 70X, 84X.

The Long Hall ★★ PUB   The polished walnut-and-brass interior of this Victorian pub elicits purrs of delight from thirsty patrons as soon as they walk through the door. One of Dublin's most gorgeously, seductively . . . well, *Irish* of pubs, the Long Hall is named for the bar that runs the entire length of the interior. Regulars have to fight for space alongside the tourist crowd, but it's more than worth squeezing in for a look at the interior. Not that staying here for a few pints is anything like a chore.

51 South Great George's St., Dublin 2. ⓒ **01/475-1590.** Mon–Wed 4–11:30pm; Thurs 1–11:30pm; Fri–Sat 1pm–12:30am; Sun 1–11pm. Bus: 11E, 15F, 16, 16A, 19, 19A, 39X, 65, 65B, 65X, 83, 122.

McDaid's ★ PUB   This was Brendan Behan's favorite pub—and if there ever was a man to be trusted to know a thing or two about such matters, it was surely he. A lively atmosphere prevails under the high ceilings of this satisfyingly traditional place, so drop in for a slow pint and maybe a browse through one of the antiquarian books on the shelves in the corner. Not that you'll have chance to do much browsing once the evening heats up—ever since Behan spilled the beans, hordes of contented visitors come here to try it for themselves. Still, it's a welcoming, traditional spot.

3 Harry St., off Grafton St. ⓒ **01/679-4395.** Mon–Thurs 10:30am–11:30pm; Fri–Sat 10:30am–12:30am; Sun 12:30–11pm. Luas: St. Stephen's Green. Bus: 11, 11A, 11B, 14, 14A, 15A, 15C, 15X, 20B, 27C, 33X, 39B, 40A, 40C, 41X, 46B, 46C, 46N, 46X, 51X, 58X, 67X, 70X, 84X.

The O2 ★ CONCERT HALL   This enormous indoor concert space is the biggest venue in Dublin for major international acts, standup comedy, and other big-ticket entertainment events. It's all top-of-the-bill stuff.

North Wall Quay, Dublin 1. www.theo2.ie. ⓒ **Box Office: 081/871-9300; Enquiries: 01/819-8888.** Ticket prices vary greatly, from around €5–€110, but generally about €30–€50 for major shows. Event times vary; call ahead. Luas: The Point. Bus: 151.

Outlying Attractions

Casino Marino ★★ ARCHITECTURE   This unexpected little architectural gem in the middle of a suburban park has nothing at all to do with gambling; "casino" simply means "little house." Built around 1770, the tiny neoclassical exterior is exquisitely proportioned, with Corinthian columns and elaborate detail around the white stone cornices. Unlikely though it seems from the compactness of the exterior, inside are a full 16 rooms—decorated with rich 18th-century architectural details such as exquisite plasterwork ceilings and subtly curved windows. Entry is by tour only, but the cheerful guides help put it all into context.

Casino Park (signposted from R107, Malahide Rd.), Dublin. www.heritageireland.ie. ⓒ **01/833-1618.** Admission €3 adults, €2 seniors, €1 children and students, €8 families. Mid-Mar–Oct daily 10am–5pm. Last admission 45 min. before closing. Closed Nov–mid-Mar except to prebooked groups. Bus: 20B, 27, 27B, 27C, 127, 129.

Dalkey Castle & Heritage Centre ★ CASTLE   Housed in a 15th-century tower house, this center tells the history of venerable Dalkey town in a few sweet, if unsophisticated, displays. Tours run by costumed guides tell the tale of the building (complete with live performance), or you can duck out of the tour and take in the view from the battlements instead. Adjoining the center is a medieval graveyard and the Church of St. Begnet, Dalkey's patron saint, whose foundations date back to Ireland's early Christian period. Dalkey itself is worth a wander; it's a heritage town with plenty of historic buildings, charming pubs, restaurants, and pricey little boutiques.

Castle St., Dalkey (16km/10 mi southeast of Dublin on R119). www.dalkeycastle.com. ⓒ **01/285-8366.** Admission €8 adults, €7 seniors and students, €6 children, €23 families. Apr–May and

Sept–Oct Mon–Fri 10am–5:30pm, Sat, Sun, and public holidays 11am–5:30pm; June–Aug Mon–Fri 10am–6pm, Sat, Sun, and public holidays 11am–6pm; Jan–Mar and Nov–Dec Mon–Fri 10am–5pm, Sat, Sun, and public holidays 11am–5pm. Last tour 50 min. before closing. DART: Dalkey. Bus: 7D, 59.

Dún Laoghaire ★ TOWN The bustling harbor town of Dún Laoghaire (pronounced Dun *Lear*-y) is one of a string of Dublin commuter towns that, in the 2000s, became known as "Bel Eire" for their beauty and for the density of Irish celebrity residents. It boasts plenty of interesting shops, a bucolic park, and a lovely promenade along the harbor.

13km (8 mi) southeast of Dublin on R118. Rail: Dún Laoghaire. DART: Sandycove & Glasthule. Bus: 7, 7N, 46A, 46N, 59, 63, 75, 111.

Hill of Tara ★ HISTORIC SITE Legends and folklore place this atmospheric place at the center of early Irish history. Ancient tombs have been discovered on the hill that date back to the Stone Age. Pagans believed that the goddess Queen Maeve lived and reigned from here. By the 3rd century, it was home to the most powerful men in Ireland—the high kings. They had a ceremonial residence on the hill and ruled as much by myth as by military strength. Every 3 years they would hold a *feis* (a kind of giant party-*cum*-government session), at which more than 1,000 princes, poets, athletes, priests, druids, musicians, and jesters celebrated for a week. A *feis* wasn't all fun and games, though: Laws were passed, disputes settled, and matters of defense decided. The last *feis* was held in A.D. 560. Thereafter, Tara went into a decline as the power and popularity of Christianity rose. Although little is left to see except grassy mounds, some ancient pillar stones, and depressions where the Iron Age ring forts stood, it's still a magnificent spot. A visitor center is in the old church beside the entrance to the archaeological area.

Signposted on N3, about 12km (7½ mi) south of Navan, Co. Meath. www.hilloftara.org. ℭ046/902-5903 (summer); 041/988-0300 (winter). Admission €3 adults, €2 seniors, €1 students and children, €8 families. Mid-May to mid-Sept daily 10am–6pm.

Knowth ★★★ HISTORIC SITE This extraordinary prehistoric burial site contains the longest passage tombs ever discovered in Ireland. Knowth was closed to the public for many years as archaeologists explored its depths, but at last it is now open, at least in part. It is mainly composed of two massively long underground burial chambers, the longest of which stretches for 40m (131 ft.) and was only discovered in 1968. In the mound itself, scientists found the largest collection of passage tomb art uncovered thus far in Europe, as well as a number of underground chambers and 300 carved slabs. The mound is surrounded by 17 satellite graves in a complex pattern. And still, nobody can give a definitive answer to the biggest mystery of all: What was it all for? Even now, all of Knowth's secrets have not been uncovered—excavation work is quite constant here, and you may get a chance to see the archaeologists at work. All tickets for here and Newgrange (see below) are issued at the Brú na Bóinne Visitor Centre near Donore. As with Newgrange, there is no direct access to the monument; visitors are taken there by shuttle bus.

Brú na Bóinne Visitor Centre: on N51, 2km (1¼ mi) west of Donore, Co. Meath. www.knowth.com. ℭ041/988-0300. Visitor center and Knowth: €5 adults, €3 seniors, €3 students and children, €13 families. Combined ticket with Newgrange: €11 adults, €8 seniors, €6 students and children, €28 families. Feb–Apr and Oct daily 9:30am–5:30pm; May daily 9am–6:30pm; June–mid-Sept daily 9am–7pm; mid–end Sept daily 9am–6:30pm; Nov–Jan daily 9am–5pm.

Newgrange ★★★ HISTORIC SITE   Ireland's best-known prehistoric monument is one of the archaeological wonders of Western Europe. Built as a burial mound more than 5,000 years ago—long before the Egyptian Pyramids or Stonehenge—it sits atop a hill near the Boyne, massive and mysterious. The mound is 11m (36 ft.) tall and approximately 78m (256 ft.) in diameter. It consists of 200,000 tons of stone, a 6-ton capstone, and other stones weighing up to 16 tons each, many of which were hauled from as far away as County Wicklow and the Mountains of Mourne. Each stone fits perfectly in the overall pattern, and the result is a watertight structure, an amazing feat of engineering. The question remains, though: Why? Archeologists are still trying to figure out whether it was built for kings, political leaders, or long-lost rituals. Inside, a passage 18m (59 ft.) long leads to a central burial chamber that sits in pitch-darkness all year, except for 5 days in December. During the winter solstice (December 19–23), a shaft of sunlight travels down the arrow-straight passageway for 17 minutes when it hits the back wall of the burial chamber. You can register for a lottery to be in the tomb for this extraordinary event, although competition is fierce. As part of the daily tour, you'll walk down the passage, past elaborately carved stones and into the chamber, which has three sections, each with a basin stone that once held cremated human remains. *Tip:* There's no direct access to the site; you have to come via the Brú na Bóinne Visitor Centre near Donore.

Brú na Bóinne Visitor Centre: on N51, 2km (1¼ mi) west of Donore, Co. Meath. www.newgrange.com. Ⓒ **041/988-0300.** Visitor center and Newgrange: €6 adults, €5 seniors, €3 students and children, €15 families. Combined ticket with Knowth: €11 adults, €8 seniors, €6 children and students, €28 families. Feb–Apr and Oct daily 9:30am–5:30pm; May daily 9am–6:30pm; June–mid-Sept daily 9am–7pm; mid–end Sept daily 9am–6:30pm; Nov–Jan daily 9am–5pm.

The Powerscourt Estate ★★★ ARCHITECTURE   The 20th century was not kind to this magnificent estate; abandoned and then gutted by fire, it took more than 30 years to restore the Palladian house to its former glory. The gardens are magnificent, with classical statuary everywhere, a shady grotto made of petrified moss, a Japanese garden, and an over-the-top fountain from which statues of winged horses rise. The landscaper Daniel Robertson designed the gardens between 1745 and 1767. Legend has it that due to terrible gout, he oversaw the work while being carted around in a wheelbarrow, sipping port as he went. When the bottle was empty, work was done for the day. A few rooms of the house are open to the public, including an exhibition that tells the history of the house and its restoration. There's also a playground and gift shops. If you feel energetic, follow the well marked path over 7km (4 miles) to the picturesque **Powerscourt Waterfall**—the highest in Ireland at 121m (397 ft.). Or you can drive, following signs from the estate.

On R760, Enniskerry, Co. Wicklow. www.powerscourt.com. Ⓒ **01/204-6000.** Gardens: €8.50 adults, €7.50 seniors and students, €5 children 15 and under, €25 families, free for children 4 and under. Waterfall: €5.50 adults; €5 seniors and students; €2.50 children 15 and under; €16 families. Gardens: daily 9:30am–5:30pm (or at dusk if earlier). Garden Pavilion: Mon–Sat 9:30am–5:30pm, Sun 10am–5:30pm. Ballroom and Garden Rooms: May–Sept Sun–Mon 9:30am–1:30pm; Oct–Apr Sun 9:30am–1:30pm. Powerscourt Waterfall: Jan–Feb and Nov–Dec 10:30am–4:30pm; Mar–Apr and Sept–Oct 10:30am–5:30pm; May–Aug 9:30am–7pm. About 20km (12½ mi) south of Dublin. Bus: 44, 185 (nearest stop is Enniskerry village, approx. 1–2km/⅔–1½-mi walk).

Russborough House ★★ ARCHITECTURE   This impressive villa was built between 1741 and 1751, designed by the great Richard Cassels, who also designed Powerscourt House (see listing above). In the 1950s, the house was bought by Sir

Alfred Beit, a member of the De Beers diamond family. He had inherited a massive collection of art and wanted someplace to keep it. He thought this rural mansion was just the spot. Thus began one of the most exquisite small rural art collections you're likely to find anywhere, with paintings by Vermeer, Gainsborough, and Rubens, although most of the paintings have been moved out over the last decade to other museums after a series of robberies. You can see the house only by guided tour, and there is certainly a lot to see—ornate plaster ceilings by the Lafranchini brothers, huge marble mantelpieces, inlaid floors, and lavish use of mahogany in the doors and staircase, as well as fine displays of silver, porcelain, and furniture. Kids will be kept amused by a 3-D exhibition and a fiendish maze.

Signposted from N81, 3.2km (2 mi) south of Blessington, Co. Wicklow. www.russboroughhouse.ie. ⒸΦ **045/865-239.** House: €10 adults, €6 seniors and students, €6 children 15 and under, €25 families. 3-D exhibition: €6 adults, €4 seniors and students, €4 children 15 and under, €15 families. Combined ticket: €12 adults, €8 seniors and students, €8 children 15 and under, €30 families. Maze: €3. House and gardens Mar–Sept 10am–5pm; tours on the hour, Mon–Fri 10am–5pm, Sat noon–3pm; 3-D maze daily 10–5. Bus: 65.

THE SOUTHEAST

Dramatic coastline, misty mountains, and evocative historic monuments characterize the lush counties south of Dublin. The area also has a distinctive, musical dialect, peppered with unique words and phrases—remnants of the ancient Yola language that was once spoken here. The three main tourist centers of the Southeast—**Waterford, Wexford,** and **Kilkenny**—are close enough together that you could use any as a base for exploring the region by car. And make no mistake: It's not long before you really start to feel like you've left the city behind and entered the real countryside. But "city" is a relative term out here; Waterford, the biggest population center in the region, has a population of just 46,000.

ESSENTIALS

Arriving

BY BUS Bus Éireann (www.buseireann.ie; ✆ 01/703-2420) operates direct service several times a day from the central bus station ("BusÁras") on Store Street, Dublin, into Kilkenny, Wexford, and Waterford. The journey to Kilkenny takes upward of 2 hours; to Wexford and Waterford, closer to 3 hours.

BY TRAIN Irish Rail (www.irishrail.ie; ✆ 1850/366-222) operates several trains daily between Dublin and Kilkenny, Wexford, and Waterford. The journey to Kilkenny takes about 1½ hours; to Waterford, a little over 2 hours; and to Wexford, 2½ hours.

BY FERRY Ferries from Britain sail to Rosslare Harbour, 19km (12 miles) south of Wexford Town. Call **Irish Ferries** (www.irishferries.ie; ✆ 0818/300-400) or **Stena Line** (www.stenaline.com; ✆ 01/204-7777) for bookings and information. Irish Ferries also sail to Rosslare from northern France.

BY CAR The journey from Dublin to Kilkenny, Waterford, or Wexford is nearly all motorway. For Kilkenny, take E20, then M7 southwest out of Dublin, then split off onto M9. If you're heading to Waterford, stay on M9 for another 50km (31 miles) after the turnoff for Kilkenny. From Dublin to Wexford, take N11 south (you may want to loop around and join it via N81 and M50 if you're starting on the northside), then keep heading south on this road until you reach Wexford. The drive to Kilkenny is about 1½ hours, and to Waterford or Wexford, about 2 hours—but remember traffic can be terrible around Dublin, especially during rush hour.

BY PLANE Tiny **Waterford Airport** is in Killowen (www.waterfordairport.ie; ✆ 051/846-600) 9km (5⅔ miles) south of Waterford Town. The

British budget airline **Flybe** (www.flybe.com) flies here a few times per week from Manchester and Birmingham in the U.K.

Getting Around

Getting from Dublin to the center of Kilkenny, Wexford, or Waterford by public transport is easy. It's also relatively simple to travel between them; however, as with most rural areas in Ireland, getting *around* the countryside by public transport once you're here is extremely challenging. Unless you're sticking to the big towns, your best option is to rent a car.

BY BUS   A handful of buses per day run between Kilkenny and Waterford; the journey takes 1 to 2 hours, depending on if you have to change buses (which you almost always do). No convenient bus routes connect Kilkenny and Wexford. A couple of direct services per day run between Waterford and Kilkenny, plus slightly more if you don't mind changing buses; journey times are also 1 to 2 hours. Direct buses connect Waterford and Wexford every couple of hours; most journeys take 1 hour.

BY TRAIN   A half-dozen or so trains daily go between Kilkenny and Waterford; the journey takes 35 minutes. Getting from Kilkenny or Waterford to Wexford by train is a laborious, all-day process involving multiple changes and should be avoided if at all possible.

BY CAR   To rent a car from Dublin, try **Hertz** (www.hertz.ie) at Dublin Airport (© **01/844-5466**); 151-157 South Circular Rd., Dublin 8 (© **01/709-3060**); or Baggot St. Bridge, 2 Haddington Rd., Dublin 4 (© **01/668-7566**). **Europcar** also has branches at Dublin Airport (© **01/812-2800**) and Marks St. (off Pearse St.), Dublin 2 (© **01/648-5900**). In Kilkenny, try **Enterprise-Rent-a-Car** at Barlo Nissan, Dublin Rd. (www.enterprise.ie; © **056/775-3318**). **Hertz** has a branch in Wexford Town, on Ferrybank (www.hertz.ie; © **053/915-2500**), or you can try **Budget Car Rental** at Rosslare Ferryport (www.budget.ie; © **053/913-3318**). In Waterford, Enterprise has a branch on Tranmore Rd.

BY FERRY   The drive between Waterford and Wexford requires you to take a circuitous route via New Ross that doubles the distance. Unless, that is, you take the handy car ferry from the poetically named **Passage East,** about 12km (7½ miles) east of Waterford (www.passageferry.ie; © **051/382-480**). Regular crossings are April to September, Monday to Saturday 7am to 10pm, Sunday and public holidays 9:30am to 10pm; October to March, Monday to Saturday 7am to 8pm, Sunday and public holidays 9:30am to 8pm. Tickets per car are €8 one-way, €12 round-trip; on a bicycle €2–€3; and camper vans €12–€16.

[FastFACTS] THE SOUTHEAST

ATMs/Banks   Convenient locations include the **Allied Irish Bank (AIB)** on Dublin Rd., Kilkenny, and 72 The Quay, Waterford; and **Bank of Ireland** at 29 Parnell St., Waterford, and Custom House Quay, Wexford.

Dentists   For dental emergencies, your hotel will usually contact a dentist for you; otherwise, in Kilkenny, try **Market Cross Dental Surgery,** James St. (© **056/772-1386**); in Waterford, try **O'Connell Street Dental Clinic,** 38 O'Connell St. (© **051/856-800**); and in Wexford, try **Allsmile Dental Practise,** 27 St. John's Gate (© **053/912-1748**).

Doctors   For emergencies, dial © **999.** For

nonemergencies, any good hotel will contact a doctor for you. Otherwise, in Kilkenny, try **Friary Court Clinic,** Friary St. (✆ **056/776-5613**); in Waterford, try **Catherine Street Medical Centre,** 18 Catherine St. (✆ **051/875338**); and in Wexford, try **Whiterock Family Practise,** Whiterock Hill (✆ **053/916-0070**).

Emergencies For police, fire, or other emergencies, dial ✆ **999.**

Pharmacies In Kilkenny, try **White's Chemist,** 5 High St. (✆ **056/772-1328**); in Waterford, try **Gallagher's Late Night Pharmacy,** 29 Barronstrand St. (✆ **051/878103**); and in Wexford, try **Boots the Chemist,** 54 North Main St. (✆ **053/914-7851.**

Taxis In Kilkenny, call **Ray Cabs** (✆ **086/888-2777**) or **Town & County Taxi** (✆ **056/776-5714**); in Waterford, call **Rapid Cabs** (✆ **051/858-585**) or **Swift Cabs** (✆ **051/898-989**); and in Wexford, call **Wexford Cabs** (✆ **053/912-3123**) or **Wexford Taxi Services** (✆ **053/914-6666**).

A Note on Listings

Given that the main attractions in the Southeast are close enough together that you could use either Waterford, Wexford, or Kilkenny as a base to explore the region by car, we have grouped together the hotel and restaurant listings for all three in this chapter. However, to reflect the wealth of attractions in each of those areas, sightseeing listings have been separated out.

WHERE TO STAY

Waterford and Kilkenny both have some high-quality, reasonably priced accommodations within the town centers. In Wexford, choice within the town is limited; you're much better opting for a place in the countryside, where there is a satisfying mixture of bucolic farmhouses and luxurious getaways worth splurging for.

Where to Stay in County Kilkenny

Lawcus Farm Guesthouse ★★★   Make no mistake: You're staying on a real farm at this guesthouse ("helping us on the farm at feeding time is greatly appreciated," says the website). But that's a big part of its appeal, as it means the setting is lovely and the breakfasts (which use many products from the farm) are unusually delish. As for the B&B, it's set in an early-19th-century building that has been artfully renovated. Guest rooms are cozy and decent-sized, with plenty of natural light; some have original fireplaces; one has exposed gray stone walls and an antique-style brass bed. You're right next to a river, where you can go wild water swimming, or even try your hand at fishing for trout. There's only one snag to this rural idyll: Lawcus Farm doesn't accept credit cards or checks, so make sure you're able to pay in cash.

Stoneyford, Co. Kilkenny. www.lawcusfarmguesthouse.com. ✆ **086/603-1667.** 5 units. €100. Parking (free). Rates include breakfast. Discounts for stays of 2 or more nights. Children under 5 free (1 per party). **Amenities:** Wi-Fi (free). Driving from Dublin: After passing Stoneyford sign, take turn to the right of the small bridge and follow signs to B&B. From Waterford: As Dublin, but approach to Stoneyford is from opposite direction. From Cork: At Colnmel, take N76 (toward Kilkenny), then turn off through Callan and Kells. When entering Kells, look for sign pointing to Lawcus Farm beside pub on right. Keep following signs past priory on left.

Rosquil House ★★   Comfortable and friendly, this modest little B&B is an outstanding value for money. No, it's not fancy, but it was custom-built by the owners, so bedrooms are spacious and well-proportioned (one is accessible for travelers with disabilities). And the same care that went into the design of the home goes into the hospitality: hosts Rhoda and Phil greet guests with genuine warmth and enthusiasm, making them feel immediately at home. Public areas, including a large guest lounge, are tastefully decorated in color schemes of chocolate and cream with polished wood floors. Breakfasts, cooked by Phil, are delicious. The only downside? It's a 15-minute walk into town (so not right in the heart of the action).

Castlecomer Rd., Kilkenny, Co. Kilkenny. www.rosquilhouse.com. © **056/772-1419.** 7 units. €70–€85. Parking at nearby lots (no discount) €3.50–€5 overnight; €5–€16 for 24 hrs. Rates include breakfast. **Amenities:** Wi-Fi (free).

Where to Stay in Waterford City

Granville Hotel ★★ You'll know as soon as you see the elegant, Sienna-colored frontage of this welcoming hotel that it's a historic property. Built in the late 1700s, it has been in business continuously since 1865. The interior retains something of a manor house feel, with sweeping draperies, deep red carpeting, and antique furniture. Guest rooms are comfortable and reasonably spacious—although not all have air conditioning, so make sure you request this when you book if it's important to you. Some rooms overlook Waterford Quay, with its field of gently bobbing yacht masts. The hotel bar is popular with locals, and the modern Irish **Bianconi Restaurant** is excellent. Staff could hardly be friendlier or more helpful. You can book a relaxing (and reasonably priced) massage beauty treatment in the Therapy Room.

Meagher's Quay, Waterford, Co. Waterford. www.granville-hotel.ie. © **051/305-555.** 98 units. €90–€100. Parking at nearby lots (no discount) €3.50–€5 overnight; €5–€16 for 24 hrs. Breakfast not included in lower rates. Dinner, bed and breakfast packages available. **Amenities:** Wi-Fi (free), restaurant, bar, room service, a/c.

Sion Hill House ★★ The liberal scattering of handsome antiques around this 18th-century house tells you something about its storied past. Ask your host, George, to tell you the rest—it has enough history to fill a small book. The elegant guest rooms are decorated with tantalizing elements of that past in mind, and it feels like there's a new story to be told around each corner. One room has a large bell outside the window that was used to signal the start and end of the day for the gardeners who once worked the grounds; another has antique French furnishings, to reflect a connection between the house and Princess Letizia Bonaparte, niece of Napoleon. The 5 acres of gardens are peaceful, with lovely views across the river to Waterford. They're quite famed locally; George and his wife, Antoinette, even run tours for non-residents. Check the website for some excellent off-season deals, including almost half-price room rates.

Dock Rd., Ferrybank, Waterford, Co. Waterford. www.sionhillhouse.net. © **051/851-558.** 4 units. €80–€96. Free parking. Rates include breakfast. **Amenities:** Wi-Fi (free).

Waterford Marina Hotel ★ This modern, well-run hotel, overlooking the River Suir, isn't particularly characterful—but it's in a great location, a short walk from the center of Waterford. Rooms are clean and have everything you need, with comfortable beds. Family rooms are an exceptionally good value—they sleep up to four, for only €10 or so more than the standard double rates. (You'll pay a €25 supplement for kids between 12 and 16.) Some bedrooms have lovely views over the water. Special offers are often listed on the website, including packages that cover dinner in the excellent restaurant. *Tip:* Ask for an upper-floor room—the views are better, and since there can be street noise at night, you're above the ruckus there.

Canada St., Waterford, Co. Waterford. www.waterfordmarinahotel.com. © **051/856-600.** 81 units. €79–€100. Parking (free). Breakfast not included in lower rates. **Amenities:** Wi-Fi (free), restaurant, bar, room service, accessible rooms.

Where to Stay in County Wexford

Monart Spa ★★★   A luxurious, grown-up retreat, Monart is consistently named among the top spas in Ireland—and for good reason. It's a sumptuous, impeccably designed place, set beside a lake and a verdant forest. Guest rooms are surrounded by woodland, and some have little balconies overlooking the grounds. The restaurant is excellent, though expensive (€40 for three courses, and many dishes cost extra). The heavenly spa has a thermal suite (free to use for guests) equipped with two pools, a salt grotto, indoor and outdoor saunas, and an aroma steam room. Packages and short breaks are a good value—for example, a 3-night stay, including breakfast, dinner, and a spa treatment, is around €315. To maintain the air of serenity, no children are allowed at Monart. This is a strictly adults-only zone.

On L6124, The Still, Enniscorthy, Co. Wexford. www.monart.ie. ℂ **053/923-8999.** 70 units. Doubles €95–€170. Parking (free). Rates include breakfast. Dinner, bed and breakfast, and spa treatment packages available. **Amenities:** Restaurants (2), bar, room service, afternoon tea, café, spa, pool. About 5.2km (3⅓ miles) west of Enniscorthy.

Riverbank House Hotel ★★   This cozy midsize hotel just outside the town center in Wexford has lovely views of the River Slaney. (Rooms overlooking the river have suitably huge picture windows.) Beds are comfortable and very large; some are four-poster. Family rooms cost just €30 more than doubles (though they are not that much bigger, with one double and one single bed). The bar and restaurant are pleasant spaces, filled with polished wood and natural light. The casual pub-style food is good, too—think unfussy, international dishes of the something-for-everyone variety—and in good weather you can dine on the terrace overlooking the river. The genuinely cheerful staff helps things run smoothly. All in all, this is a thoroughly decent, near-budget option about a 10-minute walk from central Wexford.

The Fridge, Wexford, Co. Wexford. www.riverbankhousehotel.com. ℂ **053/912-3611.** 23 units. Doubles €79–€130. Parking (free). Rates include breakfast. **Amenities:** Wi-Fi (free), restaurant, bar, room service.

WHERE TO EAT

Waterford's restaurant scene is impressive for such a small city. Restaurants such as **Rinuccini,** a winning combination of Irish and Italian, really raise the bar—although it's perfectly possible to find a decent meal without stretching the wallet. Likewise, the wonderful **Campagne in Kilkenny** mixes French cuisine with innovative Irish influences.

Where to Eat in County Waterford

Bodega! ★★ MODERN IRISH/EUROPEAN   Precisely as you'd expect from a restaurant with an exclamation point in the name, Bodega! cultivates an upbeat, funky vibe. The menu is similarly vivacious: smoked salmon cured in gin to start, followed by piri-piri–marinated tiger prawns, or maybe an order of chicken wings flavored with honey and a kick of ginger. Subtler, more traditional bistro-style choices are also on the menu, along with plenty of daily specials. The long cocktail list should help maintain the buzz.

54 John's St., Waterford. www.bodegawaterford.com. ℂ **051/844-177.** Main courses €16–€28. Mon–Sat noon–10pm. Closed Sun.

The Munster ★ BISTRO This cozy bar, across the street from the House of Waterford Crystal visitor center (p. 97), serves a smallish menu of unpretentious, traditional pub grub—think sandwiches, Irish stew, seafood pie, and an enormous house burger. The early-evening menu has a few slightly more ambitious choices, such as chicken breast with chorizo and Parmesan cream, or salmon fishcake served with chili jam. It may lack frills, but everything's well prepared.

Bailey's New St., Waterford, Co. Waterford. www.themunsterbar.com. ℭ **051/874-656.** Main courses €12–€14. Mon 12:30am–2:30pm; Tues–Fri 12:30–2:30pm and 5–9pm; Sat 5–9pm; Sun 4–8pm.

Richmond House ★★★ MODERN IRISH This is something of a destination restaurant for people in this part of Ireland, and it's easy to see why—the menu is a hugely successful combination of Irish and Continental flavors. Menus change daily according to what's fresh and in season, and when we say "fresh," we mean fresh: The grounds of this 18th-century mansion hide a productive garden, where the chef gets most of the fruit and vegetables for the kitchen. This produce is served alongside locally sourced lamb, beef, and seafood. The expert wine list has a better than average selection of wines by the glass—a relief, given the price of dinner. Those wanting to sample some of this sumptuous cooking on a budget may want to check out the €33 early-bird menu, served until 7:30pm.

Singposted from N72, Cappoquin, Co. Waterford. www.richmondhouse.net. ℭ **058/54278.** Fixed-price menus: 2 courses €25; 3 courses €55. Daily 6–9pm. Closed Dec 22–Jan 10.

Where to Eat in County Wexford

The Yard ★★ BRASSERIE There are two sides to this place; drop in at lunchtime for a hearty but informal meal (beer-battered cod and chips, perhaps, or a tasty burger), or come in the evening for a more elaborate, brasserie-style menu, albeit with Irish inflections. Specials might include confit duck with crispy truffled potatoes, local lamb with minted peas, or fish stew with a white wine and chili broth. Come on Thursday or Friday night for the great value set menu—4 courses for just €25.

3 Lower Georges St., Wexford, Co. Wexford. ℭ **053/914-4083.** Main courses €16–€29. Mon–Sat noon–10pm.

Where to Eat in County Kilkenny

Campagne ★★★ BISTRO The chef at this outstanding French-Irish restaurant, about a 10-minute walk from Kilkenny Castle, used to run the kitchen at the superlative Chapter One in Dublin (see p. 61). You'll see that influence in the short but inventive menu, which features such items as duck with cabbage, turnips, and blackberries; turbot served with a rich crab bisque; or lime parfait served with deliciously tart lemon curd ice cream. The dining room is sleek and atmospherically lit, with colorful modern art on the walls. The only downside is that it's quite pricey, but plenty of locals will tell you it's their go-to place for a special dinner. The wine list is extensive and well chosen, with particularly strong French options.

5 The Arches, Gashouse Lane, Kilkenny, Co. Kilkenny. www.campagne.ie. ℂ **056/777-2858.** Main courses €28–€30. Tues–Thurs 6–10pm; Fri 12:30–2:30pm and 6–10pm; Sat 12:30–2:30pm and 5:30–10pm; Sun 12:30–3pm. Closed Sun for dinner except on public holiday weekends. Closed Tues nights following public holiday Mondays.

Gourmet Store ★ DELI/CAFE Very good for a quick lunch on the go, this little cafe in the center of Kilkenny is popular with local office workers who come for tasty sandwiches and bagels. There's also a great stock of deli goods, so you can put together your own picnic hamper, or they'll even do it for you—perfect for when you need to snatch a quick bite on the road. A lot of the off-the-shelf products are local and small-brand, including jams, chutneys, and other upscale nibbles, so stock up on gifts and edible souvenirs to take home.

56 High St., Kilkenny, Co. Kilkenny. www.thegourmetstorekilkenny.com. ℂ **056/777-1727.** Main courses €5–€10. Mon–Sat 8am–6pm.

Kyteler's Inn ★ PUB This atmospheric old inn has been in business for over 6 centuries. They serve decent pub food, but it's the vibe you really come for—all exposed flagstones and cozy nooks, it's hard to think of a more satisfyingly Irish-looking pub. The place is named after former resident, Alice Kyteler, who died in 1324. She poisoned at least three of her husbands, ran the Inn as a den of debauchery, and was sentenced to be burned as a witch. She escaped, but nobody saw or heard from her again. Unless, that is, you believe some of the more colorful tales about this place after dark . . .

Kieran St., Kilkenny, Co. Kilkenny. www.kytelersinn.com. ℂ **056/772-1064.** Daily noon–around midnight.

Mocha's Vintage Tea Rooms ★ CAFE A good choice for a quick light lunch—or, even better, a slice of cake—this popular little cafe opposite Kilkenny railway station has a delightfully shabby-chic vibe. The walls are crammed with antique prints and mismatched ornaments, giving the place the feel of a broken dollhouse. Lunches are tasty and healthful with a variety of sandwiches, quiches, and salads. To indulge, choose from one of the homemade cakes, tarts, or desserts—each delectable.

4 the Arches, Kilkenny, Co. Kilkenny. ℂ **056/777-0565.** Main courses €5–€12. Mon–Sat 8:30am–5:30pm.

Rinuccini ★★★ ITALIAN This extremely popular restaurant, opposite Kilkenny Castle, packs in diners for its delicious Italian food. The basement-level dining room can get crowded, but the food more than makes up for it. Fresh spaghettini might be served with Kilmore Quay prawns, basil, and chili, or perhaps a simple fettuccine with the house Bolognese sauce and fresh cream. Desserts are equally good—try the home-made chocolate mousse, or if your belt buckle will go out that far, the tasty cheese plate, filled with specialty selections imported from Italy and sprinkled with black truffle. It's a bit of a splurge, but worth it. Due to Rinuccini's popularity with locals, you should book reservations if you're coming on a weekend.

1 The Parade, Kilkenny, Co. Kilkenny. www.rinuccini.com. ✆ **056/776-1575.** Main courses €20–€30. Mon–Fri noon–3pm and 5–10pm; Sat noon–3:30pm and 5–10pm; Sun noon–3:30pm and 5–9:30pm.

Where to Eat near Glendalough and the Rock of Cashel

Roundwood Inn ★ MODERN IRISH/EUROPEAN   This cozy, welcoming inn has been in business since the 1600s, and it still retains a wonderfully traditional atmo-sphere. An open fire roars in the grate, while the menu doesn't stray far from tradition—and why should it? Roast meats, seafood, game, and hearty stews are all unpretentious and deliciously prepared. The Roundwood Inn is not far from Glendal-ough (see box below), so the resulting mix of hungry hikers, chatty locals, and passing tourists makes for a cheerful crowd.

Main St., Roundwood, Co. Wicklow. ✆ **01/281-8107.** Main courses €9–€14. Daily noon–9:30pm.

Ryan's Daughter ★ IRISH/CAFE   Good for a satisfyingly traditional lunch, this cute little cafe is not far from the Rock of Cashel (see box, later in this chapter). The food is hearty and old-school: homemade pies, stews, roast chicken, pork, or beef, piled high with steaming hot vegetables. Portions are so generous you probably won't be hungry for dinner. The flat-rate €10 per main course is a great value; alternatively, you could reward yourself for making the climb up and down from the Rock with a restorative coffee and a tasty slice of cake for just a couple of euro.

Ladyswell St., Cashel, Co. Tipperary. www.ryansdaughter.ie. ✆ **062/62688.** Main courses €3–€10. Daily 9am–4pm.

EXPLORING COUNTY WATERFORD

The main seaport of southeast Ireland, Waterford City's unprotected proximity at the edge of the ferocious Atlantic Ocean makes it Ireland's Windy City, as a sea breeze is always blowing here. Its oceanside location has a lot to do with its status as the oldest city in the country, founded by Viking invaders in the 9th century.

Tourism Office

The **Waterford Tourist Office** is at the Granary, the Quay, Waterford (www.waterford tourism.com; ✆ **051/875788**). In May, June, and September it's open Monday to Sat-urday 9:30am to 5:30pm; July and August, Monday to Friday 9pm to 6pm, Saturday 9:30 and to 5:30pm, and Sunday 11am to 5pm from late July to mid-August; and from October to April, Monday to Saturday 9:15am to 5pm.

Top Attractions in Waterford City

Bishop's Palace ★★ MUSEUM   One of three separate museums that are known collectively as *Waterford Treasures*, the Bishop's Palace focuses on life in the city from 1700 until the mid–20th century. The collection covering the 18th century is by

A WALK TO mahon falls

These impressive, 80m (262½ ft.) water-falls are in the Comeragh Mountains, on R676 between Carrick-on-Suir and Dungarvan. At the tiny village of Mahon Bridge, 26km (16 miles) south of Carrick-on-Suir, turn west on the road marked for Mahon Falls, then follow signs for the falls and Comeragh Drive. In about 5km (3 miles), you reach a parking lot along the Mahon River (in fact, just a tiny stream). The trail, indicated by two boulders, begins across the road. Follow the stream along the floor of the valley to the base of the falls. From here you can see the fields of Waterford spread out below you, and the sea a glittering mirror beyond. Walking time is about 30 minutes round-trip.

far the most impressive, including furniture, art, fashion, and some exquisite glass and silverwork. Appropriately enough, given the close proximity to the famous factory (see listing below), it also holds the earliest surviving pieces of Waterford Crystal, a decanter dating from 1789. The Bishop's Palace, itself an elegant example of Georgian architecture, was built by Richard Cassels (1690–1751), who was also the architect of Leinster House in Dublin (p. 77).

The Mall, Waterford, Co. Waterford. www.waterfordtreasures.com/bishops-palace.📞**051/849650.** Admission €7 adults, €6 seniors and students, children 13 and under free, €14 families. Jun–Aug Mon–Sat 9am–6pm; Sun and public holidays 11am–6pm. Sept–May Mon–Sat 10am–5pm; Sun and public holidays 11am–5pm. Last admission 1 hr. before closing.

Garter Lane Arts Centre ★ ARTS COMPLEX One of Ireland's largest arts centers, the Garter Lane occupies two buildings on O'Connell Street. Number 5 holds exhibition rooms and artists' studios, and no. 22a, a former Friends Meeting House, is home of the Garter Lane Theatre, along with an art gallery and outdoor courtyard. The gallery showcases works by contemporary and local artists, plus a varied program of music, dance, and films.

O'Connell St., Waterford, Co. Waterford. www.garterlane.ie. 📞 **051/855038.** Many events and exhibitions free; ticketed events around €5 to €20. Tues–Sat 11am–10pm; Sun 7–10pm; individual performance times vary.

House of Waterford Crystal ★ FACTORY TOUR One of the best-known Irish brands in the world, Waterford Crystal has been made in the city (with significant periods of hiatus) since 1783. In 2009, the company filed for bankruptcy—perhaps Ireland's most high-profile victim of the financial crisis—but new owners were soon found, and with them came this shiny, purpose-built factory and visitor center, right in the heart of Waterford. You can tour the factory to watch the glittering products being molded, blown, cut, and finished—or just drop by the enormous shop for some sparkly souvenirs.

The Mall, Waterford, Co. Waterford. www.waterfordvisitorcentre.com. 📞 **051/317000.** Admission €12.50 adults, €9.50 seniors and students, €4.50 children 6–18, children 5 and under free, €32 families. Tour: Apr–Oct Mon–Sat 9am–4:15pm; Sun 9:30am–4:15pm. Nov–Dec Mon–Fri 9:30am–3:15pm. Jan–Feb Mon–Fri 9am–3:15pm. Mar Mon–Sat 9am–3:15pm; Sun 9:30am–3:15pm. Shop stays open 1 hr. 45 min. after start of last tour.

Medieval Museum ★★ MUSEUM The latest addition to the multisite Waterford Treasures, the Medieval Museum has some exquisite artifacts from the city's medieval period, but they're not the only attraction here. Just as interesting is the

PEACE AND LIGHT: glendalough

Nestled within is an ancient, abandoned monastery, built on the edge of dark lakes, and surrounded by hills and forests, this evocative, misty glen is a magical place. The ruins date from the 6th century, when a monk who became known as St. Kevin chose this secluded setting, which was already used as a Bronze Age tomb, for his home. Over the next 4 centuries, Kevin's church became a center of religious learning, attracting thousands of students from all over Europe. Unfortunately, its success, as with so many early Irish religious sites, was its downfall, and Glendalough soon came to the attention of Vikings, who pillaged it repeatedly between A.D. 775 and 1071. But it was always rebuilt stronger than ever, until 1398, when English forces in Ireland virtually wiped it out. Attempts were made to resuscitate it, and it limped on as just a shadow of all it had been until the 17th century, when it was abandoned altogether.

The combination of so many years of history and such an evocative setting means that there's plenty to see here. Your first step should be to stop by the visitor center at the entrance to the ruins to pick up a map. There are many walking trails, each one taking in different ruins, as the chapels were scattered over several miles. The oldest ruins, the **Teampall na Skellig,** can be seen across the lake at the foot of towering cliffs, but because there's no boat service, they cannot be visited. There's also a cave known as Kevin's Bed, which is believed to be where the saint lived when he first arrived at Glendalough. Follow the path from the upper lake to the lower lake and walk through the remains of the monastery complex. Although much of the monastic city is in ruins, there's a nearly perfect round tower, 31m (102 ft.) high and 16m (52 ft.) around the base, as well as hundreds of timeworn Celtic crosses and several chapels. One of these is St. Kevin's Chapel, often called **St. Kevin's Kitchen,** a fine specimen of an early Irish barrel-vaulted oratory with a miniature round belfry rising from a stone roof.

Glendalough is signposted from R756, 2km (1.3 miles) west of Laragh, Co. Wicklow. Admission is €3 adults, €2 students, €1 children, and €8 families. It's open mid-March to mid-October, daily 9:30am–6pm; and the rest of the year, daily 9:30am to 5pm. Last admission is 45 minutes before closing. For more information, see www.glendalough.ie or call the visitor center at ✆ **040/445-600.**

13th-century Choristor's Hall with its vaulted stone ceiling. Closed off for years, it now forms one of the main areas of the museum, together with a 15th-century wine vault. Highlights of the permanent collection include medieval art, clothes (including a velvet cap given to the Mayor of Waterford by Henry VIII), and the city's original charter, dating from 1373.

Cathedral Sq., Waterford, Co. Waterford. www.waterfordtreasures.com/medieval-museum. ✆ **051/849501.** Admission €7 adults, €6 seniors and students, children 13 and under free, €14 families. Jul–Aug Mon–Sat 9am-6pm, Sun and public holidays 11am–5pm; Sept–May Mon–Sat 10am–5pm, Sun and public holidays 11am–5pm.

Reginald's Tower ★★ MUSEUM   Claimed to be Ireland's oldest building that's still in day-to-day use, Reginald's Tower was built around the year 1000 by the Viking invaders who founded the city. Today it houses a museum devoted to that period in Waterford's history; inevitably, much of it is interpretive in nature, with displays that tell the story in absorbing detail, but a surprising number of actual items is on display, too. Highlights include fragments of Viking pottery, coins, and jewelry—including a stunning ornamental clasp, intricately patterned with fine threads of gold and silver.

The Quay, Waterford, Co. Waterford. www.waterfordtreasures.com/reginalds-tower. ℂ **051/ 304220.** Admission €3 adults, €2 seniors, €1 students and children, €8 families. Easter–May daily 10am–5pm; Jun–mid-Sept daily 10am–6pm; mid-Sept–Easter Wed–Sun 10am–5pm.

EXPLORING COUNTY WEXFORD

Although it's within easy reach of County Wexford, Dublin might as well be hundreds of miles away—the countryside in this area feels so bucolic and peaceful. Wexford is known for its long stretches of pristine beaches and for the evocative historic monuments in Wexford Town and on the Hook Head Peninsula. The modern English name of Wexford evolved from *Waesfjord,* which is what the Vikings called it when they invaded in the 9th century. The Normans captured the town at the end of the 12th century, and you can still see remnants of their fort at the Irish National Heritage Park.

Tourism Office

The **Wexford Tourist Office** is on Crescent Quay, Wexford (www.visitwexford.ie; ℂ **053/912-3111**). It's open Monday to Friday from 9am to 6pm and Saturday from 10:30am to 5pm. From late July to mid-August it's also open on Sunday from 10:30am to 5pm.

Top Attractions in County Wexford

Hook Lighthouse & Heritage Centre ★★ LIGHTHOUSE The Hook Head Peninsula is one of southern Ireland's loveliest drives, full of captivating vistas and hidden byways to discover. Nestled at the end of it all is this picturesque old lighthouse, the oldest part of which dates from the 13th century, making it the world's oldest lighthouse still in continuous use. Guided tours do an excellent job of telling the history of the lighthouse and the surrounding peninsula, which has been occupied since at least the 5th century A.D. There is an active program of special events, from art courses to ghost tours. *Tip:* The drive from Waterford is drastically shorter if you take the Passage East car ferry; see "Getting Around: By Ferry" earlier in this chapter for details.

Hook Head, Co. Wexford. www.hookheritage.ie. ℂ **051/397-055.** Admission €6 adults, €4.50 seniors and students, €3.50 children 5–16, children 4 and under free, €18–€20 families. Visitor center: Jun–Aug daily 9:30am–6pm; May and Sept daily 9:30am–5:30pm; Oct–Apr daily 9:30am–5pm. Lighthouse tours: Jun–Aug half-hourly 10am–5:30pm; Sept–May hourly 11am–5pm.

Irish Agricultural Museum and Famine Exhibition ★★ MUSEUM An extremely absorbing and at times affecting place, this excellent museum on the grounds of Johnstown Castle tells the story of agriculture and how important it was to the history of this region. There are rooms devoted to, among other things, dairy farming, country furniture, traditional crafts, and historic machinery. Of course, no museum devoted to farming in Ireland would be complete without mention of its greatest catastrophe—the Great Famine, which killed about a million people in the mid–19th century (and was responsible for the emigration of a million more). A special section puts it all into perspective in a thought-provoking way. Johnstown Castle was built in

JFK: son OF NEW ROSS

New Ross was the birthplace of Patrick Kennedy (1823–58), great-grandfather of John F. Kennedy, the 35th President of the United States. You can visit the **Kennedy Homestead** (www.kennedy homestead.ie; ℂ **051/388264**), where Patrick and his family lived, in the tiny village of Dunganstown, 8km (5 miles) south of New Ross. It's open daily from 9:30am to 5:30pm; entry costs €7.50 adults, €6.50 seniors, €5 students, and €20 families. Another JFK site of interest is the **Kennedy Memorial Arboretum** (www.heritageireland.ie; ℂ **051/388171**), a beautiful lakeside garden and wildlife haven dedicated to the late President. It's signposted from R733, about 12km (7½ miles) south of New Ross. It's open May to August, daily 10am to 8pm; April and September, daily 10am to 6pm; and October to March, daily 10am to 5pm. Entry costs €3 adults, €2 seniors, €1 students and children, and €8 families.

the 1400s; today, it's used as a government building, but you can still wander the verdant grounds.

Johnstown Castle Estate, Bridgetown Rd., off Wexford-Rosslare Rd. (N25), Wexford, Co. Wexford. www.irishagrimuseum.ie. ℂ **053/918-4671**. Gardens and museum: Apr–Oct €8 adults, €6 seniors, €4 students and children, €24 families; Nov–Mar €6 adults, €5 seniors, €4 students and chiildren, €20 families. Gardens only: Apr–Oct €3 adults, €2 seniors, €1 students and children, €8 families; Nov–Mar free. Museum: Apr–Jun and Sept–Oct Mon–Fri 9am–5pm, Sat–Sun and public holidays 11am–5pm; Jul–Aug Mon–Fri 9am–5:30pm, Sat–Sun and public holidays 11am–5:30pm; Nov–Mar Mon–Fri 9am–4pm, Sat–Sun and public holidays noon–4pm. Gardens: Apr–Jun and Sept–Oct daily 9am–5:30pm; Jul–Aug daily 9am–7pm; Nov–Mar daily 9am–4:30pm.

Irish National Heritage Park ★★ LIVING HISTORY PARK   This 14-hectare (35-acre) living-history park on the banks of the River Slaney outside of Wexford Town provides an ideal introduction for visitors of all ages to life in ancient Ireland, from the Stone Age to the Norman invasion. Each reconstructed glimpse into Irish history is well crafted and has its own natural setting and wildlife. There's also a nature trail and interpretive center, complete with gift shop and cafe. Kids can easily be amused for half a day here.

Ferrycarrig (about 4.8km/3 miles west of Wexford, signposted from N11), Co. Wexford. www.inhp. com. ℂ **053/912-0733**. Admission €9 adults, €7 seniors and students, €4.50 children 13–16, €4 children 4–12, children under 4 free, €24 families. May–Aug 9:30am–6:30pm. Sept–Apr 9:30am–5:30pm. Last admission 1½ hrs. before closing.

SS Dunbrody Famine Ship ★★ HISTORIC SITE   This huge, life-sized reconstruction of a 19th-century tall ship is exactly the kind of vessel on which a million or more people emigrated from Ireland to escape the Great Famine. An interpretive history center, the SS *Dunbrody* is an engaging way to learn about that history—particularly for youngsters, who will find it less stuffy than a conventional museum. Actors in period dress lead the tours, describing in great detail what life on board was like for the passengers. The SS *Dunbrody* is in New Ross, 36 km (22⅓ miles) west of Wexford.

The Quay, New Ross, Co. Wexford. www.dunbrody.com. ℂ **051/425239**. Admission €8.50 adults, €7 seniors, €5 students and children, €20–€25 families. Apr–Sept daily 9am–6pm (first tour 9:45am, last tour 5pm); Oct–Mar daily 9am–5pm (first tour 10am, last tour 4pm).

5

Exploring County Wexford

THE SOUTHEAST

Wexford Opera House ★ PERFORMING ARTS This shiny, modern opera house is a somewhat awkward addition to the Wexford skyline, with its large but rather garish copper-plated tower. The biggest event in the calendar of the opera house is, unsurprisingly, the Wexford Festival Opera. Held over two weeks each October/ November, this prestigious event attracts aficionados from all over Ireland and beyond. Opera lovers will be in heaven—but book early if there's something you want to see. Tickets start at around €10, rising to about €100 for the best seats.

High St., Wexford, Co. Wexford. www.wexfordoperahouse.ie. ℂ **053/912-2144.** Ticket prices vary; generally between €10 and €40. Event times vary; call ahead.

Wexford Walking Tours ★★ TOUR Proud of their town's ancient streets and antique buildings, the people of Wexford began conducting guided tours for visitors more than 30 years ago. Now the tourism office runs the tours on a more formal basis, but they're still led by locals, whose knowledge of the town and its history is unrivaled. The regular historical tour runs March to October and costs €5 per person. It departs daily at 11am from the Wexford Tourist Office, which also handles booking. The whole tour takes about 90 minutes. They also offer ghost tours and a walk of the surviving sections of the medieval town walls.

Departs from the Wexford Tourist Office on Crescent Quay, Wexford Town, Co. Wexford. www.wexfordwalkingtours.net. ℂ **086/352-6133.** Mar–Oct Mon–Sat 11am. Tour €5.

EXPLORING COUNTY KILKENNY

Like so many Irish towns, Kilkenny City stands on the site of an old monastery from which it takes its name. A priory was founded here in the 6th century by St. Canice: In Gaelic, *Cill Choinnigh* means "Canice's Church." In medieval times it was a prosperous walled city. Much of its medieval architecture has been skillfully preserved, including long sections of the medieval wall. Further afield from the county seat, the gentle countryside is full of captivating old ruins, from the majestic Kells Priory to the haunting remains of Jerpoint Abbey.

Tourism Office

The **Kilkenny Tourist Office** is at Shee Alms House, Rose Inn Street, Kilkenny (www.kilkennytourism.ie; ℂ **056/775-1500**). It's open May to September, Monday to Saturday 9am to 6pm, Sunday 10.30am to 4pm; October to April, Monday to Saturday 9:15am to 5pm.

Top Attractions in County Kilkenny

Jerpoint Abbey ★★ HISTORIC SITE About 18km (11 miles) southeast of Kilkenny is this outstanding Cistercian monastery, founded in the 12th century. Preserved in a peaceful country setting, the abbey's highlights include a sculptured cloister arcade, unique stone carvings on medieval tombs, and Romanesque architecture in the north nave. The staff is as friendly and knowledgeable about the local area as they come. Ask for details of where to find the mysterious ruins of the **Church of the Long Man,** about 16km (10 miles) away. If you're lucky, they'll be able to direct you—it's nearly impossible to find otherwise, and a local secret you may find yourself sworn to keep. *Tip:* If you're here in spring or autumn, plan your visit for toward the end of the day. Wandering around these ancient places as the setting sun blushes the walls in shades of peach and gold is an unforgettable experience.

On N8, 2.5km (1½ miles) southwest of Thomastown. www.heritageireland.ie. © **056/772-4623.** Admission €3 adults, €2 seniors, €1 students and children, €8 families. Early Mar–Sept 9am–5:30pm; Oct daily 9am–5pm; Nov–early Dec daily 9:30–4pm. Closed Dec–early Mar.

Jerpoint Glass Studio ★ FACTORY TOUR   Here you can witness the creation of Jerpoint glass, which you've probably been admiring in shops all across Ireland. The lines of the glasses, goblets, and pitchers are simple and fluid, highlighted with swirls of color. You can watch the glass being blown and then blow your budget next door at the shop.

Stoneyford, Co. Kilkenny. www.jerpointglass.com. © **056/772-4350.** Free admission. Shop and gallery: Mar–Oct Mon–Sat 10am–6pm; Sun and public holidays noon–5pm. Nov–Feb Mon–Sat 10am–5:30pm; Sun and public holidays noon–5pm. Glassblowing demonstrations: Mon–Thurs 10am–4pm; Fri 10am–1pm.

Kells Priory ★★ HISTORIC SITE   With its encompassing fortification walls and towers, as well as complex monastic ruins enfolded into the sloping south bank of the King's River, Kells is a glorious ruin. In 1193 Baron Geoffrey FitzRobert founded the priory and established a Norman-style town beside it. The current ruins date from the 13th to 15th centuries. The priory's wall has been carefully restored, and it connects seven towers, the remains of an abbey, and foundations of chapels and houses. You can tell by the thick walls that this monastery was well fortified, and those walls were built for a reason—it was frequently attacked. In the 13th century, it was the subject of two major battles and burned to the ground. The priory is less than a half-mile from the village of Kells, so if you have some time to spare, cross the footbridge behind it, which takes you on a swell stroll across the river and intersects a riverside walk leading to a picturesque old mill.

Kells, Co. Kilkenny. No website. © **056/775-1500.** Free admission. Take N76 south from Kilkenny, follow signs for R699/Callan and stay on R699 until you see signs for Kells.

Kilkenny Castle ★★★ CASTLE   Standing majestically beside the River Nore on the south side of Kilkenny City, this landmark medieval castle was built in the 12th century and remodeled in Victorian times. From its sturdy corner towers to its battlements, Kilkenny Castle retains the imposing lines of an authentic fortress and sets the tone for the city. The exquisitely restored interior includes a library, drawing room, and bedrooms, all decorated in 1830s style. The former servants' quarters are now an art gallery. The 20-hectare (49-acre) grounds include a riverside walk, extensive gardens, and a well-equipped children's playground. Access to the main body of the castle is by guided tour only, prefaced by an informative video on the rise, demise, and restoration of the structure. This is a very busy site, so arrive early (or quite late) to avoid waiting. From November to January entry is by guided tour only.

The Parade, Kilkenny, Co. Kilkenny. www.kilkennycastle.ie. © **056/770-4100.** Admission €6 adults, €4 seniors, €2.50 students and children 6 and over, €14 families. Apr–May and Sept 9:30am–5:30pm; Jun–Aug 9am–5:30pm; Oct–Feb 9:30am–4:30pm; Mar 9:30am–5pm.

St. Canice's Cathedral ★★ CHURCH   At the northern end of the city, this is the church that gave Kilkenny its name. It was built in the 12th century, but was restored after the English invasion led by Oliver Cromwell in the mid–17th century. It is noteworthy for the rich interior timber and stone carvings, its colorful glasswork, and the structure itself. On the grounds, amid the tombstones in the churchyard, is a massive

THE rock OF CASHEL

Worth the long drive it takes to get here from almost anywhere useful, this is one of Ireland's most iconic—and most impressive—medieval ruins. The extraordinary, dramatic outline of this craggy abbey, atop a hill in the center of Cashel, dominates views for miles around.

An outcrop of limestone reaching some 60m (197 ft.) into the sky, the so-called "Rock" tells the tales of 16 centuries. It was the seat of the kings of Munster at least as far back as A.D. 360, and it remained a royal fortress until 1101, when King Murtagh O'Brien granted it to the church. Among Cashel's many great moments was the legendary baptism of King Aengus by St. Patrick in 448. Remaining on the rock are the ruins of a two-towered chapel, a cruciform cathedral, a 28m (92-ft.) round tower, and a cluster of other medieval monuments. Inside the cathedral, extraordinary and detailed ancient carvings survive in excellent condition. The views of and from the Rock are spectacular.

Cashel is located 72km (45 miles) northeast of Waterford on R688. Entry to the Rock costs €6 adults, €4 seniors, €2 children and students, and €14 families. It's open mid-March to early June daily 9am–5:30pm; early June to mid-September daily 9am–7pm; mid-September to mid-October daily 9am–5:30pm; and mid-October to mid-March daily 9am–4.30pm. Last admission is 45 minutes before closing. For more information see www.heritageireland.ie or call ✆ **062/61437**

round tower, believed to be a relic of the ancient church (although its original conical top has been replaced by a slightly domed roof). If you want to climb to the tip of the tower, it will cost you a couple of euro and more calories than you can count. The steps up to the cathedral were constructed in 1614, and the carvings on the wall at the top of the stairs date from medieval times.

The Close, Coach Rd., Kilkenny, Co. Kilkenny. www.stcanicescathedral.com. ✆ **056/776-4971.** Cathedral: €4 adults; €3 seniors, students, and children; €12 families. Round Tower: €3 adults; €2.50 seniors, students, and children; €12 families. Combined ticket: €6 adults; €5.50 seniors, students, and children; €15 families. May–Sept Mon–Sat 9:30am–5pm, Sun 9:30am–4:30pm. Apr–May and Sept Mon–Sat 10am–1pm and 2–5pm; Sun 2–5pm. Jun–Aug Mon–Sat 9am–6pm; Sun 1–6pm. Oct–Mar Cathedral: Mon–Sat 10am–1pm and 2–4pm; Sun 2–4pm. Round Tower: Mon–Sat noon and 3pm; Sun 3pm. No children under 12 allowed to climb the tower.

COUNTY CORK

Cork is the largest of Ireland's counties, and one of its most diverse. It encompasses a lively capital city, quiet country villages, rocky hills, picturesque beaches, and long stretches of flat, green farmland. Here, modern tourism (this is where you find the Blarney Castle, after all) meets workaday Irish life, and somehow they manage to coexist side by side in peace. St. Finbarre founded Cork in the 6th century, when he built a monastery on a swampy estuary of the River Lee. He gave the place the rather generic Gaelic name of *Corcaigh*—which, unromantically, means "marsh." Cork City is worth a day or so to explore, but it can feel congested and gritty. Far more captivating is Kinsale, a pretty harbor town with a reputation as something of a gourmet's paradise, due to its plethora of outstanding restaurants. Farther afield, a clutch of historic sites, the storied seaport of Cobh, and the barren beauty of Cape Clear Island provide more to explore.

ESSENTIALS

Arriving

BY BUS From Dublin Airport, **AirCoach** (www.aircoach.ie; ✆ 01/844-7118) runs a regular, nonstop service to the center of Cork City. One-way tickets are €20 adults, €8 children. The journey time is 3¾ hours. In Cork City, **Bus Éireann** (www.buseireann.ie; ✆ 021/450-8188) runs from the **Parnell Place Bus Station** (www.buseireann.ie; ✆ 021/450-8188) to all parts of the Republic. Bus 249 connects Cork with Kinsale. Buses also arrive on Pier Road, across from the tourist office.

BY TRAIN **Iarnród Éireann/Irish Rail** (www.irishrail.ie; toll-free ✆ 185/036-6222) travels to Cork from Dublin and other parts of Ireland. Trains arrive at Kent Station, Lower Glanmire Road, in eastern Cork City (✆ 021/455-7277). Kinsale does not have a train station.

BY FERRY Ferry routes into Cork from Britain include service from Swansea on Fastnet Line (www.fastnetline.com; ✆ 021/487-8892); and from Roscoff, France, on Brittany Ferries (www.brittany-ferries.com; ✆ 021/427-7801). Boats dock at Cork's Ringaskiddy Ferryport.

BY CAR Cork is reachable on the N8 from Dublin, N25 from Waterford, and N22 from Killarney. To hire a car in Cork, try **Enterprise Rent-A-Car,** Kinsale Road (✆ 021/497-5133) or **Hertz** at Cork Airport (✆ 021/496-5849).

BY PLANE **Cork Airport,** Kinsale Road (www.cork-airport.com; ✆ 021/413131) is served by **Aer Lingus** and **Ryanair.**

ATMs/Banks In Cork City, try **Ulster Bank** (88 Patrick St.; ℭ **021/427-0618**). In Kinsale try **Bank of Ireland,** Emmett Place (ℭ **021/477-2521**).

Dentists For dental emergencies, your hotel will usually contact a dentist for you; otherwise, in Cork, try **Smiles Town Dental,** 112 Oliver Plunkett St., Cork (ℭ **021/427-4706**); in Kinsale, **Catherine McCarthy,** Market Sq. (ℭ **021/477-4133**).

Doctors For medical emergencies, dial ℭ **999.** For nonemergencies, your hotel should call you a doctor. Otherwise, in Cork, you

could try the **Patrick Street Medical Centre,** 9 Patrick St., Cork (ℭ **021/427-8699**); and in Kinsale, **The Medical Centre,** Emmet Place (ℭ **021/477-2253**).

Emergencies For police, fire, or other emergencies, dial ℭ **999.**

Internet Access Cork City Library at 57 Grand Parade (ℭ **021/492-4900**) has Internet terminals that nonmembers can use for €1 per half-hour.

Pharmacies In Cork, you can try **Murphy's Pharmacy,** 48 North Main St. (ℭ **021/427-4121**) or **Marian Pharmacy** on Friar's Walk (ℭ **021/496-3821**) In

Kinsale, try **John Collins,** Market Place (ℭ **021/477-2077**).

Post Office In Cork, the main post office is on Oliver Plunkett St. (ℭ **021/485-1032**). In Kinsale, it's at 10 Pearse St. (ℭ **021/477-2246**).

Taxis The main taxi ranks are along St. Patrick's Street, along the South Mall, and outside major hotels. In Cork, try **ABC Cabs** (ℭ **021/496-1961**) or **Cork Taxi Co-Op** (ℭ **021/427-2222**). In Kinsale, try **Kinsale Cabs** (ℭ **021/477-2642**) or **Cab 3000** (ℭ **021/477-3000**).

WHERE TO STAY

Cork City is filled with B&Bs and small hotels, particularly along Western Road. They vary in quality, but among them are some interesting, decently priced options. Away from the city, the pretty harbor town of Kinsale contains several elegant, high-quality B&Bs and boutique-style accommodations.

Where to Stay in Cork City

Avondale ★★ The exterior of this little B&B next door to Cork's University College is so generic-looking that you could almost miss it. The welcome you get from the owner Dolores will quickly expel any thoughts that you are in the wrong place, however. She's a charming host, with a talent for making travelers feel at home. Guest rooms are modern and uncluttered, with cushy duvets and good-quality beds. The hearty breakfasts are served in a tiny room overlooking the garden, which feels more akin to a family lounge than a formal dining area. But by that point, you may feel so much like a houseguest that you don't even notice.

1 St. Mary's Villas, Western Rd., Cork. www.avondalebb.com. ℭ **021/490-5874.** 4 units. €70–€80. Free parking. Rates include breakfast. **Amenities:** Wi-Fi (free).

Garnish House ★★ One of several B&Bs and hotels in this neighborhood, Garnish House is a sweet and friendly place to stay. You're hardly through the door before being offered an afternoon tea, complete with delicious homemade scones. Guest rooms are pleasant, with good-sized beds, and some rooms even have Jacuzzi baths. Breakfasts are the selling point, though. They are outstanding; in addition to the usual hearty "full Irish" options, you can have French toast, pancakes, lentil ragout, stuffed tomatoes, salmon and dill tarts, scrambled eggs with avocado—more choices than plenty of restaurants around here would offer at dinner. There are self-catering options available for those who want a little extra freedom, including a one-bedroom apartment and a full town house directly across the street.

1 St. Mary's Villas, Western Rd., Cork. www.garnish.ie. © **021/427-5111.** 14 units. €70–€172. Free parking. Rates include breakfast. **Amenities:** Wi-Fi (free).

Lancaster Lodge ★   Another small hotel on Western Road, Lancaster Lodge is modern, well run, and a good value for money. The purple color scheme in some of the public areas might be a bit garish for some, but guest rooms are more subdued and quite spacious (always a plus). Suites, which aren't a great deal more than the standard doubles, come with Jacuzzi baths. Breakfast is better than you might expect from a budget hotel, and while they don't serve dinner, central Cork is only a short walk away.

Lancaster Quay, Western Road, Cork. www.lancasterlodge.com. © **021/425-1125.** 48 units. €91–€139. Free parking. Breakfast not included in lower rates. **Amenities:** Wi-Fi (free), room service.

Where to Stay in Kinsale

Actons Hotel ★   This pleasant, well-run property looks out over Kinsale Harbour. Built in the mid–19th century, it's been a hotel since the 1940s, though a recent renovation has smoothed out a few old wrinkles. Guest rooms aren't huge, but they're nicely designed, with very large beds and lovely harbor views. In a town where it's easy to find accommodations with character but not modern conveniences, there are a couple of welcome extras including an elevator (you'd be surprised how rare that is around here) and a swimming pool. The hotel's two restaurants are fine, but Kinsale is full of better restaurants within a short walk.

Pier Road, Kinsale, Co. Cork. www.actonshotelkinsale.com. © **021/477-9900.** 74 units. €110–€170. Free parking. Rates include breakfast. Dinner, bed and breakfast packages available. **Amenities:** Wi-Fi (free), restaurants (2), bar, room service, gym, swimming pool, a/c (public areas only), accessible rooms.

The Blue Haven ★★   There's something wonderfully old-school about this chic town house hotel in the middle of Kinsale. It may be that the rooms are traditionally decorated with antique-style furniture and heritage print wallpaper. Or perhaps it's the friendliness of the staff. Whatever the source, it makes the Blue Haven a *true* haven. Add to that the fact that the in-house restaurant, the Fishmarket (see listing later in this chapter), is excellent, and you have a real reason to stay here. *Tip:* Frequent special offers can bring the prices down considerably. For example, midweek dinner, bed-and-breakfast deals for well under €100 are common, and enticing package deals for golfers, including access to one of the best courses in Ireland, can be had. The only snag is that you can get street noise here, so ask for an upper-floor room if you're a light sleeper.

3-4 Pearse St., Kinsale, Co. Cork. www.bluehavenkinsale.com. © **021/477-2209.** 17 units. €120–€140. Parking at nearby lots (no discount) around €1.30 per hour. Rates include breakfast. Dinner, bed and breakfast packages and 2-night midweek and weekend deals available. **Amenities:** Wi-Fi (free), restaurants (2), bar, room service.

Desmond House ★★   This lovely, historic B&B is one of the best places to stay in Kinsale. Desmond House was built in the mid–18th century, and, according to host Michael McLaughlin, is one of the oldest and best-preserved Georgian buildings in

Cork City

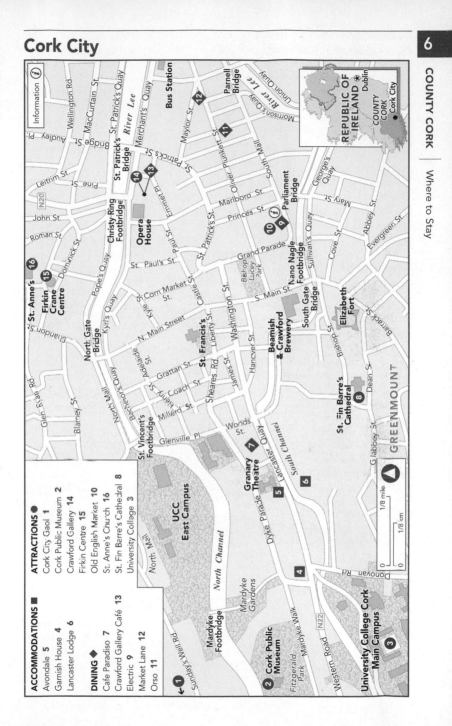

REPUBLIC OF IRELAND ● Dublin

COUNTY CORK

● Cork City

Parnell Bridge

Bus Station

Opera House

Christy Ring Footbridge

Firkin Crane Centre

St. Anne's

North Gate Bridge

St. Francis's

Beamish & Crawford Brewery

South Gate Bridge

Elizabeth Fort

St. Fin Barre's Cathedral

Granary Theatre

St. Vincent's Footbridge

UCC East Campus

Mardyke Footbridge

Cork Public Museum

University College Cork Main Campus

GREENMOUNT

Parliament Bridge

Nano Nagle Footbridge

St. Patrick's Bridge

ACCOMMODATIONS ■
Avondale **5**
Garnish House **4**
Lancaster Lodge **6**

DINING ◆
Cafe Paradiso **7**
Crawford Gallery Café **13**
Electric **9**
Market Lane **12**
Orso **11**

ATTRACTIONS ●
Cork City Gaol **1**
Cork Public Museum **2**
Crawford Gallery **14**
Firkin Centre **15**
Old English Market **10**
St. Anne's Church **16**
St. Fin Barre's Cathedral **8**
University College **3**

1/8 mile
1/8 km

town. Michael is a genuine and charming man; his policy of charging American visitors according to whichever exchange rate works out best with the euro—on the day you booked or the day you check out—is a typically considerate gesture. Guest rooms are generous, with big, comfortable beds (a full 6 feet from side to side), and the up-to-date bathrooms are furnished with whirlpool tubs. Many of the ingredients for the delicious breakfasts come straight from the Old English Market in Cork (see listing later in this chapter).

42 Cork St., Kinsale, Co. Cork. www.desmondhousekinsale.com. ℭ **021/477-3575.** 4 units. €140. Parking at nearby lots (no discount) around €1.30 per hour. Rates include breakfast. **Amenities:** Wi-Fi (free).

Pier House ★★ Hosts Pat and Anne have done a splendid job in converting this 19th-century town house into a B&B; chic color schemes and subtle splashes of modern art lift the mood beautifully. A few of the bedrooms have little balconies, and guests are welcome to bring wine back with them if they want to spend a leisurely hour admiring the views of the harbor or garden. Breakfasts are delicious and plentiful. You'll have to fend for yourself at dinner, but that's hardly a chore in foodie-friendly Kinsale.

Pier Road, Kinsale, Co. Cork. www.pierhousekinsale.com. ℭ **021/477-4169.** 10 units. €100–€140. Parking for bikes and motorbikes only; car parking at nearby lots around €1.30 per hour. Rates include breakfast. **Amenities:** Wi-Fi (free).

WHERE TO EAT

Cork's reputation as a kind of cultural "Dublin South" is burnished by its restaurant scene, smattered with trendy eateries. However, it's Kinsale where the county really goes to let its collective belt out. Over the last 20 years, the town has transformed itself from a sleepy fishing village into one of Ireland's premier food destinations.

Where to Eat in Cork City

Cafe Paradiso ★★ VEGETARIAN An inventive, classy vegetarian restaurant, Cafe Paradiso does such magnificent things with veggies that even passionate carnivores will find plenty to love. Start with roast eggplant with honey and cardamom or cauliflower soup with braised shiitake mushrooms, before moving on to deep-fried squash blossoms with smoked pepperonata and green onion polenta. Desserts are heavenly, especially the rich chocolate mousse (made with olive oil—trust us, it works) and spicy almond brittle. The excellent wine list is reasonably priced. If you can't quite run to dinner here, come before 7pm for the early-bird menu. Or for those who prefer to roll straight from table to bed, they also have guest rooms for €100 per night (dinner included).

16 Lancaster Quay, Cork. www.cafeparadiso.ie. ℭ **021/427-7939.** Fixed-price menus: 2 courses €33, 3 courses €36–€40. Mon–Fri 5:30–10pm; Sat noon–2:30pm and 5:30–10pm. No children after 7pm.

Crawford Gallery Café ★★ CAFE A big step up from the average cafe tacked onto an art gallery, the Crawford is as much a great little bistro as it is a convenient spot for a coffee or light nibble. It's open for breakfast, which certainly provides some excellent options if you can't face another hotel morning meal. You'll find spiced scones, American-style pancakes, and delicious eggs Florentine with organic spinach on the menu. Lunchtime is when this place gets busiest, though, and the lineup changes

Kinsale

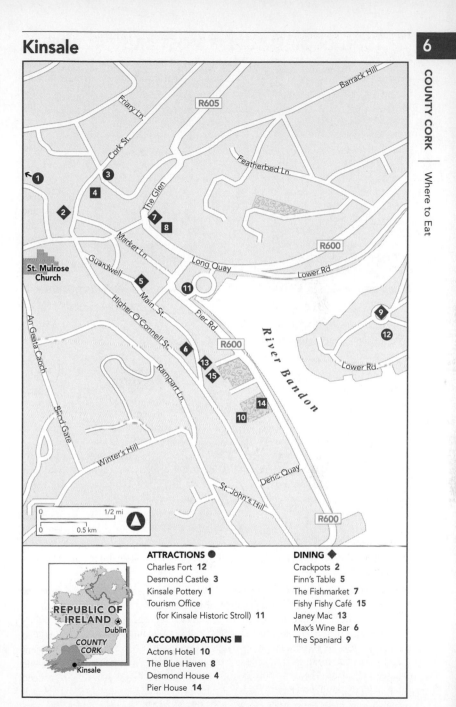

ATTRACTIONS ●
Charles Fort **12**
Desmond Castle **3**
Kinsale Pottery **1**
Tourism Office
(for Kinsale Historic Stroll) **11**

ACCOMMODATIONS ■
Actons Hotel **10**
The Blue Haven **8**
Desmond House **4**
Pier House **14**

DINING ◆
Crackpots **2**
Finn's Table **5**
The Fishmarket **7**
Fishy Fishy Café **15**
Janey Mac **13**
Max's Wine Bar **6**
The Spaniard **9**

6 a tuneful pint: CORK'S MOST MUSICAL PUBS

Cork has a deserved reputation as home to some of Ireland's best pubs for live, traditional music. It's virtually a rite of passage to catch a session while enjoying a pint or two (and it's stout in these parts, by the way—Murphy's or Beamish, not Guinness—if you really want to fit in). You can just follow your ears to find the best places, but here are a few of the most respected to get you started. **An Bodhran** (the name refers to a type of drum made from goatskin) at 42 Oliver Plunkett St. (© **021/427-4544**) has live sessions nightly, as does the cozy **An Spailpín Fánach** (which means "The Wandering Migrant Worker") at 27 South Main St. (© **021/427-7949**). **Sin é** (literally, "That's It"), 8 Coburg St. (© **021/450-2266**) has been one of Cork's top live-music pubs for decades, long before it became a popular tourist activity. They have sessions most nights, but those on Tuesdays, Fridays, and Sundays tend to be particularly good. And if you've had enough live music at the atmospheric **Long Valley** (© **021/427-2144**), you could go upstairs to watch a poetry slam. They are generally held on Monday nights, along with a lively program of spoken-word events; see www.obheal.ie for more details.

regularly, with plenty of daily specials like chorizo bean cassoulet or smoked salmon salad with horseradish dressing. On Thursdays the café stays open until 8pm for early-evening suppers.

At the Crawford Gallery, Emmet Place, Cork. www.crawfordgallerycafe.com. © **021/427-4415.** Breakfast: €3–€11. Lunch: €11–€15. Mon–Wed and Fri–Sat 8:30–11:30am and noon–3pm; Thurs 8:30am–8pm.

Electric ★★ SEAFOOD/MODERN IRISH With a dining room overlooking the river and the city skyline beyond, it's easy to get swept up in the romantic atmosphere of this trendy but unpretentious restaurant. The menu isn't large, but it's honest and beautifully done with steaks, cider, dill-battered fish and chips, and a juicy house burger topped with Wicklow blue cheese. There are actually two dining spaces here; in addition to the main restaurant, there's the **Fish Bar** (Wednesday to Saturday only), where you can eat super-fresh seafood while perched on bar stools overlooking the river. Despite its popularity, you can usually get a table at Electric if you arrive early—a full fifth are held back every night—and no reservations at all are taken for the Fish Bar.

41 South Mall, Cork. www.electriccork.com/restaurant. © **021/422-2990.** Main courses €15–€25. Wed–Sat noon–10pm; Sun–Tues noon–9pm. No children in the Fish Bar.

Market Lane ★★ IRISH This friendly, informal restaurant serves Irish-inflected bistro food. It's a let-your-hair-down kind of place, and the menu strikes a good line between traditional, unpretentious cooking with just a few more adventurous touches. Typical mains include gin-marinated pork with black pudding and hake with summer greens and roasted garlic. Lunches are just as good, and if you're not in the mood to linger over a full meal, pick something from the small but well-judged menu of sandwiches and salads. The early-bird menu is an outstanding value at just €20 for three courses (daily until 7pm, except Friday and Saturday).

5-6 Oliver Plunkett St., Cork. www.marketlane.ie. © **021/427-4710.** Main courses €14–€26. Mon–Thurs noon–10pm; Fri–Sat noon–10:30pm; Sun 1–9pm (10pm on public holidays).

THE GREAT GOURMET GATHERING: kinsale food festival

Food lovers from all over Ireland—and even farther afield—descend on Kinsale for a weekend each October when the Kinsale Gourmet Festival takes over town. The event's calendar changes every year, but there are always plenty of cooking demonstrations and other lively activities. Restaurants join in the fun by hosting parties, special tastings, "meet the chef" events, and other culinary goodies. Many of them are free, although some of the bigger events and banquets charge about €20 to €100 per ticket. It's magnificent, Bacchanalian fun. Learn more and book tickets at www.kinsalerestaurants.com.

Orso ★★★ IRISH/MEDITERRANEAN This place is like a ray of warm Mediterranean sunshine. Traditional flavors of southern Europe are mixed with Irish influences, and the result is nothing short of delightful. It's open all day, so you can pop in for a breakfast of flatbread with banana and cinnamon or granola with Greek yogurt and berry compote. The lunch menu is long and varied, but it's really at dinnertime when the excellent cooking comes into its own. Plates include *schiacciata* (a type of gossamer-thin pizza made with olive oil and sea salt) alongside lamb encrusted with sesame seeds. Nearly everything on the wine list is available by the glass, and the small cocktail menu is intriguing—try the zingy mint and lime spritzer.

8 Pembroke St., Cork. www.orso.ie. © **021/243-8000.** Main courses €8–€12. Mon 8:30am–6pm; Tues–Thurs 8:30am–10pm; Fri–Sat 8:30am–10:30pm; Sun (Dec only) noon–9. Closed Sun, Jan–Nov.

Where to Eat in Kinsale

Crackpots ★★★ SEAFOOD/MODERN IRISH A happy marriage of designer pottery shop and outstandingly good restaurant, Crackpots specializes in fresh, delicious seafood. The ingredients are all locally sourced, so exactly what appears on the menu depends on what's freshest, but grilled langoustine with spinach and lime pesto or baked salmon flavored with lemongrass and served with potato rosti are few favorites. It's not all seafood; the menu is also filled with items like roast duck, lamb, or a simple steak served in a sauce of brandy and peppercorn, plus a vegetarian option or two. The dining room is decorated with some interesting art (most of which is for sale), or you can sit in a heated garden terrace out back if the weather's fine.

3 Cork St., Kinsale. www.crackpots.ie. © **021/477-2847.** Main courses €14–€29. Mon–Sat 6–9pm; Sun 1–3pm. No dinner Sun.

Finn's Table ★★★ MODERN IRISH The menu here is ambitious without being overly complicated and with plenty of space to let the ingredients breathe. As you'd expect from Kinsale, the seafood on the menu comes directly from the harbor, so you never know exactly what will end up in the kitchen. However, on a typical night plates can include tender squid fried with salt and pepper, monkfish and scallops served with Parmesan cream, or lemon sole with glazed asparagus and a carrot and lime buerre blanc. Though the standout dishes tend to be seafood, there's plenty more to choose from, and the meats are all sourced from the owner's parents, who run a butcher shop in nearby Mitchelstown.

6 Main St., Kinsale. www.finnstable.com. © **021/470-9636.** Main courses €20–€35. Wed–Mon 5:30–10pm. Closed Tues.

The Fishmarket ★★ SEAFOOD/INTERNATIONAL   Another excellent seafood restaurant packed with the grand choices Kinsale is known for, the Fishmarket is the in-house restaurant at the Blue Haven hotel (see listing above). The short menu has a nice balance of traditional seafood dishes—classic fish and chips or hake filet with lemon and chive butter—together with some meatier options such as Thai red curry or steak in peppercorn sauce. There are vegetarian choices and celiac-friendly dishes, too. The tempting dessert menu features such diet-busting delights as a Guinness and Belgian chocolate pecan brownie served with ice cream and chocolate sauce.

3-4 Pearse St., Kinsale. www.bluehavenkinsale.com. ℂ **021/477-2209.** Main courses €19–€48. Daily 6–10pm.

Fishy Fishy Café ★★★ SEAFOOD   Widely respected, hugely popular, and yet brilliantly simple, the Fishy Fishy is one of the best restaurants in Kinsale. The owners also have a gourmet store and fish-and-chip shop on Guardwell Street, but this is their flagship. The expertly prepared, fresh seafood comes from a small number of trusted suppliers. And we do mean local. Shane catches the cod and turbot; Maurice provides the crab; Christy, David, and Jimmy catch the prawns— you get the idea. Exactly what's cooking that day depends on the catch, but you can expect to find the signature Fishy Fishy pie of salmon and shellfish in a creamy sauce with a bread-crumb topping. Reservations are only taken for dinner, so this place gets packed during lunchtime.

Crowleys Quay, Kinsale. www.fishyfishy.ie. ℂ**021/470-0415.** Main courses €16–€25. Mar–Oct daily noon–9pm. Nov–Feb Sun–Wed noon–4pm; Thurs–Sat noon–9pm. No lunch Sun–Wed, Nov–Feb.

Janey Mac ★★ CAFE   There's a nice little story behind the name of this artisan bakery and cafe. "Janey Mac" isn't a person, rather it was a phrase invented by the residents of Kinsale in the 1950s as an alternative expletive to the blasphemous (and therefore, in those days, verboten) "Jesus Christ." Since then, this building has housed several businesses of wildly disparate kinds, but most of them have kept the same name. The homemade cakes, scones, brownies, and other baked treats here are delicious, and they serve great sandwiches at lunchtime, too. The little dining room is decorated in a shabby-chic style, scattered with cushions and other appealing touches. Look for the wry "thought for the day," scrawled on a blackboard at the back.

38 Main St., Kinsale. www.janeymackinsale.com. ℂ **086/811-1848.** Main courses €3–€9. Mon–Sat 9am–5pm.

Max's Wine Bar ★★★ MODERN IRISH   A husband-and-wife team has run Max's since the '90s, and they're still effortlessly adept at making diners feel welcome. The menu changes seasonally, but the main flavors are French, with dishes like black sole with herb butter or lobster broth prepared with Chardonnay and tarragon. There are also Irish influences, with regionally sourced meats and wild game, some prepared with local cider. The specials board invariably features a selection of fresh, local seafood. The early-bird menu (a thoroughly reasonable €30 for three courses) is served from 6pm until 7:30pm (7pm on Saturdays).

48 Main St., Kinsale. www.maxs.ie. ℂ 021/477-2443. Main courses €21–€30. Apr–mid-Dec daily 6–10pm. Closed mid-Dec to Mar and public holidays.

The Spaniard ★★ BISTRO   The portrait on the sign of this atmospheric old inn shows Don Juan de Aguila, the Spanish commander who led a force of 4,000 men, assisted by local Irish revolutionaries, against the English at the Battle of Kinsale in

1601. The English won, but Don Juan became a hero in local folklore. The present inn dates from around 50 years after the battle, and it's still a satisfying place with an old-world look. They serve excellent, homey pub food in the restaurant, but the bar menu is just as good, and cheaper, too. An eclectic program of live music features everything from straight-up Irish folk to Russian Gypsy bands.

Junction of Scilly and Lower rds., Kinsale. www.thespaniard.ie. ℂ **021/477-2436.** Main courses €18–€25. Mon–Fri 12:30–3pm and 6–9pm; Sat 12:30–3pm and 6–10pm; Sun 12:30–3pm and 6:30–10pm.

EXPLORING COUNTY CORK

A busy, artsy hub where urban conveniences are seasoned by an appreciation for rural life, Cork City is also home to a major university, which keeps the population young, the creative class dynamic, the pubs interesting, and the number of affordable restaurants plentiful. Not far from the city, Blarney Castle is an impressive sight—although it would take a starry-eyed Medievalist indeed to claim that the experience wasn't somewhat marred by the rather cynical, touristy atmosphere. Meanwhile, 25km (15½ miles) to the south of the city, the adorable harbor town of Kinsale is both an attractive hideaway and a major restaurant destination. The only disadvantage is that it's hardly undiscovered, but that somehow fails to dent its charm. To the east of Cork City, the two great attractions are Fota Island, a brilliantly designed wildlife park, and Cobh, which was the last port of call in Ireland for millions of emigrants in the 19th and early-20th centuries.

Tourism Offices

The **Cork Discover Ireland Centre** is at the appropriately named Tourist House at 42 Grand Parade, Cork (www.corkcity.ie; ℂ **021/425-5100**). The **Kinsale Tourist Office** is on Pier Road (www.kinsale.ie; ℂ **021/477-2234**). Both are open year-round.

Top Attractions in Cork City

Cork City might as well be called Dublin South. It's far smaller than the capital, with 125,000 residents, but it's a busy, attractive, cultured place. However, Cork also has severe traffic congestion and can feel gritty and crowded. For its fans, these flaws merely make Cork a more interesting place, underscoring the sense that it's a real, working city.

Cork City Gaol ★ HISTORIC SITE Like something straight out of a Victorian novel, this early-19th-century jail is an austere, impressive, and highly atmospheric building. It opened in 1824 as a women's prison. Its famous inmates included the extraordinary Constance Markievicz, the first woman elected to the British parliament. She was sentenced to execution after the 1916 Easter Rising, in which she took part—though her sentence was commuted. Earlier in its history, this was the last place in Ireland many convicts were held before being shipped off to Australia. This colorful history is well presented, with the (perhaps inevitable) aid of costumed mannequins in key positions. Somewhat incongruously, in 1927, after the building ceased to be used as a prison, it became the site of Ireland's first radio station. A small museum tells this story, complete with a restored studio from the period.

Convent Ave., Sunday's Well, Cork, Co. Cork. www.corkcitygaol.com. ℂ **021/430-5022.** Admission €8 adults, €7 seniors and students, €5 children, €25 families. Radio Museum €2. Mar–Oct daily 9:30am–5pm; Nov–Feb daily 10am–4pm.

THE GUINNESS CORK jazz festival

Held every year since 1978, this is Ireland's biggest and most prestigious jazz festival. Big names such as Ella Fitzgerald, Oscar Peterson, and Stephane Grappelli have played here over the years, and more than 1,000 performers from all over the world take part annually. It's held at various citywide venues in late October. Visit www.corkjazzfestival.com for details. Tickets go on sale in early September; prices vary and some events are free.

Cork Public Museum ★ MUSEUM This simple, rather endearing civic museum is a good place to get an overview of the city's history. Displays include a few objects from Cork's ancient past, but it's strongest when it comes to the traditional crafts made in the city during the 19th and 20th centuries—including silverware and intricate lace from the Victorian period. There are also very good collections relating to the lives of local revolutionaries, including Michael Collins (see the box on p. 120). The museum is located on the west side of Cork, in the middle of Fitzgerald Park—parallel to the Western Road, where many of the city's B&Bs are located (see "Where to Stay," earlier in this chapter).

Fitzgerald Park, Cork, Co. Cork. www.corkcity.ie. ✆ 021/427-0679. Free admission. Apr–Sept Mon–Fri 11am–1pm and 2:15–5pm, Sat 11am–1pm and 2:15–4pm, Sun 3–5pm; Oct–Mar Mon–Fri 11am–1pm and 2:15–5pm, Sat 11am–1pm and 2:15–4pm.

Crawford Art Gallery ★★★ MUSEUM One of the best art galleries in Ireland, the Crawford has impressive collections of sculpture and painting. The Irish School is particularly well represented, with works from John Butts (1728–65), including his beautiful 1755 panorama of Cork City, and Harry Clarke (1889–1931), a Dubliner who was not only one of the most celebrated illustrators of the early–20th century, but who also produced some extraordinary, early Deco-influenced stained glass. There's also a strong collection of works by female Irish artists from the mid–19th century onward; check out the extraordinary abstract work of Mainie Jellet (1897–1944) and the Cubist painter Norah McGuinness (1901–80). There is also a program of temporary exhibitions, and the excellent Crawford Gallery Café (see listing above) is a good spot for a light lunch.

Emmet Place, Cork. www.crawfordartgallery.ie. ✆ 021/480-5042. Free admission. Mon–Wed and Fri–Sat 10am–5pm; Thurs 10am–8pm. 2nd floor closes 4:45pm daily. Closed Sun and public holidays.

The Firkin Crane Cultural Centre ★ PERFORMING ARTS Dating from the 1840s, this unique rotunda was part of Cork's original Butter Exchange, and the building's name derives from Danish words pertaining to measures of butter. Although destroyed by fire in 1980, the site was rebuilt and opened as a cultural center in 1992. Today, it is dedicated to contemporary dance and serves as a venue for new dance works and for touring national and international dance companies, plus occasional performance art and other installations. They also run one-off classes, workshops, and interactive exhibitions. Performances are irregular; the best are usually reserved for the Guinness Cork Jazz Festival in October (see box above). Ticket prices range from around €5 to €20, though many events are free.

John Redmond St., Shandon, Cork, Co. Cork. www.firkincrane.ie. ✆ 021/450-7487. Ticket prices and performance times vary by event.

milking it: **AN UNLIKELY DEBUT**

A neat story about the birth of radio broadcasting in Ireland is told at the Radio Museum, in Cork City Gaol (see listing above). Meticulous planning went into the launch of Station 2RN, in 1926, right down to a permanent armed guard to make sure nothing went wrong. However, the first Irish radio star turned out to be an unlikely participant. In order to test the signal, very early one morning a technician pointed a microphone out of the window—just as a horse and cart from the local dairy happened to be passing by. Thus, the first sound broadcast in Ireland was those of an unwitting milkman, quietly making his rounds.

Old English Market ★★ MARKET   The name of this bustling food market harks back to the days of English rule. Quite a long way back, in fact: It was first granted a charter in 1610 during the reign of King James I. The current market building dates from 1788, although it was redesigned after being gutted by fire in the 1980s. Inside is a cornucopia of fresh produce, including super-traditional Cork delicacies—some of them tempting, others less palatable to outsiders. Tripe, anyone? How about pig's trotters? Happily, more modern refreshments and takeaway snacks are readily available.

Grand Parade; enter from Patrick St., Grand Parade, Oliver Plunkett St., or Princes St., Cork. www.theenglishmarket.ie. (C) **005/763-2259,** Free admission; individual food stall prices vary. Mon–Sat 8am–6pm. Closed public holidays.

St. Anne's Church ★ CHURCH   Cork's most recognizable landmark, also known as Shandon Church, is famous for its giant pepper pot steeple and eight melodious bells. No matter where you stand in the downtown area, you can see the stone tower crowned with a gilt ball and a unique fish weather vane. Until a few years ago, due to a quirk of clockworks, it was known as "the four-faced liar" because each of its four clock faces showed a different time—except on the hour when they all managed to synchronize. Somewhat sadly, that charming quirk has now been repaired. Climb the 1722 belfry for the chance to play a tune on the famous Shandon Bells. If you continue on the somewhat precarious climb past the bells, you'll be rewarded with spectacular views over the surrounding countryside.

Church St., Shandon, Cork. www.shandonbells.ie (C) **021/450-5906.** Admission €5 adults, €4 seniors and students, €2.50 children, €12 families. Mar–May and Oct Mon–Sat 10am–4pm; Sun 11:30am–3:30pm; June–Sept Mon–Sat 10am–5pm; Sun 11:30am–4:30pm; Nov–Feb Mon–Sat 11am–3pm; Sun 11:30am–3pm.

St. Fin Barre's Cathedral ★ CHURCH   This Church of Ireland cathedral sits on the spot St. Finbarre chose in A.D. 600 for his church and school. A much smaller medieval tower was demolished to make way for the current building, which dates from the early 1860s—there's nothing left of the original, although a few pieces of decorative stonework that were salvaged during the demolition can be viewed inside. The architect, William Burges (1827–81), was the winner of a competition that was staged to create a new Anglican cathedral in the city; his winning design embraced the French Gothic style that was popular at the time, including its most prominent feature—three soaring spires, which still dominate the skyline. The interior is highly ornamented with unique mosaic work. The bells were inherited from the 1735 church that previously stood on this site. The Cathedral also hosts occasional exhibitions; check the website for listings of what's on.

Bishop St. www.cathedral.cork.anglican.org. ℃ **021/496-3387.** Admission €5 adults, €3 students and children. Apr–Nov Mon–Sat 9:30am–5:30pm, Sun 12:30–5pm; Dec–Mar Mon–Sat 9:30am–5:30pm. Closed certain bank holidays; call to check.

University College Cork ★★ HISTORIC SITE Part of Ireland's national university, with about 7,000 students, this center of learning is housed in a pretty quadrangle of Gothic Revival–style buildings. Colorful gardens and wooded grounds grace the campus. An audio tour of the grounds takes in the Crawford Observatory, the Harry Clarke stained-glass windows in the Honan Chapel, a landscaped garden, and the Stone Corridor, a collection of stones inscribed with the ancient Irish *ogham* written language. Also on the campus is the **Lewis Glucksman Gallery** (www.glucksman.org; ℃ **021/490-1844**), an innovative art center that has an excellent program of exhibitions. Expect to see innovative photography, painting, sculpture, and a few items from the university's ever-expanding permanent collection. There is also a good cafe and shop on-site. Admission to the Glucksman is free, though a donation of €5 per person is requested.

Visitor Centre: North Wing, Main Quad, Western Rd., Cork, Co. Cork. visitorscentre.ucc.ie. ℃ **021/490-1876.** Self-guided tours €10. Visitor Centre: Mon–Fri 9am–5pm, Sat noon–5pm. Glucksman Gallery: Tues–Sat 10am–5pm; Sun 1–5pm.

Top Attractions in Kinsale

This former fishing village is enchanting, with its narrow, winding streets, well-kept 18th-century houses, imaginatively painted shop fronts, window boxes overflowing with colorful flowers, and harbor full of sailboats. Kinsale has a more eventful history than you might think, however. In 1601, it was the scene of a major sea battle between Protestant England and Catholic Spain—one in which Irish rebels played a covert part. You can learn all about this fascinating conflict on one of local man Don Herlihy's absorbing "Historic Strolls" (see listing below).

Charles Fort ★ HISTORIC SITE Southeast of Kinsale at the head of the harbor, this coastal landmark dates from the late–17th century. A classic star-shaped fort, it was constructed after the Battle of Kinsale to prevent foreign invaders from entering the port. The building was strengthened throughout the 18th and 19th centuries, and the fort remained in use as a military garrison right up until the British left in 1921. Charles Fort was named after Charles II, who was king of England and Ireland at the time it was built. Across the river is the smaller James Fort that dates back to the reign of King James I (1603–25). Local lore has it that until the 19th century, access to this stretch of water was controlled by a massive chain floating on timber kegs between the two shores that could be drawn tight at a moment's notice.

Summercove, Kinsale. www.heritageireland.ie. ℃ **021/477-2263.** Admission €4 adults, €3 seniors, €2 students and children, €10 families. Mid-Mar–Oct daily 10am–6pm; Nov–mid-Mar daily 10am–5pm.

Desmond Castle ★ CASTLE This small, squat stone fortress doesn't really look like a castle, in part because it incongruously sits halfway up a residential street. It was built around 1500 as the customs house for Kinsale Harbour. In the late–17th century it was turned into a prison, at which time its history took several dark detours, including a fire that gutted the building in 1747, roasting alive the 54 French soldiers who were imprisoned within. Later, during the potato famine, it was used as a workhouse.

This signposted pedestrian path runs along the sea from Scilly, the community across the harbor from Kinsale, to Charles Fort. You can pick up maps of the full route at the Kinsale Tourist Office.

Technically a separate village, Scilly is effectively a miniscule suburb of Kinsale, but it retains a strong sense of its own identity. Pronounced "silly," its unusual name is thought to hark back to fishermen from the Scilly Isles (off the coast of Cornwall, England) who settled here during the 17th century.

Take the right-hand road around the village, skirting along the coast, and join the marked pedestrian trail by the waterside. Along here there are lovely views across to Kinsale, and across the harbor you'll see the stout remains of **James Fort.** Named for King James I, it was built by the English shortly after the Battle of Kinsale to guard the entrance to the port and ensure against further insurrection. It was captured by the forces of the (Protestant) King William I during his war with the deposed (Catholic) James II in 1690—part of the same conflict that is still commemorated today by the Protestant "Orange marches" in Northern Ireland.

Another tiny hamlet on the outskirts of Kinsale, **Summer Cove** is as sweet a place as its halcyon name suggests. Black-and-white toy town houses, with splashes of green and red, face the harbor as gulls circle overhead and the waves froth and bubble along the harbor walls.

A short walk uphill from Summer Cove lies **Charles Fort** (see listing above). This impressive military structure was once the site of Ringcurran Castle in medieval times, an important defensive position used by the Spanish during the Battle of Kinsale in 1601. After a lengthy fight, the allied Irish and Spanish troops were defeated by the English army, who reduced the castle to rubble. In 1678, a permanent fortress was built here to reinforce the defenses of James Fort. Charles Fort remained in use as a barracks until the end of British rule in the early 20th century. It suffered extensive damage during the civil war, and has only recently been restored.

The Scilly Walk ends here. If you continue to walk south along the sea, you'll find another path that follows the headland to the tip of **Frower Point,** which affords great views across the harbor to the Old Head of Kinsale.

There's an unusual but interesting little museum inside, detailing the story of the Irish exiles who helped transform the global wine trade from the 17th century onward. Cork St., Kinsale. www.heritageireland.ie. ℰ **021/477-4855.** Admission €3 adults, €2 seniors, €1 students and children, €8 families. Mid-Apr–Sept daily 10am–6pm; last admission 1 hr. before closing.

Kinsale Historic Stroll ★★★ TOUR   One of the most pleasant ways to spend an hour in these parts is to take local resident Don Herlihy's excellent walking tour—or Historic Stroll, as he prefers to call it—of Kinsale town. Don and his fellow guide, Barry Moloney, have been leading visitors around the main sights since the mid-1990s, and their local knowledge is second to none. Highlights include the 12th-century St. Multose Church; a walk past Desmond Castle (see listing above); and the harbor, where the 17th-century Battle of Kinsale is recounted with an enthusiasm only found in people who really love their subject. The tour starts outside the tourist office at 11:15am every day. On weekdays from May to September there's also an earlier tour at 9:15am. The cost is €6 adults, €1 children. You pay at the end or, in their words, "drop out for free if you're not delighted." That probably doesn't happen very often. If you prebook, you're given a free historic chart designed by Don.

Departs from Kinsale Tourist Office, Pier Road, Kinsale. www.historicstrollkinsale.com. ℰ**021/477-2873** or 087/250-0731. Admission €6 adults, €1 children. May–Sept Mon–Sat 9:15 and 11:15am; Sun 11:15am. Oct–Apr daily 11:15am.

Kinsale Pottery and Arts Centre ★ STORE This excellent ceramics workshop on the outside of Kinsale sells beautiful, original items of pottery from delicate tea sets and tableware to ornamental masks. The shop is full of surprises, and prices aren't too steep for the quality of what's on offer. A two-floor gallery always has some interesting pieces on display. If you're looking for an alternative way to spend a day or more, the workshop also offers pottery courses where you can learn the basics of the craft and go home with your own creations at the end. Prices start at €75 for a 6½-hour course, including all materials.

Ballinacurra, Kinsale. www.kinsaleceramics.com. ℰ **021/477-2771.** Free admission. Daily 10am–6pm. From Kinsale: From Pearse St., turn left at the junction with the Blue Haven hotel on your right, then follow signs to Bandon and Innishannon. Take this road up the big hill, past Woodlands B&B and the Kinsale GAA sports ground, then look for signs to Kinsale Pottery after about ⅓km (⅕ mile) on the left.

Out from Cork & Kinsale

Further afield from the county's two most visited hubs, the brawny, verdant County Cork countryside is a place of natural beauty—yet many of its most impressive sites are little known outside Ireland. Beauty spots such as Gougane Barra and Mizen Head have a real sense of drama, as do ancient sites such as the Dromberg Stone Circle. Meanwhile, a more recent past can be explored in the bittersweet museum at Cobh— which once was the main point of departure for Irish people emigrating to the New World. And if you don't mind treading a well-beaten path on the tourist trail, County Cork is also home to one of Ireland's most famous attractions: Blarney Castle.

Bantry House ★★ HISTORIC HOME This Georgian house was built around 1750 for the earls of Bantry. It holds furniture and objects d'art from all over Europe, including Aubusson and Gobelin tapestries said to have been made for Marie Antoinette. The gardens, with original statuary, are beautifully kept—climb the steps behind the building for a panoramic view of the house, gardens, and Bantry Bay. There is also an informative exhibition on the ill-fated Spanish Armada, which, led by the Irish rebel Wolfe Tone, attempted to invade the country near Bantry House in 1769. If you really love it, you can spend the night (rooms are €170–€200).

Bantry, Co. Cork. www.bantryhouse.com. ℰ**027/50047.** House and garden €11 adults, €8 seniors and students, €3 children 6–16, children 5 and under free, €26 families. Guided tours €15 (includes general admission). Apr–Oct Tues–Sun and public holiday Mon 10am–5pm.

Blarney Castle ★ CASTLE Though a runaway favorite for the title of "cheesiest tourist attraction in Ireland," Blarney Castle is still an impressive building. Constructed in the late–15th century, it was once much bigger, but the massive square tower is all that remains today. The famous "Blarney Stone" is wedged far enough underneath the battlements to make it uncomfortable to reach, but not far enough that countless tourists don't bend over backward, hang upside down in a parapet, and kiss it in hopes of achieving lifelong loquaciousness. It's customary to tip the attendant who holds your legs (you might want to do it *before* he hangs you over the edge). If you need a break from the masses, the gardens are pretty and much less crowded. Also check out the dungeons penetrating the rock at the base of the castle. You can easily get here by bus, and the number 215 stops about twice an hour (once per hour on Sundays). Ask the driver to let you off at the stop nearest the castle.

Blarney, Cork. www.blarneycastle.ie. ⓒ **021/438-5252.** Admission €12 adults, €10 seniors and students, €5 children 8–14, €30 families. May and Sept Mon–Sat 9am–6:30pm; Sun 9am–5:30pm. June–Aug Mon–Sat 9am–7pm; Sun 9am–5:30pm. Oct–Apr Mon–Sat 9am–5:30pm (or dusk if earlier); Sun 9am–dusk. 8km (5 miles) from Cork City on R617.

Cape Clear Island (Oileán Chléire) ★★ ISLAND

The southernmost inhabited point in Ireland, 13km (8 miles) off the mainland, Cape Clear Island has a permanent population of just a hundred residents. It is a bleak place with a craggy coastline and no trees to break the rush of sea wind, but it's also starkly beautiful—rough, irregular, and graceful. In early summer, wildflowers brighten the landscape, and in October, passerine migrants, some on their way from North America and Siberia, fill the air. Seabirds are abundant during the nesting season, especially from July to September. You can get to the island by ferry (see below) and explore it all at your own pace; alternatively, **Fastnet Tours** (www.fastnettour.com; ⓒ **028/39159**) run a tour up to three times a week. After visiting the island's tiny heritage center, you're taken out for a boat ride around **Fastnet Rock,** a craggy outcrop in the Atlantic. Home to nothing but a weather-beaten lighthouse, Fastnet was traditionally known as "Teardrop Island," not for its shape, but because it was the last piece of Ireland that emigrants saw on their way to America. The tours, which only go ahead in good weather, leave from the pier in Baltimore on Tuesdays, Thursdays, and Sundays at 10, 10:30, and 11, but frustratingly, you can only book online. They cost €32 per person.

Cape Clear Island, Co. Cork. www.oilean-chleire.ie. ⓒ **Ferry: 028/39159** or 41923. Return ferry: £16 adults, €8 children, €40 families. Generally 4 times daily, sometimes less in winter. Schedule may change according to weather.

Cummingeera ★ HISTORIC SITE

Stark and eerie, Cummingeera is an abandoned village near Lauragh at the base of a cliff in a wild, remote valley. The walk to the village gives you a taste for the rough beauty of this mountainous area, and a sense of the extent to which people in pre-famine Ireland would go to find a patch of arable land. To get to the start of the walk, take R571 heading east from the village of Derreen. From this road, take the turning for Glanmore Lake, signposted on the left after approximately 1km (⅔ mile). Then turn right at the road posted for STONE CIRCLE. Continue 2km (1¼ miles) to the point at which the road becomes dirt, and park on the roadside. From here, there is no trail—just walk up the valley to its terminus, about 2km (1¼ miles) away, where the ruins of a village hug the cliff's base. Where the valley is blocked by a headland, take the route around to the left, which is less steep. Return the way you came; the whole walk—4km (2½ miles)—is of moderate difficulty.

Near Lauragh, Co. Cork.

The Donkey Sanctuary ★ SANCTUARY

A real heartbreaker, this one: a charity that rescues abandoned and abused donkeys and nurses them back to health. A few of the beasts of burden here have been voluntarily relinquished by owners who are no longer able to care for them, but the majority have sadder histories. The donkeys live out their days at this quiet and bucolic place, where they receive medical aid and plenty of TLC. Visitors can meet the gentle patients and learn their stories. The

who was MICHAEL COLLINS?

Much of County Cork, and particularly the little town of Clonakilty, seems obsessed with Michael Collins, but when you learn a bit about him, you can understand why. Collins, also known as "the Big Fella," was one of the heroes of the Irish struggle for independence—the commander in chief of the army of the Irish Free State, which under his command won the Republic's independence from Britain in 1921.

Collins was born in 1890 and, along with his seven brothers and sisters, was raised on a farm in Sam's Cross, just outside Clonakilty. He emigrated to England at 15 and, like many other young Irish men, found work in London. In his 20s, he joined the Irish revolutionary group, the Irish Republican Brotherhood (I.R.B.). He first came to fame in 1916 as one of the planners and leaders of the Easter Rising, fighting alongside Patrick Pearse at the General Post Office in Dublin. It may have roused passions among the population, but the Rising was a military disaster, and Collins—young but clever—railed against its amateurism. He was furious about the seizure of prominent buildings—such as the GPO—that were impossible to defend, impossible to

escape from, and difficult to get supplies into.

After the battle, Collins was arrested and sent to an internment camp in Britain, along with hundreds of other rebels. There his stature within the I.R.B. grew, and by the time he was released, he had become one of the leaders of the Republican movement. In 1918, he was elected a member of the British Parliament, but like many other Irish members, refused to go to London, instead announcing that he would sit only in an Irish parliament in Dublin. Most of the rebel Irish MPs (including Eamon de Valera) were arrested by British troops for their actions, but Collins avoided arrest, and later helped de Valera escape from prison. Over the subsequent years, de Valera and Collins worked together to create an Irish state.

After lengthy negotiations and much bloodshed (Collins orchestrated an assassination that essentially wiped out the British Secret Service in Ireland), Collins was sent by de Valera in 1921 to negotiate a treaty with the British government. In the meeting, British Prime Minister David Lloyd George agreed to allow Ireland to become a free republic,

emphasis is on happy endings. Seeing these animals given a new lease on life can be a touching and even quite profound experience for kids.

Liscarroll, nr. Mallow, Co. Cork. www.thedonkeysanctuary.ie. ℂ **022/48398.** Free admission. Mon–Fri 9am–4:30pm; Sat, Sun, and bank holidays 10am–5pm.

Drombeg Stone Circle ★★ HISTORIC SITE   This ring of 13 standing stones is the finest example of a megalithic stone circle in County Cork. The circle dates from 153 B.C., and little is known about its ritual purpose. However, the remains of two huts and a cooking place, just to the west of the circle, give some clue; it is thought that heated stones were placed in a water trough (which can be seen adjacent to the huts), and the hot water was used for cooking. This section has been dated to sometime between A.D. 368 and 608. While you're out this way, consider stopping at the charming little village of **Ballydehob (Béal Átha Dá Chab).** An arty place with an ancient stone bridge and some brightly painted houses, it's one big photo opportunity. Ballydehob is also signposted from R597 between Rosscarbery and Glandore.

Off R597 between Rosscarbery and Glandore, Co. Cork. No phone. Free admission (open site). The turning for Drombeg Stone Circle is signposted just after the sign for Drombeg (if as long as that republic did not include the counties of Ulster (a move designed to appease the Unionists in Northern Ireland). Those largely Protestant counties would remain part of the United Kingdom. Knowing he could not get more at the time and hoping to renegotiate later, Collins reluctantly agreed to sign the treaty, deciding that it was time to stop the bloodshed. (Along with Lloyd George, Winston Churchill, then a government minister, also signed the treaty.) After signing the document, Collins said, "I have just signed my death warrant."

As he'd expected, the plan tore the new Republic apart, dividing the group now known as the IRA into two factions—those who wanted to continue fighting for all of Ireland, and those who favored the treaty. Fighting soon broke out in Dublin, and the civil war was underway.

Collins had learned many lessons from the Easter debacle, and now his strategy was completely different. His soldiers operated as "flying columns," waging a guerrilla war against the enemy—suddenly attacking, and then just as suddenly withdrawing, thus minimizing their losses, and leaving the opposition never knowing what to expect next, but the battle stretched on for 10 months.

In August 1922, Collins was weary of the war and on a peace mission in his home county. After visiting various factions and stopping at a pub near his mother's birthplace, he and his escort were on the road near Béal na Bláth when Collins was shot and killed. Precisely who killed him—whether it was his own men or the opposition—is not known. He had made, on his rapid rise to the top, too many enemies. He was 31 years old.

The **Michael Collins Centre** (www.michaelcollinscentre.com; © **023/884-6107**), located on the farm where he grew up, is a good place to learn more about the man. In addition to an hour-long tour, featuring a film and a visit to actual ambush site, the center runs in-depth, 3½-hour guided trips around the local area. These are probably for Collins devotees only, though, due to the 3½-hour running time. The center is sign-posted off N71, 5.6km (3½ miles) west of Clonakilty. It's open mid-June to mid-September, Mondays to Fridays from 10.30am to 5pm, and Saturdays from 11am to 2pm. Admission is free.

approaching from the direction of Rosscarbery); if approaching from Glandore, it's about 0.5km (⅓ mile) after the whitewashed church in Drombeg village.

Fota Island & Wildlife Park ★★ ZOO If only all zoos were like the Fota Wildlife Park. Most of the animals at this thoughtfully designed park are free to roam without any apparent barriers, mingling with each other and human visitors. Kangaroos, macaws, and lemurs have the run of 16 hectares (40 acres) of grassland; only the cheetahs are behind conventional fencing. If close contact with a menagerie of exotic creatures doesn't delight the kids (unlikely though it sounds), try the small amusement park, tour train, picnic area, or gift shop on-site. The Park's Savannah Café has a view of the meerkat exhibition, so you may find yourself being watched by curious eyes while eating your lunch.

Fota Island, Carrigtwohill. www.fotawildlife.ie. © **021/481-2678.** Admission €14.50 adults; €9.50 seniors, disabled, and children; €44–€56 families. Mon–Sat 10am–6pm; Sun 10:30am–6pm. Last entry 1 hr. before closing.

Gougane Barra ★★ ISLAND One of Ireland's most beautiful spots, Gougane Barra (which means "St. Fin Barre's Cleft") is the name of both a tiny old settlement

point of departure: A DAY IN COBH

If you're a foreigner with an Irish surname, this bustling seaside town could be more important to you than you realize. Cobh (pronounced cove, meaning "haven") used to be called Queenstown, and it was once Ireland's chief port of emigration. During the early–20th century, several transatlantic liners departed from here every week. It was also the last port of call for the RMS *Titanic* before it sank in April 1912. That story is expertly told at **Cobh: the Queenstown Story** (Deepwater Quay; www.cobhheritage.com; ℂ **021/481-3591**). Part of the Cobh Heritage Centre, the exhibition is open Monday to Saturday from 9:30am to 6pm and Sunday and bank holidays from 11am to 6pm.

Defining the Cobh skyline, **St. Colman's Cathedral** (www.cobhcathedral.ie; ℂ **021/481-3222**) is an excellent example of neo-Gothic church architecture. Started in 1868, the cathedral was the country's most expensive religious building of its time. The largest of its 47 bells weighs 3½ tons, and the organ has nearly 2,500 pipes. The interior is vast and ornate, including a beautiful nave and precipitously high chancel arch. It is also a popular venue for concerts and recitals.

A short walk from St. Colman's Cathedral, the **Lusitania Memorial** (Casement Sq.) commemorates the British passenger liner sunk by a German U-boat on May 7, 1915, killing 1,198 passengers, including several victims buried in Cobh cemetery.

And if you want to discover more about Cobh's role in the *Titanic* story, there's an hour-long **walking tour** that takes in a variety of related sites, putting it all into the context of the town's maritime history. In truth, this is more of a general historical tour of the town with just a couple of actual *Titanic* connections, but it's informative nonetheless. The tour departs from the Commodore Hotel, 4 Westbourne Place, at 11am and 2pm daily. (The tour doesn't run from October to March if there are no prebookings.) It costs €9.50 adults, €4.75 children for the 11am tour; €12.50 adults, €6.25 children for the 2pm tour. For bookings, visit www.titanic.ie or call ℂ **021/481-5211.**

and a forest park a little northeast of the Pass of Keimaneigh, 24km (15 miles) northeast of Bantry, and well signposted off R584, about halfway between Macroom and Glengarriff. Its most beautiful feature is a still, dark, romantic lake, which is the source of the River Lee. This is where St. Fin Barre founded a monastery, supposedly on the small island connected by a causeway to the mainland. Though nothing remains of the saint's 6th-century community, the setting is idyllic, with rhododendrons spilling into the still waters where swans glide by. The island now holds an elfin chapel and eight small circular cells dating from the early 1700s, as well as a modern chapel. There are signposted walks and drives through the wooded hills, although you have to pay a small admission charge per car to enter the park.

7km (4½ miles) west of Ballingeary, Co. Cork (signposted off R584).

Ilnacullin (Garinish Island) ★★ ISLAND Officially known as Ilnacullin, but usually referred to as Garinish (or "Garnish"), this little island is a beautiful and tranquil place. It used to be little more than a barren outcrop, whose only distinguishing feature was a Martello tower left over from the Napoleonic Wars. Then, in 1919, the English landscaper Harold Peto was commissioned to create an elaborately planned Italianate garden, with classical pavilions and myriad unusual plants and flowers. The island's unusually mild microclimate allows a number of subtropical plant species to thrive here; indeed, George Bernard Shaw is said to have written *St. Joan* under the shade of its palm trees. The island can be reached for a round-trip fee of around €10 per person (€5 children age 6–15) on a covered ferry operated by **Blue Pool Ferry,** the Blue Pool, Glengarriff (www.bluepoolferry.com; *©* **027/63333**), or **Harbour Queen Ferries,** the Harbour, Glengarriff (www.harbourqueenferry.com; *©* **027/63116**). Boats run back and forth about every 20 minutes. *Note:* The Harbour Queen doesn't take credit cards. The nearest ATMs are in Bantry and Kenmare, Co. Kerry (see p. 125).

Glengarriff, Co. Cork. www.garnishisland.com. *©* **027/63040.** Admission (gardens) €4 adults,€3 seniors, €2 students and children, €10 families. Apr Mon–Sat 10am–5:30pm, Sun 1–6pm; May and Sept Mon–Sat 10am–6pm, Sun noon–6pm; June Mon–Sat 10am–6pm, Sun 11am–6pm; July–Aug Mon–Sat 9:30am–6pm, Sun 11am–6pm; Oct Mon–Sat 10am–4pm, Sun 1–5pm. Last landing 1 hr. before closing.

Mizen Head ★★★ VIEWS   At Mizen Head, the very extreme southwest tip of Ireland, the land falls precipitously into the Atlantic breakers in a procession of spectacular 210m (689-ft.) sea cliffs. You can cross a suspension bridge to an old signal station, now a visitor center, and stand on a rock promontory at the southernmost point of the mainland. The sea view is spectacular, and it's worth a trip regardless of the weather. On wild days, tremendous Atlantic waves assault the cliffs, while on a clear day, dolphins may leap from the waves and seals bask on the rocks. A huge renovation a couple of years ago added new bridges, viewing platforms, and a ship's bridge simulator. On the way out to Mizen Head, you'll pass Barleycove Beach, a gorgeous stretch of sand and rock.

From Cork: Take N71 to Ballydehob, then R592 and R591 to Golleen and follow signs to Mizen Head. www.mizenhead.ie. *©* **028/35115** or **35225.** Admission €6 adults, €4.50 seniors and students, €3.50 children 6–11, children under 5 free, €18 families. Mid-Mar–May, Sept, and Oct daily 10:30am–5pm. June–Aug daily 10am–6pm. Nov–mid-Mar Sat–Sun 11am–4pm.

COUNTY KERRY

7

With its softly rolling green fields, sweeping seascapes, and vibrant little towns, it's easy to see why so many visitors make a beeline for County Kerry. Charming villages like colorful Kenmare and bustling historic towns like Killarney seem as familiar as the Irish folk songs written about them. Craggy mountain ranges punctuated by peaceful green valleys are just what you hope for when you come to Ireland. Unfortunately, this idyllic beauty cuts both ways: This is extremely well-trodden territory, and up to a couple of million tourists flock here every year. With that in mind, the height of summer can be the worst time to visit—ideally, you want to hit these hills in the late spring or autumn. However, even at the busiest times, there's an antidote. Should you find that the crowded roads on the Ring of Kerry are getting to you, simply turn off onto a small country lane, and within seconds, you'll find yourself virtually alone in the peaceful Irish countryside.

ESSENTIALS

Arriving

BY BUS **Bus Éireann** (www.buseireann.ie; ✆ **064/663-0011**) operates regularly scheduled service into Killarney and Dingle from all parts of Ireland.

BY TRAIN Trains from Dublin, Cork, and Galway arrive daily at the Killarney Railway Station (www.irishrail.ie; ✆ **064/663-1067**), Railway Road, off East Avenue Road. There are no train stations in Kenmare or Dingle.

BY CAR Unless you join an organized tour (see p. 125), a car is the only feasible way to get around the Ring of Kerry. Getting to Killarney from Cork is easy—just head northeast out of the city on N22; the distance is about 85km (53 miles). To get to Killarney from Dublin, take M7 southwest to Limerick and then N21; the journey is about 310km (193 miles). Kenmare and Killarney are connected by the main N71 Ring of Kerry Road; they're only 33km (20½ miles) apart, but allow plenty of time due to the winding nature of the road (and, in summer, tour-bus traffic). To hire a car in Killarney, try **Budget** on Kenmare Place (www.budget.ie; ✆ **064/663-4341**) or **Enterprise** on Upper Park Road (www.enterprise.ie; ✆ **066/711-9304**).

BY PLANE **Aer Lingus** (www.aerlingus.com; ✆ **081/836-5000**) has two flights per day from Dublin into the miniscule Kerry County Airport, Farranfore, County Kerry (www.kerryairport.ie; ✆ **066/976-4644**), about 16km (10 miles) north of Killarney. Flights from London's Luton

Airport are operated by **Ryanair** (www.ryanair.com; ℂ **0871/246-0000** in the U.K. or ℂ 1520/444-004).

Organized Tours

If you're not confident in renting a car and driving yourself around the Ring of Kerry, a plethora of companies will take you to see the major sights on organized bus tours. Most depart from **Killarney**, the most popular base for exploring the Ring (see p. 136). Prices vary enormously according to what you choose, but expect to pay somewhere in the region of €20 to €40 per person.

Two recommended operators are **Corcoran's Chauffeur Tours,** 8 College St. (www.corcorantours.com; ℂ **064/663-6666**); and **Dero's Tours,** 22 Main St. (www.derostours.com; ℂ **064/663-1251** or 663-1567). Both run full-day tours of the Ring of Kerry, and tours to Dingle and the Slea Head Peninsula, in addition to a variety of tours centered around Killarney National Park. The downside, of course, is that you may not have enough time to see everything properly.

[FastFACTS] COUNTY KERRY

ATMs/Banks In Killarney, a branch of Allied Irish Banks (**AIB**) is at 25 Main St. ((ℂ **064/663-1047**). In Kenmare, try **Bank of Ireland** in the Square (ℂ **064/664-1255**). On Main St. in Dingle is a **Bank of Ireland** (ℂ **066/915-1100**) and an **AIB** (ℂ **066/915-1400**).

Dentists For dental emergencies, your hotel should contact a dentist for you; otherwise, in Killarney, try the **Torc View Dental Surgery,** Park Rd., Killarney (ℂ **066/662-6999**); in Kenmare, try **Con O'Leary,** the Square (ℂ **064/664-2621**); in Dingle, try **Bryan Long,** Main St. Upper (ℂ **066/915-1527**).

Doctors For medical emergencies, dial ℂ **999.**

For nonemergencies, your hotel should call you a doctor. Otherwise, in Killarney, try the **Killarney Medical Centre** at 47 New St. (ℂ **064/662-0628**); in Kenmare, **The Medical Centre** on Railway Rd. (ℂ **064/664-1514**); and in Dingle, try the **Dingle Medical Centre** (ℂ **066/915-2225**).

Emergencies For police, fire, or other emergencies, dial ℂ **999.**

Internet Access O'Sheas on Main St., Kenmare (ℂ **064/664-0808**) has a small Internet cafe; in Dingle, try **The Old Forge Internet Café** on Holyground (ℂ **066/915-0523**).

Pharmacies In Killarney, try **O'Sullivan's Pharmacy,**

81 New St. (ℂ **064/663-5886**); in Kenmare, try **Brosnan** on Henry St. (ℂ **064/664-1318**); in Dingle, try **O'Keefe** on Strand St. (ℂ **066/915-1310**).

Post Office In Killarney, the main post office is on New St. (ℂ **064/663-1461**); in Kenmare, it's on Henry St. (ℂ **064/664-1490**); and in Dingle, it's on Main St. (ℂ **066/915-1661**).

Taxis In Killarney, taxis line up at the rank on **College Square** (ℂ **064/663-1331**). You can also phone **Killarney Cabs** (ℂ **064/663-7444**) or **Kerry Autocabs** (ℂ **087/296-3636**). In Kenmare, try the **Kenmare Taxi Service** (ℂ **087/614-7222**). In Dingle, try **Dial-a-Cab** (ℂ **087/222-2248**).

WHERE TO STAY

As the main tourist hub of County Kerry, it should come as no surprise that it's in and around Killarney where you'll find the greatest choice of accommodations. However, if you have the freedom of a car, consider nearby Kenmare as an alternative base. It's quieter and just as convenient for exploring the Ring of Kerry. A little farther afield, Dingle has some delightful B&Bs and small hotels.

Where to Stay in Killarney

Aghadoe Heights ★★★ This seductive retreat just north of Killarney is worth the splurge; luxurious and welcoming, it's one of the best spas in Ireland. The large guest rooms are decorated in soothing tones of white, gray, and oatmeal. Beds are extremely comfortable and bathrooms impeccably modern. It's worth spending a little extra to get a room at the front to appreciate the stunning views of the Lower Lake in Killarney National Park. There is a huge list of treatments in the opulent, futuristic spa (they even have a "precious stone chamber" for the more exotic-sounding options), and the thermal suite is full of high-tech touches such as showers infused with refreshing essential oils. On-site are two excellent restaurants and a bar overlooking the lake.

Aghadoe, Killarney, Co. Kerry. www.aghadoeheights.com. © **064/663-1766.** 74 units. €150–€330. Free parking. Rates include breakfast. Spa and dinner, bed and breakfast packages available. **Amenities:** Wi-Fi, restaurants (2), bar, pool, spa, room service. Head north out of Killarney on N22; Aghadoe Heights is signposted about 2.7km (1 mile) after the second of the two roundabouts on the north side of the town center (just after the turn for Birch Hill).

Cahernane House ★★★ A neo-Gothic mansion on the outskirts of Killarney National Park, Cahernane was once home to the Earls of Pembroke, and it's still evocative of bygone days. The public areas, in particular, have the feel of an old gentlemen's club filled with antique furniture, stag heads on the wall, and roaring fires in the open grates. Guest rooms are more modern, though no less elegant, and some bathrooms come with deep claw-foot tubs. Many rooms have private patios. Cahernane has two restaurants: the excellent, formal **Herbert Room,** and the more relaxed **Cellar Bar,** where you can take lighter meals under the carved arches of the old wine cellar. Fields and farmland surround the hotel, and the misty mountains of the park linger in the distance. Dinner, bed and breakfast packages start at around €115 per person.

Muckross Rd., Killarney. www.cahernane.com. © **064/663-1895.** 38 units. €130–€194. Free parking. Rates include breakfast. **Amenities:** Restaurant, bar, room service.

Earls Court House ★★ Just outside the center of Killarney, on a quiet street with views of the mountains, Earls Court House is a pleasingly old-fashioned B&B. Guest rooms are simple but elegant, featuring polished wood furniture and buttermilk-colored walls. A few have canopy or four-poster beds. Flatscreen TVs mounted to the walls add a touch of modern convenience. You can take afternoon tea in one of the two guest lounges (included in the price of your room), and light suppers are served until early evening. The excellent, varied breakfasts include fresh, home-baked bread and pastries. Check the website for special offers.

Woodlawn Rd., Killarney. www.killarney-earlscourt.ie. © **064/663-4009.** 24 units. €100–€140. Free parking. Rates include breakfast. 2-night minimum on some summer weekends. **Amenities:** Wi-Fi (free), guest lounges, library.

Friars Glen ★★★ Nestled in the cleft of a lush and verdant glen inside Killarney National Park, this delightful B&B could hardly be friendlier or better run. Hosts John and Mary (and their two dogs) welcome guests like old friends; they really enjoy what they do and take pride in helping visitors plan their explorations of the park and the Ring of Kerry. They will even organize tours on your behalf and can provide babysitting in the evenings with a bit of notice. The building itself looks like an old farmhouse (exposed stone, woodsy feel), but it is actually recently built. Guest rooms are cozy and simple, boasting knotted wood furniture and decent-size bathrooms. The views of the surrounding glen are inspiring. Breakfast is served until a very civilized 10am. Dinner isn't offered, but the place is only a short drive

County Kerry

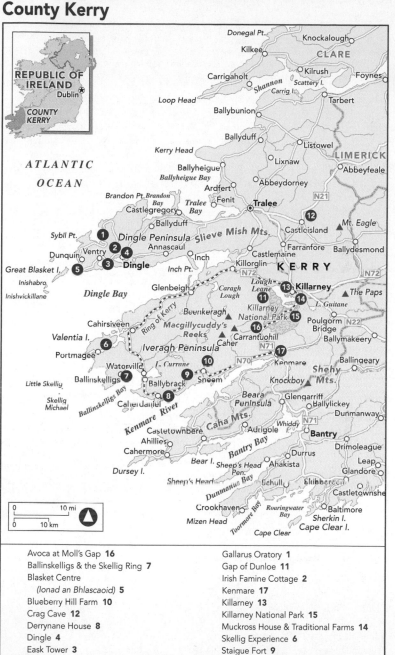

Avoca at Moll's Gap **16**
Ballinskelligs & the Skellig Ring **7**
Blasket Centre
  (Ionad an Bhlascaoid) **5**
Blueberry Hill Farm **10**
Crag Cave **12**
Derrynane House **8**
Dingle **4**
Eask Tower **3**

Gallarus Oratory **1**
Gap of Dunloe **11**
Irish Famine Cottage **2**
Kenmare **17**
Killarney **13**
Killarney National Park **15**
Muckross House & Traditional Farms **14**
Skellig Experience **6**
Staigue Fort **9**

from Killarney, and Molly Darcy's pub (see listing later in this chapter) is within walking distance.

Mangerton Rd., Muckross, Killarney. www.friarsglen.ie. ℂ 064/663-7500. 10 units. €100–€110. Free parking. Rates include breakfast. **Amenities:** Wi-Fi (free). Head south from Killarney on N71 for about 4km (2½ miles), then turn left immediately after Molly Darcy's pub. The turn for Friar's Glen is on the right, immediately after the Muckross Garden Centre. (From Kenmare, take N71 toward Killarney and then take a right immediately before Molly Darcy's pub.)

Larkinley Lodge ★★   A swell option just a few blocks from the center of Killarney, Larkinley Lodge is a stylish, modern B&B in a converted town house. Guest rooms are spotlessly clean with muted, neutral color schemes and excellent orthopedic beds. Toni and Danny Sheehan are gregarious owners whose warm personalities shine through. Breakfasts are traditional and top-notch. The location is only about a 10-minute walk or less into central Killarney, not far from pubs and restaurants. However, it's in a quiet neighborhood, so you can easily escape the evening street noise that can sometimes be a problem in this lively town.

Lewis Rd., Killarney. www.larkinley.com. ℂ 064/663-5142. 6 units. €80–€90. Free parking. Rates include breakfast. **Amenities:** Wi-Fi (free).

Where to Stay in Kenmare

Sallyport House ★★   This peaceful 1930s mansion-turned-B&B in Kenmare is an extremely good value for the money. It's filled to the brim with interesting antiques, lending a touch of old-school luxury to its already traditional charms. (Thanks to a wealthy industrialist ancestor, there's a story behind the presence of most of them.) Guest rooms are comfortable and spacious. A few have intricately carved antique four-poster beds. The house is surrounded by verdant countryside, and some rooms look out over an idyllic lake. Breakfasts are delicious, and the service is warm and accommodating without ever being intrusive.

Shelbourne St., Kenmare (just south of junction with Pier Rd.). www.sallyporthouse.com. ℂ 064/664-2066. 5 units. €110–€130. Free parking. Breakfast included. **Amenities:** Wi-Fi (free).

Sea Shore Farm ★★   A modern house overlooking Kenmare Bay and the mountains beyond, this is a special place to stay. Big floor-to-ceiling windows take full advantage of the magnificent surroundings. The guest rooms are large (very large in some cases) and tastefully furnished. The guest lounge has a library of travel books, though you may find yourself too distracted by the views to concentrate. Kenmare is a short drive away or just a captivating, 15-minute walk through the countryside—the better to work off those indulgent breakfasts. Hosts Mary and Owen make everything run smoothly and are always full of helpful suggestions for things to do. They have an encyclopedic knowledge of the local area.

Sea Shore, Tubrid, Kenmare. www.seashorekenmare.com. ℂ 064/664-1270. 5 units. €90–€120. Free parking. Breakfast included. **Amenities:** Wi-Fi (free).

Shelburne Lodge ★★   This cozy 18th-century house has quite a storied history. It was originally the country home of William Petty, the Lord Shelburne (1737–1805), a Dublin-born landowner who was responsible for building much of the modern town of Kenmare. He later became Prime Minister of Great Britain and Ireland, and he signed the Treaty of Paris that formally ended the American War of Independence in 1783 and brought peace between Britain and the U.S. His home is in good hands nowadays, thanks to wonderful hosts Tom and Maura Foley. Rooms have an old-fashioned air with color schemes of yellow and peach, antique furniture, and huge beds. Public

Killarney

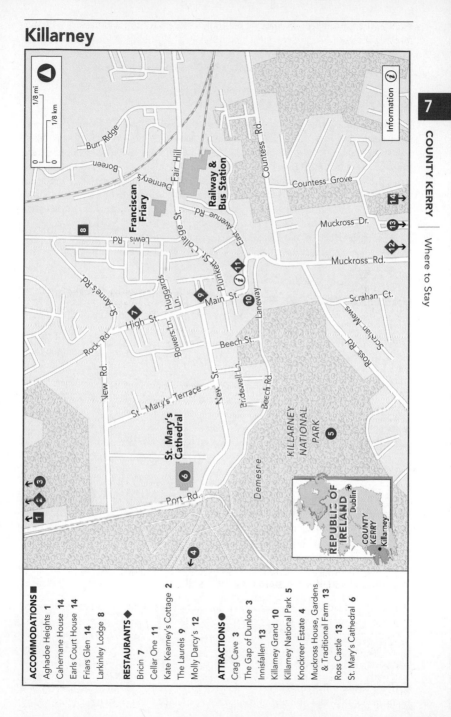

Information ⓘ

ACCOMMODATIONS ■
Aghadoe Heights **1**
Cahernane House **14**
Earls Court House **14**
Friars Glen **14**
Larkinley Lodge **8**

RESTAURANTS ◆
Bricin **7**
Cellar One **11**
Kate Kearney's Cottage **2**
The Laurels **9**
Molly Darcy's **12**

ATTRACTIONS ●
Crag Cave **3**
The Gap of Dunloe **3**
Innisfallen **13**
Killarney Grand **10**
Killarney National Park **5**
Knockreer Estate **4**
Muckross House, Gardens
& Traditional Farm **13**
Ross Castle **13**
St. Mary's Cathedral **6**

areas have a similar feel, like the guest sitting room, so packed with handsome furniture that it's like walking through an antique shop. There's a manicured lawn out back, and the center of Kenmare is only a short walk away.

Cork Rd., Kenmare. www.shelburnelodge.com. ℭ **064/664-1013.** 9 units. €100–€160. Free parking. Breakfast included. **Amenities:** Wi-Fi (free).

Where to Stay in Dingle

Castlewood House ★★★   Overlooking the glassy expanse of Dingle Bay, this handsome, whitewashed house is filled with art and antique knickknacks. The location is just breathtaking; views of the shimmering water, framed by distant mountains, are fully exploited by the huge bay windows, flooding the bright guest rooms with natural light. Beds are unusually comfortable, and accommodations are heavy on designer furniture and well-chosen art. Bathrooms have Jacuzzi tubs. Breakfasts are outstanding— porridge with a dash of whiskey, homemade breads, oranges in caramel, kippers with scrambled eggs, or even a light and fluffy omelet with smoked salmon. Husband-and-wife team Brian and Helen Woods-Heaton are expert and charming hosts. Despite the delightfully rural feel to the location, Dingle Marina is only about a 10-minute walk away.

The Wood, Dingle. www.castlewooddingle.com. ℭ **066/915-2788.** 14 units. €138–€160. Free parking. Rates include breakfast. **Amenities:** Wi-Fi (free).

Greenmount House ★★★   A welcoming B&B overlooking Dingle Bay, Greenmount House is one of the best places to stay in the area. The view from the front is like a cliché of what you might imagine all of Ireland to be like; rolling green slopes falling gently into the sea at Dingle Bay with the streets of quaint Dingle Town curving around the coastline below. The public areas are arranged at the front as much as possible so that you can admire the view from the guest lounge or breakfast room. The garden has an enclosed hot tub where you can savor a glass of wine. Guest rooms are bright and spacious; some have polished wood floors and others have skylights, letting the daylight pour in. Breakfasts are delicious and plentiful (a fave: tasty smoked salmon and scrambled eggs). Hosts Mary and John are incredibly friendly and will even arrange personal tours of the area for you, escorted by a member of their own family.

Upper John St., Dingle. www.greenmounthouse.ie. ℭ **066/915-1414.** 14 units. €100–€150. Free parking. Rates include breakfast. **Amenities:** Wi-Fi (free).

Where to Stay in the Rest of County Kerry

Ballygarry House ★★   On the outer edge of the otherwise unlovely Tralee, this pleasant country inn is surrounded by gardens. Built as a manor house in the 18th century, plenty of the original features have been retained, even though the facilities are thoroughly modern. Elegant guest rooms maintain the country mansion air; superior rooms are surprisingly spacious, with king-size beds. Family rooms are an excellent value at (usually) the same price as doubles. The in-house spa is a relaxing, revitalizing hideaway (as is the outdoor hot tub). Special inclusive spa offers change monthly—massage, facial, and access to the spa facilities for around €100 is the kind of deal you can expect. The **Brooks** restaurant serves top-quality, modern Irish food.

Signposted off N21, Leebrook, approx. 3.3km (2 miles) west of central Tralee. www.ballygarry house.com. ℭ **066/712-3322.** 46 units. €114–€172. Free parking. Rates include breakfast. **Amenities:** Wi-Fi (free), spa, restaurant, bar.

Coffey River's Edge ★★   A bright, cheery building overlooking the River Laune in the center of Killorglin, one of the main stops on the Ring of Kerry, Coffey's is an exceptional value for the money. Owners Finbarr and Anne are congenial hosts, and nothing seems like too much trouble to make their guests feel at ease. Rooms are decently sized with large beds and contemporary wood furniture. Breakfasts are served in the dining room overlooking the river and a picturesque stone bridge, and a large guest balcony and deck outside. No evening meal is on offer, but the rest of pretty Killorglin is just a short, leisurely stroll away. Finbarr and Anne are both keen golfers and will happily arrange a game for you at a local course.

The Bridge, Killorglin. www.coffeysriversedge.com. © **066/976-1750.** 11 units. €53–€65. Free parking. Breakfast included in rates. **Amenities:** Wi-Fi (free).

Derrynane Hotel ★   The view from this place is striking—perched on a promontory overlooking Kenmare Bay, guests look out across a dramatic coastal inlet streaked with tiny green islands and a smattering of pleasure boats cruising around the coast. It's also a savvy pick for families, as standard rooms that actually sleep up to three go for the same cost as doubles; and there's a small outdoor pool (along with a sauna and seaweed bath treatment center). That's the good news. As for the accommodations: they have few frills. Some are nicely designed, if rather spartan, and others could do with an upgrade (so ask to switch if you're not pleased). A small herb garden on the grounds provides ingredients for the in-house restaurant. *Tip:* Package deals are available, including "Golden Breaks," with special discounts for seniors.

Signposted from N70 Ring of Kerry Rd., Caherdaniel. www.derrynane.com. © **066/947-5136.** 70 units. €72-€108. Free parking. Breakfast not included in lower rates. **Amenities:** Restaurant, bar, room service, swimming pool, gym, treatment room.

Iskeroon ★★★   In an eye-poppingly beautiful setting on the Ring of Kerry, looking out across the Derrynane coast and out to the Skellig Islands, this bed and breakfast is a serene and special place to stay. Built in the 1930s, the house isn't large, but this merely adds to the feeling of special care and attention you experience from the moment you walk through the door. The two suites, with stone floors, king-size beds, handmade furniture, and well-chosen pieces of art, have been expertly renovated. Fresh ingredients are provided for breakfast, but you prepare it yourself in the little kitchenette that comes with your suite, as there's no better location to enjoy a leisurely breakfast than your balcony overlooking the sea. The only downside is the 3-night minimum stay, but it hardly feels like a negative once you're here. The former coach house on the grounds is rented out as a full self-catering accommodation for €400-€450 per week (depending on the time of year).

Bunavalla (halfway between Waterville and Caherdaniel). www.iskeroon.com. © **066/947-5119.** 2 units. €100. Free parking. Breakfast included. 3-night minimum stay. **Amenities:** Wi-Fi, DVD player and DVD library, kitchenette. At the Scariff Inn, follow signs for Bunavalla Pier, then follow signs to Iskeroon near the bottom of the hill.

QC's ★★   More of a restaurant-with-rooms than a small hotel, QC's is nonetheless a stylish place to stay. Accommodations are open-plan spaces with a minimalist vibe and feature polished wood floors, huge skylights, and claw-foot tubs next to the bed. High-tech extras include Bose stereos. The guest lounge looks like it's tumbled from the pages of a magazine, featuring deep velvet sofas and a cozy wood-burning stove. The downstairs **restaurant** is superb and specializes in fresh seafood. They take pride in local flavors cooked to perfection, such as roast hake with samphire and lemon risotto or local meats served with seasonal vegetables and delicious sauces.

Main St., Cahersiveen. www.qcbar.com. © **066/947-2244.** 5 units. €80-€112. Free parking. Breakfast included. **Amenities:** Wi-Fi.

WHERE TO EAT

Though relatively light on standout, first-class restaurants, Kerry has a wide variety of options—including great pubs and family-friendly eateries. Kenmare and Killarney take the lion's share of the best places, but the countryside has some enticing surprises. Dingle is one of the best places in Ireland for gourmet seafood, not to mention its more low-rent (but delicious) cousin, fish and chips.

Where to Eat in Killarney

Bricin ★★ IRISH   Rather incongruously located above a craft shop, this is a long-standing favorite of the Killarney dining scene. Plates often feature locally raised meat, usually served with intriguing sauces—rack of roast lamb with Madeira and rosemary sauce, for example, or steak with brandy, bourbon, and pepper. However, it's the house specialty for which this place is renowned: boxty, a classic pancake stuffed with several different types of filling. The dining room is an old-fashioned type of space, complete with stained-glass windows and an open fireplace. There are two early-bird menus (€19 for two courses) served until 6:30pm.

26 High St., Killarney. www.bricin.com. ✆ **064/663-4902.** Fixed-price menus €19–€35. Tues–Sat 6–9pm. Closed Mon. Closed early Jan–early Mar.

Cellar One ★★ MODERN EUROPEAN   The decor of this basement dining room elicits strong emotions: Some see it as a wry, colorful design statement, others consider it garishly camp. The food, however, is not controversial, it's just delish, a successful fusion of a number of influences from Europe, Asia, North Africa, and even Latin America. You might opt for some spicy chickpea cakes to start, followed by tiger prawns prepared in chili, garlic, and tequila, or maybe some crab-encrusted cod with wilted spinach in a coconut and ginger sauce. Desserts go a more traditional route with choices like chocolate pudding or the wonderfully named "knickerbocker glory"—a retro-style ice cream sundae served with fruit, chocolate brownies, and meringue. Service is excellent.

At The Ross Hotel, Church Lane, Killarney. www.theross.ie. ✆ **064/663-1855.** €19–€28. Daily noon–9:30pm.

Kate Kearney's Cottage ★ INTERNATIONAL   Unofficially considered the gateway to the Gap of Dunloe, this cheerful pub is a little touristy (there's even an in-house souvenir shop—a dead giveaway). But the atmosphere is upbeat, and the traditional—and filling—pub food is pretty tasty. Think steaks, ribs, burgers, and bistro-style classics, all washed down with a restorative pint. In summer there's a full "Traditional Irish Night" every Wednesday, Friday, and Sunday. Dinner is accompanied by a show of live music and Irish dancing. The pub is named after a feisty local woman who carved out a reputation as a maker of illegal potcheen (moonshine) that she called Mountain Dew.

Gap of Dunloe, Gap of Dunloe, signposted from N72 (Ring of Kerry Rd.), Beaufort, Killarney. www. katekearneyscottage.com. ✆ **064/664-4146.** €12–€17. Daily noon–11pm (food 6:30–9:30pm).

The Laurels ★ INTERNATIONAL   The menu at this busy pub in the center of Killarney is a mix of bistro dishes and more populist fare. Starters include deep-fried brie with red currant sauce and chicken wings, while mains range from a generous steak served with peppercorn sauce to a tureen of white wine–poached mussels with citrus cream sauce. They also serve stone-baked pizzas, made fresh to order—none of this menu business, you just choose the toppings you want. The lunch offerings are much simpler, consisting of "doorstop" (very thick-cut) sandwiches, burgers, salads, and the like. In summer there are lively music sessions several times a week.

Main St., Killarney. www.thelaurelspub.com. ℂ **064/663-1149.** €14–€29. Mon–Thurs 10:30am–11:30pm; Fri–Sat 10:30am–12:30am; Sun 12:30–11pm. (Food served until about 9:30pm.)

Molly Darcy's ★ IRISH Set on the outskirts of Killarney National Park, Molly Darcy's manages to retain its festive vibe despite being quite touristy (don't come here looking for much in the way of authenticity). That said, the interior has a rustic charm to it, and the service is kindly. The menu sticks to traditional pub food—fish and chips, catch of the day, homemade pies, lamb stew—though the house burger served with mozzarella, rocket (arugula), and basil shakes things up a bit. Vegetarians are catered to with almost as many options as the meat and fish dishes. From July to September there is a show of live music and Irish dancing every night except Sunday and Monday; during October, the show is on Tuesdays and Thursdays.

At the Muckross Park Hotel, Muckross Rd., Killarney. www.mollydarcy.ie. ℂ **064/662-3400.** €14–€24. Daily noon–11pm (food 6:30 to about 9:30pm).

Where to Eat in Kenmare

The Boathouse ★ BISTRO/SEAFOOD This pleasant seafood bistro at Dromquinna Manor has an outside seating area overlooking Kenmare Bay. The menu serves dishes like creamy seafood chowder or local crab claws served with ginger, lime, and coriander butter. Or you could just have a cheeseburger served with sea-salted french fries and take in the wonderful view. This is a good stop for lunch on a sunny day, especially when the weather's fine and you can sit outside.

On N70, 5km (3 miles) west of Kenmare. www.dromquinnamanor.com. ℂ **064/664-2889.** €11–€30. May–June and Sept–Oct Thurs–Sun 12:30–9pm; Jul–Aug daily 12:30–9pm.

The Lime Tree ★★★ MODERN IRISH An outstanding restaurant housed in a historic building, the Lime Tree has been one of the area's go-to fine dining establishments since 1985. The modern Irish menu is sophisticated without being overly complicated. You'll find plenty of locally sourced ingredients and plates such as rack of Kerry lamb served with a mini shepherd's pie (a traditional dish made with minced lamb and mashed potatoes) and garlic confit. The free-range duck breast is accompanied by a zingy rhubarb and ginger chutney. Desserts consist of upscale comfort food: a rich terrine of white and dark chocolate with black currant sorbet or a classic crème brûlée. The wine list is unsurprisingly excellent, but surprisingly filled with plenty of very affordable choices.

Shelbourne St., Kenmare. www.limetreerestaurant.com. ℂ **064/664-1225.** €19–€27. Thurs–Mon 6–9pm. No children after 8:30pm.

Ocean Blue Seafood Bar ★★ FISH & CHIPS This fish-and-chip shop in Kenmare is one of the best fast-food restaurants in the region. There's nothing fancy, but that's the point; it's all about perfectly made, crispy fish and chips. Choose from fresh wild cod, plaice, hake, or whiting, all battered and served with chunky chips (thick fries). There are a couple of more unusual options like tempura-battered crab and a small menu of Chinese dishes, but it's the classics that keep the locals coming back.

Main St., Kenmare. ℂ **085/139-6121.** €7–€18. Daily noon to around 11pm.

Packie's ★★ IRISH One of the best and most durable restaurants in Kenmare, Packie's has been a favorite in this town for years. The candlelit dining room is atmospheric, and the crowd is as much local as visitors. It's easy to understand why—the food is unpretentious but delicious, and uses a bounty of local ingredients. Think steak, lamb, or perhaps super-fresh seafood, all simply prepared but melt-in-your-mouth tasty. Desserts are worth adding an extra notch to your belt for. The reasonably priced wine list does the job and offers plenty of choices available by the glass.

Henry St., Kenmare. www.kenmarerestaurants.com/packies. ℂ **064/664-1508.** €16–€30. Tues–Sat 6–10pm. Closed Mon. Closed Feb.

Purple Heather ★ IRISH   This sweet little place in Kenmare is simple and cozy. Its popularity with locals speaks to its authenticity. There's a bar at the front where you can sit with a leisurely pint, but at lunchtime, venture toward the back to sample the menu of tasty snacks like salads, hearty sandwiches, fluffy omelets, homemade soups, and bowls of chowder. It's nothing complicated, but it's all well done, with a cordial, unpretentious atmosphere to boot.

Henry St., Kenmare. ℂ **064/664-1016.** €7–€18. Mon–Sat 11am–5:30pm.

Where to Eat in Dingle

The Chart House ★★ IRISH   Almost everything on the menu here is sourced from providers within the Dingle peninsula. That's one of the reasons the Chart House, a friendly restaurant on the outskirts of Dingle, remains one of the region's most popular eateries. Yes, the menu is short, but it's impeccably curated, and often, quite creative. Dishes include mussels served with lemongrass and coconut broth, beef filet with colcannon (a traditional Irish dish made with potato and cabbage), and duck with juniper gravy. *Tip:* The early-bird deal has almost as much choice as the evening service and costs €32.50 for three courses.

The Mall, Dingle. www.thecharthousedingle.com. ℂ **066/915-2255.** €19–€28. Daily 6–10pm. Times may vary in winter. Closed Jan–mid-Feb.

Doyle's Seafood Bar ★★★ SEAFOOD   This is one of the best places in Dingle to go for seafood. Period. It's not cheap, but the food is beautifully prepared. As you'd expect, what you find on the menu will depend on the local catch of the day; however, specialties often reappear, including fish stew made with white wine and saffron, turbot with red pepper and chive sauce, and black sole with a lemon and parsley butter. Carnivores are catered to with simple steaks and lamb dishes—expertly cooked, but hardly the reason why people flock here. The wine list is extensive, and the early-bird menu is served until 7:30pm (€28 for three courses).

4 John St., Dingle. www.doylesofdingle.ie. ℂ **066/915-2674.** €20–€35. Mon–Sat 5–9:30pm.

Reel Dingle Fish ★★ FISH & CHIPS   My favorite "chipper" in Dingle, everything's cooked the traditional way here: fish in batter, with piping-hot chips, and no messing around. But there's a greater-than-average choice of fresh fish to choose from, including hake, monkfish, pollock, and locally smoked haddock. They also sell homemade burgers crafted from local beef.

Bridge St., Dingle. ℂ **066/915-1713.** €5–€12. Daily noon to around 11pm.

Where to Eat in the Rest of County Kerry

The Blind Piper ★ IRISH   This friendly and lively pub is one of the top places to eat in Caherdaniel. The high-quality bar menu strikes a nice balance between straightforward traditional pub grub and something a little more sophisticated. Think Guinness stew with fresh soda bread, fish and chips, excellent hamburgers, and Thai fish cakes. The charming staff makes you feel right at home, and in summer the bar is often enlivened by live traditional music sessions. The Blind Piper is a bit hard to find, partly because it doesn't have a proper street address. Take the main N70 road through Caherdaniel, and then take the turn next to the big red building in the center of the village. (There's usually a handmade sign here pointing you in the right direction.) The pub is painted bright yellow.

Off main Ring of Kerry Rd. (N70), Caherdaniel. www.blindpiperpub.com. *ℂ* **066/947-5126.** €11–€22. Daily about 11am–midnight; food served Mon–Thurs, noon–4pm; Fri–Sun noon–8pm.

The Blue Bull ★ IRISH   This great little pub in tiny, picturesque Sneem doesn't deviate too far from Irish pub classics, but it does them all very well—fish and chips, mussels in garlic sauce, steaks, sandwiches, and salads. The crowd, a good mix of hungry tourists and easy-going locals settling down at the bar, makes for a congenial atmosphere. It's a great spot for standing at the bar, eavesdropping on a few conversations, and possibly being asked your opinion about the topic of the day.

South Sq., Sneem. *ℂ* **066/947-5126.** €6–€20. Mon–Sat 11am–around midnight; Sun noon–11pm (food until about 9pm).

Jack's Coastguard Restaurant ★★★ SEAFOOD/MODERN IRISH   This cheery restaurant lists "Water's Edge" as its address. That's not so much a name as a description; it's right on the harbor in Cromane, a tiny village near Killorglin. The dining room is a bright, modern space with stellar views of the bay; adding to the atmosphere, a pianist plays in the corner. The menu strikes elegant notes, too, with choices like hake filet with an almond and herb crust and turbot with a side of potatoes, prepared with raisins and orange. Meat dishes are kept more simple, such as lamb with potatoes boiled in sea salt topped with rosemary jus. The restaurant is attached to a popular local pub.

Water's Edge, Cromane Lower, Killorglin. www.jackscromane.com. *ℂ* **066/976-9102.** €17–€32. May–Sept Wed–Mon noon–9pm; Oct Wed–Sun noon–9pm; Nov–Dec Thurs–Sun noon–9pm; Feb–Apr Thurs–Sun noon–9pm. Closed Jan.

Nick's Restaurant and Piano Bar ★★ SEAFOOD/IRISH   The Rat Pack feel to this restaurant's name says everything about its old-school credentials. Nick's is quite famous in Ireland—it's been here since 1978—and while you won't find cutting-edge cuisine, it's still deserving of its reputation as one of the better places to eat along the Ring of Kerry. There are two dining areas: a formal restaurant and a bar, where a simpler (and less expensive) selection is served in more relaxed surroundings. On the main menu you'll find several catches of the day (naturally), grilled sole, shellfish mornay, or a classic seafood platter. It's not all about the fruits of the sea, though, and you can also order steaks, lamb, and a chicken supreme with whiskey cream sauce. The bar menu is more of the fish and chips or steak sandwich variety, but it's still good. Everything is served to the gentle melodies of a live piano accompaniment. Just the same as it ever was.

Lower Bridge St., Killorglin. www.nicks.ie. *ℂ* **066/976-1219.** €20–€34. Wed–Sun 5:30–10pm.

Smuggler's Inn ★ SEAFOOD/IRISH   Overlooking the beach in Waterville, the menu here, appropriately enough, is mostly seafood caught fresh from Ballinskelligs Bay; think oysters, black sole, and seafood chowder. The conservatory dining room has lovely views of the bay, or you can sit outside and take in the full glory of it all. The Smuggler's Inn also does bed-and-breakfast accommodations for around €70–€110 per night.

Cliff Rd., Waterville. www.the-smugglers-inn.com. *ℂ* **066/947-4330.** €15–€30. Daily noon–3pm and 6–9pm. No children after 8pm. Closed Nov–Easter.

TAKING A (moon) shine TO POTCHEEN

"Keep your eyes well peeled today, the excise men are on their way, searching for the mountain tay, in the hills of Connemara . . . "

—From "The Hills of Connemara"

Potcheen is a potent form of Irish moonshine, traditionally brewed from grain or potatoes. It was banned by the English crown in 1661, an act that effectively criminalized thousands of distillers overnight. Unsurprisingly, that didn't stop people from making the stuff, and after 336 years on the wrong side of the law, potcheen was finally made legal again in 1997.

One 17th-century writer said of potcheen that "it enlighteneth ye heart, casts off melancholy, keeps back old age and breaketh ye wind." Its usefulness didn't stop there, evidently, as history records the drink being used as everything from a bath tonic to a substitute for dynamite.

Potcheen has long been used in fiction as a symbol of Irish nationalism, its contraband status rich with rebellious overtones. The traditional folk song "The Hills of Connemara" describes potcheen being secretly distributed under the noses of excise men.

In 2008, the European Union awarded the drink "Geographical Indicative" protection. This means that only the genuine Irish product is allowed to carry the name (the same status enjoyed by champagne and Parma ham).

You'll find potcheen for sale in a few souvenir stores. Like most liquors it can be drunk straight, on the rocks, or with a mixer, but at anything from 80 to a massive 180 proof, potcheen packs a mean punch, so enjoy . . . cautiously.

EXPLORING COUNTY KERRY

The Ring of Kerry is the name for the small highway that skirts the edges of the Iveragh Peninsula. It is both the actual name of the road—or, if you want to be pedantic, a section of the N70, N71, and N72 highways—and the collective name given to the many attractions in the area. Nearly all of County Kerry's most popular sights are either on or within a short distance of the Ring.

At the western end of county, the less-visited **Dingle Peninsula** also has much to offer. To call it "undiscovered" would be too generous—in the summer Dingle Town is packed with travelers—but it's not as ruthlessly jammed as the Ring of Kerry, and, from time to time, even in the high season, you can find yourself blissfully alone amid its natural beauty.

Tourism Offices

The **Killarney Tourist Office** is on Beech Road, Killarney (www.killarney.ie; (C) **064/663-1633**). The **Kenmare Tourist Office** is at the Kenmare Heritage Centre, Market Square, Kenmare (www.kenmare.ie; (C) **064/664-1233**). The The **Dingle Tourist Office** is on the Quay, Dingle (www.dingle-peninsula.ie; (C) **066/915-1188**). All three stay open year-round.

The Ring of Kerry

Undoubtedly Ireland's most popular scenic route, the Ring of Kerry winds its way along a panorama of rugged coastline, tall mountains, pristine lakes, and beautiful small towns and villages. What you won't find, at least in the summertime, is much in

killarney NATIONAL PARK

A bucolic refuge with breathtaking scenery just steps from the fracas of Killarney, this national park is the essential stop along the Ring. If peace and quiet is what you seek, you could skip the Ring altogether and spend the whole day here. Cars are banned from most of the ferny trails, so take a hike or hire a "jarvey," or "jaunting car"—an old-fashioned horse-and-buggy available at not-too-steep prices. The drivers congregate behind the visitor center at Muckross House (see below).

Within the park's limits are two estates, **Muckross** and **Knockreer** (p. 139), along with the romantic remains of medieval abbeys and castles. At almost every turn, you'll see Killarney's own botanical wonder, the arbutus, or "strawberry tree," plus eucalyptus, redwoods, and native oak.

For many, the main attractions are the park's three lakes. The largest of these, the **Lower Lake,** is sometimes called Lough Leane or Lough Lein, translated as "the lake of learning." It's more than 6km (3¾ miles) long and is dotted with 30 small islands. The most celebrated of Killarney's islands, **Innisfallen** (see listing below), seems to float peacefully in the Lower Lake. Nearby is the Middle Lake, also called Muckross Lake, and the smallest of the three, the Upper Lake.

The main visitor center for the park is at **Muckross House** (✆ **064/663-1440**) and is clearly signposted from the main Ring of Kerry Road (N71), a couple of miles south of Killarney. Drop by here to pick up maps and other information about the park to explore the many walking trails (see p. 140). The visitor center is open daily from 9am–5:30pm; hours may vary in winter.

For more information on the park, visit **www.killarneynationalpark.ie.**

the way of peace. Bicyclists avoid the route because of the scores of tour buses thundering down it from early morning until late in the day. Most people traveling the route start and finish at its largest hub, **Killarney,** but the town of **Kenmare** makes for a more charming (and certainly more quiet) base. You can drive either way along the Ring of Kerry, but a counterclockwise route gives you the most spectacular views. Very large vehicles are always meant to travel this way to avoid accidents and nasty traffic jams around the Ring's perilously narrow bends.

Top Attractions in Killarney

The 18th-century sidewalks of western Ireland's busiest tourist town are spacious and pleasant in winter, when the resident population of 7,000 goes about its business. But in summer, this all changes and the streets overflow with visitors. Nonetheless, Killarney—with its good restaurants, pubs, hotels in every price range, and outstanding traditional music scene—is a convenient base for exploring Killarney National Park. Amid the wilds, lakes, and mountains of this extraordinarily beautiful nature reserve, it's easy to forget the noise and haste of commercialized civilization.

Gap of Dunloe ★★ BYWAY   A narrow pass between the Purple Mountains and the fabulously named mountain range, MacGillycuddy's Reeks, the winding Gap of Dunloe rises through mountains and wetlands on the western side of Killarney National Park. The route through the gap passes craggy hills, meandering streams, and deep gullies, and it ends in the park at the Upper Lake. Some of the roads can be difficult around here, so many people choose to explore by bicycle (try **Killarney Rent-a-Bike,** Lower New Street, Killarney (www.killarneyrentabike.com; ✆ **064/663-1282**)

WHAT'S IN A name: MACGILLYCUDDY'S REEKS

This marvelously named range of mountains just west of Killarney is beautiful to look at—they were formed by red sandstone that was gradually shaved down by glaciers until they reached the gentle shape they hold today. The name, though, is a bit baffling. It turns out the mountains were named after an ancient clan that once predominated in this area—the Mac Gilla Machudas. The word "reek" is an old Irish term for a peaked hill. So these are the mountains of the Mac Gilla Machudas, just in case you were wondering.

or by "jarvey" (see the box on p. 137). These can be booked at the National Park Visitor Centre at Muckross House (see listing below) or from **Killarney Jaunting Cars,** Muckross Close (www.killarneyjauntingcars.ie; ✆ **064/663-3358**).

Signposted from N72 (Ring of Kerry Rd.), Killarney.

Innisfallen ★★ ISLAND   Shrouded in forest, this small island appears to float peacefully in the Lower Lake. Behind the trees is what's left of a monastery that was founded in the 7th century and flourished for 1,000 years. It's thought that Brian Boru, the great Irish chieftain, and St. Brendan the Navigator were educated here. From 950 to 1320, the "Annals of Innisfallen," a chronicle of early Irish history, was written at the monastery. You can reach Innisfallen by rowboat, available for rental at Ross Castle (see listing below).

Lower Lake, opposite Ross Castle, Ross Rd., (signposted from N71, Ring of Kerry Rd.), Killarney.

Killarney Grand ★ PUB/LIVE MUSIC   This hugely popular pub in Killarney—officially known as Sheehan's Bar, although the signs out front say both—is one of the best places in the region to hear traditional Irish music. There are lively sessions nightly at 9pm; after 11pm it turns into a nightclub. The atmosphere gets pretty raucous, and the crowds can really pack in here (definitely standing room only), but the music is always good. Some of the biggest names in Irish music have played here over the years, and you never know when you might catch the next big thing. A "neat" dress code is enforced at the door. In other words, you don't have to wear your best duds, but don't be too scruffy, either.

Main St., Killarney. www.killarneygrand.com. ✆ **064/663-1159.** Admission free until 11pm; price varies after that, according to who's playing. Mon–Sat 7:30pm–2:30am; Sun 7:30pm–1:30am.

Killarney Lakes Cruise ★ TOUR   From the harbor at Ross Castle (see listing below), the **MV Pride of the Lake** takes you on a waterborne tour that lasts about an hour. The covered boat ride is a little on the touristy side—and very popular, so you might want to make reservations—but the views of the park from the lake are gorgeous. You can also take a tour that combines a lake cruise with a "jaunting car" ride around the park. *Note:* You can get to the pier by Ross Castle on a free shuttle bus from Killarney town center. It leaves Scotts Street (by the junction with East Avenue Road) a quarter of an hour before each sailing.

The Pier, Ross Castle, Ross Rd., off N71 (Ring of Kerry Rd.), Killarney. www.killarneylaketours.ie. ✆ **064/662-7737.** €14 adults, €8 children 11 and under. Apr–Oct sailings 11am, 12:30pm, 2:30pm, 4pm, and 5:15pm. Times may change according to weather.

Knockreer Estate ★ GARDENS The grand old house that once stood here burned down in the early–20th century. There's a modern building of the same name on the same site that serves as the park's education center, but the lovely old gardens of the estate still exist. Here 200-year-old trees mix with sweet wildflowers and azaleas to fragrant effect. A signposted walk takes you past beautiful views of the Lower Lake and the valley; a pathway leads down to the River Deenagh. Main access to Knockreer is through Deenagh Lodge Gate, opposite the cathedral.

Main entrance near St. Mary's Cathedral on Cathedral Place, off New St., Killarney. Free admission.

Muckross House & Gardens ★★ HISTORIC HOME This elegant, neo-Gothic Victorian house at the entrance to Killarney National Park was built in 1843. The rooms are presented much as they would have been in the mid–19th century, from the grand, *Downton Abbey*–like formal dining room to the stark contrast of the Victorian kitchens and servants' quarters below the stairs. The landscaped gardens are beautiful and a riot of color in high summer. The pleasant cafe, overlooking some manicured flower beds, is a lovely spot to linger. There's also a traditional weavers and craft shop on the grounds. The ruin of the 15th-century **Muckross Abbey,** founded about 1448 and burned by Cromwell's troops in 1652, is also near the house. The abbey's central feature is a vaulted cloister around a courtyard that contains a huge yew tree, thought to be as old as the abbey itself. William Makepeace Thackeray once called it "the prettiest little bijou of a ruined abbey ever seen."

On N71 (Ring of Kerry Rd.), 6km (3.6 miles) south of Killarney. www.muckross-house.ie. © **064/667-0144.** Admission €7.50 adults, €6 seniors, €4 students and children, €22 families. Joint ticket with Muckross Traditional Farms: €12.50 adults, €10.50 seniors, €7 students and children, €35 families. Sept–Jun daily 9am–5:30pm; Jul–Aug daily 9am–7pm.

Muckross Traditional Farms ★★ LIVING HISTORY PARK Not far from the Muckross House estate, these farms are designed to demonstrate traditional life as it was in previous centuries in County Kerry. It's cleverly done—the farmhouses and barns are authentically detailed, and work really does go on here. Farmhands work the fields, while the blacksmith, carpenter, and wheelwright ply their trades. Women draw water from the wells and cook meals in historically accurate kitchens. There's also a petting zoo where kids can get to handle some of the animals. A coach constantly circles the grounds, ferrying those with mobility problems between the different areas of the farm. *Note:* A combination ticket allows you to visit Muckross House & Gardens for a small extra fee.

Kenmare Rd. (N71), Killarney, County Kerry. www.muckross-house.ie. © **064/663-0804.** Admission €7.50 adults, €6 seniors, €4 students and children, €22 families. Joint ticket with Muckross House & Gardens: €12.50 adults, €10.50 seniors, €7 students and children, €35 families. Mar–Apr and Oct weekends and bank holidays 1–6pm; May and Sept daily 1–6pm; Jun–Aug daily 10am–6pm. Closed Nov–Apr.

Ross Castle ★ CASTLE Just outside Killarney Town, this 15th-century fortress still guards the edge of the Lower Lake. Built by the O'Donoghue chieftains, the castle was the last stronghold in Munster to surrender to Cromwell's forces in 1652. But it could not withstand time as well as the English army, and all that remains today is a tower house surrounded by a fortified *bawn* (walled garden) with rounded turrets. The tower has been furnished in the style of the late–16th and early–17th centuries. While you can wander the grounds at will, you can only see inside the castle on a guided tour. The tours tend to be a bit tedious, as the guides seem to scrounge around a bit for facts

walk this way: THE TRAILS OF KILLARNEY NATIONAL PARK

Cars are banned on most of Killarney National Park's walking trails, where the ground is a soft carpet of moss and the air is fragrant with wildflowers. Here are some of the best walking trails. Trail maps are available at the Muckross House visitor center.

Blue Pool Nature Trail: This trail starts behind the Muckross Park Hotel and winds for a relaxing 2.3km (1.5 miles) along a path of coniferous woodland beside a small lake. The trail is named for the lake's unusually deep blue-green color, a result of copper deposits in the soil.

Cloghereen Nature Trail: Incorporated into a small section of the Blue Pool trail (see above), this walk is fully accessible to blind visitors. A guide rope leads you along the route, lined by plants identifiable by scent and touch. An audio guide is available from the Muckross House visitor center for a small deposit.

Mossy Woods Nature Trail: One of the park's gentler trails, this route starts from Muckross Lake and runs just under 2km (1.3 miles). The moss-covered trees and rocks it passes are a major habitat for bird life. You'll also see several strawberry trees (*Arbutus*), something of a botanical mystery, along the route. They're commonplace around these parts but found almost nowhere else in Northern Europe. The route offers some incredible views of the Torc Mountains and the memorably named MacGillycuddy's Reeks.

Serious hikers might be interested in the **Kerry Way,** a long-distance trail that roughly follows the Ring of Kerry. Ireland's longest marked hiking trail, the 202km (126-mile) route follows several "green roads" (old, unused roads built as make-work famine relief projects and now converted into walking paths). For more information, see **www.kerryway.com.**

interesting enough to justify the ticket price. In good weather, the best way to reach it is via a lakeside walk—it's 3km (2 miles) from Killarney to the castle. From the castle, you can take boat tours of the lake (see p. 138).

Ross Rd., signposted from N71 (Ring of Kerry Rd.), Killarney. www.heritageireland.ie. © **064/663-5851.** €4 adults, €3 seniors, €2 students and children, €10 families. Mid-Mar–Oct daily 9:30am–5:45pm. Last admission 45 min. before closing. No photography.

St. Mary's Cathedral ★ CHURCH

If you think this limestone cathedral looks more Castle Dracula than parish church, it may be because New Street was once the home of Bram Stoker. He spent summers in Killarney while he was a student at Trinity College. Officially known as the Catholic Church of St. Mary of the Assumption, it's designed in the Gothic Revival style and laid out in the shape of a cross. Construction began in 1842, was interrupted by the famine, and finally concluded in 1855 (although the towering spire wasn't added until 1912).

Cathedral Place, off New St., Killarney. © **064/663-1014.** Free admission. Daily 10:30am–6pm.

Torc Mountain Walk ★★ HIKE

Rising steeply from the south shore of Muckross Lake, Torc Mountain provides spectacular views of the Killarney Lakes and nearby MacGillycuddy's Reeks, a moody mountain range. Start at the Torc Waterfall parking lot, about 6km (3¾ miles) south of Killarney, and follow the trail to the top of the falls. At a T-intersection, turn left toward the top parking lot, then almost immediately turn right onto Old Kenmare Road, following a small stream along the south slopes of Torc Mountain. After leaving the woods, you'll see Torc Mountain on your right. Look for a crescent-shaped gouge in the side of the road, about 9m (30 ft.) across, with a small cairn at its far edge. This is the beginning of the path to the ridge top, marked somewhat erratically by cairns. Return the way you came; the whole moderately difficult trip is just under 10km (6 miles) and takes about 4 hours.

In Killarney National Park. Start at Torc Waterfall parking lot, about 6km (3¾ miles) south of Killarney on N71 (Ring of Kerry Rd.). Also accessible on 4.5km (2.8-mile) looped walking trail from Muckross House.

Top Attractions in Kenmare

Originally called *Neidin* (pronounced Nay-deen, meaning "little nest" in Irish), Kenmare is indeed a little nest of verdant foliage and colorful buildings nestled between the River Roughty and Kenmare Bay. It's an enchanting little place with flower boxes at every window, sparkling clean sidewalks, and great little shops.

Avoca at Moll's Gap ★ SHOP   Creative, colorful, and with what must be one of the world's best-appointed parking lots, this branch of Avoca is on a mountain pass just off the main Ring of Kerry Road, north of Kenmare. Though quite small, it sells a good selection of the crafts, knitwear, and upscale knickknacks for which the Wicklow-based company is famous. (See p. 81 for a review of their flagship department store in Dublin.) The cafe upstairs is also a swell pit stop for a light lunch or restorative cup of tea and slice of cake.

Moll's Gap (on R568, signposted from main N71 Ring of Kerry Rd.), Kenmare. www.avoca.ie. ℰ 064/663-4720. Mid-Mar–mid-Nov weekdays 9:30am–5:30pm; Sat–Sun and public holidays 10am–6pm. Cafe closes 5pm.

De Barra Jewellery ★ SHOP   Young jewelry designer Shane de Barra runs this exquisite little boutique in the center of Kenmare. His creations in gold and other precious materials have a unique, subtle beauty. He has an especially deft touch with freshwater pearls that he forms into lovely necklaces strung together with tiny threads of gold. Prices aren't too high, considering the quality. A true original.

Main St., Kenmare. ℰ 064/664-1867. Mon–Sat 9:30am–6pm.

Kenmare Druid Circle ★ HISTORIC SITE   On a small hill near the market square (see below), this large Bronze Age druid stone circle is magnificently intact, featuring 15 standing stones arranged around a central boulder that still bears signs (circular holes, a shallow dent at the center) of having been used in ceremonies. To find it, walk down to the market square and follow signs on the left side of the road. There's no visitor center, and no admission fee; it's just sitting in a small paddock, passed by the traffic of everyday life.

Off the Square, Kenmare.

Kenmare Farmer's Market ★ MARKET   If you're visiting midweek, be sure to check out this small but lively open-air market held every Wednesday in Kenmare's main square. The emphasis is on food from small, artisan producers from across the region and beyond. You'll also find rustic crafts. Traders can come here from quite far afield to sell their wares, although the bulk of what's on offer is locally sourced. It's a fun and lively market to browse your way through the stalls.

The Square, Kenmare. Wed 10am–5pm. Some stalls may close in bad weather.

Seafari ★★ TOUR   This is a good option for families who want to interest their kids in Kenmare Bay—aboard a 15m (49-ft.) covered boat. The 2-hour cruise covers 16km

ALL'S fair IN KENMARE ON AUGUST 15TH

One day of the year Kenmare is no less overrun with visitors than Killarney: August 15, **Fair Day.** This is a working agricultural market, and the streets are taken over by farmers selling all manner of livestock, while a small army of onlookers descends on the town to witness the picturesque congregation. Stalls and other amusements provide fresh food, souvenirs, and even fortune-telling.

(10 miles) and features guides well versed in local history and wildlife such as dolphins, sea otters, and gray seals frolicking nearby. Boats depart from the pier next to the Kenmare suspension bridge. The family ticket includes coffee, tea, cookies, lollipops for the kids, and a drink of rum for the grown-ups. They'll also lend you a pair of binoculars if you need one. Live entertainment sometimes follows you on board, from kid-friendly puppet shows to traditional Irish music. Reservations recommended.

3 The Pier, Kenmare. www.seafariireland.com. ℂ **064/664-2059.** €20 adults, €17.50 students, €15 teenagers, €12.50 children 11 and under then €7.50 per extra child, €60 families. Apr–Oct, 2 sailings daily; call or check website for departure times.

Quills Woollen Market ★ MARKET   This long-standing business is housed in a delightfully multicolored row of shops in the center of Kenmare. They specialize in traditional Irish knitwear—particularly heavy-knit Aran sweaters, coats, and cardigans. They also sell Irish tweeds, shawls, linens, and various pieces of home goods like plush sheepskin rugs. It's a great place to stock up on authentic souvenirs. There are other branches of Quills in Killarney, Glengarriff, Ballingeary, and Sneem.

Main St., Kenmare. www.irishgiftsandsweaters.com. ℂ **064/664-1078.** Mon–Sat 9:30am–5:30pm.

The Rest of the Ring of Kerry

The next major stop on the Ring north of Killarney, **Killorglin** is a smallish town that lights up in mid-August when it has a traditional horse, sheep, and cattle fair (see box later in this chapter).

Continue on N70, and glimpses of Dingle Bay will soon appear on your right. **Carrantuohill,** Ireland's tallest mountain at 1,041m (3,414 ft.), is to your left, while bleak views of open bog land fill the rest of the landscape. The Ring winds around cliffs and the edges of mountains with nothing but the sea below—another reason you will probably average only 50kmph (31 mph) at best. As you continue, you'll notice the remnants of many stone cottages dotting the fields along the way. Most date from the mid-19th-century Great Famine, when millions of people starved to death or were forced to emigrate. This area was particularly hard hit, and the peninsula alone lost three-quarters of its population.

Glenbeigh is next on the Ring, and it's a cozy seafront town with streets lined with palm trees and a sandy beach. It makes a good spot for a break, or you can continue along the sea's edge to **Cahersiveen,** where you can zip across to the little island of **Valentia.** In the 18th century, the Valentia harbor was notorious as a refuge for smugglers and privateers.

From Valentia you can hop a ferry to arguably the most magical site of the Ring of Kerry, an island just off its shore called **Skellig Michael.** This rocky pinnacle towering over the sea is where medieval monks built a monastery in exquisite isolation (see box below).

Head next for **Waterville,** an idyllic beach resort located between Lough Currane and Ballinskelligs Bay. For years it was a favorite retreat of Charlie Chaplin (1889–1977), and there's a statue of him near the beach.

If you follow the sea road north of town to the Irish-speaking village of **Ballinskelligs,** you'll see where the medieval monastery is slowly rotting away. There's a sandy Blue Flag beach just past the post office by Ballinskelligs Bay, and at the end of the beach are the remnants of a 16th-century castle.

Continuing on N70, the next point of interest is **Derrynane,** at **Caherdaniel.** Derrynane is the former seat of the O'Connell clan and erstwhile home to Daniel O'Connell ("the Great Liberator" who freed Irish Catholics from the last of the English Penal Laws in the 19th century). From there, watch for signs to **Staigue Fort,** a 3,000-year-old stone fort.

Sneem, the next village on the circuit, is a colorful little hamlet boasting houses painted in vibrant shades. The colors—blue, pink, yellow, and orange—burst out on a rainy day like a little touch of the Mediterranean. From here, you're almost back to your starting point, and you've made your way around the Ring.

Top Attractions

The following points of interest are listed alphabetically, though all are on, or within easy reach of, the route described above.

Ballinskelligs and the Skellig Ring ★★ HISTORIC SITE   West of Waterville, across a small bay, the coastal village of **Ballinskelligs** contains the absurdly picturesque ruins of St. Michael Ballinskelligs, a medieval priory overlooking the sea. A sandy beach also features the remnants of a 16th-century castle. Ballinskelligs is a starting point for the so-called **Skellig Ring,** a stunning coastal drive that takes in some of the best views of the mysterious Skellig Islands (see below). It also passes through some of the most spectacular scenery in the county, and with the merest fraction of the traffic that can clog the Ring of Kerry. However, be warned: Its very remoteness means this route can be tough going, and the roads are very mountainous in places. This is also the edge of Gaeltacht territory, where Irish is the primary language on road signs. To find the Ring, head south through Ballinskelligs. About 0.5km (⅓ mile) after the pink An Post building, you'll come to a crossroads. The Skellig Ring (*Morchuaird na Sceilge* in Gaelic) is signposted to the right. The signs continue throughout the route.

Visitor Information Point: Barbara's Beach Café, Ballinskelligs Beach, Ballinskelligs, Co. **Kerry. Tourist Office:** Cahersiveen Community Centre, Church St., Cahersiveen, Co. Kerry. www.visit ballinskelligs.ie. (C) **066/947-2589** (Cahersiveen, summer only).

Blueberry Hill Farm ★★ FARM   A good way to amuse younger children for half a day, this working farm still does as much as possible according to traditional methods. As part of the half-day tours, you can help milk cows, make butter, and take part in a treasure hunt. Children get to interact with the animals and even help out at feeding time. There's also a cafe selling tasty homemade scones and other treats. The whole experience is very friendly, authentic, and can be quite delightful for the little ones. Full-day courses in such skills as basket making, blacksmithing, food preserving, and beekeeping are available for adults.

Signposted from R568 (Sneem-Killarney Rd.,) Sneem. www.blueberryhillfarm.ie. (C) **086/356-1150** or 086/316-0224. €15 adults and children, €60 families. Tours start at 10am and 3pm.

Crag Cave ★★ CAVES   Although they are believed to be more than a million years old, these limestone caves were not discovered until 1983. Today, they're open

GREAT, mysterious WONDER: A TRIP TO THE SKELLIG ISLANDS

"Whoever has not stood in the grave-yard on the summit of that cliff, among the beehive dwellings and beehive ora-tory, does not know Ireland through and through . . . "
—George Bernard Shaw

The craggy, inhospitable Skellig Islands rise precipitously from the sea. Here gray skies meet stormy horizons about 14km (8 miles) off the coast of the Iveragh Peninsula. From the mainland, Skellig Michael and Little Skellig appear impossibly sharp-angled and daunting even today, even though the mere act of getting there isn't perilous, as it was in the 6th and 7th centuries. Back then a group of monks built a community on the steepest, most wind-battered peaks. Over time, they carved 600 steps into the cliffs and built monastic buildings hundreds of feet above the ocean. The complex is now a UNESCO World Heritage Site.

Landing is only possible on **Skellig Michael,** the largest of the islands. There is something tragic and beautiful about the remains of the ancient oratories and beehive cells there. Historians know very little about these monks and how they lived, although they obviously sought intense isolation. Records relating to the Skelligs indicate that even here, all but completely hidden, the Vikings found the monastery and punished it as they did all the Irish monastic settlements. Monks were kidnapped and killed in attacks in the 8th century, but the settlement always recovered. To this day, nobody knows why the monks finally abandoned the rock in the 12th century.

Start your exploration at the **Skellig Experience** (www.skelligexperience.com; ✆ **066/947-6306**) on Valentia Island, which is reached via road bridge in Port-magee. The well-designed visitor center

tells you all about the extraordinary his-tory of these ancient edifices and also offers boat trips out to see the islands. It's open May, June, and September, daily from 10am to 6pm, and until 7pm in July and August; in March, April, October, and November it's open on weekdays only from 10am–5pm. Last entry is 45 minutes before closing. Admission costs €5 adults, €4 seniors and students, €3 children, and €14 families.

If you add a cruise to see the Skelligs, the cost is €27.50 adults, €24.50 seniors and students, €14.50 children, and €71.50 families—but note that, at pres-ent, the visitor center's own boat trips only cruise *around* the Skelligs, and **do not make landfall.** If you want to see the ruins on Skellig Michael up close, you have to go with one of the many independent boat operators who work the route. There is a list of endorsed skippers in the "Local Information" sec-tion of the Skellig Experience website. If you use **Des Lavelle** (✆ **086/947-6124** or 087/237-1017) or **Eoin Walsh** (✆ **066/947-6327** or 087/283-3522), the fee includes entry to the visitor center. They both charge around €50 per person. Whichever provider you use, you should check that the boat is in good condition and that you're confident in their safety procedures (for example, the provision of life jackets). The crossing is beautiful in calm seas but can quickly become very rough if the weather turns.

There are also "unofficial" ways of reaching the islands, although they're very much at your own risk. For a negoti-ated fee, you can almost always find a fisherman who's willing to take you over, wait, and then bring you back. The cross-ing will be rougher, but certainly more adventurous.

KILLORGLIN: THE puck STOPS HERE

The first major stop on the Ring of Kerry northward from Killarney, **Killorglin** is a sleepy little town—until August 10, at least, when the annual **Puck Fair** (www. puckfair.ie) incites a 3-day explosion of merrymaking and pageantry.

One of Ireland's last remaining traditional fairs, it's technically an agricultural show; the apex of the event involves capturing a mountain goat (which symbolizes the *puka* or *puki*, a mischievous Celtic sprite) that is then declared *King Puck* and paraded around town on a throne, wearing a crown. It's bonkers but quite a lot of fun.

Nobody knows how the fair began, but one story dates it to Cromwell's invasion of Ireland in the mid–17th century. English soldiers were foraging for food in the hills above the town and tried to capture a herd of goats. One escaped to Killorglin and alerted the villagers to mount a defense. Others say the fair is pre-Christian, connected with the Pagan feast of Lughnasa on August 1.

For the rest of the year, Killorglin is a pretty, quiet town, well worth a wander. The River Laune runs straight through the town center. As you cross the old stone bridge, look out for the whimsical statue of the goat on the eastern side—and know that it stands in honor of this town's love for the *puka*.

---

for the wandering (via guided tour only, of course). The guides accompany you 3,753m (12,310 ft.) into the well-lit cave passage on a 40-minute tour revealing massive stalactites and fascinating caverns. If you simply can't do without a souvenir fix, even here there's a crafts shop. There is also a children's play area (endearingly called **"Crazy Cave"**), although it costs extra. The Garden Restaurant is a useful stop for lunch if you need a quick bite. It's very touristy but interesting nonetheless. On the same site is the **Kingdom Falconry** center, where you can watch birds of prey fly and be guided by handlers.

College Rd., Castleisland. www.cragcave.com. © **066/714-1244. Caves:** €12 adults, €9 seniors and students, €5 children, €30–€35 families. **Kingdom Falconry:** €8 adults, seniors, and students; €5 children. **Crazy Cave:** €8 children (accompanying adults free). **Combination tickets:** €20 adults, €17 seniors and students, €18 children (includes Crazy Cave). Apr–Dec daily 10am–6pm; Jan–Mar Fri–Sun 10am–6pm. Tour times: May–Aug, every half hour; Jan Apr and Sept–Dec 10:45am, noon, 2:30, 4, and 5:30pm.

Derrynane House National Historic Park ★★ MUSEUM   Daniel O'Connell (1775–1847) was an Irish political leader and member of Parliament, who became known as "the Great Liberator" for his successful campaign to repeal the laws that barred Catholics from holding office. He became particularly famous in his lifetime for his so-called "monster meetings," vast public rallies held across the country (one, on the Hill of Tara, was reckoned to have been attended by nearly a million supporters). His house, at Caherdaniel, is open to the public. It contains a museum devoted to his life featuring various artifacts and items from his personal archives. Not everything will be of interest to those who aren't already familiar with his story, but a few pieces—such as the gilded carriage from which he triumphantly greeted crowds after a brief spell as a political prisoner—are definitely worth seeing. The vast grounds are a scenic spot to wander through.

Signposted from N70 (Ring of Kerry Rd.), approx. 2.5km (1.5 miles) from Caherdaniel. www. heritageireland.ie. © **066/947-5113.** Admission €3 adults, €2 seniors, €1 students and children,

€8 families. Apr and Oct–mid-Nov Wed–Sun and public holidays 10:30am–5pm; May–mid-Sept daily 10:30am–6pm. Last admission 45 min. before closing.

Staigue Fort ★★ HISTORIC SITE   This well-preserved, surprisingly large, pre-historic fort is built of rough stones without mortar of any kind. The walls are 4m (13 ft.) thick at the base. Historians are not certain what purpose it served—it may have been a fortress or just a kind of prehistoric community center—but experts think it probably dates from around 1000 B.C. It's an open site with no visitor center; just this ancient structure, alone and open to the elements in the middle of a farmer's field.

4 km (2½ miles) off N70 just outside Castlecove on a small farm road (follow signs).

The Dingle Peninsula

A quieter, shorter alternative to the Ring of Kerry, the Dingle Peninsula loop is an exhilarating, sometimes vertigo-inducing drive full of heart-stopping dips and breath-taking panoramas (acrophobes should avoid the R561 coast road between Milltown and Annascaul). The peninsula's main town, **Dingle (*An Daingean*)**, is a brightly colored place at the foot of steep hills and on the edge of a gorgeous stretch of coast. There's not much to do here, but it makes a good base for exploring the region. The town's most famous resident is a dolphin that adopted the place years ago and has been bringing in animal-loving tourists ever since.

Exploring Dingle Town

Brian de Staic Jewellery Workshop ★ SHOP   Brian is a highly respected jewelry designer who has built up quite a following since he first appeared on the scene over 30 years ago. He specializes in modern interpretations of ancient Celtic motifs, and you'll find everything from pendants and brooches to earrings, bracelets, and crosses. Some of his work is based on instantly recognizable designs; others are more subtle and abstract. It's all exquisite quality.

Green St., Dingle. www.briandestaic.com. ⟨⟩ **066 915-1298.** Mon–Sat 9am–5:30pm.

Dingle Dolphin Boat Tours ★★ TOUR   The story of Fungie the Dingle Dol-phin is strange and heartwarming. The bottlenose dolphin was first spotted by Dingle's lighthouse-keeper in 1983 as he escorted fishing boats out to sea and then back again at the end of their voyages, day after day. The sailors named the dolphin, and he became a harbor fixture. Fishermen took their children out to swim with him, and he seemed to love human contact. Now people come from miles around to have a few minutes' time with Fungie, and the fishermen ferry them out to meet him. Trips last about 60 minutes and depart roughly every 2 hours in low season and as often as every half-hour in high season. Fungie swims right up to the boats that stay out long enough to afford views of the picturesque bay. You pay at the end, and there's no charge if he doesn't show. However, while the little fella is still merrily packing in the crowds at the time of this writing, nobody quite knows how old Fungie is. So before you get the little ones too excited, you might want to call ahead . . . discreetly.

The Pier, Dingle. www.dingledolphin.com. ⟨⟩ **066/915-2626**. Tour starts at €16 adults, €8 children 11 and under. Daily 11:30am–4pm, weather permitting.

Eask Tower ★ VIEWS   Built in 1847 as a famine-relief project, this is a remark-able edifice, a 12m (39-ft.) tower built of solid stone nearly 5m (16-ft.) thick with a wooden arrow pointing to the mouth of the harbor. It is certainly interesting to look at, but the main reason for making the 1.6km (1-mile) climb to the summit of Carhoo Hill

THE slea head DRIVE

When leaving Dingle by car, head west along R559 and you'll encounter the **Slea Head Drive,** a spectacular stretch of road known for its collection of ancient sites—including the **Gallarus Oratory** (see listing below), one of the best-preserved pieces of early Christian architecture in Ireland. At any tourist information center, you can get a guide to the various ruined abbeys and old forts along the way. **Note:** This is serious Gaeltacht territory, so by law, all signs—even road hazard signs—are in Gaelic only.

is not to see the tower, but the incredible views of Dingle Harbour, Connor Pass, and, on the far side of the bay, the peaks of the Iveragh Peninsula. This is a great place to get your bearings, but save a trip here for a clear day.

Carhoo Hill, Dingle. From Dingle, follow Slea Head Rd. 3.2km (2 miles), turn left at road signposted for Coláiste Ide, and continue another 3.2km (2 miles).

Louis Mulchay Workshop ★ POTTERY Now a big name in designer Irish pottery, Louis Mulchay has been making interesting creations from his seaside studio since the 1970s. He still designs everything on sale and personally crafts a great deal of the pieces—chances are you'll be able to come away with a true original. It's all beautifully made, from Deco-influenced vases to kitchenware, tea sets, and ornaments. Considering what a name he is, Louis's prices are pretty reasonable, too. The workshop also has a handy cafe (open daily until 5pm).

On R559, Clogher, Ballyferriter, near Dingle. www.louismulcahy.com. © **066/915-6229.** Workshop: May–Sept Mon–Fri 9am–7pm, Sat–Sun 10am–7pm; Oct–Feb, Mon–Fri 9am–5:30pm, Sat–Sun 10am–5:30pm; Mar and Apr Mon–Fri 9am–6pm, Sat–Sun 10am–6pm. Clogher is 16.5km (10½ miles) northwest of Dingle on R559.

The Rest of the Dingle Peninsula

The Blasket Islands ★★ ISLANDS Overshadowed by the more famous Skelligs (see box earlier in this chapter), the Blaskets are another group of mysterious, abandoned islands off the Kerry coast, but with a more recent story to tell. For hundreds of years these were home to an isolated community with a rich tradition of storytelling and folklore that was well documented in the late 1800s. In the 1950s, however, the Irish government ordered a mandatory evacuation when the islands were considered too dangerous for habitation. You can visit the largest of the islands, **Great Blasket,** where a few crumbling buildings and skeletal edifices remain. The main attraction is the eerie, ghost-town–like atmosphere in an outstandingly beautiful setting. It's all capped off by a stunning 13km (8-mile) walking route that stretches to the west end of the island, passing sea cliffs and beaches of ivory sand. You can pick up maps and other information from the **Blasket Centre** on the mainland in Dunquin. **Marine Tours** (www.marinetours.ie; © **086/335-3805**) in Ventry runs return trips to Great Blasket, with a 3-hour stop on the island, for €50.

The Blasket Centre (Ionad an Bhlascaoid): Dunquin (Dún Chaoin). www.heritageireland.ie. © **066/915-6444.** Admission €4 adults, €3 seniors, €2 children, €10 families. Apr–Oct daily 10am–6pm. Last admission 45 min. before closing.

Gallarus Oratory ★ HISTORIC SITE This small, beehive-shaped church is one of the best-preserved pieces of early Christian architecture in Ireland. Built between

what's in a name: A GRUESOME TALE IN BALLYFERRITER

The unassuming village of **Ballyferriter** (*Baile an Fheirtearaigh*), part of the Slea Head Drive, is named after a local rebel named Piaras Ferriter. He was a poet and soldier who fought in the 1641 rebellion and ultimately became the last area commander to surrender to Oliver Cromwell's English troops.

Just north of the village, you can follow signs to the moody ruins of the **Dún an Oir Fort,** a defensive citadel dating from the Iron Age. There's also a small memorial to 600 Spanish and Irish troops who were massacred here by the English in 1580. Most were beheaded—a fact commemorated by the highly gruesome local names for two adjacent fields nearby. The first, where the executions were carried out, is called "the Field of the Cutting." The second, where their partial remains were buried, is "the Field of the Heads."

the 7th and the 9th centuries A.D., its walls and roof are made entirely from dry stones without mortar—yet the interior stays remarkably dry. The small visitor center features displays on the history of the Oratory, plus the obligatory information film. Nearby is the single surviving tower of the 15th-century **Gallarus Castle.**

4.8km (3 miles) east of Ballyferriter. www.heritageireland.ie. ℂ **064/663-2402.** Free admission. May–Aug daily 10am–6pm. Signposted down small farm road off R559, just east of Gallarus. Approx. 6.3km (3.9 miles) northeast of Dingle, turn off R559 at signs for *Boile an Fheirteoraigh,* Wine Strand, and Louis Mulcahy Pottery; then after about 0.1km (100 yards), take the right-hand fork in the road. Gallarus Oratory is signposted on the right a short distance down this road, up a small track.

Irish Famine Cottage ★ HISTORIC SITE   This cottage isn't a replica; it's a real dwelling, maintained as it would have been at the time it was abandoned (including eerie, scattered pieces of furniture) during the famine years of the mid–19th century. The humble stone building is a stark and haunting sight, perched on a windswept cliff, overlooking the coast, while sheep and horses graze nearby. You can't go inside, but looking in through the windows gives a powerful enough impression of what life was really like for the rural poor. The ticket price includes a bag of feed you can take up with you for the curious farm animals who watch your approach. *Note:* The cottage is a 2-minute walk uphill from the parking lot, so it may not be suitable for those with mobility problems.

Signposted from R559 (Slea Head Dr.), Ventry. www.famine-cottage.com. ℂ **066/915-6241.** €4 adults, €3 children. Apr–Oct daily 10am–6pm. If approaching from the west, sign is just after the turn for Dunbeg Fort.

COUNTIES LIMERICK & CLARE

North of Kerry and Cork lies County Limerick, a name with poetic associations (of a sort). But despite the 50,000 bad jokes and dirty songs for which it can arguably be blamed, Limerick is actually rather a quiet, rural county, distinguished by the swirls and eddies of the Shannon River and its valley—although you may want to give its eponymous capital city a miss. County Clare, however, could hardly be a starker contrast. The region's biggest draw is the unique, wild region known as the Burren. Dotted with mysterious ancient stone dolmens and graced with stark, breathtaking vistas, its lunar landscape is quite unlike anywhere else in the country. As if that wasn't enough to impress, Clare also has the famous Cliffs of Moher, a place of high drama and majestic beauty. Those who don't mind a bit of cheesy fun will also find rich pickings; this part of the world is medieval banquet central, with at least two of its biggest castles packing in the crowds for a nightly dose of ye olde funne.

ESSENTIALS

Arriving

BY PLANE Several major airlines operate regular, scheduled flights into **Shannon Airport,** off the Limerick-Ennis road (N18), County Clare (www.shannonairport.com; © **061/712000**), 24km (15 miles) west of Limerick. Aer Lingus and Ryanair operate flights to London, Birmingham, and Bristol in England. A taxi from the airport to the city center costs about €35; you can catch one at the airport or prebook with **Shannon Airport Cabs** (www.shannonairportcabs.com; © **061/333-366**).

BY BUS Bus Éireann (www.buseireann.ie; © **061/313333**) provides the regular Shannonlink bus service from Shannon Airport to **Colbert Station,** Limerick's railway station, on Parnell Street. Bus services from all parts of Ireland come to this station. In County Clare, most of the small towns and countryside attractions listed in this chapter—including Bunratty, Kilfenora, Doolin, and the Cliffs of Moher—are accessible on Bus Éireann, although the frequency of service can be low in the most rural areas.

BY TRAIN **Irish Rail** operates direct trains from Dublin, Cork, and Killarney, with connections from other parts of Ireland. They arrive at Limerick's **Colbert Station,** Parnell Street (www.irishrail.ie; ⓒ **061/315555**).

BY CAR Although several of the major sights in this region can be reached on public transportation, you really need a car for the more remote and hard-to-get-to places. Shannon Airport has offices of: **Avis** (www.avis.ie; ⓒ **061/715600**), **Budget** (www.budget.ie; ⓒ **061/471361**), and **Hertz** (www.hertz.ie; ⓒ **061/471369**). Several local firms also maintain desks at the airport; among the most reliable is **Dan Dooley Rent-A-Car** (www.dan-dooley.ie; ⓒ **061/471098**).

8 [FastFACTS] COUNTIES LIMERICK & CLARE

ATMs/Banks A handy ATM is at Bunratty Castle and Folk Park. Otherwise, ATMs are frustratingly rare in the countryside, so make sure you get cash when you can.

Doctors For medical emergencies, dial ⓒ **999.** For nonemergencies, your hotel should call you a doctor. Otherwise, in Limerick City, try the **Abbeygrove Surgery** in Sir Harry's Mall, off Island Road (ⓒ **061/419121**). In Ballyvaughan, try the **Ballyvaughan Medical Centre**

(ⓒ **065/707-7035**). In Doolin, try **Dr. Catherine O'Loughlin** on Fisher Street (ⓒ **065/707-4990**).

Emergencies For police, fire, or other emergencies, dial ⓒ **999.**

Internet Access In Galway City, **Chat 'R Net,** 2 Eyre Square (ⓒ **091/539-912**) offers Internet access and low-cost international calls. You'll be lucky to find any place in the countryside, although the majority of even the small rural B&Bs listed in this chapter have Wi-Fi.

Pharmacies In the rural areas of County Clare covered in this chapter, drugstores are fairly scarce, though in Ballyvaughan you could try the **Burren Pharmacy** on Ennis Road (ⓒ **065/707-7029**).

Taxis In Limerick City, try **Munster Cabs** (ⓒ **061/639474**). Taxis further out into the countryside in small towns and villages are rare; the best bet is to ask your hotel, B&B, or restaurant to call you one.

WHERE TO STAY

Limerick City's economic growth spurt in the 1990s and 2000s led to the construction of several large, impersonal chain hotels there. But why would you bother? The real finds are to be had in the rural parts of County Limerick, where you can hide away in a lovely old cottage on a tranquil farm, or splurge on a night in a grand country house retreat. Around County Clare, the best small hotels and B&Bs are to be found out in the countryside—including a few real standouts.

Where to Stay in County Limerick

Adare Manor ★★★ Surrounded by a whopping 840 acres of landscaped grounds, on the very edge of lovely Adare village (see p. 156), this luxurious resort looks impressively Victorian Gothic from the outside. Indoors you'll find a beautifully restored and converted manor house; mostly 19th century, although check out the elaborately-carved 15th-century doors on the ground floor. Guest rooms are

LOVED-UP IN lisdoonvarna

If you've been looking for love in all the wrong places, clearly you've never been to Lisdoonvarna. This County Clare town lives for *l'amour*. There's a Matchmaker Pub on the main street (inside the Imperial Hotel); two local residents call themselves professional matchmakers (Willie Daly, a horse dealer, and James White, an hotelier); and every autumn, the town hosts the month-long **Lisdoonvarna Matchmaking Festival** (www.matchmakerireland.com). Thousands of love-lorn singletons come in search of The One, and locals cheer them on. Up and down each street, every atmospheric corner is used for mixers and minglers. Residents stir the pot by hosting romantic breakfasts, dinners, games, and dances. So good are their intentions and so charming is their belief in true love—in the idea that there really is somebody out there for everybody, and that they should all come together in a far-flung corner of western Ireland to find one another—that you may just fall for it. Lisdoonvarna can be found on the main N67 road, between Ballyvaughan and Ennistimon.

spacious and individually decorated in traditional (some might say fussy) style. Hidden away on the grounds are 15 modern 3-bedroom self-catering villas, plus 18 town houses. There's also a swimming pool and a pampering spa. Adare Manor is renowned as something of a golfer's paradise, with a highly rated 18-hole championship course. Archery, clay pigeon shooting, and horseback riding can all be easily arranged. The Oak Room restaurant is one of the best in the area (see listing below). *Tip:* Stays at Adare Manor are sometimes offered as part of air-hotel packages that reduce the price considerably. You might want to check to see if it's listed when choosing a package.

Adare, Co. Limerick. www.adaremanor.com. © **061/605200.** 62 units. €440–€700 double; €300–€720 villas. Free parking. Breakfast included. **Amenities:** Restaurants (2), bar, room service, spa, pool, gym, golf course.

Echo Lodge ★★ This place was once a convent, before being converted into a chic and stylish hotel. Bedrooms are quite small, but decorated in such a way that they could be described as "traditional" without the acres of chintz that sometimes implies—instead, they use vintage-print wallpapers, tasteful color schemes, and pleasantly eccentric, objets d'art touches here and there, such as mini-Ionic columns for bedside tables. There's usually a good handful of deals and special offers listed on the website. The Mustard Seed restaurant (see listing below) is one of the best in the area.

Ballingarry, Co. Limerick (13km/ 8 miles south of Adare). www.mustardseed.ie. © **069/68508.** 76 units. €130–€320 doubles. Free parking. Breakfast included. **Amenities:** Wi-Fi (free; public areas only), restaurant, bar, room service.

Where to Stay in County Clare

Aran View House Hotel ★★ The clue's in the name at this small but friendly hotel in Doolin: The house looks across an expanse of lawn and sea, out to the Aran Islands in the distance. It was built in the mid–17th century; the good-sized guest rooms maintain a traditional feel, with heavy wood furniture and color schemes of peach or buttermilk. The bar wisely takes full advantage of the amazing view out front, making this a lovely spot for an early-evening pint as the sun goes down. The helpful staff runs things very efficiently, and breakfasts are good, too. Doolin is about 10 minutes' drive up the coast from the Cliffs of Moher.

Coast Rd., Doolin, Co. Clare. www.aranview.com. *C* **065/707-4420.** 13 units. €100–€110. Free parking. Breakfast included. Amenities: Restaurant, bar.

Gregan's Castle Hotel ★★★   An elegant 18th-century house set amid the austere beauty of the Burren, Gregan's is one of the most unique places to stay in this region of Ireland. Manager Simon Haden is the second generation of hoteliers in his family to run this place, although it's been a hotel for much longer—famous guests of the 20th century included J. R. R. Tolkien, who was apparently so inspired by the lunar-like views of the surrounding Burren that he drew on them to describe Mordor in *The Lord of the Rings*. Guest rooms are design-magazine chic, with modern furnishings and bay windows. Televisions are banned in the hotel to enable guests to get maximum benefit from the peace and tranquility of the surroundings. Even if you can't stretch the cost of a night here, consider booking a table in the superb restaurant, **Gregan's Castle** (see listing below). Chef David Hurley's modern Irish cooking is superlative. Check the website for some attractive dinner, bed and breakfast packages, and midweek deals.

Ballyvaughan, Co. Clare. www.gregans.ie. *C* **065/707-7005.** 22 units. €255–€330. Free parking. Breakfast included. **Amenities:** Wi-Fi (free), restaurant, bar.

Moy House ★★   An extraordinary, squat tower house built in the 19th century, Moy House overlooks the crashing waves of the Atlantic Ocean. You can climb the four-story central tower for the best view out to sea, although the view from some of the guest rooms is almost as good. (The cheaper ones have views of the grounds, not the sea.) Rooms are decorated in muted, modern tones, with large beds and modern bathrooms. One bathroom even has an original, glass-covered well. You can walk down to the beach for a stroll along the dramatic shoreline, or relax in the drawing room—the house is packed with bookshelves filled with interesting tomes. The restaurant is excellent, with a very strong emphasis on seasonal produce, but it's certainly not cheap at €75 per person for a five-course, fixed-price menu. Check the website for good package deals that can really lower the price, including 2-night getaways for around €230.

On N67, 1 mile south of Lahinch, Co. Clare. www.moyhouse.com. *C* **065/708-2800.** 9 units. €185–€234. Free parking. Breakfast included. **Amenities:** Restaurant.

WHERE TO EAT

Dutifully demolishing the rule of thumb that the best restaurants are usually found in cities, the rural byways of Counties Claire and Limerick contain several places to eat that would be serious contenders on any "best of" lists for Ireland.

Where to Eat in County Limerick

The Mustard Seed ★★★ MODERN EUROPEAN   The in-house restaurant of the excellent Echo Lodge hotel (see listing above) is one of the best-loved and most widely known in the region. The restaurant has its own kitchen garden that supplies many of the ingredients. The four-course menus are imaginative; after a starter of warm strawberry salad, made with beet meringues and elderflower syrup, you could go for spring lamb with chargrilled zucchini cream or guinea fowl with Parmesan custard and a vegetable fricassee. Special packages including overnight accommodation are usually offered on the website.

At the Echo Lodge hotel, Ballingarry, Co. Limerick (13km/8 miles south of Adare). www.mustard seed.ie. ℂ **069/68508.** Fixed-price 4-course dinner €60. Daily 6:45–9:15pm.

The Oak Room ★★★ MODERN IRISH   Another superb hotel restaurant, the Oak Room is part of Adare Manor (see listing above). The high stone windows and silver candelabra of the dining room here should leave no doubt that this is a place where you're expected to sit up straight—gentlemen, a tie if you please. The food certainly lives up to the promise of being something special. Herb and citron–marinated salmon makes a deliciously piquant starter before a main of beef filet with cracked pepper jus or rack of lamb with a wild garlic crust. And if you're liking the place too much to leave at the end of the meal.. . . . well, you probably should anyway; the cheapest rooms here often cost about €400.

Adare, Co. Limerick. www.adaremanor.com. ℂ **061/605200.** Main courses €25–€35. Daily 6:30–10pm.

The Wild Geese ★★★ MODERN IRISH   What is it about Adare that breeds superlative restaurants? The Wild Geese, in the center of the village, serves outstanding modern Irish food with plenty of local ingredients. A main of roast chicken could be stuffed with soft Bluebell Falls goat's cheese, a specialty from County Clare; or some monkfish may arrive accompanied by a potato and spinach pancake, finished off with lemongrass sauce. Sunday lunch, which often features dishes seen on the evening menu, is significantly cheaper than dinner service, at just €20 for two courses.

Adare, Co. Limerick. www.adaremanor.com. ℂ **061/605200.** Main courses €25–€32. May Sept Tues–Sat 6:30–10pm, Sun noon 3pm and 5:30–10pm; Oct–Apr Tues–Sat 6:30–10pm, Sun noon–3pm. Closed most of Jan. On R523, about 4km (2½ miles) southwest of Rathkeale, Co. Limerick.

Where to Eat in County Clare

Barrtra Seafood Restaurant ★★ SEAFOOD   A friendly, family-run place with a good line in simple, tasty seafood, this restaurant looks out over Liscannor Bay. Just glance at a map and you'll quickly see why that makes this such a lovely spot in the evening—the sun sets over the sea on a virtually direct line to the dining room. The menu is simple and fresh, focusing on locally caught seafood served with tasty sauces or unadorned, and a few well-chosen vegetables on the side. It's not all fishy; you could go for a hearty steak and horseradish crème fraiche instead, or perhaps mix the two up with the popular surf 'n' turf (steak served with scallops and garlic butter). It's advisable to call ahead to check opening times outside the summer season.

Miltown Malbay Rd., Lahinch, Co. Clare. www.barrtra.com. ℂ **065/708-1280.** Fixed-price 3-course menu €35. Daily noon–2:30 and 6–10pm. Closed Jan–Feb.

Bay Fish & Chips ★ FISH & CHIPS   A 10-minute drive from the Cliffs of Moher, the Bay serves extremely fresh fish and chips. There's nothing fancy here—battered seafood and chunky, steaming chips—but it's the simplicity of this dish that makes it such a universally loved staple in this part of the world. Specials always include a fresh catch of the day. Portions are formidable, and staff will happily chat with you while you wait for the batter to turn that irresistible shade of golden brown. To get here from the Cliffs, just head south on R478 for a little over 5.5km (3½ miles). It's on the main street as you drive through Liscannor—look for the small white building with a blue wave painted on one end.

Main St., Liscannor, Co. Clare. ℂ **083/112-3351.** €5–€10. Daily noon to around 11pm.

leprechauns: YOU'RE DOING IT ALL WRONG

The word "leprechaun" comes from the Irish *leath bhrógan*, meaning "shoemaker." In folklore, leprechauns were often depicted as shoemakers by trade. They were mischievous creatures, not evil exactly, but certainly not averse to some malicious practical jokes.

Different regions of Ireland all had their own versions of leprechaun folklore. There was disagreement over how they looked, too, although there were a few elements of common ground—including, most interestingly, a fondness for *red* coats, not green ones. The green came to be added later, presumably by foreigners, out of an association with Ireland in general.

Today, the word also has less whimsical connotations. It's used to describe the more crass side of the tourism industry (with good reason—after all, the Ring of Kerry really does have LEPRECHAUN CROSSING signs). And on an even less pleasant note, it's used by some Northern Irish Unionists as a term of abuse for the Gaelic language.

The Cherry Tree ★★★ MODERN IRISH   Overlooking a lake in the sweet village of Killaloe, the Cherry Tree has raked in awards over the years, and with good reason. The menu, which uses plenty of local ingredients, is simple yet sophisticated, wisely giving space for those local flavors to come to the fore. A starter of crab cakes with chili jam could lead on to sea bass filet served with braised leeks and lemon butter sauce, or maybe some pan-roasted Tipperary steak with horseradish mash. The early-bird menu, served until 9pm on Thursday and 7:30pm on Friday and Saturday, is a great value at €26 for three courses. Reservations are advisable.

Lakeside, Ballina, Killaloe, Co. Clare. www.cherrytreerestaurant.ie. ✆ **061/375688.** Main courses €16–€27. Wed–Sun 6–10pm (also Tues, Jun–Aug only). Closed Sun–Mon.

Durty Nelly's ★ IRISH   You don't walk into a pub called Durty Nelly's expecting haute cuisine. Nonetheless, a few welcome surprises are to be found here. Genuine, appetizing pub food is the order of the day—fish and chips, steak sandwiches, burgers, or salads. Those who don't mind a bit of cheesy tourist novelty can have their picture taken while pouring their own pint of Guinness. Its proximity to Bunratty Castle (see p. 158) means that most travelers will probably see it as more of a lunch spot than a dinner destination, but there are actually three dining rooms here—the more refined Oyster and Loft restaurants offer an upmarket version of the same food (good steaks, Thai curries, fresh seafood, and so on). And if you're wondering about the name, "Durty Nelly" was a somewhat ribald heroine of Irish folklore, said to have invented the magical cure-all (and highly alcoholic) moonshine, potcheen (see p. 136).

Next to Bunratty Castle, Bunratty, Co. Clare. www.durtynellys.ie ✆ **061/364-861.** €14–€29. Mon–Thurs 10:30am–11:30pm; Fri–Sat 10:30am–12:30am; Sun non–11pm. (Food noon–10pm.) Oyster Restaurant: daily noon–10pm. Loft Restaurant: daily 5:30–10pm.

Gregan's Castle ★★★ MODERN IRISH   The hugely talented David Hurley is the head chef at the exceptional in-house restaurant of the Gregan's Castle Hotel in Ballyvaughan (see listing above). His menus are exquisite; easily the equal of the kind of top-level restaurants one may mistakenly think are confined to major cities. The seven-course tasting menu forms the entirety of the dinner service, although a slightly

LIMERICK CITY: worth A VISIT?

Its name is synonymous the world over with a particular brand of cheerful verse, but spend much time in Limerick's eponymous capital and you might find yourself making up a few off-color rhymes of your own. In such a small country, its population of 60,000 is enough to make it the Republic's fourth largest city (only Dublin, Cork, and Galway are bigger), yet it has the kind of gritty, urban feel usually associated with much larger places. It also has a crime problem, including gang-related crime. During the economic crash, what had been a sharply growing business sector in the city collapsed, leading to a population drain of around 5%.

Simply put, Limerick City just isn't very nice. Sorry, Limerick.

That said, there are genuine efforts to make things better. The Tourist Board is doing its part to clean the place up, with a certain amount of success. A prime example is **King John's Castle** ★ (Nicholas Street, www.shannonheritage.com, ✆ **061/411201**). The stern riverside fortress, dating from 1210, is the centerpiece of Limerick's historic area. But rarely has an historic building been so poorly treated in the modern age; during the 1950s, in an astonishing act of government vandalism, it even had a public housing project built within its central courtyard. Thankfully, that's long gone, but the big, modern visitor center building that's gone up in its place still rather spoils the effect. That said, a recent renovation has greatly modernized and improved the visitor facilities, including high-tech interactive displays. Admission costs €8 adults, €7 seniors, €4.50 children, €21 to €24 families, free for children 4 and under. It's open April to September from 9:30am to 5:30pm, and October to March from 9:30am to 4:30pm (last admission 1 hour before closing).

The **Limerick City Gallery of Art** ★ (People's Park, at the corner of Perry Square and Mallow Street, www.gallery.limerick.ie; ✆ **061/310633**) has a good, regularly changing program of contemporary art exhibitions. Its permanent collection includes work by Irish painters Jack B. Yeats and Sir John Lavery. Its opening times are Monday, Wednesday, and Friday 10am to 5:30pm; Tuesday 11am to 5:30pm; Thursday 10am to 8:30pm; Saturday 10am to 5pm; and Sunday noon to 5pm (closed on public holidays). Admission is free.

Perhaps the greatest attraction in Limerick is the **Hunt Museum** ★★, Rutland Street (www.huntmuseum.com; ✆ **061/312833**). Located in the old customs building, the museum's 18th-century Palladian front is modeled on the Petit Trianon at the Palace of Versailles in France. It has exhibits dating as far back as ancient Greece and Rome, and paintings by Picasso and Renoir. Admission costs €5 adults, €3.50 seniors and students, €2.50 children, and €12 families. It's open Monday to Saturday from 10am to 5pm and Sunday from 2 to 5pm.

cheaper, three-course dinner menu is available until 7:30pm. A typical meal could start with a few expertly prepared impeccable canapés, before moving on to chicken and sweetbread terrine, wild Wicklow venison, or perhaps some perfectly prepared local seafood. Desserts are sumptuous; compressed pineapple with coconut and lime, for instance. If you love Gregan's so much that you don't want to leave (and that would be perfectly understandable), rooms start at just under €200 per night during high season.

Main St., Liscannor, Co. Clare. ✆ **083/112-3351**. €70; 7-course tasting menu €75, or €115 with wines. Daily 6–9pm (last orders).

EXPLORING COUNTY LIMERICK

The majority of County Limerick is peaceful, pleasant farmland. The picture-postcard village of Adare is definitely worth a visit, as are Lough Gurr and Rathkeale. Sadly, the same cannot be said of Limerick City; despite the best efforts of the Tourist Board to shake up its image (see box above), the city remains a rather gritty, unpleasant place.

Visitor Information

The **Limerick Tourist Information Centre** is on Arthur's Quay, Limerick (© **061/317522**). It is open Monday to Friday 9am to 5pm; in summer it's usually open weekends, too, but call ahead to check.

Another office is located in the **Adare Heritage Centre,** Main Street, Adare (www.adareheritagecentre.ie; © **061/396225**). It is open daily, year-round, from 9am to 6pm.

Top Attractions in County Limerick

Adare ★★ TOWN   *"O sweet Adare,"* wrote the poet Gerald Griffin (1803–40), *"O soft retreat of sylvan splendor/ Nor summer sun nor morning gale/ E'er hailed a scene more softly tender."* Like a town plucked from a book of fairy tales, Adare has thatched cottages, black-and-white timbered houses, lichen-covered churches, and romantic ruins strewn along the banks of the River Maigue. Drop in at the **Adare Heritage Centre** while you're there—part visitor center, part museum on the history of the town, part craft store. The center is on the main street through Adare village center. Yes, this place has been seriously discovered by the tour-bus crowds (even by May, which is still officially off season, the roads can get clogged at times), but it's still absolutely worth a stop.

Adare, Co. Limerick. Heritage Centre: www.adareheritagecentre.ie. © **061/396666.** Historical Exhibition: €4.50 adults; €3.50 seniors, students, and children. Daily 9am–6pm (sometimes closed for lunch).

Foynes Flying Boat Museum ★★ MUSEUM   When Shannon Airport was just a remote patch of undeveloped farmland, this was the center of international aviation in Europe. The first commercial flight from the U.S. to Europe touched down at Foynes Airport one hot July morning in 1937; five years later this became one end of the first-ever regular service between the two continents. (It's no coincidence that, in the same year, Foynes was also the birthplace of the Irish coffee. The story goes that a flight to New York had to turn back after a particularly violent storm. The bartender was asked to hurriedly prepare something to both warm up and steady the nerves of the passengers—so he served hot coffee and threw shots of whiskey in for good measure.) At this engaging museum you can see a replica of the original Pan Am "flying boat," which may make you swear never to complain about a modern flight again. You can also tour the actual terminal building, kept as it was when the airport closed in 1945, and experience a replica 1940s cinema.

Foynes, Co. Limerick. www.flyingboatmuseum.com. © **069/65416.** Admission €11 adults, €9 seniors and students, €6 children 5–13, children 4 and under free, €28 families. Mar–May daily 9:30am–5pm; Jun–Sept 9am–6pm; last admission 1 hr. before closing.

Lough Gur ★★ LAKE   An unusual preponderance of ancient sites surrounds this lovely lake. Most of the sights are well signposted on R512, the drive that skirts around

THE lough derg DRIVE

At the meeting point of counties Clare, Limerick, and Tipperary, Lough Derg creates a stunning waterscape. Often called an inland sea, Lough Derg is the Shannon River's largest lake and widest point: 40km (25 miles) long and almost 16km (10 miles) wide.

The road that circles the lake for 153km (95 miles), the **Lough Derg Drive,** is another of Ireland's great scenic drives. It's one continuous photo opportunity, where panoramas of hilly farmlands, gentle mountains, and glistening waters are unspoiled by commercialization.

The drive is also a collage of colorful shoreline towns, starting with **Killaloe, County Clare,** and **Ballina,** County Tipperary. They're so close that they are essentially one community—only a splendid 13-arch bridge over the Shannon separates them. In the summer, its pubs and bars are filled with weekend sailors.

Kincora, on the highest ground at Killaloe, was the royal settlement of Brian Boru and the other O'Brien kings, although no trace of any buildings survives. Killaloe is a picturesque town with lakeside views at almost every turn and restaurants and pubs perched on the shore.

Eight kilometers (5 miles) inland from Lough Derg's lower southeast shores is **Nenagh,** the chief town of north Tipperary. It lies in a fertile valley between the Silvermine and Arra mountains.

On the north shore of the lake in County Galway, **Portumna** is worth a visit for its forest park and castle.

Memorable little towns and harborside villages like **Mountshannon** and **Dromineer** dot the rest of the Lough Derg Drive. Some towns, like **Terryglass** and **Woodford,** are known for atmospheric old pubs where spontaneous sessions of traditional Irish music are likely to break out. Others, like **Puckane** and **Ballinderry,** offer unique crafts.

The best way to get to Lough Derg is by car or boat. Although there is limited public transportation in the area, you will need a car to get around the lake. Major roads that lead to Lough Derg are the main Limerick-Dublin road (N7) from points east and south, N6 and N65 from Galway and the west, and N52 from the north. The Lough Derg Drive, which is well signposted, is a combination of R352 on the west bank of the lake and R493, R494, and R495 on the east bank.

the lake's edge. Lough Gur was occupied continuously from the Neolithic period to late medieval times. Archaeologists have uncovered foundations of a small farmstead built around the year 900, a lake island dwelling built between 500 and 1000, a wedge-shaped tomb that was a communal grave around 2,500 B.C., and the extraordinary Grange Stone Circle, which is a 4,000-year-old site with 113 upright stones forming the largest prehistoric stone circle in Ireland. An interesting Heritage Centre helps put it all into context. To find the center, head south through the village of Ballyneety; about 6.5km (4 miles) on you'll come to Reardons Pub in Holycross. Take the first left afterward, keep to the left, and this road will take you straight there.

11km (6¾ miles) SE of Limerick City on R512, Lough Gur, Co. Limerick. www.loughgur.com. ℂ **061/385386.** Free access to Lough; Heritage Centre €5 adults, €4 seniors and students, €3 children, €15 families. Heritage Centre Mar–Oct Mon–Fri 10am–5pm, Sat–Sun noon–6pm; Nov–Feb Mon–Fri 10:30am–4:30pm, Sat–Sun noon–5pm. Site open year-round.

EXPLORING COUNTY CLARE

With its miles of pasture and green, softly rolling fields, Clare seems, at first, a pleasantly pastoral place. But head to the coast and a dramatic landscape awaits you, with plunging cliffs and crashing waves. Turn north, and you'll find visual drama of a different kind, courtesy of the otherworldly landscapes of the Burren.

Tourism Offices

The **Burren Centre** in Kilfenora (☏ **065/708-8030**) is the place to go for information on the Burren region. In addition, there are visitor information points on Main Street in **Ballyvaughan** (☏ **065/707-7464**) and at the **Cliffs of Moher** (☏ **065/708-1171**).

Top Attractions in County Clare

Clare has a remarkable coastline, including the spectacular **Cliffs of Moher.** In truth, the visitor experience there is somewhat overdone, but the views are undeniably stunning.

The **Burren National Park,** meanwhile, is by far the county's greatest attraction. You could spend several days exploring its profound wilderness, although a day is plenty to hit the high points.

Traditional Irish music is always on heavy rotation in Clare, which is well known for a vibrant music scene, especially in the charming village of **Doolin.**

Clare is also an excellent place for those fascinated by the country's ancient history, as it's littered with historic and prehistoric sites, from the **Poulnabrone Dolmen** to **Bunratty Castle,** with its better-than-you-probably-expected folk park.

Aillwee Cave ★★ CAVE   This deep cave was undiscovered for thousands of years until a local farmer followed a dog into it 50 years ago. Inside he found a huge cavern with 1,000m (3,280 ft.) of passages running straight into the heart of a mountain. He kept it to himself for decades before eventually spreading the word. Professional cave explorers later uncovered its magnificent bridged chasms, deep caverns, a frozen waterfall, and hollows created by hibernating brown bears. (Brown bears have been extinct in Ireland for 10,000 years.) Guided tours are excellent here—generally led by geology students from area universities. There's a scary moment when they turn out the lights for a minute so you can experience the depth of the darkness inside. Tours last approximately 30 minutes, and are conducted continuously. There are a couple of other attractions on the same site. The **Burren Birds of Prey Centre** is a working aviary designed to mimic the natural habitat of the buzzards, falcons, eagles, and owls that live there. *Tip:* Save up to 10% by booking tickets online.

Ballyvaughan, Co. Clare. www.aillweecave.ie. ☏ **065/707-7036.** Admission to caves: €12 adults, €5.50 children, €29–€35 families. Birds of Prey Centre: €10 adults, €8 children, €25 families. Combined ticket for both: €18 adults, €10 children, €44–€55 families. Mar–Jun and Sept–Oct daily 10am–5:30pm; Jul–Aug daily 10am–6:30pm; Nov–Feb daily 10am–5pm (times are first and last tour). Flying display times Mar–Apr and Sept–Oct noon and 3pm; May–Aug noon, 2, and 4pm; Nov–Feb noon and 3pm. Call to check times in winter.

Bunratty Castle and Folk Park ★★ LIVING HISTORY PARK   An impressive, early-15th-century castle, Bunratty is the home of two major tourist attractions: a "living history" recreation of a 19th-century village, and a riotous nighttime medieval banquet. You can tour the interior of the castle, which is surprisingly complete, and the

Counties Clare & Limerick

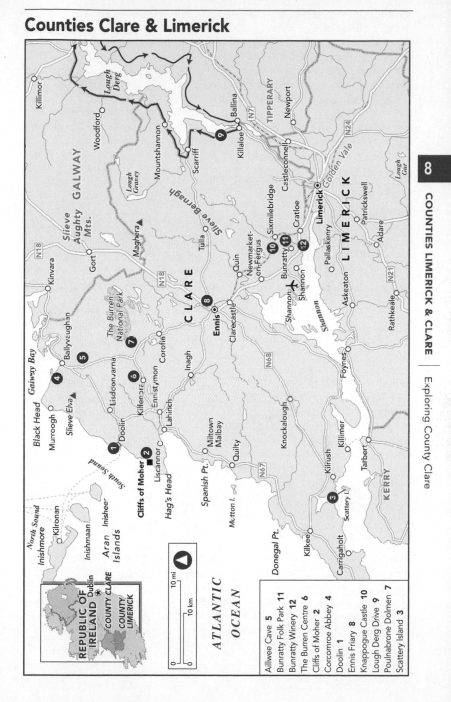

Killimor

Lough Derg

TIPPERARY

Newport

Ballina

N7

Woodford

Killaloe

Castleconnell

N24

GALWAY

Mountshannon

Scarriff

9

Lough Gur

Slieve Aughty Mts.

Lough Graney

Slieve Bernagh

Sixmilebridge

Cratloe

Limerick

Patrickswell

N18

Maghera

Tulla

Newmarket-on-Fergus

Bunratty

11

10

12

LIMERICK

Adare

Gort

Quin

Kinvara

CLARE

The Burren National Park

7

Shannon

Shannon

Pallaskenry

N21

Ballyvaughan

Corofin

Clarecastle

Shannon

Askeaton

Rathkeale

5

Ennis

8

Galway Bay

Lisdoonvarna

6

Ennistymon

Inagh

N68

Foynes

Black Head

4

Killenora

Lahinch

Knockalough

Killimer

Tarbert

Murroogh

Doolin

Slieve Elva

Miltown Malbay

Kilrush

1

Liscannor

2

Quilty

Spanish Pt.

N67

KERRY

Cliffs of Moher

Hag's Head

Mutton I.

Scattery I.

3

Carrigaholt

Donegal Pt.

South Sound

Kilkee

North Sound

Inishmore

Kilronan

Inishmaan

Inisheer

Aran Islands

ATLANTIC OCEAN

REPUBLIC OF IRELAND

Dublin

COUNTY CLARE

COUNTY LIMERICK

10 mi

10 km

Aillwee Cave 5
Bunratty Folk Park 11
Bunratty Winery 12
The Burren Centre 6
Cliffs of Moher 2
Corcomroe Abbey 4
Doolin 1
Ennis Friary 8
Knappogue Castle 10
Lough Derg Drive 9
Poulnabrone Dolmen 7
Scattery Island 3

beautiful, restored walled garden. However, the folk park is the big attraction here. Actors in period costume wander around as you walk through the impressive-looking village center, complete with everything from a post office and schoolroom to a doctor's office. You can go inside each one and chat with the occupants. Meanwhile, professional craftspeople work their trades, using authentically traditional methods. There's even a Victorian-style pub. It's all excellent fun, and a brilliant way to imbue kids with a sense of history. In the evenings, the medieval banquet takes over the castle's Great Hall. After a full sit-down meal, there's a lively a show of music, dancing, and folk stories—all performed by actors and musicians in medieval garb. There are two sittings nightly, at 5:30 and 8:45pm. Reservations are essential.

Signposted from N18 (Shannon-Limerick Rd.), Bunratty, Co. Clare. www.shannonheritage.com. ✆ 061/361-511. Admission €15 adults, €10 seniors and students, €9 children, €34–€38 families. Medieval banquet: €49 adults, €37 children 10–12, €25 children 6–9, children 5 and under free. Daily 9am–5:30pm. Last admission 4pm.

The Burren National Park ★★★ PARK   This stark, otherworldly landscape spreads across 1,653 hectares (4,083 acres) and continually acquires more land as it becomes available. The remarkable rocky land is dotted with picturesque ruined castles, tumbling cliffs, rushing rivers, lakes, barren rock mountains, and plant life that defies all of nature's conventional rules. The park is particularly rich in archaeological remains from the Neolithic through the medieval periods—dolmens and wedge tombs (approximately 120 of them), ring forts (500 of those), round towers, ancient churches, high crosses, monasteries, and holy wells. The park is centered at Mullaghmore Mountain, but there are no official entrance points—and like all National Parks in Ireland, it's completely free to enter. **The Burren Centre,** on R476 to Kilfenora, is a fine place to get acquainted with all facets of the area. Using films, landscape models, and interpretive displays, it gives an informative overview of the Burren's unique landscape and history. There is also a craft shop and tearoom on site. Local guide **Tony Kirby** leads 2½-hour guided walks from outside the center at 12:30pm on Saturdays, Sundays, Tuesdays, and Thursdays in summertime. The cost is €20, including entry to the exhibition. Contact the visitor center for more details.

Visitor center: Kilfernora, Co. Clare. www.theburrencentre.ie. ✆ **065/708-8030.** Admission €6 adults, €5 seniors and students, €4 children 6–16, €20 families, children 5 and under free. Mid-Mar–May, Sept, and Oct daily 10am–5pm; Jun–Aug daily 9:30am–5:30pm.

Cliffs of Moher ★★ NATURAL WONDER   The cries of nesting seabirds are faintly audible amid the roar of the Atlantic crashing against the base of these breathtaking cliffs that undulate for 8km (5 miles) along the coast, some towering as high as 214m (702 ft.). On a clear day, you can see the Aran Islands in Galway Bay as misty shapes in the distance. Look the other way, and you'll see a constant throng of tour buses, cars, and tacky souvenir stalls set up along the footpath. The enormous visitor center houses gift shops, a high-tech "Cliffs of Moher Experience," and various other exhibits. Furthermore, the visitor center has the only (legal) car park, which you can't use without buying entry tickets to the whole center—effectively turning it into a steep *per person* parking charge. If this doesn't put you off the whole place, head up the path beside the visitor center to **O'Brien's Tower** for the best view of the cliffs. The 19th-century tower is a knockout spot for photos—though you have to pay an extra couple of euro to climb the stairs.

Nr. Liscannor, Co. Clare. www.cliffsofmoher.ie. ✆ **065/708-6141.** Admission €6 adults; €4 seniors, students, and disabled visitors; children 15 and under free. Price includes parking and visitor center admission. Mar and Oct Mon–Fri 9am–6pm, Sat–Sun 9am–6:30pm; Apr Mon–Fri 9am–6pm, Sat–Sun 9am–7pm; May and Sept Mon–Fri 9am–7pm, Sat–Sun 9am–7:30pm; Jun Mon–Fri 9am–7:30pm, Sat–Sun 9am–8pm; Jul and Aug daily 9am–9pm; Nov–Feb daily 9am–5pm.

Corcomroe Abbey ★★ HISTORIC SITE Set jewel-like in a languid green valley bounded by rolling hills, the jagged ruins of this Cistercian abbey are breathtaking. Donal Mór O'Brien founded the abbey in 1194, and his grandson, a former king of Thomond, is entombed in the structure's northern wall. There are some interesting medieval and Romanesque carvings in the stone, including one of a bishop with a crosier. Corcomroe is a lonely spot, except for Easter morning, when people come from miles around to celebrate Mass. It's meant to be quite a sight. Look for a mound, surrounded by trees, beside the road on the way out—it's the remains of an ancient ring fort.

Signposted from L1014, near Oughtmama, Co. Clare. No phone. Free admission (open site).

Doolin ★★ TOWN Doolin's old pubs and restaurants ring with the sound of fiddle and accordion all year long, earning this secluded fishing village a reputation as the unofficial capital of Irish traditional music. Most famous among them is **Gus O'Connor's Pub** (Fisher St.; www.gusoconnorsdoolin.com; ✆ **065/707-4168**), set among a row of thatched fishermen's cottages, about a 10-minute walk from the seafront. Great though the craic is here, the pub's fame inevitably draws crowds, and it can get packed to the rafters on a busy night. If you're looking for something a little more authentic, head up the road to **McGann's** (Main St.; www.mcgannspubdoolin. com; ✆ **065/707-4133**); it's less well known and not so unrelentingly jammed as Gus O'Connor's. In fact, on many nights, there are no locals in Gus's at all—they're all here, downing pints of Guinness and listening to the fiddles. Feel free to join them. Doolin is on R479, about 7.8km (4¾ miles) west of Lisdoonvarna.

Tourist Information Point: At the Hotel Doolin, Fitz's Cross, Doolin, Co. Clare. ✆ **065/707-4111** or 086/856-9725.

Ennis Friary ★ HISTORIC SITE When you walk around Ennis Friary, it can be hard to get a sense of scale, but if it helps you to understand it, consider that records show that in 1375 it was the home and workplace for 350 friars and 600 students. Founded in 1241, this Franciscan abbey, a famous seat of learning in medieval times, made Ennis a focal point of Western Europe for many years. It was finally forced to close in 1692, and thereafter fell into ruin. It's been partly restored and contains many beautifully sculpted medieval tombs, decorative fragments, and carvings, including the famous McMahon tomb with its striking representations of the Passion. The nave and chancel are the oldest parts of the friary, but other structures, such as the 15th-century tower, transept, and sacristy, are also rich in architectural detail.

Abbey St., Ennis, Co. Clare. www.heritageireland.ie. ✆ **065/682-9100.** Admission €4 adults, €3 seniors, €2 children and students, €9 families. Easter–Sept daily 10am–6pm; Oct daily 10am–5pm. Last admission 45 min. before closing.

Knappogue Castle and Walled Gardens ★★ CASTLE Midway between Bunratty and Ennis, this regal castle was built in 1467 as the home of the MacNamara clan—who, along with the O'Briens, dominated the area for more than 1,000 years. Oliver Cromwell used the castle as a base in the mid–17th century while pillaging the countryside and thus, unlike many castles, it was largely left intact. The original Norman structure also has elaborate late-Georgian and Regency wings, added in the early- and mid–19th century. Later, in the 20th century, it fell into disrepair but was rescued by Texan Mark Edwin Andrews, a former U.S. assistant secretary of the Navy. He and his wife, Lavone, an architect, worked closely with area historical societies and returned the castle to its former glory, even furnishing it with 15th-century furniture. The Andrews family then turned Knappogue over to the Irish people. The peaceful walled gardens have been meticulously restored to their Victorian condition—look for the wonderful statue of Bacchus. The gardens supply herbs for the **medieval banquets,** held nightly at 6:30pm, from April to October. Call or see the castle's website for details. *Note:* There is no cafe or restaurant on-site during the day.

Quin, Co. Clare. www.shannonheritage.com. ℭ **061/360-788.** Admission €7 adults, €4.50 seniors, €4 children 5–16, €16–€19 families, children 5 and under free. May–Aug daily 10am–4:30pm. Last admission 30 min. before closing.

Poulnabrone Dolmen ★ HISTORIC SITE   This portal tomb is an exquisitely preserved prehistoric site made all the more peculiar and arresting by the otherworldly Burren landscape on which it sits. Its dolmen (or stone table) is huge and surrounded by a natural pavement of rocks. The tomb dates back 5,000 years. When it was excavated in the 1980s, the remains of 16 people were found. And yet, the greatest mystery remains how the gigantic boulders were moved and lifted—the capstone alone weighs 5 tons. In the summer, you probably won't have much trouble finding this sight—just look for all the tour buses. At times they literally block the road.

On R480, 8km (5 miles) south of Aillwee Cave (see p. 158). Free admission (open site).

COUNTY GALWAY

With its misty, mountain-fringed lakes, rugged coastline, and extensive wilderness, County Galway is a wild and wooly area. And yet, nestled just outside its most dramatic and unkempt part—the windswept, boggy expanse of Connemara—is one of Ireland's artsiest and most sophisticated cities. The diminutive city of Galway has long been a center for culture, and the winding, medieval streets of its oldest quarter retain a seductively bohemian air. Though small, the city is a natural hub for exploring the region. For many travelers to Ireland, Galway is the farthest edge of their journey. Part of the reason they draw the line here is because the county looks so otherworldly—with its bleak bogs, heather-clad moors, and extraordinary light—they think that it must be the end of all that's worth seeing in Ireland (if not the end of the world). It isn't, of course, but Galway is just far enough from the touristy bustle to feel far away.

ESSENTIALS

Arriving

BY BUS   Buses from all parts of Ireland arrive daily at **Bus Éireann Travel Centre,** Ceannt Station, off Eyre Square, Galway, County Galway (www.buseireann.ie; ✆ **091/562000**). They also provide daily service to Clifden.

BY TRAIN   Trains from Dublin and other points arrive daily at Ceannt Station in Galway City, off Eyre Square.

BY CAR   Galway is on the main N18, N17, N63, N67, and M6 roads. Journey time from Dublin is about 2 hours; from Killarney it's about 3 hours; and from Cork it's about 2½ hours. Outside of Galway City, which is easily accessible by public transportation, your options in this region get pretty limited if you don't have a car. Buses to rural areas sometimes run only a handful of times per day, and remote sites may be completely inaccessible without a car. To hire one in Galway, try **Budget,** 12 Eyre Square (www.budget.ie; ✆ **091/564-570**) or **Irish Car Rentals** at Motorpark, Headford Road (www.irishcarrentals.com; ✆ **061/206-086**).

BY PLANE   Galway has an airport, but at this writing it has not been used for regular commercial flights since 2011. It may be worth checking www.galwayairport.com to see if the situation has changed.

ATMs/ Banks   In Galway, there's a **Bank of Ireland** (☎ **091/567-321**) and an **AIB** (☎ **091/561-151**) on Eyre Square.

Dentists   For dental emergencies, your hotel should contact a dentist for you; otherwise, in Galway City, try **Eyre Square Dental Clinic** on Prospect Hill, Eyre Square (☎ **091/562-932**).

Doctors   For medical emergencies, dial ☎ **999**. For nonemergencies, your hotel should call you a doctor. Otherwise in Galway City, try the **Crescent**

Medical Centre, 1 The Crescent (☎ **091/587-213**). In Clifden, try **Dr. Ciaran MacLoughlin** on Main Street (☎ **095/21141**).

Emergencies   For police, fire, or other emergencies, dial ☎ **999**.

Internet Access   In Galway City, **Chat 'R Net,** 2 Eyre Square (☎ **091/539-912**) offers Internet access and low-cost international calls. You'll be lucky to find any place in the countryside, although the majority of even the small rural B&Bs listed in this chapter have Wi-Fi.

Pharmacies   In Galway City, try **Eyre Square Pharmacy,** 2 Eyre Square, (☎ **091/567-740**). If you need a drugstore off-hours, the **University Late Night Pharmacy,** opposite the University College Hospital on Newcastle Road (☎ **091/ 520-115**), is open until 9pm weekdays, though it doesn't stay open late on weekends.

Taxis   In Galway City, try **Abby Taxis** (☎ **091/533-333**) or **Galway Taxis** (☎ **091/561-111**). Taxis in small towns and villages are rare; the best bet is to ask at your hotel or B&B.

WHERE TO STAY

Galway City has a handful of good, reasonably priced accommodations, although, as with many Irish cities, you'll get more for your money by staying in the 'burbs—in this case, pretty Salthill, a mile or two to the west of the center. Further afield from the region's main hub, the countryside is scattered with exceptionally beautiful and interesting places to stay.

Where to Stay in and Around Galway City

The G ★★★   When the G opened in the mid-2000s it was considered a symbol of Galway's status as a sophisticated and moneyed enclave. A modern and luxurious hotel, it's full of chic designer flourishes and contemporary art. The hotel overlooks the glassy waters of Lough Atalia and Galway Bay, and many bedrooms have floor-to-ceiling windows to take full advantage of those views, flooding the place with natural light. Service is outstanding, with charming and attentive staff. Treatments in the artfully designed spa aren't cheap, but excellent package deals are on offer, including a massage, use of the thermal suite (usually €20), dinner in the hotel restaurant, and tickets to the movie of your choice at a nearby cinema for just €120 per person. **Gigi's** restaurant serves good modern Irish food, with plenty of local meats and seafood. The menu also carries a nice innovation—you can choose from one of three set menus, which are ordered by price. "Treat" will set you back €25 for three courses, while "Indulge" is much steeper—€55 for four courses.

Wellpark, Galway, Co. Galway. www.theghotel.ie. ☎ **091/865-200**. 101 units. €125–€215 double. Free parking. Breakfast included. **Amenities:** Wi-Fi (free), restaurant, bar, room service, spa, gym.

The House Hotel ★★   This upbeat, funky hotel is set in the heart of Galway City. The public areas are filled with playful design statements, from polka-dot chairs to hot-pink sofas. Don't worry: Guest rooms are far more muted and restful, if still stylish, in oatmeal, white, or green color schemes, with the slightest hint of a retro theme. The restaurant is good and surprisingly reasonable for a hotel of this size in the center of the city. The in-house cocktail bar is a lively nightspot. That said, you're spoiled for choice when it comes to nightlife in this neighborhood—Galway's buzzing Latin Quarter is literally on your doorstep. The House Hotel runs frequent deals, such as a 2-night dinner, bed and breakfast package for an impressive €160 per person.

Spanish Parade, Galway, Co. Galway. www.thehousehotel.ie. ℂ **091/538-900.** 40 units. €129–€249. Discounted parking at nearby lot (€8 for 24 hrs.). Breakfast not included in lower rates. **Amenities:** Wi-Fi (free), restaurant, bar, room service.

Marless House ★ A congenial B&B in Salthill, the small seaside commuter town immediately to the west of Galway, Marless House offers exceptionally good value for the money. Guest rooms are spacious and spotlessly clean (though some have slightly overwhelming floral color schemes). Mary and Tom are thoughtful hosts; they have arrangements with several local tour groups, so if you want to book an organized trip to one of the major sights in the region—including the Aran Islands and the Cliffs of Moher—the coach will come and pick you up directly from here, and drop you back at the end of the day. Mary is also a great source of sightseeing information and will cheerfully help you draw up an itinerary. Breakfasts are scrumptious and filling.

8 Threadneedle Rd., Salthill, Galway, Co. Galway. www.marlesshouse.com. ℂ **091/523-931.** 6 units. €70–€80. Free parking. Breakfast included. **Amenities:** Wi-Fi (free).

Sea Breeze Lodge ★★ Another good option in Salthill, just outside Galway City, this stylish little B&B overlooks Galway Bay. Guest rooms are spacious and contemporary, with polished wood floors and big windows, looking out over the bay or garden. Beds are enormous—the larger ones are super king-size (the European equivalent of an American king-size), and all have luxurious memory foam mattresses. Breakfasts are served in a pleasant little conservatory overlooking the garden. The hotel can arrange tours of the major sights in the area, including an all-day trip to the Aran Islands for €25 per person. There's no restaurant, but the center of Galway is only about 5km (3 miles) by car or taxi.

9 Cashelmara, Salthill, Galway, Co. Galway. www.seabreezelodge.org. ℂ **091/529-581.** 6 units. €132–€160. Free parking. Rates include breakfast. **Amenities:** Wi-Fi (free).

Where to Stay in Connemara and the Aran Islands

Dolphin Beach House ★★★ All in all, this is one of our favorite guesthouses on the Emerald Isle. A splendidly restored early-20th-century homestead, Dolphin Beach House has awe-inspiring views of the bay at Clifden. The guest rooms are huge and light-filled, with handmade wood beds and high ceilings. The dining room looks out across acres of green fields, giving way to the azure sea beyond. Delicious evening meals are served here, such as local lamb or a catch of the day. The vegetables for the table are grown in the house's own organic garden. Breakfasts are good, too. Fearghus Foyle is an easy, charming host and a passionate environmentalist; the house is almost entirely powered by renewable energy sources, and there's a rainwater collection and recycling system. Check the website for good midweek discount deals. *Note:* Dinner must be booked in advance, before you arrive.

Lower Sky Rd., Clifden, Co. Galway. www.dolphinbeachhouse.com. ℂ **095/21204.** 4 units. €98–€180. Free parking. Breakfast included. 3-course dinner €40. **Amenities:** Wi-Fi (free), restaurant. No children under 12.

Kilmurvey House ★★   Overlooking Dún Aengus Fort (see p. 170), this is probably the best place to stay on the Aran Islands. At first view, the gray stone manor looks somewhat austere; inside, however, it's all cheerful, bright rooms and polished wood floors. Owner Teresa Joyce is extremely welcoming, and her home-cooked breakfasts are superb (try her porridge made with whiskey). She occasionally cooks dinner, too, although generally not for small groups—check in advance if you want to try and arrange this. She'll happily serve you a glass of wine and a plate of crackers and cheese, however, if you just want a snack. Guest rooms are enormous; you could probably fit an average European city B&B bedroom into one of these bright, light-filled spaces several times over.

Kilmurvey, Inis Mor, Aran Islands, Co. Galway. www.kilmurveyhouse.com. © **099/61218.** 12 units. €90–€110. Free parking. Breakfast included.

WHERE TO EAT

Cosmopolitan Galway City is naturally the focus of the western region's culinary scene. That's not to say that the range of options is particularly varied, but there are some excellent places—particularly if you're after fresh, local seafood. The rest of the county is not without a few top-notch places either, plus a liberal smattering of cheap and cheerful lunch spots.

Where to Eat in Galway City

Aniar ★★★ MODERN IRISH   This achingly fashionable restaurant in the center of Galway City is one of the best places to eat in the region. Head chef Ultan Cooke has won many fans both for his passionately slow-food ethos and his delicious food. The menu is tiny but smartly curated, and always designed according to what's best and in season. The central ingredients are given subtly innovative twists—duck served with dandelion, for example, or filet of John Dory with mussels and monk's beard (the leaves of the soda plant). The only downside is the cost. This is not a cheap night out, although the five-course tasting menu for €60 (€90 with a different glass of wine per course) is less expensive than you might expect from a place as on trend as this. Needless to say, reservations are essential.

53 Lower Dominick St., Galway, Co. Galway. www.aniarrestaurant.ie. © **091/535-947.** €30–€35. Tues–Sat 6–10pm.

Ard Bia at Nimmo's ★★ SEAFOOD/BISTRO/CAFE   The pleasantly rustic dining room doubles as a popular cafe during the day. At any time, the emphasis is the same: delicious, homey flavors, with local and seasonal produce. Stop in for some tasty, creative sandwiches at lunch, or maybe some fresh hummus with roast vegetables. In the evening, expect local fish with wilted greens and saffron aioli or perhaps some lamb marinated in harissa. The wine list is excellent and reasonably priced—you can pop in just for a glass or two without eating, if you don't mind perching on a barstool. They also do a popular brunch on weekends.

Spanish Arch, Long Walk, Galway, Co. Galway. www.ardbia.com. © **091/561-114.** Lunch: €5–€12. Dinner: €19–€26. Mon–Fri 10am–3:30pm (lunch served from noon) and 6–10pm. Sat–Sun 10am–3:30pm (brunch only) and 6–10pm.

G.B.C. (Galway Bakery Company) ★★ BAKERY/BISTRO   Both the cheerful bakery and cafe downstairs during the day and the busy restaurant upstairs come nightfall are hugely popular with locals. The cafe serves breakfast, fresh bakery goods, and light meals all day. It's a buzzing spot for a cup of coffee and a mid-afternoon treat. Meanwhile, upstairs is a proper sit-down bistro, albeit a pleasantly informal one, serving steak, roast chicken, fajitas, pasta, or maybe a fresh filet of salmon. The evening set menu offers much the same hearty kind of fare, but the early-bird menu tends to have a couple of different options—such as burgers, open sandwiches, and even an extremely late-in-the-day full Irish breakfast.

Williamsgate St., Galway, Co. Galway. www.gbcgalway.com. ☎ **091/563-087.** €4–€17. Cafe: daily 8am–8pm. Restaurant: Sun–Wed noon–8pm, Thurs–Sat noon–9pm.

Gourmet Tart Company ★★ BAKERY/INTERNATIONAL A French-style bakery and patisserie with a restaurant attached, the Gourmet Tart Company is very popular with locals for snacks, light meals, and sweet treats. (They also do a very good sit-down breakfast if you want to linger.) At lunch they sell sandwiches and assorted deli items to take out. At night, however, appears a full menu of delicious international fare at very reasonable prices. Think filet of sole with new potatoes, Thai curry with coconut rice, or perhaps a salad of Parma ham, pears, and Cashel blue cheese. Brunch is popular on Sundays. There are also smaller (deli/bakery only) branches in the Galway Shopping Centre on Headford Road; at 7 Lower Abbeygate Street; and on Raven Terrace, opposite the fire station.

Salthill Upper (opposite Salthill Church), Salthill, Galway, Co. Galway. www.gourmettartco.com. ☎ **091/861-667.** Breakfast: €2–€10. Lunch: €4–€12. Dinner: €8–€17. Mon–Thurs 8am–6pm; Fri–Sat 8am–9pm; Sun 8am–6pm.

Kirwan's Lane ★★ MODERN IRISH/SEAFOOD The exposed stone walls of the elegant downstairs dining room at this popular restaurant speak to the building's medieval origins. Open the menu, however, and everything suddenly seems up to date—this is one of the most reliable restaurants in Galway City for modern Irish cuisine. Seafood is a specialty, expertly prepared and presented, from prawn and clam linguine with chili, garlic, and lemon to Connemara mussels prepared with lemongrass and coconut cream. Carnivores are not overlooked, with a good selection of meat dishes (try the duckling with orange and mango purée if it's on offer).

Kirwan's Lane, Galway, Co. Galway. www.kirwanslane.com. ☎ **091/568-266.** €17–€25. Mon–Sat 12:30–2:30pm and 6–10pm; Sun 6–10pm.

Martine's Quay Street ★★ BISTRO A friendly, cozy restaurant in the center of Galway City, Martine's serves excellent, Irish-influenced bistro-style cooking, occasionally with Asian touches. The menu is short but well curated: dishes like tempura of hake or goat's cheese salad, followed by a juicy steak or catch of the day. They take their meat seriously here; the specials board includes a "cut of the day," according to what's best. The early-bird menu is an excellent value at €20 for two courses (or €25 for three). It's also not really early bird at all—it's available all night, every night. This is also a good choice for a simple but delicious lunch of salads, sandwiches, and a few more extensive, sit-down lunch dishes, all for around €10 or less.

21 Quay St., Galway, Co. Galway. www.winebar.ie. ☎ **091/565-662.** €12–€17. Daily 1–3pm and 5–10:30pm.

Oscars Seafood Bistro ★★★ SEAFOOD Another of the standout places to go for seafood in Galway City, Oscar's is a cheerful, relaxed kind of place. The dining room is filled with modern art, with fabric drapes across the ceiling providing a slightly bohemian touch. You could start with some prawns, cooked simply in garlic and butter, before moving on to some Clare Island salmon with seasonal vegetables, or perhaps some seared scallops with lime drizzle. There are always plenty of specials, which vary according to what's fresh, plus a couple of meat dishes. The ingredients are sourced from local producers and farmers markets. The fixed-price menu is an exceptional value at just €15 for two courses (served Monday to Thursday all night and Friday until 7pm).

Dominick St., Galway, Co. Galway. www.oscarsbistro.ie. © **091/852-180.** €15–€25. Daily noon–9pm.

The Pie Maker ★★ PIES   Just try and beat *this* for an authentic Irish food experience. With its old-style red-and-gold frontage and dimly lit, quirkily decorated dining room, the Pie Maker could have tumbled fully formed out of the Victorian age. The menu consists of pies, pies, and more pies, with light, fresh pastry crusts. There are a couple of sweet options, but most are savory with hot, fresh fillings of meat and vegetables, such as roast beef, curried chicken, chicken and mushroom, or sausage and mozzarella. Super-traditional sides come in the form of creamy mashed potatoes and garden peas. And if by some miracle you have room for dessert, try the amazing Banoffee pie, a heavenly combination of whipped cream, banana, and toffee with a crumbly base. Pies can also be ordered to go. The Pie Maker is open until an astonishingly late 4am on Fridays and Saturdays should you feel yourself in need of a late—or should that be early?—snack. *Note:* Cash only.

10 Cross St. Upper, Galway, Co. Galway. © **091/513-151.** €5–€10. Daily noon–10pm.

Where to Eat in Connemara and the Aran Islands

O'Dowd's ★★ SEAFOOD   There's not much room in this tiny pub in tiny Roundstone, which means you'll be fighting for space with dozens of hungry locals. But trust them, for they know exactly what they're here for: extremely good, fresh seafood, simply and beautifully prepared. There's nothing complicated about the menu, and that's part of the appeal—Connemara salmon or seafood au gratin, served with boiled potatoes or fries, or perhaps a simple lamb stew to keep carnivores happy. Try the delicious chowder if it's on offer. Needless to say, reservations are advisable.

Roundstone, Co. Galway. www.odowdsseafoodbar.com. © **095/35809.** Main courses €13–€22. Mon–Sat 10am–5:30pm.

The Steam Café ★ CAFE   This cute and simple little cafe is one of the best places in Clifden for lunch. The menu isn't fancy, but it's all good—wraps, sandwiches, light meals, and daily specials, all made with quality ingredients. The salads come from the café's own organic vegetable garden. The soups are particularly tasty, with ever-changing daily specials, but you may find minestrone, tomato and herb, or even carrot and orange. They also do tasty cakes and desserts—great to wash down the excellent coffee. The Steam Café is in the Station House Hotel, which is on the main N59 road, in Clifden town center.

Station House Hotel Courtyard, off N59 (Galway Rd.), Clifden, Co. Galway. © **095/30600.** €4–€12. Mon–Sat 10am–5:30pm.

Teach Nan Phaidi ★★ CAFE/IRISH   The Aran Islands aren't exactly awash with fine restaurants, and so as a captive audience you might be forgiven for lowering your expectations. But this little cafe-restaurant near the Dún Aengus Fort is nothing short of delightful. The Irish country cottage interior is atmospheric, with exposed wood beams and jauntily painted furniture. The menu is straightforward and unfussy but quite delicious: cakes, stews, sandwiches, and soups—comfort food, in other words, and incredibly welcome after a blustery day on the island. Most of the ingredients are locally sourced, and there's a special children's menu, too. The homemade desserts, particularly the cakes, are absolutely delicious. Service is upbeat and cheerful.

Kilmurvey, Inis Mor, Aran Islands, Co. Galway. ℂ **099/20975.** €4–€13. Daily 11am–5pm.

EXPLORING COUNTY GALWAY

The majority of top attractions in County Galway are split between two regions: the area around busy Galway City, and the wild, untamed landscapes to the west known as Connemara. Here you'll find windswept, boggy countryside peppered with breathtaking views, dramatic old buildings, and charming little towns.

Tourism Offices

The **Galway Tourist Office** is on Forster Street, Galway (www.galway.ie; ℂ **091/537-700**). The city also has a smaller tourist information point on Eyre Square. The **Aran Islands Tourist Office** is in Kilronan, Inishmore (ℂ **099/61263**). The **Clifden Tourist Office** is on Galway Road, Clifden (ℂ **095/21163**). The Clifden office is closed in winter.

Top Attractions in Galway City

A small but thriving and cultured city, Galway still has its winding medieval lanes, but it also has a cosmopolitan core. The city's hub is busy Eyre Square (pronounced *Air* Square), which is a few minutes' walk from everywhere. The charming, artsy medieval district is a tiny, tangled area, so getting lost is half the fun of going there.

Many of Galway's top attractions are outdoors and free of charge. In the center of town, for example, on Shop Street, is **Lynch's Castle,** dating from 1490 and renovated in the 19th century. It's now a branch of the Allied Irish Bank, and you can walk in and look around. The stern exterior is watched over by a handful of amusing gargoyles.

Close to the city docks, you can still see the area where Spanish merchants unloaded cargo from their galleons. The **Spanish Arch** was one of four arches built in 1594, and the **Spanish Parade** is a small open square, which, like Eyre Square, is great for people-watching.

Corrib Princess Cruise ★ TOUR   Sit back and take in the view from this 157-passenger, two-deck boat as it cruises along the River Corrib out of Galway City. The journey along the river takes in castles, historical sites, and assorted wildlife. There's a bar onboard, with an enthusiastic hostess who shows passengers how to fix the perfect Irish coffee and often tries to liven things up with a bit of traditional dancing. It's not for those averse to the tourist experience, but the 90-minute trip is very picturesque. You can buy tickets at the dock or at the *Corrib Princess* desk in the tourist office. It's advisable to call ahead or check the website for up-to-date sailing times.

Departs from Woodquay, Galway, Co. Galway. www.corribprincess.ie. ℂ **091/592-447.** €15 adults, €13 seniors and students, €7 children 4–16; €35 families. Sailings May, Jun, and Sept daily 2:30 and 4:30pm; Jul–Aug daily 12:30, 2:30, and 4:30pm.

Druid Theatre ★★ PERFORMING ARTS   Highly respected across Ireland and beyond for its original, cutting-edge productions, the Druid has been one of the region's foremost arts institutions since the 1970s. They're particularly known for premiering new work from up-and-coming writers, so expect to find challenging,

THE aran islands

"I have heard that, at that time, the ruling proprietor and magistrate of the north island used to give any man who had done wrong a letter to a jailer in Galway, and send him off by himself to serve a term of imprisonment."

—J. M. Synge

When you see the ghostly shapes of the Aran Islands floating 48km (30 miles) out at sea like misty Brigadoon, you instantly understand why the sea-battered and wind-whipped Aran Islands have been the subject of fable, song, and film for thousands of years.

The islands—**Inis Mor** (Inishmore), **Inis Meain** (Inishmaan), and **Inis Oirr** (Inisheer)—are outposts of Gaelic culture and language. All the islands are rather strange looking, with a ring of rocks around their outer edges and, inside, small farms surrounded by soft green grass and wildflowers. Life on the islands is deeply isolated. To this day, many of the 1,500 inhabitants maintain a somewhat traditional life, fishing from currachs (small crafts made of tarred canvas stretched over timber frames), living in stone cottages, relying on pony-drawn wagons to get around, and speaking Gaelic. They still wear the classic creamy hand-made *bainin* sweaters that originated here, as there's nothing better for keeping out the chill.

Of the islands, **Inishmore** is the largest and easiest to reach from Galway. Its easy transport means you can escape the crowds if you wish. Most visitors debark from the ferries at **Kilronan,** Inishmore's

main town (though it's only the size of a village). It's an easy enough place in which to arrange or rent transportation. The mode is up to you: Horse-drawn buggies can be hailed like taxis as you step off the boat, minivans stand at the ready, and bicycle-rental shops are within sight. Drop in at **Oifig Fáilte** (Aran Island Tourist Information) in Kilronan to pick up walking maps, ask questions, and generally get yourself going here.

There are some excellent geological sights on the islands, including the magnificent **Dún Aengus,** a vast 2,000-year-old stone fortress on Inishmore on the edge of a cliff that drops 90m (295 ft.) to the sea. Its original purpose is unknown—some think it was a military structure, others say it was a vast ceremonial theater. From the top, there are spectacular views of Galway Bay, the Burren, and Connemara.

Aran Island Ferries (www.aranisland ferries.com; ✆ **091/568-903**) runs daily service to Inishmore and Inishmaan. Boats leave from Rossaveal (Ros a' Mhíl) 23 miles west of Galway City. The crossing takes 40 minutes. Call for daily sailing times. The booking office is at 4 Forster Street in Galway. A shuttle bus goes from nearby Queen's Street to the ferry port, but you must check in at the booking office least 90 minutes before sailing time if you want to take it. The return crossing costs €25 adults, €20 seniors and students, €13 children. Round-trip shuttle bus fares are €8 adults, €7 seniors and students, €5 children.

intelligent material being staged here. They also produce new versions of classic plays by Irish, British, and European dramatists. Shows can sell out some time in advance, however, and are often out on the road (the Druid is a touring company), so it's advisable to check out what's on and make reservations as far in advance as possible. Ticket prices range from around €15 to €45.

Flood St., Galway, Co. Galway, www.druid.ie. ✆ **091/568-660.** Ticket prices and performance times vary by show.

County Galway

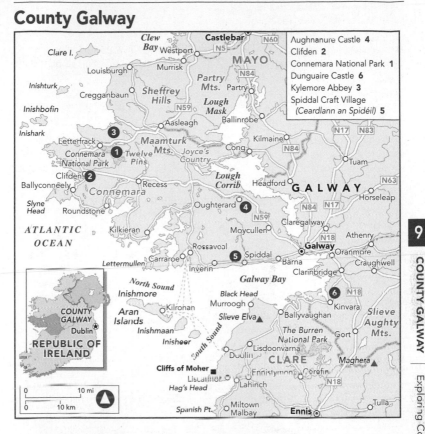

Aughnanure Castle **4**
Clifden **2**
Connemara National Park **1**
Dunguaire Castle **6**
Kylemore Abbey **3**
Spiddal Craft Village
(Ceardlann an Spidéil) **5**

Galway Arts Centre ★★ ARTS COMPLEX   Once the home of W. B. Yeats's patron, Lady Gregory, this attractive town house housed local governmental offices for many years. Today it offers an excellent program of concerts, readings, and exhibitions by Irish and international artists, returning, in a way, to a form Lady Gregory would have appreciated. Usually two or three exhibitions run at any one time. The Arts Centre also manages a second building at 23 Nuns Island. The permanent home of the Galway Youth Theatre, it's used by them and other groups for performances, concerts, and films. For details, call the main arts center number.

47 Dominick St., Galway, Co. Galway. www.galwayartscentre.ie. ⓒ **091/565-886.** Free admission. Mon–Fri 10am–5:30pm, Sat 10am–2pm.

Galway Atlantaquaria ★★★ AQUARIUM   Also known as the National Aquarium of Ireland (the largest in the country), this is a fantastic way to reward kids for trudging around all those historic ruins. One's imagination is captured right from the first exhibit—a dramatic "splash room" where a large, one-tonne (just under a ton) capacity tank goes off every minute or so with a giant splash, which is designed to imitate the natural movement of waves on the Galway coast. The exhibits are thoughtfully presented throughout. Highlights include the enormous ocean tank, set over two floors and housing a couple of hundred sea creatures, including small sharks; a "wreck" tank that's home to dangerous conger eels; and touch pools in which kids can handle tame sea creatures such as starfish and hermit crabs, under supervision from the aquarium staff. There's also the opportunity to tickle some inquisitive rays—make sure your hands are wet first or your touch can burn their skin.

The Promenade, Salthill, Galway, Co. Galway. www.nationalaquarium.ie. © **091/585-100.** €11.50 adults, €8 seniors and students, €7.50 children 3–16, €4.50 extra children, €22–€33 families. Mon–Fri 10am–5pm; Sat–Sun 10am–6pm.

Galway Cathedral ★ CHURCH   It's easy to understand why this church's nickname is so short and simple, given that its official name is "Cathedral of Our Lady Assumed into Heaven and St. Nicholas." The impressive, domed exterior is classical in style, although it was built in the 1960s. The interior is striking, with rows of symmetrical stone archways and dramatic lighting. Contemporary Irish artisans designed the statues, colorful mosaics, and stained-glass windows. The limestone for the walls was cut from local quarries, while the polished floor is made from Connemara marble.

University and Gaol rds. beside the Salmon Weir Bridge on the river's west bank. www.galway cathedral.ie. © **091/563-577** (select option 4). Free admission; donations welcome. Daily 8:30am–6:30pm.

Galway City Museum ★ MUSEUM   A rather endearing little museum overlooking the Spanish Arch, this is a good place to spend half an hour acquainting yourself with the city's history. The permanent galleries downstairs relate to Galway's prehistoric and medieval periods, while the upper levels deal with the city's more recent past, including its relationship with the arts. Highlights include a large collection of intricate embroidered textiles made by a local order of nuns between the 17th and 20th centuries, and some engaging exhibits relating to the history of cinema going in the city. A lively program of special events includes talks, touring exhibitions, and hands-on arts workshops.

Spanish Parade, Galway, Co. Galway. www.galwaycitymuseum.ie. © **091/532-460.** Free admission. Jun–Aug Tues–Sat 10am–5pm, Sun noon–5; Sept–May Tues–Sat 10am–5pm. Closed Mon.

Lynch's Castle ★ CASTLE   Dating from 1490 and renovated in the 19th century, this impressive structure was once home to the Lynch family, who ruled the city for many years. It's one of the oldest medieval town houses in Ireland and is now a branch of the Allied Irish Bank. The stern exterior is watched over by a handful of amusing gargoyles; inside is a small display telling the building's history.

Abbeygate and Shop sts. Free admission. Mon–Wed and Fri 10am–4pm; Thurs 10am–5pm.

Spiddal Craft Village (Ceardlann an Spidéil) ★★ ARTS COMPLEX   On the main road as you enter Spiddal from Galway is this fantastic collection of cottage-style crafts stores and workshops. The artists in residence here change, but there's always a diverse selection. At this writing, they include a basket maker; a store selling Irish language books and creative, artsy gifts; a wonderful contemporary ceramicist; a jeweler specializing in pieces made from pre-euro Irish coins; a traditional weaver; a stained-glass artist; and a couple of very talented painters. There are plenty of affordable items, in addition to some more exclusive work. Even if you're not buying, it's an inspiring place to browse. The on-site **Builín Blasta Café** sells delicious bakery goods,

Galway City

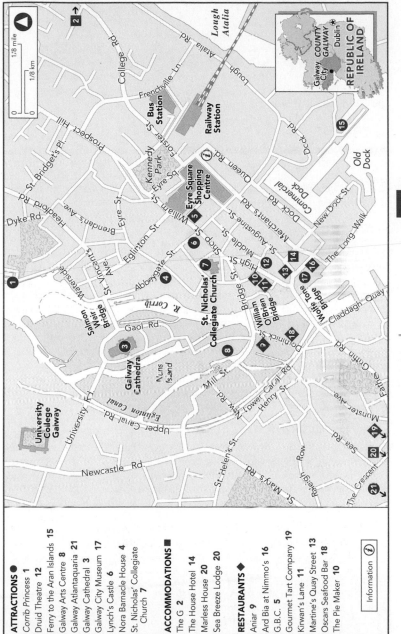

ATTRACTIONS ●

Corrib Princess **1**
Druid Theatre **12**
Ferry to the Aran Islands **15**
Galway Arts Centre **8**
Galway Atlantaquaria **21**
Galway Cathedral **3**
Galway City Museum **17**
Lynch's Castle **6**
Nora Barnacle House **4**
St. Nicholas' Collegiate
Church **7**

ACCOMMODATIONS ■

The G **2**
The House Hotel **14**
Marless House **20**
Sea Breeze Lodge **20**

RESTAURANTS ◆

Aniar **9**
Ard Bia at Nimmo's **16**
G.B.C. **5**
Gourmet Tart Company **19**
Kirwan's Lane **11**
Martine's Quay Street **13**
Oscars Seafood Bar **18**
The Pie Maker **10**

Information ⓘ

A DAY AT THE races

Almost as big a social event as it is a sporting one, the **Galway Races** are a big deal on the Irish horse-racing calendar. People dress up in posh frocks and big hats, and the crowds cheer enthusiastically as the competing racehorses pound the turf. Horse lovers and high rollers still pour in from around the country for the race weeks in July, August, and October. The animals are the best around, and the atmosphere is electric. Ticket prices vary depending on the event and day of the week, but expect to pay from around €20 to upward of €40 for a ticket. There are also multiday and season tickets available. The racetrack is in Ballybrit, on the north side of the city. See www.galwayraces.com or call the track directly at ✆ **091/735-870** for more details.

snacks, and light meals, in addition to takeaway deli items. You can contact the individual artists via the main website.

About 15km (9.3 miles) west of Galway on R336, Spiddal, Co. Galway. www.ceardlann.com. ✆ **086/806-7352.** Mon–Sat 9:30am–6pm, Sun noon–5pm.

St. Nicholas' Collegiate Church ★★ CHURCH   This is Galway's oldest church—it's said that Christopher Columbus prayed here in 1477 before sailing away on one of his attempts to reach the New World. Established in about 1320, it has changed from Roman Catholic to Church of Ireland and back again at least four times. Currently, it's under the aegis of the latter denomination. Inside are a 12th-century crusader's tomb with a Norman inscription, a carved font from the 16th or 17th century, and a stone lectern with barley-sugar twist columns from the 15th century. Guided tours, conducted by a knowledgeable and enthusiastic church representative, can be arranged. Call or ask at the church for details.

Jcn. of Mainguard and Lombard sts., Galway, Co. Galway. www.stnicholas.ie. ✆ **086/389-8777.** Free admission (donations requested). Mar–Dec 9am–7pm; Jan–Feb 9am–5pm. Opening times may vary in winter. No tours available Sun morning.

Top Attractions in Connemara

If you look for Connemara on road signs, you may be looking forever, because it's not a city or county, but rather an area or region. Like the Burren in County Clare, the boundaries are a bit hazy, but most agree that Connemara is west of Galway City, starting at Oughterard and continuing toward the Atlantic. You know it when you see it, as it's an area of heartbreaking barrenness and unique beauty, with dark bogs and tall, jagged mountains punctuated by curving, glassy lakes dotted with green islands. The desolate landscape is caused, in part, by an absence of trees that were felled and dragged off long ago for building ships, houses, and furniture. Connemara is part of the **Gaeltacht,** or Irish-speaking area, so many signs are in Gaelic only.

Aughnanure Castle ★ CASTLE   Standing on an outcrop of rock surrounded by forest and pasture, this sturdy fortress is a well-preserved Irish tower castle, with an unusual double *bawn* (fortified enclosure) and a still-complete watchtower that you can climb. It was built around A.D. 1500 as a stronghold of the "Ferocious" O'Flaherty clan, who dominated the region and terrified the neighbors in their day. The castle's fireplaces are so big that you could fit a double bed in them. The ruined banqueting hall contains the remains of a dry harbor.

Oughterard, Co. Galway. www.heritageireland.ie. ℂ **091/552-214.** Admission €3 adults, €2 seniors, €1 children, €8 families. apr–late-Oct daily 9:30am–6pm.

Clifden (An Clochán) ★ TOWN   This pretty little seaside town has an enviable location at the edge of the blue waters of Clifden Bay, where miles of curving, sandy beaches skirt the rugged coastline. It's a small, attractive place with colorful Victorian shop fronts and church steeples thrusting skyward through a veil of trees. With its plentiful restaurants, shops, hotels, and pubs, there's plenty to keep you amused here for a few hours. Though undeniably handsome and worth a visit, the downside is that Clifden is also quite touristy. If you prefer somewhere more off the beaten path, take a detour to **Roundstone (_Cloch na Rón_)** on your way out of town. About 24km (15 miles) south on R341, it's a smaller, sleepier fishing port, with pristine beaches. To reach Clifden from Galway City, take N59, the stunning drive, which takes just over 1 hour, passes through the heart of Connemara National Park (see below).

Clifden, Co. Galway.

Connemara National Park ★★★ PARK   This gorgeous national park encompasses over 2,000 hectares (4,940 acres) of mountains, bogs, grasslands, and hiking trails. Some of the best lead through the peaceful **_Gleann Mór_ (Big Glen),** with its River Polladirk, or up to the **Twelve Bens** (also called the Twelve Pins), a small, quartzite mountain range north of the Galway-Clifden road. Nearby are the lesser-known, equally lovely **Maumturk** range and the breathtaking **Killary Fiord**—the only fiord in Ireland. None of the Twelve Bens rises above 730m (2,392 ft.), which makes their summits quite accessible to those who don't mind walking at a steep incline. Frequent rainfall produces dozens of tiny streams and waterfalls, and the views are spectacular. The excellent Visitor Centre south of the crossroads in **Letterfrack** dispenses general information on the park and sustenance in the form of tea, sandwiches, and fresh-baked goods.

Visitor Centre: Signposted from N59, Letterfrack, Co. Galway. www.connemaranationalpark.ie. ℂ **095/41054** or 076/100-2530. Free admission. Visitor Centre: Mar–Oct 9am–5:30pm. Park: daily, year-round.

Kylemore Abbey ★★ HISTORIC SITE   As you round yet another bend on the particularly barren stretch of country road around Kylemore, this extraordinary neo-Gothic abbey looms into view, at the base of a wooded hill across the mirror-like

A TRIP TO clonmacnoise

Resting somberly on the east bank of the Shannon, this is one of Ireland's most profound ancient sites. St. Ciaran founded the monastic community of **Clonmacnoise** in A.D. 548 at the crucial intersection of the Shannon and the Dublin-Galway land route, and it soon became one of Europe's great centers of learning and culture.

For nearly 1,000 years, Clonmacnoise flourished under the patronage of Irish chiefs. The last high king, Rory O'Connor, was buried here in 1198. Clonmacnoise was raided repeatedly by native chiefs, Danes, and Anglo-Normans, until it was finally destroyed by English troops in 1552. Previously the monks always had something to rebuild, but this time the English carried away everything—the roofs from the buildings, the doors, even the panes from the windows. By the time they'd finished, according to a report written by a monk from that time, "There was not left a bell, small or large, an image or an altar, or a book, or a gem, or even glass in a window, from the wall of the church out, which was not carried off."

Today you can see what was left of the cathedral, a castle, eight churches, two round towers, three sculpted high crosses, and more than 200 monumental slabs, including some stones on which the old carvings can still be seen with thoughtful messages in ancient Celtic writing saying things like "A prayer for Daniel."

Clonmacnoise is on R357, 6.5km (4 miles) north of Shannonbridge, County Offaly. The drive from Galway City is mostly motorway and takes about 1 hour. Entry costs €6 adults, €4 seniors, €2 students and children, €14 families. It's open mid-March to May and September and October daily from 10am to 6pm; June to August daily 9am to 6:30pm; and November to mid-March daily from 10am to 5:30pm. For more information, call the visitor center at ℭ **090/9674195.**

Kylemore Lake. The facade of the main building—a vast, crenelated 19th-century house—is a splendid example of neo-Gothic architecture. In 1920, its owners donated it to the Benedictine nuns, and the sisters have run a convent boarding school here ever since. You can see a little of the interior, but it's disappointingly plain; the exterior and the grounds are the attraction here, and impressive enough to justify a visit. The highlight is the restored Gothic chapel, an exquisite cathedral in miniature with a plain, somber cemetery to one side, a lavish Victorian walled garden, and the breathtaking views of it all from across the lake. The complex includes a decent restaurant that serves produce grown on the nuns' farm, as well as tea and good scones; a shop with a working pottery studio; and a visitor center. The abbey is most atmospheric when the bells are rung for midday office or for vespers at 6pm.

Kylemore, Co. Galway (follow signs from N59). www.kylemoreabbey.com. ℭ **095/52011.** Admission €12.50 adults, €10 seniors, €9 students and children 11–17, €25–€34 families, children 10 and under free. Mar and Oct 9am–5:30pm; Apr–Jun and Sept 9am–6pm; Jul–Aug 9am–7pm; Nov and Feb 9:30am–5pm; Dec 9:30am–4:30pm; Jan 10am–4:30pm.

COUNTIES MAYO & SLIGO

The strikingly beautiful landscape of Galway continues to the strikingly beautiful landscape of southern Mayo without fanfare. Like Galway, Mayo is marked by dramatic scenery, which terminates in rocky cliffs plunging down into the opaque blue waters of the icy sea. If you head farther north, you'll reach the smooth pastures of County Sligo. The main appeal here is not its towns, which tend to be functional farm communities, but the countryside. This is the landscape that inspired the poet William Butler Yeats. Its unspoiled marvels are still a healing tonic—though the region is rich with fairy-tale castles and mysterious prehistoric sites, its biggest gift to the visitor is tranquility.

ESSENTIALS

Arriving

BY BUS   **Bus Éireann** runs daily bus service to Sligo Town from Dublin, Galway, and other points including Derry in Northern Ireland. It provides daily service to major towns in Mayo. The bus station in Sligo is on Lord Edward Street.

BY TRAIN   Trains from Dublin and other major points arrive daily at Westport in Mayo, and Sligo Town in Sligo. The train station in Westport is on Altamont Street; about a 10-minute walk from the town center; in Sligo it's on Lord Edward Street, next to the bus station.

BY CAR   Four major roads lead to Sligo: N4 from Dublin and the east, N17 from Galway and the south, N15 from Donegal to the north, and N16 from Northern Ireland.

BY PLANE   **Ireland West Airport Knock** in Charlestown, County Mayo (www.knockairport.com; ℓ **094/936-8100**) is becoming quite a popular hub for budget airlines from the U.K. **Aer Lingus** (www.aerlingus.com; ℓ **081/836-5000**) or **Ryanair** (www.ryanair.com; ℓ **0871/246-0000** in the U.K. or ℓ 152/044-4004) run daily scheduled flights from London, Liverpool, Edinburgh, and Bristol. **Flybe** (ℓ **087/1700-2000** in the U.K. or ℓ 0044/1392-683-152) also has three flights per week from Manchester and Edinburgh. There are no flights to the airport from other points within Ireland.

ATMs/Banks In Westport, there is a branch of **AIB** on Shop Street (𝄐 098/25466). In Ballina, there's a **Bank of Ireland** on Pearse Street (𝄐 096/21144). In Sligo Town, try the **AIB** on Stephen Street (𝄐 071/914-2157).

Doctors For medical emergencies, dial 𝄐 999. For nonemergencies, your hotel should call you a doctor. Otherwise in Westport, try the **Westport Medical Clinic,** Market Lane (𝄐 098/27500); in Ballina, there's

the **Moyview Family Practise** on Dillon Terrace (𝄐 095/22933). In Sligo Town, the **Medicentre** is on Barrack Street (𝄐 071/914-2550).

Emergencies For police, fire, or other emergencies, dial 𝄐 999.

Pharmacies In Westport, try **Treacy's** on James Street (𝄐 098/25474). In Ballina, **Quinn's Chemist** is on Pearse Street (𝄐 096/21365). In Sligo Town, there's a branch of **Boots**

on O'Connell Street (𝄐 071/914-9445).

Taxis If you need a cab home from a restaurant, the management should be able to call a recommended one for you—particularly in rural areas, where taxi firms can be few and far between. Otherwise, in Ballina, you could try the **Ballina Taxi Company** (𝄐 087/295-8787). In Westport, there's **AA Taxis** (𝄐 087/237-7070). In Sligo Town, try **Ace Cabs** (𝄐 071/914-4444).

WHERE TO STAY

This region of Ireland has few pickings when it comes to the quantity of top places to stay. Even the major towns have only a smattering of decent B&Bs and small hotels. However, in the deepest reaches of the countryside, there are gems to be found. Places like Ashford Castle and Temple House in County Sligo, or the Bervie in County Mayo, are among the most unique and special places to stay in all of Ireland. It takes effort to get to these places, but the journey will be worth it.

Where to Stay in County Mayo

Ashford Castle ★★★ This fairytale-like castle has entertained plenty of famous guests over the years; Grace Kelly, Ronald Reagan, Brad Pitt, Pierce Brosnan, and Tony Blair are just a few of the luminaries to have been cosseted within its luxurious walls. It was also named the best resort hotel in Europe by *Condé Nast Traveler* in 2010, and if you've got a spare couple of hundred euros burning a hole in your wallet, you too can join the ranks of its illustrious fans. Ashford Castle was built in the 13th century and still looks every inch the palatial abode; suits of armor and priceless antiques line the walls and the sumptuous guest rooms have huge four-poster beds. The grounds are stunning—the castle overlooks Lough Corrib, and there are acres of forest and landscaped gardens in which to get lost. A range of spa treatments is available. The restaurant is as excellent as you'd expect (don't even think about dressing down, although there's a less formal eatery on the grounds, too). Hotel experiences in Ireland don't come much more splurge-y than this, but that's the cost of living like royalty—even for a night. Check the website for special deals, especially in the off season.

On R346, on the eastern approach to Cong, Co. Mayo. www.ashford.ie. 𝄐 094/954-6003. 83 units. €174–€726. Free parking. Breakfast included. **Amenities:** Wi-Fi (free), restaurants (2), bar, gym, massage treatments, estate sports including golf, fishing, and clay-pigeon shooting.

10

The Bervie ★★★   Overlooking the Atlantic Ocean on Achill Island, reached by a road bridge across Achill Sound, the Bervie is an inspiring place to stay. Husband-and-wife hosts, Elizabeth and John Barrett, spent years lovingly restoring the place. Elizabeth actually grew up here; it's been a B&B since the 1930s, although today it's a far more sophisticated place than she remembers from her childhood. Guest rooms are spacious, with well-chosen furniture (most of it made locally) and tasteful art. Some rooms directly overlook the sea—and what a view! You can see some of the other islands dotted around the bay from some rooms, while others have a dramatic viewpoint of cliffs. Light pours in from huge windows, and the whispering of the waves soothes you off to a restful sleep. Elizabeth's home-cooked breakfasts are to die for, and after years of being advance notice-only, the outstanding dinners are a permanent fixture. (Roast lamb served with Madeira jus, or rib-eye steak with onion marmalade blue cheese mushrooms—all with excellent use of local ingredients. There's a reasonably priced wine list too.)

The Strand, Keel, Achill, Co. Mayo. www.bervie-guesthouse-achill.com. ℂ **098/43114.** 14 units. €110–€130. Free parking. Breakfast included. Dinner €45. **Amenities:** Wi-Fi (free), restaurant. Take N59 to Achill Island, then follow R319 to Keel. The Bervie is signposted from the edge of the village.

Enniscoe House ★★   Flanked by Mount Nephin on one side and the shimmering waters of Lough Conn on the other, Enniscoe is a stunningly restored mid-18th-century mansion. Very little has been significantly altered from the original structure, so the place is overflowing with wonderful period details (one room even has its original silk wallpaper). Bedrooms are oversized with big windows and antique, half-canopied beds. Bathrooms are modern and elegantly designed. Susan Kellett and her son, DJ, run the place with a natural flair for hospitality. Susan is a great cook, too; make sure you book one of her excellent dinners. The grounds are big, and with enough to do that you could spend a day here without leaving, should you wish. They're open to the public, with a cafe and even a **Heritage Centre,** complete with a local history museum, a genealogical service, and a small antiques shop. The Enniscoe estate also has a couple of self-catering cottages available if you want even more privacy.

Castlehill, Ballina, Co. Mayo. www.enniscoe.com. ℂ **096/31112.** 6 units. €200–€240. Dinner €50. Free parking. Breakfast included. **Amenities:** Guest lounge.

Windmill Cottages ★★   Your host, Pierre Blezat, fell so in love with the area when he first came here that he left his native France to run Windmill Cottage as a B&B. He restored the small complex of farm buildings, and each displays a personal touch. The effect is like a series of cozy, contemporary country cabins; exposed pine walls, modern art on the walls, and up-to-date furniture. The cottages are a stone's throw (literally) from the sea, and the views of the water, with mountains in the distance, are seductive. The breakfast room takes full advantage of the view and sometimes doubles as a dining room in the evenings, when Pierre serves delicious French-Irish meals that must be booked in advance. Pierre can also arrange a chauffeur service to Westport train station for €15; transfers from further afield are possible, too.

Carraholly, about 2km (1.2 miles) west of Westport Golf Club, Co. Mayo. www.windmill-cottage.com. ℂ **098/56006.** 6 units. €100–€150. Dinner €30. Free parking. Breakfast included. **Amenities:** Wi-Fi (free), bike hire. Closed Oct–Mar.

Where to Stay in County Sligo

Ross Farmhouse ★★   Not far from Carrowkeel, Ross Farmhouse is a restored 19th-century cottage, surrounded by acres and acres of rolling farmland. The cheerful owners, Nicholas and Oriel Hill-Wilkinson, see this place as their pride and joy, and it shows in the wholehearted welcome they give guests. Bedrooms are reasonably sized, with simple, unfussy furnishings. One is a family room, and another is fully accessible to wheelchairs. Downstairs are two lovely guest lounges filled with antiques. An open peat fire warms the hearth in winter. Breakfasts are good, and they'll cook for you in the evenings if you book in advance (very reasonable at €35 per person; there's a good wine list, too, or you can bring your own if you prefer). In addition to all the countryside walks, ancient ruins, and sweet little towns you could wish for, the area has some of the best horseback riding in Ireland—ask if you'd like recommendations for local riding centers. *Note:* Not all bedrooms have a private bathroom, so specify when you book if you want one.

Riverstown, Co. Sligo. (Follow signs from Drumfin on N4 or Coola on R284.) www.rossfarmhouse sligo.com. ✆ **071/916-5140.** 6 units. €90. Free parking. Breakfast included. **Amenities:** Wi-Fi (free).

Temple House ★★★   This is quite simply *the* place you need to try and stay in the northwest if you're after a truly unique and historic B&B experience. Temple House is not the sort of place that's full of five-star extras, but you'll find it hard to beat for historical authenticity, beautiful surroundings, and sheer charm. The 1665 manor house has been restored, bit by painstaking bit, by the amiable young custodians of the estate, Roderick and Helena Perceval. The place is dripping with history; once a thriving country estate, it fell slowly into near-ruin during the turbulent years of the 20th century. Guest rooms are huge, packed with unusual antiques, and bathrooms are completely modern. Nightly dinners are more akin to parties, with all guests seated around an enormous old table, and the food is outstanding. Breakfasts hit the spot, too, with plenty of homemade treats. The beautiful grounds are full of secrets, including a boating lake, a walled garden, and even a ruined Knights Templar castle. There are supposedly a couple of resident ghosts, too, although they must be of a very friendly sort, with such a convivial atmosphere as this. There is also a self-catering cottage on the grounds.

Ballymote, Ballinacarrow, Co. Sligo. www.templehouse.ie. ✆ **071/918-3329.** 6 units. €140–€180. Dinner €45. Free parking. Breakfast included. **Amenities:** Wi-Fi (free). Closed Dec–Mar. No dinner Sun.

The Glasshouse ★   Depending on your point of view, this place is either a stylish retreat in a part of Ireland sorely lacking contemporary hotels or it resembles an explosion in a kitsch factory. The exterior, which juts out from beside River Garavogue, resembles a gleaming, modern ship; within, it's all multicolored circles on the carpet, misshapen blue sofas, and a bright orange, towering atrium. Bedrooms are a little more refined, with muted tones and modern art on the walls. There is an in-house restaurant, although it's somewhat pricey for Sligo. The appropriately named View Bar looks out over the town; it has live music, too, although that can be a drawback due to noise, so ask for a room away from the bar when you book.

Swan Point, Sligo, Co. Sligo. www.theglasshouse.ie. ✆ **071/919-4300.** 116 units. €79–€129. Free parking. Breakfast not included in lower rates. **Amenities:** Internet (broadband/via TV), restaurant, bars (2), room service, air conditioning (some rooms).

WHERE TO EAT

Standout restaurants in this part of the country are few and far between. However, they often can be found in hotels and the better B&Bs. Westport, in County Mayo, has some good, reliable choices, and the dining scene in Sligo Town has improved dramatically over the last couple of years.

Where to Eat in County Mayo

An Port Mor ★★ SEAFOOD/MODERN IRISH   This multi-award-winning restaurant in Westport specializes in seafood. Local catches dominate the menu, so you could easily find Clew Bay crab cakes and scallops, or blue trout (yes, *blue*) from Curran served with tarragon and canola. The seafood is excellent, but it's not all that's on offer; expect to find a juicy sirloin served with red onion marmalade, or perhaps some local lamb. Everything is impeccably presented, and the atmosphere in the cheerful dining room is relaxed. Service is excellent, too.

Bridge St., Westport, Co. Mayo. www.anportmor.com. © **098/26730.** €15–€28. Mon–Fri 5:30pm–midnight; Sat–Sun 5pm–midnight.

Bayside Bistro ★ BISTRO   There aren't many restaurants on Keel, the main town on little Achill Island, so we were pleased to find this cheerful and reasonably inexpensive option. The menu is far more varied than it has to be at dinner, ranging from stir-fried squid with sweet chili to duck in cranberry and red wine. There's always a wide selection of daily seafood specials, too. Lunches are simpler—salads, ciabatta sandwiches, crostini (grilled bread with assorted toppings), or even fish tacos.

On R319, Keel, Achill Island, Co. Mayo (next to the general store and post office in the center of the village). www.baysidebistro.ie. © **098/43798.** €14–€20. Daily noon–10pm.

The Helm ★ SEAFOOD/BISTRO   This laid-back bar-restaurant specializes in local seafood. Portions are generous: Tackle the delicious fisherman's platter only if you're very hungry or traveling with a small army. Creamy seafood chowder is a specialty. And for those who can't bear fish, there's the usual lamb or steak on the menu (though the fruits of the sea will be better). Lunch service is heartier and more traditional, with Irish stew and mash alongside lasagna and chips. Desserts are all comfort food like pies, crumbles, and even jelly and ice cream. The Helm is also a B&B with a few self-catering apartments available, too.

The Harbour, Westport, Co. Mayo. www.thehelm.ie. © **098/26398.** €19–€23. Sun–Thurs 8am–11:30pm; Fri–Sat 8am–12:20am. (Food served until about 9:30pm.)

The Lodge at Ashford Castle ★★★ CONTEMPORARY IRISH   If you can't quite swing a night at Ashford Castle (see listing earlier in this chapter), then, like the other 99% of us, you might consider dining here to get a peek at how the "set" set lives. And eats! The modern Irish cooking is deliciously inventive, and just a glance at the menu is enough to give you an idea of the celebratory approach to fine, locally sourced food here. A starter of Killary Fjord mussels and urchin is served with a sauce made with licorice and squid ink, while the Atlantic sea spray hogget (mature lamb) comes with wild garlic, seaweed, and lemon. The dining room has a fantastic view of Lough Corrib. If you want to spend the night, doubles start at around €130.

On the grounds of Ashford Castle, Cong, Co. Mayo. www.lisloughreylodge.com/fine-dining-mayo.html. © **094/954-5400.** Fixed-price menus (3 courses) €42. Mon–Sat 6–10pm; Sun 1–3:30pm and 6–10pm

Where to Eat in County Sligo

Coach Lane at Donaghy's Bar ★★ IRISH/INTERNATIONAL   A very popular spot with locals, Coach Lane has two dining rooms: a bar, serving easy crowd-pleasers such as burgers, fish and chips, and shepherd's pie; and a more upmarket, gastropub-style restaurant. There the menu is divided into salad, pasta, meat, or seafood options, so after an appetizer of buffalo wings or smoked salmon, you could move on to a Caesar salad or rib-eye steak. There's always a varied selection of seafood, too, including black sole in a white wine sauce, buttered shrimp with garlic and lemon, and salmon teriyaki.

1-2 Lord Edward St., Sligo, Co. Sligo. www.coachlane.ie. *©* **071/916-2417.** €18–€25. Bar food: daily 3–10pm. Restaurant: daily 5:30–10pm.

Eala Bhan ★ INTERNATIONAL   Surf and turf are the mainstays at the popular Eala Bhan. Enormous T-bones or tender sirloins come with satisfyingly traditional steakhouse sides—onion rings, french fries, or maybe a creamy potato gratin. The seafood is good: local (of course) hake or a catch of the day. The lunch menu is almost as extensive as dinner, with a few lighter options such as roast chicken salad or seafood chowder. The early-bird menu (served until 6:30 daily) is a great value at just €20 for three courses.

Rockwood Parade, Sligo, Co. Sligo. www.ealabhan.ie. *©* **071/914-5823.** €17–€25. Daily noon–3:30pm and 5–9:30pm.

Osta Café and Wine Bar ★ CAFE   The owners of this sweet cafe overlooking the river in Sligo are big believers in the slow food and organic movements. This is reflected in their delicious, healthful food that makes superb use of ingredients from small, local producers. Daily specials could include boxty, a traditional Irish potato pancake made with leeks and cheese, a delicious spinach quiche, or just a plate of fresh sandwiches. (The bread comes from a local bakery.) They also serve wonderful homemade soups. The cafe stays open until well into the evening on most days.

Garavogue Weir, off Stephen St., Sligo Town, Co. Sligo. www.osta.ie. *©* **071/914-4639.** €4–€12. Mon–Wed 8am–7pm; Thurs–Fri 8am–9pm; Sat 8am–8pm; Sun 9am–6pm.

Trá Bán ★★ INTERNATIONAL   Another fine place for steaks and seafood, Trá Bán is above a popular bar in Strandhill, a little seaside town about 8km (5 miles) west of Sligo Town. Typical starters include crab claws in garlic butter or salmon sushi. For your main course we recommend the "reef on beef" (sirloin, filet, or beef medallions with a lobster tail on top), or red snapper served with stir-fried vegetables and red-pepper coulis. There's also a special children's menu (three courses for €14). The atmosphere is easygoing, thanks to the cheery and efficient staff. Reservations are recommended, especially on weekends.

Above the Strand Bar, Strandhill, Co. Sligo. www.trabansligo.ie. *©* **071/912-8402.** €17–€25. Tues–Sun 5–9:30pm. Closed Mon and early Jan–early Feb.

EXPLORING COUNTY MAYO

Serenely beautiful, County Mayo sits in the shadow of its more famous neighbor, Galway, and doesn't seem to mind. For experienced Ireland travelers, Mayo is a kind of Galway Lite—its rugged coastal scenery is similar to that of Galway, but it has less of the traffic or tourist overload from which Galway suffers in the summer. This is peaceful, pleasant Ireland, with striking seascapes and inland scenery that ranges from

County Mayo

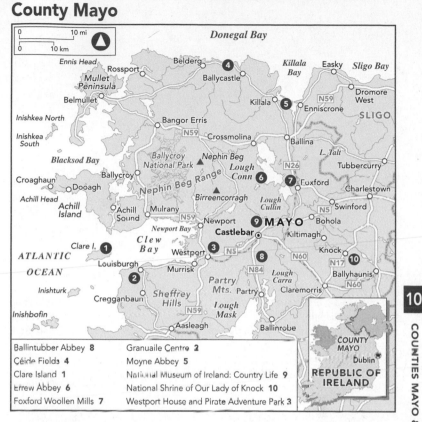

Map legend:

Ballintubber Abbey **8**	Granuaile Centre **2**	
Céide Fields **4**	Moyne Abbey **5**	
Clare Island **1**	National Museum of Ireland: Country Life **9**	
Errew Abbey **6**	National Shrine of Our Lady of Knock **10**	
Foxford Woollen Mills **7**	Westport House and Pirate Adventure Park **3**	

Map labels: Donegal Bay, Ennis Head, Rossport, Belderg, **4**, Killala Bay, Easky, Sligo Bay, Mullet Peninsula, Ballycastle, Killala **5**, Dromore West, Belmullet, Enniscrone, SLIGO, N59, Inishkea North, Bangor Erris, Crossmolina, Ballina, L. Talt, Inishkea South, N59, Tubbercurry, Blacksod Bay, Ballycroy National Park, Nephin Beg, Lough Conn **6**, **7** Foxford, Croaghaun, Ballycroy, Nephin Beg Range, Charlestown, Achill Head, Birreencorragh, Lough Cullin, N5 Swinford, Achill Island, Achill Sound, Mulrany, N59, Newport, **9** MAYO, Bohola, Newport Bay, Castlebar, Kiltimagh, Clare I. **1**, Clew Bay, Westport **3** N5, **8**, N60, Knock **10**, ATLANTIC OCEAN, Louisburgh, Murrisk, N84, Lough Carra, N17, Ballyhaunis, **2**, Partry Mts., Partry, Claremorris, N60, Inishturk, Cregganbaun, Sheffrey Hills, N59, Lough Mask, Inishbofin, Aasleagh, Ballinrobe

COUNTY MAYO, Dublin, REPUBLIC OF IRELAND

lush and green to stark, desert-like, and mountainous. It's an unpredictable place, where the terrain changes at the turn of a steering wheel.

Because it's a rural county with no major cities or many large towns, County Mayo feels a bit like a place without a center. Towns like **Westport** (*Cathair na Mart*) and **Ballina** (*Béal an Átha*) make good bases. Of the two, Westport is the more attractive; it's also home to one of the county's biggest (and most touristy) attractions, **Westport House.** Ballina, meanwhile, is within easy reach of some atmospheric historical sites—including **Céide Fields,** a superbly preserved and explicated footprint of an advanced Stone Age farming community.

Visitor Information

The main tourist information center for County Mayo is the **Westport Tourist Office,** James Street, Westport (www.mayo.ie; ✆ **098/25711**). There is also office on Pearse Street in **Ballina** (✆ **096/72800**).

Top Attractions in County Mayo

Ballintubber Abbey ★★ HISTORIC SITE   This abbey is a real survivor—one of only a few Irish churches in continuous use for almost 800 years. Founded in 1216 by Cathal O'Connor, king of Connaught, it has endured fires, numerous attacks, illnesses, and anti-Catholic pogroms. Although Oliver Cromwell's forces so thoroughly dismantled the abbey that they even carried off its roof in 1653 in an effort to finally suppress it, clerics continued discreetly conducting religious rites. Today it's an impressive church, with 13th-century windows on the right side of the nave and a doorway dating to the 15th century. It was completely restored in 1966. A helpful visitor center illuminates its troubled and fascinating history. Guided tours are available weekdays from 10am to 5pm; there's no charge but donations of €4 per person are requested.

Off the main Galway-Castlebar Rd. (N84), about 21.5km (13½ miles) east of Westport, Ballintubber, Co. Mayo. www.ballintubberabbey.ie. (© **094/903-0934.** Free admission. Daily 9am–midnight.

Céide Fields ★★ HISTORIC SITE   In a breathtaking setting, above huge chalk cliffs that plunge hundreds of feet down into a deep blue sea, ancient people once lived, worked, and buried their dead—a fact that nobody knew until the 1930s, when a local farmer noticed stones piled in strange patterns in his fields. More than 40 years later, his archaeologist son explored the discovery further. Under the turf, he found Stone Age fields, megalithic tombs, and the foundations of a village. Standing amid it now, you can see a pattern of farm fields as they were laid out 5,000 years ago (predating the Egyptian pyramids). Preserved for millennia beneath the bog, the site is both fascinating and inscrutable. To a casual observer, it's little more than piles of stones, but the visitor center makes it meaningful in a series of displays, films, and tours. The pyramid-shaped center itself is designed to fit in with the dramatic surroundings—you can see the building from miles away. It also contains a cafeteria, which comes as a relief since this site is 20 hilly, rocky kilometers (12 miles) of winding roads from anywhere.

On R314, 8km (5 miles) west of Ballycastle, Co. Mayo. www.heritageireland.ie. (© **096/43325.** Admission €4 adults, €3.50 seniors, €2 students and children, €10 families. Apr, May and Oct daily 10am–5pm; Jun–Sept daily 10am–6pm; last tour 1 hr. before closing. Céide Fields is about 34km (21 miles) northwest of Ballina.

Clare Island ★★ ISLAND   Floating about 5km (3 miles) off the Mayo coast, just beyond Clew Bay, Clare Island is a place of unspoiled splendor. Inhabited for 5,000 years and once quite populous—1,700 people lived there in the early 19th century—Clare is now home to 150 year-round islanders, plus perhaps as many sheep. But the island is best known as the haunt of Grace O'Malley, the "Pirate Queen," who controlled the coastal waters 400 years ago (see box below). O'Malley's modest castle and the partially restored Cistercian abbey where she is buried are among the island's few attractions. The rest of the draw is its remote natural beauty. Two ferry services operate out of Roonagh Harbour, 29km (18 miles) south of Westport: **O'Malley's Ferry Service** (www.omalleyferries.com; (© **098/25045**), and **Clare Island Ferries** (www.clare islandferry.com; (© **098/26307**). The round-trip fare for the 15-minute journey is around €15. For more information on Clare Island, visit www.clareisland.info. Co. Mayo.

The National Museum of Ireland: Country Life ★★ MUSEUM   The countryside outpost of Ireland's multisite national museum (the others are all in Dublin, see chapter 4), this one specializes in Irish life, trade, culture, and tradition since the mid–19th century. Permanent exhibitions deal with folklore; the natural environment and how communities relied on it for survival; political and social upheaval,

Exploring County Mayo

COUNTIES MAYO & SLIGO

local hero: GRACE O'MALLEY, THE PIRATE QUEEN

Grace O'Malley, the "Pirate Queen," was born in 1530 on **Clare Island.** She was, by all accounts, ahead of her time. A heroine, adventurer, pirate, gambler, mercenary, traitor, chieftain, and noblewoman, she is remembered now with affection, although at the time she was feared and despised. Even as a child, she was fiercely independent. When her mother refused to let her sail with her father, she cut off her hair and dressed in boys' clothing. Her father called her "*Grainne Mhaol*," or "Bald Grace," later shortened to Granuaile (pronounced *Graw-nya-wayl*), a nickname she'd carry all her life.

At 16, Grace married Donal O'Flaherty, second in line to the O'Flaherty clan chieftain, who ruled all of Connacht. A few years later, her career as a pirate began when the city of Galway, one of the largest trade centers in the British Isles, refused to trade with the O'Flahertys. Grace used her fleet of fast galleys to waylay slower vessels on their way into Galway Harbour. She then offered safe passage for a fee in lieu of pillaging the ships.

She is most fondly remembered for refusing to trade her lands in return for an English title, a common practice of the day.

When the English captured her sons in 1593, she went to London to try to secure their release. In an extraordinary turn of events, she actually secured a meeting with Queen Elizabeth. History records that, just as remarkably, the two women got on quite well (although legend has it that Grace initially tried to smuggle a knife in with her, in case things went differently). A deal was struck; Elizabeth agreed to release her sons and to return some captured lands, if Grace would agree to renounce piracy. This she did and returned to Ireland triumphantly.

The truce did not last, however. She got her sons back, but not her property. She took up piracy again and continued it until her death from natural causes in 1600.

The small but charming Granuaile Centre, Church St., Louisburgh (© **098/66341**) does an engaging job of telling Grace's colorful story. It's open weekdays from 10am to 4pm; entry costs €4 adults, €2 seniors and students. Kids go free.

particularly in the years preceding the Great Famine; traditional trades and crafts; and the changing life of the Irish people at home and at work. They also have a thoughtful program of changing exhibitions. Like all the National Museum sites, entry is completely free.

Signposted from N5, Turlough Park, about 8km (5 miles) east of Castlebar, Co. Mayo. www.museum.ie. (© **094/903-1755.** Free admission. Tues–Sat 10am–5pm; Sun 2–5pm. Closed Mon.

Westport House and Pirate Adventure Park ★★ AMUSEMENT PARK At the edge of the town of Westport, this late-18th-century residence is the home of Lord Altamont, the Marquess of Sligo and a descendant, it is said, of Pirate Queen Grace O'Malley (witness the bronze statue of her on the grounds). The work of Richard Cassels and James Wyatt, the house has a graceful staircase of ornate white Sicilian marble, unusual Art Nouveau glass and carvings, family heirlooms, and silver. The grandeur of the residence is undeniable, but purists might be put off by the fact

A TRIP TO achill island

The rugged, bog-filled, sparsely populated coast of counties Mayo and Sligo makes for scenic drives to secluded outposts. Leading the list is **Achill Island,** a heather-filled slip of land with sandy beaches and spectacular views of waves crashing against rocky cliffs. The drive from the mainland and then across the island to the little town of **Keel** requires patience and skill but rewards you with a camera full of photos. The unrelenting wind off the Atlantic Ocean means that Achill Island is ideal for windsurfing, hang gliding, or any activity that involves a breeze.

About 5.7km (3½ miles) west of Keel is the secluded Blue Flag beach of **Keem Bay.** It was once a major fishing ground—basking shark were being caught here commercially up until the 1950s—but no more. You can reach the bay along a small cliff-top road, which passes by cliff faces containing, so we're told, rich seams of glittering amethyst. Apparently it's not uncommon to find chunks of the stuff lying loose after heavy rainfall.

Hidden on the slopes of **Mount Slievemore,** Achill's tallest mountain, is a remarkable find—the remains of an **abandoned village.** The hundred or so crumbling stone cottages of the nameless ghost town date back to sometime around the 12th century. It was deserted during the Great Famine, although some cottages are known to have been in occasional use until the very early years of the 20th century, as the traditional practice of "booleying"—seasonal occupation by farming communities—continued here long after it had died out in the rest of Ireland. Mount Slievemore is between Keel and Doogort, in the central northeastern part of Achill Island.

At Kildavnet, between Derreen and Coughmore, in the southeastern corner of the island, you'll find **Granuaile's Tower.** This impressive 15th-century tower house was owned by Grace O'Malley, the "Pirate Queen," who caused all manner of havoc for the English around these parts in the 16th century (see box above). There's not a great deal to see, but it's a stunning spot to admire. Nearby **Kildavnet Church** is thought by some archaeologists to date from the 8th century.

To get to the Achill Island crossing, take N59 heading northwest out of Westport, then join R319, signposted to Achill. The drive from Westport to the crossing is about 42km (26 miles) and should take around 40 minutes. Once you're on Achill Island, Keel is about another 14km (8⅔ miles) down the same road.

that the sprawling gardens are a commercial enterprise these days, home to the **Pirate Adventure Park.** Kids, however, will be far more interested in the log ride, the swinging pirate ship, swan-shaped pedal boats on the lake, giant bouncy castle, and a child-size train tooting its way through the gardens. Probably because of that, prices are quite high (and a few attractions, such as the Pirate's Den play area for young children, cost extra).

The Westport Demense, Westport, Co. Mayo. www.westporthouse.ie. © **098/27766.** House and Gardens: €12.50 adults, €10 seniors and students, €6.50 children. House, Gardens and Pirate Park: €21 adults, €19 seniors and students, €16.50 children, €60–€75 families. Pirate's Den play area: €6.50 children 3 and over, €3.50 children 2 and under. Pitch and Putt Golf: €6.50. Mar–May and Sept–Oct daily 10am–4pm; Jun–Aug daily 10am–6pm; Nov–Dec and Feb Sat–Sun 10am–4pm. Also open 2-week Easter school holidays daily 11am–6pm; first weekend in May (May bank holiday) Fri–Mon 11am–6pm. Closed Jan.

Exploring County Mayo

COUNTIES MAYO & SLIGO

EXPLORING COUNTY SLIGO

County Sligo is known for its extraordinary concentration of ancient burial grounds and pagan sites, most of which are within easy reach of the county capital. Chief among these are the Stone Age cemeteries at **Carrowmore** and **Carrowkeel,** but just driving down the country lanes, you can't help spotting a **dolmen** (ancient stone table) in some pasture or other, with sheep or ponies grazing casually around it. **Sligo Town** isn't busy, historic, or pretty enough to require much of your time, but it is a handy place to base yourself if you want to explore the bucolic farmland that has become, thanks to the impressive energy of the County Sligo tourism offices, "Yeats Country." Although he was born in Dublin, the poet W. B. Yeats spent so much time in County Sligo that it became a part of him, and he a part of it—literally, as he is buried here. As you'll quickly discover, every hill, cottage, vale, and lake seems to bear a plaque indicating its relation to the poet or his works.

Top Attractions in and Around Sligo Town

Carrowmore Megalithic Cemetery ★★★ HISTORIC SITE   This is one of the great sacred landscapes of the ancient world. At the center of the Coolera Peninsula sits a massive passage grave that once had a Stonehenge-like stone circle of its own. Encircling that were as many as 200 additional stone circles and passage graves arranged in an intricate and mysterious design. Over the years, some of the stones have been moved, but more than 60 circles and passage graves still exist, although the site spreads out so far that many of them are in adjacent farmland. Look out for your first dolmen in a paddock next to the road about a mile before you reach the site. The dolmens were the actual graves, once covered in stones and earth. Some of these sites are open to visitors, and you can get a map to them from the visitor center. On the main site, Tomb 52A (which was only excavated in 1998) is estimated to be 7,400 years old, making it the earliest known piece of free-standing stone architecture in the entire world. From Carrowmore, you can see the hilltop cairn grave of **Knocknarea** in the distance. The visitor center has good exhibits and guided tours.

Carrowmore, Co. Sligo. (Follow signs from Woodville Rd. heading west out of Sligo Town, or from R292 at Ransboro.) www.heritageireland.ie. ℂ **071/916-1534.** Admission €3 adults, €2 seniors, €1 students and children, €8 families. Apr–early Oct daily 10am–6pm. Closed mid-Oct–Mar.

Carrowkeel Passage Tomb Cemetery ★★ HISTORIC SITE   Atop a hill overlooking Lough Arrow, this ancient passage tomb cemetery is impressive, isolated, and frequently empty. Its 14 cairns, dolmens, and stone circles date from the Stone Age (ca. 5000 B.C.), and it's easy to feel that history, standing among the cold, ageless rocks. The walk uphill from the parking lot takes about 20 minutes, so be ready to get a little exercise. It's worth the effort. This is a simple site—no visitor center, no tea shop, no admission fee—nothing but ancient mystery.

Signposted on N4 between Sligo Town and Boyle, Co. Sligo. No phone. Free admission (open site).

Drumcliffe Church ★ CHURCH   This small stone church is the final resting place of W. B. Yeats (1865–1939) and as no surprise, has become something of a pilgrimage site for his legions of fans. As you walk in, Yeats's grave is marked with a dark, modest stone just to the left of the church. He's buried alongside his young wife, Georgie Hyde-Lee (when they married in 1917, he was 52 and she was 23). The moving epitaph, "Cast a cold eye on life, on death . . ." comes from his poem "Under Ben

poetic license: THE LIFE OF WILLIAM BUTLER YEATS

The landscape of County Sligo deeply influenced the work of Ireland's first of four Nobel laureates, **William Butler Yeats** (1865–1939). The poet, playwright, and two-term Irish senator grew up amid Sligo's verdant hills and dales, now known as "Yeats Country"—a moniker the tourism board won't let you forget, through signposts and plaques mounted throughout the region and a plethora of Yeats-related activities. You can cruise Lough Gill while listening to a live recital of Yeats's poetry; take Yeats trails and buy a hundred items of Yeats memorabilia; and visit dozens of his purported haunts—some reputedly still spooked by his ghost, and some of which have only tenuous connections with the man.

Yeats died in Menton, on the French Riviera, in 1939. Knowing he was ill, he stated, "If I die here, bury me up there on the mountain, and then after a year or so, dig me up and bring me privately to Sligo." True to his wishes, in 1948 his body was moved to Sligo, and reinterred at Drumcliffe Church (see listing below), where his great-grandfather had been a rector.

Bulben." The church sits atop the 6th-century foundations of the monastery St. Columba, and the round tower on the main road dates from that earlier building. The high cross in the churchyard is from the 11th century, and its faded eastern side shows Christ, Daniel in the lions' den, Adam and Eve, and Cain murdering Abel. The little visitor center has a few gifts and doodads and an excellent teashop with marvelous cakes, hearty sandwiches, and fresh hot soup.

Drumcliffe Churchyard, Drumcliffe (on N15), Co. Sligo. No phone. Free admission.

The Model ★★ MUSEUM   One of Ireland's most renowned contemporary art museums, the Model houses an impressive collection of paintings and other visual art. It includes probably the best collection of works by Jack B. Yeats (1871–1957) outside the National Gallery in Dublin (see p. 70). Brother of William, Jack was one of the foremost Irish painters of the 20th century. Other luminaries of the Irish art world who are represented here include Louis le Brocquy (1916–2012), an extraordinary figurative painter; and the portraitist Estella Solomons (1882–1968). Their program of temporary and special exhibitions is varied and imaginative. The Model is also a venue for live music and film screenings. Check the website for up-to-date listings.

The Mall, Sligo, Co. Sligo. www.themodel.ie. ✆ **071/914-1405.** Free admission to exhibitions; tickets to other events free to around €25. Tues–Sat 10am–5:30pm; Sun noon–5pm. Closed Mon. Event times vary.

Parke's Castle ★ CASTLE   On the north side of the Lough Gill Drive (see box below), just over the County Leitrim side of the border, Parke's Castle stands out as a lone outpost amid the natural tableau of lake view and woodland scenery. Named after an English family that gained possession of it during the 1620 plantation of Leitrim (when land was confiscated from the Irish and given to favored English families), this castle was originally the stronghold of the O'Rourke clan, rulers of the Kingdom of Breffni. Beautifully restored using Irish oak and traditional craftsmanship, it exemplifies the 17th-century fortified manor house. In the visitor center, informative exhibits

County Sligo

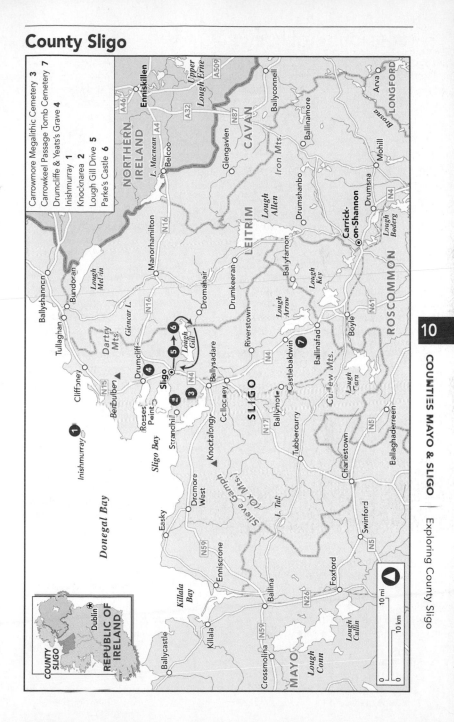

Carrowmore Megalithic Cemetery **3**
Carrowkeel Passage Tomb Cemetery **7**
Drumcliffe & Yeats's Grave **4**
Inishmurray **1**
Knocknarea **2**
Lough Gill Drive **5**
Parke's Castle **6**

THE lough gill DRIVE

This beautiful lake figured prominently in the writings of W. B. Yeats, and this 42km (26-mile) drive-yourself tour around the perimeter is well signposted.

To start, head 1.6km (1 mile) south of town and follow the signs for Lough Gill. Within 3.2km (2 miles) you'll be on the lower edge of the shoreline. Among the sites are **Parke's Castle** (see above); **Dooney Rock,** with its own nature trail and lakeside walk (inspiration for the poem "Fiddler of Dooney"); the **Lake Isle of Innisfree,** made famous in Yeats's poetry and in song; and the **Hazelwood Sculpture Trail,** a unique forest walk along the shores of Lough Gill, with 13 wood sculptures. The storied Innisfree is one of 22 islands in Lough Gill.

You can drive the lakeside circuit in less than an hour, or you can stop at the east end and visit **Dromahair,** a delightful village on the River Bonet. The road along Lough Gill's upper shore brings you back to the northern end of Sligo Town. Continue north on the main road (N15), and you'll see the graceful profile of **Ben Bulben** (519m/1,702 ft.), one of the Dartry Mountains, rising off to your right.

If you prefer to see all this beautiful scenery from the water itself, **Lough Gill Cruises** take you around Lough Gill and the Garavogue River aboard the 72-passenger *Wild Rose* waterbus as you listen to the poetry of Yeats. The boat departs from Parke's Castle (see above); visit www.roseoffinnisfree.com or call *C* **071/916-4266** for departure times and booking. Trips to the Innisfree, sunset cruises, and dinner cruises are also scheduled. Tickets start at around €15 adults, €13 seniors and students, €8 children, and €45 families.

and a splendid audio-visual show illustrate the history of the castle and introduce visitors to the rich, diverse sites of interest in the surrounding area.

On R286, 11.2km (7 miles) east of Sligo Town, Co. Leitrim. www.heritageireland.ie. *C* **071/916-4149.** Admission €3 adults, €2 seniors, €1 students and children, €8 families. Apr–mid-Sept daily 10am–6pm; last admission 45 min. before closing.

Sligo Abbey ★ HISTORIC SITE   Founded as a Dominican house in 1252 by Maurice Fitzgerald, Earl of Kildare, Sligo Abbey was the center of early Sligo Town. It thrived for centuries and flourished in medieval times when it was the burial place of the chiefs and earls of Sligo. But, as with other affluent religious settlements, the abbey was under constant attack, and it was finally destroyed in 1641. Much restoration work has been done in recent years, and the cloisters contain outstanding examples of stone carving; the 15th-century altar is one of few intact medieval altars in Ireland.

Abbey St., Sligo, Co. Sligo. www.heritageireland.ie. *C* **071/914-6406.** Admission €3 adults, €2 seniors, €1 students and children, €8 families. Apr–mid-Oct daily 10am–6pm; last admission 45 min. before closing.

Sligo County Museum ★ MUSEUM   This museum in the center of Sligo Town does a good job of giving you an overview of the county's history, from ancient times to the present day. The most interesting sections cover the region's extraordinary prehistoric heritage, including a couple of ancient artifacts. (Sligo is, after all, where you'll find the world's oldest building by some measures—see the listing for Carrowmore Megalithic Cemetery earlier in this chapter.) The other standout sections are devoted to two of Sligo's most famous residents: W. B. Yeats, one of the 20th century's

A SOMBER SORT OF GRANDEUR:
strokestown park

Strokestown Park House (www.strokes townpark.ie; ② **071/963-3013**) was the seat of the Pakenham-Mahon family from 1600 to 1979. King Charles II granted the vast estate, which stretches for miles in every direction, to Nicholas Mahon after the Restoration in appreciation of his support of the House of Stewart during the bloody English Civil War. It was quite a reward. The original house, completed in 1697, was considered to be too small and unimposing by Nicholas's grandson, Thomas. So he hired Richard Cassels (also known as Richard Castle) to build him something bigger and more impressive. The result is this 45-room Palladian mansion.

The north wing houses Ireland's last existing galleried kitchen (where the lady of the house could observe the culinary activity without being part of it). The south wing is an elaborate vaulted stable so magnificent that it has been described as an "equine cathedral."

These days Strokestown is also the permanent home of the **Irish National Famine Museum,** one of the country's very best museums devoted to that deadly period in Irish history. It sets out the terrible mixture of natural disaster and shocking cruelty of the British establishment that led to the deaths of around a million people and the emigration of a million more. Exhibits include letters penned by some of the tenants of Strokestown during the famine years.

The reasoning behind this somber but incongruous pairing of historic attractions becomes clearer when you understand a little more of the history behind the grand Strokestown estate— particularly the behavior of one man, Major Denis Mahon, who was the landlord at Strokestown during the 1840s. When the potato blight struck and famine started to spread, Mahon and his land agents could have done many things to help the hundreds of starving peasants who lived and worked on the property, but instead they evicted them as soon as it became clear they would not be able to pay their rent. He even went so far as to charter ships to send them away from Ireland. In 1847, Major Mahon was shot to death near Strokestown, and two men were hastily (and dubiously) convicted of the crime. But it seems clear that many hungry people had motives.

Strokestown Park is on the main Dublin-Castlebar Road (N5), in Strokestown, County Roscommon. It's about 77km (41 miles) south of Sligo Town. Admission costs €13.50 adults, €5.50 children, and €27.50 families. It's open from March through October, daily from 10:30am to 5:30pm, and November to February, daily from 10:30am to 4pm. The house can only be seen on a guided tour (call to check times; there are usually a handful per day in summer, but only one in winter). The museum can be visited all day.

foremost poets, whose mother was from Sligo and whose affinity with the county drastically influenced his work; and Constance Markievicz (1868–1927), an aristocrat who grew up in Sligo and went on to become both the first woman elected to the British Parliament and a prominent Irish revolutionary.

Stephen St., Sligo, Co. Sligo. ② **071/914-2212.** Free admission. Tues–Sat 10am–noon and 2–4:30pm. Closed Sun and Oct–May.

COUNTY DONEGAL

Beyond Sligo, the topography changes and the roads twist and turn through tortuous corkscrews. When the signs switch into Gaelic, the landscape opens up into great sweeping views of rocky hills and barren shores, and a freezing mist blows off the sea. You know you've reached Donegal. The austere beauty of this county can be almost too bleak, but it is also unforgettable. On a sunny day, you can stand at the edge of the sea at Malin Head and, despite the sun, the sea spray will blow a chill right through you—it feels as if you're standing at the edge of the world. County Donegal's natural wonders include the magnificent Slieve League cliffs and the remote beaches tucked into the bays and inlets of its sharply indented coast.

ESSENTIALS

Arriving

BY BUS **Bus Éireann** (www.buseireann.ie; ✆ **074/912-1309**) operates daily bus service to Donegal Town from Dublin, Derry, Sligo, Galway, and other points.

BY TRAIN Trains in this part of the country are extremely scarce. Donegal Town no longer even has a train station.

BY CAR The only practical way to get around the remote attractions of County Donegal is by car. If you're driving from the south, Donegal is reached on N15 from Sligo or A46 or A47 from Northern Ireland; from the east and north, it's N15 and N56; from the west, N56 leads to Donegal Town.

BY PLANE **Donegal Airport,** Carrickfin, near Letterkenny, Co. Donegal (www.donegalairport.ie; ✆ **074/954-8284**), also known as Carrickfinn Airport, is slowly growing as a budget airline hub. Currently a couple of scheduled flights connect per day with Dublin; **Flybe** (✆ **087/1700-2000** in the U.K. or ✆ 0044/1392-683-152) also operates regular flights from Glasgow, Scotland.

[FastFACTS] COUNTY DONEGAL

ATMs/Banks Donegal Town's central shopping area—known as "The Diamond"—has branches of **Permanent TSB** and **AIB.** ATMs get seriously few and far between in the Donegal countryside, so get cash before you strike out into the boondocks.

Dentists For dental emergencies, your hotel should contact a dentist for you. Otherwise, in Donegal Town, try **Dr. Brian McCaughey** on Upper Main Street (☏ **074/ 972-3066**).

Doctors For medical emergencies, dial ☏ **999.** For nonemergencies, your hotel should call you a doctor. Otherwise, in Donegal Town, try **Dr. Marie**

Drumgoole on Waterloo Place (☏ **074/972-1364**).

Emergencies For police, fire, or other emergencies, dial ☏ **999.**

Pharmacies In Donegal Town, try **Eske Pharmacy** (☏ **071/972-2033**) or **McElwee Pharmacy** (☏ **074/952-1032**), both on Main Street.

Post Offices The main post office in Donegal Town

is on Tirconaill Street ((☏ **071/972-1030**).

Taxis If you need a cab home from a restaurant or hotel, the management should call one for you—in rural areas, this is often the only reliable way of getting anywhere if you don't want to drive. Otherwise, in Donegal Town, try **Quinn's Taxis** (☏ **087/262-0670**) or **McNulty Taxis** (☏ **087/ 256-1319.**

WHERE TO STAY

As with counties Mayo and Sligo to the south (see chapter 10) the standout accommodations are to be found hidden away deep within the breathtaking, mountainous roads and tiny, bucolic seaside towns that are the real reason you came all this way in the first place.

Where to Stay in County Donegal

Ard Na Breátha ★★ The impeccable taste of the owners guided every design decision at this comfortable, modern guesthouse (set on a working farm). Bedrooms are summery and spacious, with bright color schemes, polished wood floors, and antique-style iron frame beds in some rooms. Family rooms are only about €30 more than standard doubles. The pleasant guest lounge has a fireplace and a small bar. Evening meals are sophisticated while unashamedly traditional in style, with plenty of local and seasonal ingredients, many supplied from their own farm, of course. Prebooking for dinner is essential. (See listing below for more on the restaurant.) The B&B is located right on the edge of Donegal Town, though the farm makes it feel quite rural, enhanced by views of the mountains in the distance.

Railway Park, Middle Drumrooske, Donegal Town, Co. Donegal. www.ardnabreatha.com. ☏ **074/972-2288.** 6 units. €90–€110 double. Free parking. Breakfast included. **Amenities:** Wi-Fi (free), restaurant, bar. Closed mid-Jan–mid-Feb.

Ballyliffin Lodge ★★ Prices are a lot more reasonable here than they would be in an equivalent spa lodging in a more visited part of the country. Don't believe us? You can get three treatments (totaling just over an hour) for just €70. And with impressive views of Malin Head (see p. 200), the hotel is just as relaxing as its in-house spa, **Rock Crystal.** Bedrooms, which take full advantage of those views, are nice and spacious, with muted, autumnal decor. The hotel can help organize plenty of activities, from horseback riding to surfing and golf.

Ballyliffin, Co. Donegal. www.ballyliffinlodge.com. ☏ **074/937-8200.** 40 units. €80–€166 double. Breakfast not included in lower rates. **Amenities:** Wi-Fi, restaurant, bar, room service, spa, gym, pool.

Bruckless House ★★ Another impeccably converted farmhouse, but with a slightly older pedigree, this property was built in the mid-1700s. Your hosts, Joan and Clive Evans, are cultured and well-traveled, and their house is full of the kind of art and antiques that tell a story. The gardens are beautiful and quite famous, even with locals. A walk down the main path, past flower beds and lawns, takes you down to the sea. Bedrooms are simple but tastefully decorated, and guests have use of the pleasantly old-fashioned drawing room. The former Gate Lodge to the house is available as a self-catering unit; it sleeps up to four and is a good value at between €200 and €450 per week, depending on the season.

On N56, Bruckless, Co. Donegal. www.bruckless.com. © **074/973-7071.** 4 units. €120 double. Free parking. Breakfast included. **Amenities:** Wi-Fi (free). From Donegal Town, Bruckless House is the first driveway on the left after the Bruckless village sign. Closed Oct–Mar.

Castle Grove Hotel ★★ Lancelot "Capability" Brown, the famous English landscaper who virtually invented landscape gardening in the 18th century, laid out the elegant grounds at this inviting white manor house. Inside, the decor is avowedly traditional in style, with plenty of period detail and heritage paint colors. Rooms have antique furnishings (including a four-poster bed in one). All have views of the grounds. Breakfasts are outstanding, and the restaurant (see listing below) is one of the best in the region. Check the website for dinner, bed and breakfast packages.

Ballymaleel, off Ramelton Rd., Letterkenny, Co. Donegal. www.castlegrove.com. © **074/915-1118.** 16 units. €90–€160 double. Breakfast included. **Amenities:** Wi-Fi (free), restaurant, bar, room service, access to nearby golf courses, tennis courts.

Rathmullan House ★★★ Right on the edge of Lough Swilly, this delightful mid-18th-century mansion is one of the best places to stay in the northwest. The public areas are warm and hospitable, with sumptuous period decor. Bedrooms are spacious and extremely comfortable; those in the modern extension lose nothing in terms of style and charm to the rooms in the older section of the house. Some have fireplaces and deep, antique-style bathtubs. Superior rooms have even more space, and family rooms can work out at just slightly more expensive than standard doubles. The house has a swimming pool, or you can just take a short stroll down to the beach of the Loch. The Weeping Elm Restaurant is outstanding, and deserves its reputation as one of the best places to eat in Donegal—no bad thing, as there aren't many others within a reasonable drive. Many ingredients are supplied from the house's own garden. Check the website for discounts and special rates—particularly outside the busiest times of year, when you can often find deals that work out to around €100 per person, which is an incredible value for a place as good as this. They also offer dinner, bed and breakfast packages.

On R247 (Chapel Rd.,) Rathmullan, Co. Donegal. www.rathmullanhouse.com. © **074/915-8188.** 32 units. €180–€250 double. Parking. Breakfast included. **Amenities:** Restaurant, pool.

WHERE TO EAT

The further you get into the wilds of County Donegal, the slimmer the pickings become where fine restaurants are concerned. Out in the countryside the best bets are usually to be found in the better hotels; Donegal Town and the area around Donegal Bay offers one or two memorable options.

Where to Eat in County Donegal

Ard Na Breátha ★★ MODERN IRISH The in-house restaurant at the lovely B&B of the same name (see listing above) serves up excellent modern Irish cooking. The attractive, high-beamed dining room has a great view across rolling farmland to Donegal Town. The menu is seasonal, but depending on when you're visiting, you could be offered a starter of parsnip and apple soup or a warm goat-cheese tart, followed by chicken supreme (free range, of course) or lamb shank with almonds and fresh ginger.

The little bar outside the dining room is perfect for a pre-dinner drink or a nightcap while you take in the heady scent of the peat-burning fire. Reservations are essential.

Railway Park, Middle Drumrooske, Donegal, Co. Donegal. www.ardnabreatha.com. (*C*) **074/972-2288.** Fixed-price menu (3 courses) €38. Daily 6–9:30pm. Closed mid-Jan–mid-Feb.

Castle Grove ★★★ IRISH   The eponymous restaurant of the Castle Grove Hotel (see listing above) has won plenty of awards over the years, and it's easy to see why—the food is superb, and a top recommendation if you're staying here or nearby. The menu presents classic Irish dishes, made with plenty of local ingredients, and infuses them with a hint of the global village—for example, a gateaux of crab prepared with Thai seasoning and served with couscous, or salmon filet from Lough Swilly wrapped in Parma ham and served with red-pepper coulis.

Ballymaleel, off Ramelton Rd., Letterkenny, Co. Donegal. www.castlegrove.com. (*C*) **074/915-1118.** Main courses €18–€28. Daily 6:30–9pm. No children 9 and under allowed after 7pm.

The Drift Inn ★★ IRISH/ PUB FOOD   You never quite know where you are with punning restaurant names, but this cheerful place in Buncrana can be forgiven a groan because of its top-quality pub grub. There are plenty of names on the menu that you probably will have seen on signs while driving here, and that accounts for at least some of the freshness of the flavors, too. You could opt for a 6-hour braised Donegal lamb shank served with mustard mashed potatoes, or Greencastle salmon filet with chili and coriander sauce. Buncrana is about a 15-minute drive south of Fort Dunree (see p. 200), and about 45 minutes south of Malin Head (see p. 200).

Railway Rd., Buncrana, Co. Donegal. www.thedriftinn.ie. (*C*)**074/936-1999.** Main courses €14–€20. Thurs 5:30–8:45pm; Fri–Sat 1–9:15pm; Sun 1–8:30pm. Closed Thurs in winter.

Pearl's Place ★★ MODERN IRISH   From the outside, Pearl's Place looks nondescript, more closely resembling a family home than a restaurant. But what a surprise awaits! Delicious Irish cooking, modern in style without being overdone, served by friendly and professional staff. You could start with some duck confit with spicy lentils, then follow it up with some local lamb with tomato and mint chutney, or maybe some sea bass with a side of garlic potatoes. They also have dedicated vegetarian and kids menus.

Killybegs Rd., Donegal Town, Co. Donegal. www.pearlsplace.ie. (*C*) **071/972-1200.** Main courses €17–€26. Wed-Fri 6–9pm; Sat 5:30–9:30pm; Sun 1–4 and 6–8:30pm.

The Village Tavern ★★ MODERN IRISH   It's quite possible that you'll experience a sense of déjà vu when you approach the front door to this homey gastropub— the owners claim that it's been photographed several times for postcards, to convey a sense of "authentic Irishness." The place is cozy on the inside, and the food, which comes highly recommended by locals, is terrific. Although the menu is contemporary in style and presentation, there's a strong sense of tradition, too, so wild salmon with coconut-flavored risotto and a spicy piri piri chicken share the menu with fish and chips or a simple box of cockles and mussels. The truly undaunted may attempt to tackle the "five steak" plate, made from two different cuts of meat, with two sauces plus sides.

Lower Main St., Mountcharles (5km/3.1 miles west of Donegal Town), Co. Donegal. www.village tavern.ie. (*C*) **074/973-5622.** Main courses €14–€24. Mon–Fri noon–9pm; Sat noon–9:30pm; Sun noon–7pm. Call ahead Oct–Apr. Food may not be served out of season, especially weekdays.

The Cook & Gardener ★★★ IRISH   It's entirely befitting that, as one of the very best hotels in Donegal, Rathmullan House (see listing above) would also have one of its best restaurants. Many of the ingredients have come no greater distance than the house's own gardens, and many of the rest haven't traveled all that much farther. You could start with the goat's-cheese parfait before moving on to Greencastle cod with braised lentils, or braised pork with colcannon potatoes and parsnip purée. Despite the quality, it's not the kind of place you have to sit up ruler-straight the whole time. Kids get their own menu, too (although younger ones are expected to be done by 7pm).

At Rathmullan House hotel, on R247 (Chapel Rd.), Rathmullan, Co. Donegal. www.rathmullan house.com. ℂ **074/915-8188.** Main courses €18–€28. Sun–Thurs 7–8:45pm, Fri–Sat 7–9:15pm.

EXPLORING COUNTY DONEGAL

Although far from Ireland's prettiest or most interesting town, the greatest attraction of **Donegal Town** is the town's layout itself: a happy mix of medieval and modern. Overseen by a low, gloomy castle at the edge of the picturesque estuary of the River Eske on Donegal Bay, this is a tiny burg, with just 2,500 residents.

To the north of Donegal Town, the coastal scenery around **Donegal Bay** is breath-taking. Follow the main road (N56) to the west out of Donegal for a slow, spectacularly scenic drive along the bay where the road winds past sheer cliffs, craggy rocks, bog land, panoramic mountain and sea views, and green pastures.

Even further north, the **Atlantic Highlands** is a stark and isolated expanse of stunning coastal scenery, mountain ranges, and the lunar landscape of its rocky beaches. The best place to start a tour of Donegal's Atlantic Highlands is at **Ardara** (*Árd an Rátha*), an adorable village about 40km (25 miles) northwest of Donegal Town. From there, weave your way up the coast, turning inland when a place lures you to do so.

And further still is the **Inishowen Peninsula**—the northernmost part of Ireland. To drive around the Inishowen is to traverse desolate seascapes, intimidating mountains, restful valleys, and impenetrable woodlands. This is a world apart, where residents treasure the legends of Ireland and still observe its ancient traditions. If you've made it this far, well done! You can join the few tourists to have stood on Malin Head and felt the icy mist come in on a wind that hits you like a fist. You can feel the satisfaction that comes from knowing there is no farther to go. And you can truly say that you have *done* Ireland.

Visitor Information

The **Donegal Discover Ireland Centre** is on the Quay, Donegal Town (ℂ **074/972-1148**). The seasonal **Ardara Heritage Centre** is on the main road through Ardara; it's closed from November to Easter.

Exploring Donegal Town and Donegal Bay

Donegal Bay Waterbus ★ TOUR   This modern, two-deck boat makes daily tours of Donegal Bay. The guided tour lasts 90 minutes. Points of interest along the way include the **Old Abbey** (see listing below); **Seal Island,** home to a colony of about 200 noisy seals; and **the Hassans,** a port from which many emigrants from the northern part of the country left for the New World. The guides are enthusiastic and knowledgeable; the only downside is that the commentary is nonstop, and they will even play the keyboard to fill in moments of silence. However, the views are wonderful. Sailing times are usually morning and afternoon or evening, but are dependent upon weather and the tides, so make sure you call ahead. Tickets can be obtained from the ticket office on Quay Street—it's the white and blue building next to Dom's Pier 1 Bar.

The Pier, Donegal, Co. Donegal. www.donegalbaywaterbus.com. ℂ **074/972-3666.** Tour €15 adults, €5 children 5–17, children 4 and under free. No credit cards. Closed Oct–Apr.

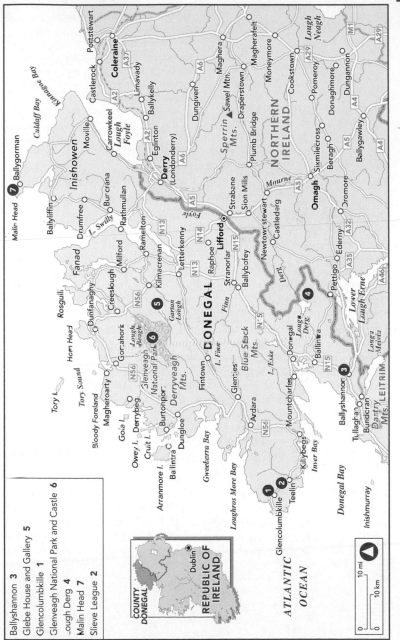

Ballyshannon **3**
Glebe House and Gallery **5**
Glencolumbkille **1**
Glenveagh National Park and Castle **6**
Lough Derg **4**
Malin Head **7**
Slieve League **2**

COUNTY DONEGAL

REPUBLIC OF IRELAND

Dublin

Old Abbey ★ HISTORIC SITE
Sitting in a peaceful spot on the quay in Donegal Town where the River Eske meets Donegal Bay, this ruined Franciscan monastery was founded in 1474 by the first Red Hugh O'Donnell and his wife, Nuala O'Brien of Munster. It was generously endowed by the O'Donnell family and became an important center of religion and learning. Great gatherings of clergy and lay leaders assembled here in 1539. It was

Irish Only!

Along with counties Mayo and Kerry, Donegal is in the **Gaeltacht,** or Irish-- language, section of the country. Increasingly, road signs in these regions are being changed to Irish only. We're including the Irish names as well as the English names for the places where you're likely to encounter this.

from this friary that some of the scholars undertook to salvage old Gaelic manuscripts and compile *The Annals of the Four Masters* (1632–36). Enough remains of its glory— ruins of a church and a cloister—to give you an idea of how magnificent it once was.

The Quay, Donegal, Co. Donegal. Free admission (open site).

Glencolumbkille (Gleann Cholm Cille) ★★ LIVING HISTORY PARK   An extraordinarily beautiful outpost overlooking the Atlantic Ocean, Glencolumbkille is a small community about 52km (33⅓ miles) west of Donegal Town. Here the dark bogs disappear, replaced by a lush green valley. It is said that St. Columba established a monastery here in the 6th century and gave his name to the glen (its Gaelic name— *Gleann Cholm Cille*—means "Glen of Columba's Church"). Today, it's home to the **Glencolumbkille Folk Park,** a wonderful "living history" park and craft village, set up and maintained entirely by the local people. In a series of small, traditional cottages, the park tells the story of this remote community in an engaging way. Guided tours are available, or you can take it at your own pace. Don't leave without browsing the *sheebeen*—a little store selling traditional, local products, including wines made from unusual ingredients such as seaweed. There are miniature playhouses to entertain the children, while a tearoom serves traditional Irish stews and *brútin* (a stew of hot milk and potatoes). Hearty Guinness cake is a house specialty.

On R263, about 26km (16 miles) northeast of Killybegs, Co. Donegal. www.gleanncholmcille.ie. ⓒ **074/973-0017.** Admission €4.50 adults, €4 seniors and students, €2.50 children 7–16, children 6 and under free, €12 families. Easter–Sept Mon–Sat 10am–6pm, Sun noon–6pm.

Slieve League ★★ NATURAL WONDER   It's surprising that these towering sea cliffs aren't better known, since they're almost three times the height of their far more feted southern cousins, the Cliffs of Moher (see p. 160), and arguably even more spectacular. Needless to say, given the remote location, they also get the tiniest fraction of the visitors. Start at the **Slieve League Cliffs Centre** (www.slieveleaguecliffs.ie; ⓒ **074/973-9077;** in Teelin, about 3km/1⅔ miles southwest of Carrick). It's a great, friendly little visitor center, full of helpful information, with a very good cafe and a crafts store. Admission and parking are both free. The summits of the Slieve League, rising almost 600m (1,968 ft.) above the sea, are often capped in clouds, and you should think twice about undertaking the walk if there is danger of losing visibility along the way. In any case, this walk should only be for the fearless and fit. Including the climb up and then back down, the hike is about 10km (6¼ miles) and takes between 4 and 5 hours. Alternatively, the visitor center runs a shuttle bus up to the best viewing point.

Slieve League Centre: Teelin, Carrick, Co. Donegal (signposted from R263), Co. Donegal. www. slieveleaguecliffs.ie. ⓒ **074/973-9077.** Free admission. Mar–Nov daily 10:30am–5:30pm.

Exploring the Atlantic Highlands

Ardara (*Árd an Rátha*) ★★ TOWN   Looking as if it were carved from stone, the charming little village of **Ardara** is known for its exceptional tweed and wool creations. Astride a narrow river in a steep gulch, it is a pleasant place to stop, chat with the locals, and do a bit of shopping or maybe have a cup of tea in its small but useful **Heritage Centre** on the N56 main road through the village.

Ardara, Co. Donegal. Heritage Centre: Ⓒ **075/41704.** Free admission. Easter–Sept Mon–Sat 10am–6pm, Sun 2–6.

Dunfanaghy Workhouse Heritage Centre ★ MUSEUM   This rather unassuming-looking building was the scene of great hardship and fear in the 19th century, when it was one of around 100,000 workhouses set up to feed and house the poor during the Great Famine. Their purpose was hardly altruistic, however; fearing that mere aid to stop the people starving would engender a "something-for-nothing" culture in the poor, the authorities decreed that they should perform backbreaking labor in return for their bread. It's estimated that workhouses killed around a million people in Ireland. This particular one housed about 300 inmates. The museum does a good job of describing their daily lives, as well as providing a history of the famine in this area. One exhibit focuses particularly on a local girl, "Wee Hannah" Herrity, who lived here and survived to tell the tale—which she did, in extensive conversation with a local biographer.

Just west of Dunfanaghy on N56, Co. Donegal. www.dunfanaghyworkhouse.ie. Ⓒ **074/913-6540.** Admission €4.50 adults, €3.50 seniors, €3 students and children, €11 families. Jun–Sept daily 10am–5pm; Oct–May Mon–Tues 9:30am–5:30pm, Wed–Fri 9:30am–4pm. Call for opening times Oct–May; actual opening times off season are unpredictable.

Glebe House and Gallery ★★ MUSEUM   What a surprise, in such a remote location, to find an art gallery as good as this. The early-19th-century house, on the shores of Lake Gartan, was once the home of the noted English painter Derek Hill (1916–2000). He donated the house, along with his personal art collection, to the Irish state in the 1980s. And it was quite a collection—highlights include paintings by Picasso, Renoir, Jack Yeats, and Oskar Kokoschka; rare Islamic and far Eastern art; and original William Morris prints. About 300 works are on display from the permanent collection, plus temporary and special exhibitions. The house itself is worth seeing, too—a handsome Regency building, surrounded by pretty woods and gardens, stretching down to the Lough. The house can only be seen on a guided tour, and space is limited to 15 people.

Church Hill, Co. Donegal. Signposted from R251, about 17km (10.5 miles) northeast of Letterkenny. www.heritageireland.ie. Ⓒ **074/913-7071.** Admission €3 adults, €2 seniors, €1 students and children, €8 families. Gallery only: Easter week daily 11am–6:30pm; Jun and Sept Sat–Thurs 11am–6:30pm; Jul–Aug daily 11am–6:30pm; last tour 1 hr. before closing. Grounds open year-round.

Glenveagh National Park & Castle ★★★ PARK/CASTLE   This thickly wooded valley is a lush forest paradise, with the lavish Glenveagh Estate at its core. It's beautiful and pleasant now, but its history is dark. Nestling at its heart, **Glenveagh Castle** was originally the home of the infamously cruel landlord John George Adair, who evicted scores of struggling tenant farmers in the freezing winter of 1861, ostensibly because their presence on his estate was ruining his view. If the tale is true, it's a form of divine justice that his estate now belongs to all of the people of Ireland. Today the fairy-tale setting includes woodlands, herds of red deer, alpine gardens, a sylvan lake, and the highest mountain in Donegal, Mount Errigal. There's a visitor center with a little shop, and a charming tearoom in the castle. You can also go on ranger-led walks of the park here for €10. Cars aren't allowed in the park past the visitor center, but a shuttle bus can take you from there straight up to the castle for €3 round-trip. Admission to the park is free, but there's a charge to visit the castle (guided tours only).

Visitor Centre and Castle: Church Hill, Co. Donegal (signposted from R251, 24.4km/15 miles northeast of Letterkenny). www.glenveaghnationalpark.ie. © **076/100-2536.** Castle: €5 adults, €3 seniors, €2 students and children, €10 families. Daily 10am–5pm. Park: Mar–Oct daily 9am–6pm; Oct–Mar daily 9am–5pm; last admission 1 hr. before closing.

Exploring the Inishowen Peninsula

Fort Dunree Military Museum ★★ MUSEUM   Rising precipitously from the cliffs beside Lough Swilly, this impressive-looking fort was constructed as a defensive lookout in case of a French invasion during the Napoleonic Wars. It later became part of Irish sea defenses in case of a German invasion during World War I. Neither came, and today Dunree serves as an informative museum. Spread partly through subsurface bunkers, the exhibitions tell the history of the fort and of the local area as a whole. It also serves as the starting point for scenic walks around Dunree Point along three recommended walking paths. The museum has a handy coffee shop overlooking the Lough.

Signposted on the coast road north of Buncrana, Co. Donegal. www.dunree.pro.ie. © **074/936-1817.** Admission €6 adults, €4 seniors and children. Daily 10:30am–6pm.

Inishowen Maritime Museum and Planetarium ★ MUSEUM   This small but engaging museum overlooks Loch Foyle. Exhibits pack all they can into the old coast guard building for the harbor town of Greencastle, taking the town's maritime history from the Armadas of the 16th century, through emigration, to the modern-day lifeboat crews and their selflessly heroic work. In something of a contrast, there's also a planetarium, complete with recently renovated digital projection. Shows run on request during the winter (minimum group size is six), but more or less all day during summer—call to confirm times.

The Harbour, Greencastle, Co. Donegal. www.inishowenmaritime.com. © **074/938-1363.** Museum only: €5 adults; €3 seniors, students, and children. Museum and planetarium: €10 adults; €6 seniors, students, and children. Easter–Sept Mon–Sat 9:30am–5:30pm, Sun noon–5:30pm; Oct–Easter Mon–Fri 9:15am–5:30pm. Last admission 30 min. before closing.

Malin Head (Cionn Mhélanna) ★★★ VIEWS   The remote Inishowen Peninsula, rarely visited but much admired, is a land of desolate seascapes, intimidating mountains, restful valleys, and impenetrable woodlands. The most far-flung of all the natural sights on the isolated Inishowen Peninsula is Malin Head, a stunning promontory where the road goes no further and the next stop west is New York. Even on a sunny day, the wind often howls and the temperature can be 10 degrees colder than it is just a few miles south. Get this far and you can say you've experienced Ireland more completely than all but a handful of visitors ever manage. To reach Malin Head, take R242 north until it turns into a small, unnamed road. Continue along this road all the way until it literally runs out and there's nowhere left to go. You'll find a place to pull over, and a little information board that tells you all about the Head. But you're unlikely to read the whole thing—you'll be too busy gazing at the incredible view.

Ballyhillin, Co. Donegal.

NORTHERN IRELAND

The vibrant and beautiful six counties of Ireland still under British rule are all the more fascinating for their troubled history. Collectively they're known as Northern Ireland—although you'll hear terms such as "Ulster" and "the North" used interchangeably. Given the seemingly endless struggle that has gone on for the soul of this place, the fact that nobody knows quite what to call it is somehow appropriate. This is a colorful, exciting region filled with lively towns and countryside of breathtaking beauty. Tourism numbers in Northern Ireland have increased greatly over the last decade, but it's still far less visited than the Republic. That's both a shame and its biggest selling point. You're likely to find yourself very welcome here—and yet, outside of the busy summer months, it's not uncommon to find yourself alone in the most spectacular places.

WHAT'S ALL THE TROUBLE?

For many years, visitors to Ireland avoided the North for obvious reasons. In so many ways, things here aren't what they used to be. And that's a good thing. There are young adults today who have spent their whole lives in Belfast or Derry and have almost no memory of a time when their cities were overshadowed by violence.

And yet, while peace reigns, the divisions remain deep. Heartbreakingly, in the most intransigent communities, this is just as true of the younger generation as it is for their parents. Time has taken away the weapons, but it has not healed all wounds.

The strife in Northern Ireland can be traced back more than 800 years, when an English army first invaded Ireland in the 12th century. The British waged a largely futile effort over the centuries to make Ireland, and the Irish, British. Their tactics included outlawing the Irish language, banning Catholicism, and barring Catholics from landownership. Finally, in the mid-1600s, Oliver Cromwell's army went for the more basic approach of killing them in droves. British families were brought over to take their land in a process the Irish called "planting." The descendants of those British settlers, generally speaking, form the Protestant population of Northern Ireland today.

After centuries of struggle, Ireland finally won independence of a sort from Britain in 1921. After much arguing, it was decided that the island would be divided. Twenty-six Irish counties would form an independent "Free State" (now the Republic of Ireland), while six counties in the Ulster province with predominantly Protestant populations would remain part of the United Kingdom to form Northern Ireland.

Northern Ireland

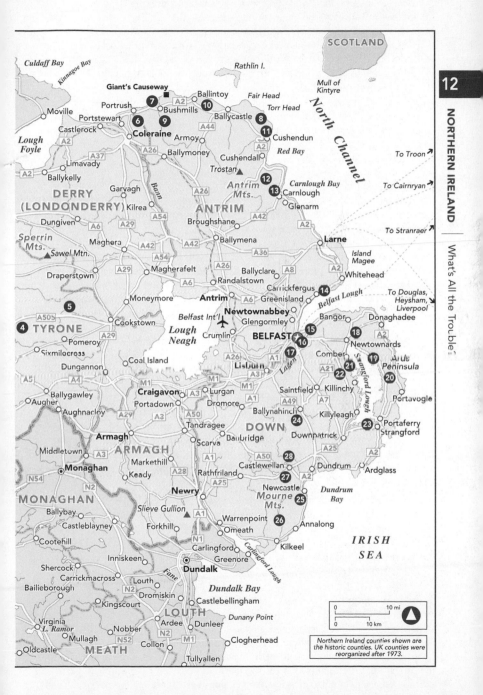

SCOTLAND

Culdaff Bay

Kinnagoe Bay

Rathlin I.

Mull of Kintyre

Giant's Causeway

Portrush **7** **A2** Ballintoy *Fair Head*
Moville Bushmills **10** *Torr Head*
Portstewart **6** **9** Ballycastle **8** North Channel
Castlerock Coleraine Armoy **11** Cushendun
Lough Foyle **A2** **A44**
Limavady **A37** **A26** Ballymoney Cushendall *Red Bay* To Troon ↗
Ballykelly Garvagh Trostan▲ *Antrim Mts.* *Carnlough Bay* To Cairnryan ↗
DERRY Kilrea **A26** **12**
(LONDONDERRY) Broughshane **13** Carnlough
Dungiven **A6** **A29** **ANTRIM** Glenarm To Stranraer ↗
Sperrin Mts. Maghera **A42** **A42** Ballymena **A42** **A2**
▲Sawel Mtn. **A54** **A36** *Island Magee*
Draperstown **A29** Magherafelt **A26** Ballyclare **A8** **A2** Whitehead
Moneymore **A6** Randalstown Carrickfergus **14** To Douglas, Heysham, Liverpool
5 **Antrim** **A6** Greenisland *Belfast Lough*
A505 Cookstown Newtownabbey **15** Bangor Donaghadee
4 **TYRONE** **A29** *Lough Neagh* Glengormley **18**
Pomeroy Crumlin **BELFAST 16** Newtownards **A2** **Ards**
Sixmilecross Coal Island **17** Comber **19** **Peninsula**
Dungannon **A26** Li**s**burn **A1** **A21 21** **20**
A5 **A4** **M1** **M1** **A3** **22** Portavogie
Ballygawley **A4** Lurgan **M1** Saintfield Killinchy
Augher **Craigavon** **A3** Dromore **A1** **A7** Portaferry
Aughnacloy **A29** Portadown **A50** Ballynahinch Killyleagh **23** Strangford
Middletown **A3** Tandragee **A49** **24** Downpatrick **A25** **A2**
Armagh Scarva Banbridge **DOWN**
ARMAGH **A1** Ardglass
Monaghan Markethill **A50** **28** Castlewellan Dundrum
Keady **A28** Rathfriland **27** **A2**
N54 **Newry** **A25** Newcastle *Dundrum Bay*
MONAGHAN **N2** Slieve Gullion▲ **A1** **25** *Mourne Mts.*
Ballybay Forkhill **26**
Castleblayney **N1** Warrenpoint Annalong
Cootehill Omeath
Inniskeen Carlingford Kilkeel *IRISH SEA*
Shercock **N2** Greenore
Carrickmacross Louth **Dundalk**
Bailieborough Dromiskin *Dundalk Bay*
Kingscourt Castlebellingham
Virginia **LOUTH** *Dunany Point*
L. Ramor Nobber Ardee Dunleer
Mullagh **N52** Collon **M1** Clogherhead
Oldcastle **MEATH** Tullyallen

0 — 10 mi
0 — 10 km

Northern Ireland counties shown are the historic counties. UK counties were reorganized after 1973.

After the division, the British police and government in Ulster were quite brutal toward the Catholic minority. Things came to a head in the late 1960s when the Catholic population began an intense civil rights campaign. Their marches and demonstrations were crushed by the authorities, sometimes with disproportionate levels of violence, thus setting the stage for the reemergence of the Irish Republican Army, a violent paramilitary group that had first appeared early in the 20th century. This modern battle between the British/Protestant authorities and the Irish resistance became known as "the Troubles." It began in 1969 and would not end for nearly 30 years.

It was a dirty fight. Throughout the 1970s and 1980s, violence on both sides was a fact of everyday life. By the 1990s, the population of Ulster—stunned by the sheer horror of an IRA bombing in the town of Omagh that killed 29 civilians on a busy shopping street—had had enough.

With the personal involvement of U.S. President Bill Clinton urging them to find a peaceful solution to their disagreements, on May 22, 1998, Northerners and their fellow islanders in the Republic voted to accept the so-called "Good Friday Agreement." It dismantled the claims of both Ireland and Britain to the North and acknowledged the sovereign right of the people of Northern Ireland to take charge of their political destiny, effectively separating their government from London.

Since the peace agreement was signed, it has been tested several times. In 2009, violence flared again in this region in a series of murders and attacks on British soldiers and others involved on one side or the other of the political landscape. The situation was quickly calmed, due to the determination of all sides not to return to the bad old days. Since then there have been sporadic incidents—including a couple of car bombs, one of which, in 2011, was outside the tourism office in Derry (although nobody was hurt). And the summer of 2013 saw some pretty serious riots in Belfast; on one night alone, 56 police officers were injured and parts of the city center were vandalized. But on the whole, despite sporadic incidents, the region remains at peace.

Is Northern Ireland Safe to Visit?

In short, yes. But you should still be savvy. From a visitor's perspective, any violence here has always been remarkably contained. Like diplomats, foreigners have always had a kind of immunity. The simple fact is that Belfast and Derry are safer for visitors than almost any comparable American city, and the Ulster countryside is idyllic and serene. Overall, Northern Ireland has one of the *lowest* crime rates in Europe. But nonetheless, you should follow these basic rules of thumb:

o **Do not** discuss the political situation with anyone you don't know well.
o **Never** get involved in political or religious arguments.
o **Avoid** venturing deep into the poorer, inner city areas of Belfast or Derry without a guide.
o **Stay informed** and follow the news to keep abreast of current events and any likely trouble spots.

BELFAST

Belfast is a lively, funky, and complicated town; a curious combination of faded grandeur and forward-looking optimism, complete with an artsy, edgy underbelly. Belfast boomed in the 19th century as prosperity flowed from its vast textile and shipbuilding industries. The 20th century was not so kind to the city, which spent many years in decline, but plenty of grand old Victorian buildings still reflect that time of wealth and

Belfast

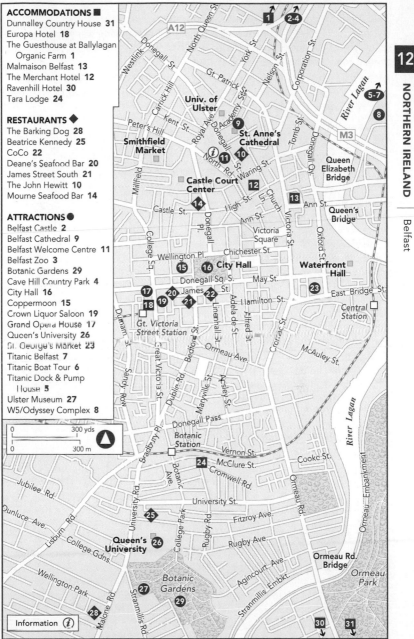

ACCOMMODATIONS ■
Dunnalley Country House **31**
Europa Hotel **18**
The Guesthouse at Ballylagan
  Organic Farm **1**
Malmaison Belfast **13**
The Merchant Hotel **12**
Ravenhill Hotel **30**
Tara Lodge **24**

RESTAURANTS ◆
The Barking Dog **28**
Beatrice Kennedy **25**
CoCo **22**
Deane's Seafood Bar **20**
James Street South **21**
The John Hewitt **10**
Mourne Seafood Bar **14**

ATTRACTIONS ●
Belfast Castle **2**
Belfast Cathedral **9**
Belfast Welcome Centre **11**
Belfast Zoo **3**
Botanic Gardens **29**
Cave Hill Country Park **4**
City Hall **16**
Coppermoon **15**
Crown Liquor Saloon **19**
Grand Opera House **17**
Queen's University **26**
St. George's Market **23**
Titanic Belfast **7**
Titanic Boat Tour **6**
Titanic Dock & Pump
  House **5**
Ulster Museum **27**
W5/Odyssey Complex **8**

Information ⓘ

205

power. Now the city's urban landscape is changing once again as the Titanic Quarter spurs new development with shiny museums and modern visitor attractions.

Arriving

BY BUS   **Ulsterbus** (www.translink.co.uk; ☏ **028/9066-6630**) runs buses from Dublin to Belfast and towns across Northern Ireland. In Belfast, the main bus station is Europa Bus Centre on Great Victoria Street.

BY TRAIN   Belfast has two train stations: Great Victoria Street Station and Belfast Central Station on East Bridge Street. Contact **Northern Ireland Railways** (☏ **028/9066-6630**) for tickets.

BY CAR   Driving from Dublin to Belfast is easy; just go north up the M1 motorway. From Dublin Airport, the journey is about 90 minutes in good traffic. From Sligo Town, take N16 and A4 west; from there it's 200km, about 2½ hours.

BY PLANE   Belfast has two airports: **Belfast International** (www.belfastairport. com; ☏ **028/9448-4848**) and **George Best Belfast City Airport** (www.belfastcity airport.com; ☏ **028/9093-9093**). United Airlines (www.united.com; ☏ **1/800/864-8331**) runs the one regular, direct flight to Belfast from North America. Aer Lingus (www.aerlingus.com; ☏ **01/814-1111**), British Airways (☏ **189/0626-747** in Ireland or ☏ 084/4493-0787 in the U.K.), Flybe (☏ **44/139-268-3152** or ☏ 087/1700-2000 in the U.K.), and Easyjet (www.easyjet.com; ☏ **084/3104-1000**) all operate regular scheduled flights from London to Belfast. Easyjet and Flybe fly to Belfast from Manchester, Birmingham, and Edinburgh in the U.K. You can fly direct to Belfast from several European cities.

Tourism Offices

The main tourist information center for the city is the **Belfast Welcome Centre** at 37 Donegall Place, BT1 5AD (www.visit-belfast.com; ☏ **028/9024-6609**). They can help book accommodations in the city, and they also have a bureau de change and left luggage facility. There are smaller visitor information points at **Belfast International Airport** (☏ **028/9448-4677**) and **George Best Belfast City Airport** (☏ **028/9093-5372**).

Getting Around

The capital city of Northern Ireland is divided into small quarters: The **City Center** spreads out from around the impressive, domed City Hall building and bustling **Donegall Square.** This is the best place for shopping, particularly along Donegall Place, which extends north from the square onto Royal Avenue. Bedford Street, which travels south from the Donegall Square, becomes Dublin Road, which, in turn, leads south to the **University Quarter,** the leafy area around Queen's University. This is where you'll find the Botanic Gardens, art galleries, and museums, as well as a buzzing nightlife scene. Heading north from Donegall Place, it's a short distance to the **Cathedral Quarter,** which surrounds Donegall Street, and holds, as the name implies, the city's most important cathedrals, as well as many vast Victorian warehouses. Finally, there's the **Golden Mile**—the area around Great Victoria Street beyond Bradbury Place. It's considered the city's best address for restaurants and pubs, although it's a bit hyperbolically named. As one local said to us, "It's not a mile and it's not golden. But it's nice enough." Some of the city's biggest attractions are now located in the new **Titanic Quarter,** a series of big commercial developments around Belfast Harbour located northeast of the city center.

[Fast FACTS] NORTHERN IRELAND

ATMs/Banks ATMs aren't hard to come by in central Belfast; there are several banks around Donegall Square, including **Ulster Bank** (𝄽 **028/9024-4112**) and **Bank of Ireland** (𝄽 **028/9043-3420**). In Derry, try **Santander** on Shipquay Street (𝄽 **084/5765-4321**).

Currency Remember that as part of the United Kingdom, Northern Ireland uses the pound sterling, not the euro. The cheapest way to get local currency is to use an ATM.

Dentists For dental emergencies, your hotel should contact a dentist for you. Otherwise, in Belfast try **Dublin Road Dental Practice,** 23 Dublin Rd., BT2 7HB (𝄽 **028/9032-5345**) or **Lisburn Road Dental Clinic,** 424 Lisburn Rd., BT9 6GN (𝄽 **028/9038-2262**); in Derry, try **Timber Quay Dental Practise,** Timber Quay, BT48 7NR (𝄽 **028/7122-1098**).

Doctors For medical emergencies, dial 𝄽 **999.** For nonemergencies, your hotel should call you a doctor. Otherwise, in Belfast, try **Ormeau Health Centre** (𝄽 **028/9032-6030**); in Derry, try **Park Medical,** 49 Great James St., BT48 7DH (𝄽 **028/7137-8500**).

Emergencies For police, fire, or other emergencies, dial 𝄽 **999.**

Internet Access In Belfast, there's **Browsers Café,** 77 Dublin Rd., BT2 7HF (𝄽 **028/9032-2272**) and **Abigail's,** 140 Upper Lisburn Rd., BT10 0BG (𝄽 **028/9061-6825**). In Derry, try **Café Connect,** 49 Strand Rd., BT48 7BN (𝄽 **028/7137-2101**).

Pharmacies In Belfast, there are branches of **Boots the Chemist** at 35-47 Donegall Place, BT1 5AW (𝄽 **028/9024-2332**) and Great Victoria St., BT2 7GN (𝄽 **028/9031-0530**). In Derry, try the **MediCare**

Pharmacy, 43 Great James St., BT48 7DF (𝄽 **028/7126-7004**).

Post Offices Main branches in Belfast include 16-22 Bedford St., BT2 7FD and 12-14 Bridge St., BT1 1LS.

Taxis In Belfast, you can catch a taxi at train stations, ports, airports, and the taxi stand in front of City Hall. Alternatively, try **Value Cabs** (𝄽 **028/9080-9080**), **Courtesy Cabs** (𝄽 **028/9002-9345**), or **Aldergrove Taxis** (𝄽 **028/9433-0950**). In Derry, there are taxi stands at the Ulsterbus station, Foyle Street, and at the train station on Duke Street; alternatively, call **City Cabs** (𝄽 **028/7126-4466**) or **Foyle Delta Cabs** (𝄽 **028/7127-9999**). Out in the countryside taxis are rarer—the best thing to do is ask for numbers from your hotel or at a pub. Most restaurants will call one for you.

Where to Stay in and Around Belfast

Belfast's hotel scene has grown in leaps and bounds during the last few years. A decade ago, expecting to find a top-quality boutique hotel or B&B from £100 per room was a tough task; today, however, you have much more to choose from. Best of all, because Belfast is still developing as a major tourist destination, the prices are still relatively low—although depending on where you're from, that advantage can be quickly wiped out by the exchange rate, which can often be more punishing to pounds than it is to euros.

Dunnanelly Country House ★★★ This delightful, Georgian-style mansion is just outside Downpatrick, about 18 miles south of Belfast, but the half-hour or so it takes to drive here from the city is a trivial price to pay for such a relaxing location. The decor inside mixes traditional, Regency-style color schemes and furnishings (love the antique rocking horse in the parlor), offset by pieces of modern art. Guest rooms are thoughtfully designed with large, modern bathrooms and have lovely views of the estate and all its allures (croquet pitch, gardens, ponds, and kennels). And you may need that exercise to help work off the hearty and delicious breakfasts. Guests have the use of a conservatory, a sitting room, and a separate game room. There's no dinner, but the owners can cheerfully point you in the direction of the best local pubs.

26 Rocks Chapel Rd., Downpatrick, Co. Down, BT30 9BA. www.dunnanellycountryhouse.com. Ⓒ 077/1277-9085. 3 units. £120. Free parking. Breakfast included. No children under 12 unless all 3 rooms booked by same group. **Amenities:** Wi-Fi (free).

Europa Hotel ★★ For some time this has been a lodging of choice for big-name politicians, diplomats, and celebrities when visiting Belfast (Hilary Clinton has stayed here several times). The large bedrooms are contemporary in style, with comfortable beds and modern furnishings. A little rubber ducky in a top hat is waiting for you as you enter the bathroom (you can take it home if you want). It's a nice touch and indicative of the attention to detail here. Downstairs there's a piano bar and the laid-back **Causerie** restaurant. Check the website for deals such as a theater package that includes tickets to the Grand Opera House (see p. 215) *and* return train travel from Dublin, for around £100 per couple.

Great Victoria St., BT2 7AP. www.hastingshotels.com/europa-belfast. Ⓒ 028/9027-1066. 240 units. £75–£260. Free parking. Breakfast not included in lower rates. **Amenities:** Wi-Fi (free), restaurant, bars (2), room service, gym, a/c (some).

The Guesthouse at Ballylagan Organic Farm ★★ Ballylagan is a working, fully certified organic farm (the first in Northern Ireland, no less), and at the center of it all is this welcoming little 1840s farmhouse. Patricia and Tom Gilbert are passionate about what they do, and boy, will you eat well here. Breakfast is made entirely from organic foods (of course), ranging from fresh baked bread to the eggs, bacon, and sausages. Home-cooked dinners can be provided, too, if booked in advance. (They can't serve wine due to licensing restrictions, but you're welcome to bring your own.) The guest rooms are painted in soothing color schemes, with modern prints on the wall. They're large enough to easily fit a sofa and a couple of chairs in addition to the extremely comfortable beds, so you certainly won't feel cramped here. For an extra charge of £10 per night you can have the use of a wood-burning stove in your room (it will be smoldering when you arrive). There's also a little guest lounge with a small library for guests to use. Ballyclare is about 13 miles north of Belfast.

12 Ballylagan Rd., Straid, Ballyclare. BT39 9NF. www.ballylagan.com. Ⓒ 028/9332-2129. 4 units. £95, children 11 and under (sharing with adult) £10. Free parking. Rates include breakfast. **Amenities:** Wi-Fi (free).

Malmaison Belfast ★ This is the only Irish outpost of Malmaison, a British mini-chain that specializes in rescuing unusual historic buildings and turning them into hip boutique hotels. This one used to be a seed warehouse, of all things, and the chic, playful design in the public areas plays up that industrial past. That means deep purple carpets, gray or black walls, and steel girders left exposed here and there. Bedrooms are decorated in masculine tones of gray and brown with low lighting, huge beds, and modern bathrooms. The in-house restaurant serves decent, brasserie-style cooking (dinner, bed and breakfast packages are available) and there's a lively bar, too.

34-38 Victoria St., BT1 3GH. www.malmaison.com/locations/belfast. Ⓒ 084/4693-0650. 64 units. £69–£145. Discounted parking at nearby lot (£10 per day). Breakfast not included in lower rates. **Amenities:** Wi-Fi (free), restaurant, bar, room service, gym.

THE red hand OF ULSTER

Around Belfast and Northern Ireland, you'll frequently come across representations of a red hand. It's carved in doorframes, painted on walls and ceilings, and even planted in red flowers in gardens. Known as the Red Hand of Ulster, it is one of the symbols of the region. According to one version of the old tale, the hand can trace its history from a battle between two men competing to be king of Ulster. They held a race (some say by boat, others say it took place on horseback) and agreed that the first man to touch Ulster soil would win. As one man fell behind, he pulled his sword and cut off his right hand, then with his left, flung the bloody hand ahead of his competitor, winning the right to rule.

The Merchant Hotel ★★★ One of Ireland's most luxurious hotels, a night at the Merchant is a real treat. The Victorian building used to be a bank; it was only turned into an hotel in 2006, with a further, £17-million upgrade in 2010. The conversion is stunning, from the extraordinary dining room with its lacquered and gilded Corinthian columns, marble floors, and ceiling friezes to the elegant cocktail lounge with chandeliers and a gently curved, dark wood bar. Guest rooms are big and thoroughly modern, but ask for an Art Deco–style room, as opposed to a traditional one—they're larger and better designed. There's an excellent **spa,** complete with hydrotherapy pool and treatment rooms, and even a hot tub on the roof with a great view over the city. The **Great Room Restaurant** serves top-notch modern Irish cuisine. Afternoon tea is also a bit of an event here, and popular, so it's advisable to book if you want to indulge. Service is impeccable. The staff could hardly be friendlier or more helpful.

16 Skipper St., BT1 2DZ. www.themerchanthotel.com. (©) **028/9023-4888.** 62 units. £160–£260. Valet parking. Breakfast not included in lower rates. Dinner, bed and breakfast packages available. **Amenities:** Wi-Fi (free), a/c, restaurant, bar, spa, gym.

Ravenhill Hotel ★★ A friendly welcome awaits from hosts Roger and Olive, whose handsome Victorian corner house has been converted into one of the best B&Bs in Belfast. Bedrooms are simple but neat as a pin with print fabrics and views of the street. You're in a residential area here, but luckily not far from the action; the city center is about a 10-minute cab or bus ride. Roger cooks delicious breakfasts and guests can expect the full "Ulster fry," in addition to a few lighter options such as kippers with parsley butter and scrambled eggs. They also bake their own traditional Irish wheaten bread from scratch, even down to milling their own flour. At certain times of year there are discounts for stays of 2 nights or more. You'll be hard-pressed to find a better or more hospitable B&B at this price.

690 Ravenhill Rd., BT6 0BZ. www.ravenhillhouse.com. (©) **028/9020-7444.** 5 units. £75–£90. Free parking. Rates include breakfast. **Amenities:** Wi-Fi (free).

Tara Lodge ★ When Tara Lodge opened in the mid-2000s, it was part of a new wave of modern, inexpensive boutique-style small hotels in Belfast, a city where good budget accommodations were scarce. It has more competition these days, but Tara Lodge still manages to get everything just about right. Guest rooms are simple but contemporary in style, if perhaps a little small, but the beds are large and comfortable. Breakfasts are very good and offer plenty of choice. The **Botanic Gardens** (see p. 214) and **Ulster Museum** (p. 217) are about 10 minutes away on foot; you could walk to the city center in about 25, or it's a short cab ride. The only downside is that there's no restaurant, but there are plenty of good options within easy reach.

36 Cromwell Rd., BT7 1JW. www.taralodge.com. ℂ **028/9059-0900.** 34 units. £79–£120. Free parking. Breakfast included. **Amenities:** Wi-Fi (free).

12 Where to Eat in Belfast

A prominent British journalist tells the story of ordering an Ulster fry in Belfast sometime in the 1970s. "No sausage," he asked the waitress. When his food arrived, there were sausages on the plate. He sent it back, asking again for no sausage. But back it came, with sausages still there. "But I said no sausages," he complained. "Chef says sausage is compulsory," replied the waitress. Today the Belfast dining scene is, happily, much more cosmopolitan. The number of top restaurants in the city seems to increase every year, from funky little gastropubs to chic fine dining. The same can't always be said for the countryside, but hidden gems, and good pubs and tea shops, can be found in even the remotest corners.

The Barking Dog ★★ IRISH/INTERNATIONAL   There's something quintessentially Belfast about this place—quirky, artsy, lively, but ultimately no-nonsense. The dining room has a funky pub feel, complete with exposed brick and old candelabras balanced on battered wood tables. If you sit in the front garden, you're separated from the street by a fence with paw prints all over it. The menu is balanced and straightforward, offering up a juicy cheeseburger with fat french fries, for example, or a simple fish pie. The slightly more original items, such as the "nibbles and tipples" combo of tapas-style sharing plates, can be paired with house cocktails. There's a good lunch menu, and the Sunday brunch is popular.

33-35 Malone Rd., Belfast, BT9 6RU. www.barkingdogbelfast.com. ℂ **028/9066-1885.** £26–£40. Mon–Thurs noon–3pm and 5:30–10pm; Fri–Sat noon–3pm and 5:30–11pm; Sun noon–9pm. No children after 9pm.

Beatrice Kennedy ★★ IRISH   A perennial favorite in the University District, Beatrice Kennedy has a genteel setting (flowery wallpaper, white napkins, and cozy dining rooms, as the restaurant is set in a Victorian row house) but a chef whose tastes are squarely in the 21st century. That means that the proteins and meats are proudly locally sourced and come in preparations both from Ireland and around the globe. Bubble and squeak on one plate, couscous on another! You might start with crab and avocado dressing slathered in mango salsa, followed by a traditional (and juicy!) ribeye, sided by thrice-fried spuds. Desserts are mostly sweet comfort foods with some touches of invention. Try the mango and chocolate mousse if it's on offer. Early-bird specials are a good value.

44 University Rd., Belfast, BT7 1NJ. www.beatricekennedy.co.uk. ℂ **028/9020-2290.** £17–£20. Tues–Thurs 5–9:30pm; Fri–Sat 5–10:30pm; Sun 12:30–2:30pm and 5–8:30pm.

CoCo ★★ MODERN EUROPEAN/INTERNATIONAL   Think contemporary here, from the posters and photo-collages that set the tone to the wide-ranging menu (it features dishes like goat-cheese fritters served with essence of bell pepper, lamb with merguez sausage and couscous, and a Thai red chicken curry served with sticky rice and bok choi). This is a particularly good place for vegetarians, who have such tasty choices as the "admiral pie," made with chili tofu, asparagus, sugar snap peas, and parsley cream. Prices are a little high for the evening service, but the pre-theater menu is a good value at three courses for £18. They also do a popular three-course Sunday lunch menu for £17. Reservations are recommended.

7-11 Linenhall St., Belfast, BT2 8AA. www.cocobelfast.com. © **028/9031-1150**. £16–£23. Mon–Fri noon–3pm and 5:30–10pm; Sat 5:30–10pm; Sun noon–9pm.

Deane's Seafood Bar ★★★ SEAFOOD Michael Deane is something of a local celebrity chef. **Eipic**, his flagship, formal restaurant on Howard Street, still serves very good Irish-French cuisine, although the adjacent **Seafood Bar** is equally good, and (even better) less expensive. Here you'll find plates such as salt cod croquettes, tempura oysters, or crispy monkfish filet served with hot and sour peppers. Also here is the excellent **Meat Locker,** a laid-back grill where you can pick up a three-course pretheater menu for an incredibly reasonable £23. Michael Deane now has several offshoots across Belfast, each cleverly going for a slightly different crowd, and sometimes sharing premises. There's the **Deli-Bistro** (© **028/902-8800**) and **Deli/Vin Café** (© **028/9024-8830**), a tapas bar, on Bedford Street; while in the University Quarter, next to the Ulster Museum, is the informal bistro, **Deanes at Queens** (© **028/9038-2111**). The newest addition to the mini-empire is his foray into Italian cooking, **Deane & Decano** (© **028/9066-3108**), on Lisburn Road. **Tip:** Seafood Bar, Deane's Deli, Deanes at Queens, and Deane and Decano share one of Belfast's best lunch deals—main dishes for just £6.50.

36-40 Howard St., Belfast, BT1 6PF. www.michaeldeane.co.uk. © **028/9033-1134**. £9–£20. Mon–Sat noon–9:30pm.

James Street South ★★★ MODERN IRISH One of Belfast's leading restaurants, James Street South has built its reputation on intriguing, highly inventive Irish cuisine. On the menu recently were such unusual (but excellent) combinations as crispy mackerel with gooseberries; razor clams served with a lime confit; loin of lamb with glazed turnip; and turbot poached in wine with *buerre rouge* (a rich sauce made with butter, shallots, and red wine). Desserts could include a deliciously sweet lemon brûlée, or you could embrace the spirit of discovery and have an assortment of Irish cheeses. Tasting menus only here (£45 for four courses, or £65 with paired wines); or eat at the cheaper and more laid back bar and grill.

21 James St. South, Belfast, BT2 7GA. www.jamesstreetsouth.co.uk. © **028/9043-4310**. £15–£24. Mon–Sat noon–2:45pm and 5:45–10:45pm.

The John Hewitt ★ IRISH/INTERNATIONAL This atmospheric bar near the Cathedral is a popular hangout with locals. The gastropub-style lunch menu is a real crowd-pleaser, serving items like soup of the day with crusty bread, crispy squid with coriander (cilantro) rice, and a steak and onion sandwich made with Italian-style ciabatta bread and served with garlic butter. They don't serve food in the evenings or any time on Sundays, but you may still want to drop by—the John Hewitt is one of the best spots in the city for live music with bands every night from 9pm or 5:30pm on Saturday. Admission to gigs is usually free.

51 Donegall St., Belfast, BT1 2FH. www.thejohnhewitt.com. © **028/9023-3768**. £4–£9. Mon–Fri 11:30am–1am; Sat noon–1am; Sun 7pm–midnight. (Food served Mon–Thurs noon–3pm, Fri–Sat noon–5:30pm.)

Mourne Seafood Bar ★★★ SEAFOOD The place in Belfast for top-quality seafood. Oysters are a specialty, served traditionally, with Tabasco and lemon, or in more elaborate ways, such as with pickled ginger and soy dressing. Alternatively, you could go for some crab claws with chili butter to start before moving on to one of the fresh daily specials like seared scallops with pea risotto. The atmosphere is relaxed and convivial, and the prices are thoroughly reasonable for food this good. They don't take reservations at lunchtime, but evening booking is essential.

34-36 Bank St., Belfast, BT1 1HL. www.mourneseafood.com. ⓒ **028/9024-8544.** £9–£20. Mon–Thurs noon–9:30pm; Fri and Sat noon–4pm and 5–10:30pm; Sun 1–6pm.

EXPLORING BELFAST

Belfast's history is at once rich, varied, and heart-wrenching. The must-sees are many, from a **Black Taxi Tour** to explore the era of the Troubles to the many, newer sights related to the famed ocean liner *Titanic* (it was built here).

Belfast Castle ★ CASTLE   Northwest of downtown and 120m (394 ft.) above sea level stands Belfast Castle; its 80-hectare (198-acre) estate spreads down the slopes of Cave Hill. Dating from 1870, this was the family residence of the third marquis of Donegall, and it was built in the style of Britain's Balmoral Castle. The estate is a lovely place to visit, offering sweeping views of Belfast and the lough. Its cellars contain a nifty Victorian arcade, a restaurant (open 11am to 5pm Wednesday to Monday, and 11am to 9pm Tuesday), and a shop selling antiques and crafts. According to legend, a white cat brought the castle residents luck, so look around for carvings featuring this much-loved feline. This is also the location of the Cave Hill Visitor Centre (see p. 214).

Signposted off Antrim Rd., 2½ miles north of the city center, Belfast, BT15 5GR. www.belfastcastle. co.uk. ⓒ **028/9077-6925.** Free admission and parking. Mon–Sun 9am–6pm; Tues–Sat 9am–10:30pm.

Belfast Cathedral ★ CHURCH   The foundation stone on this monumental cathedral, also known as St. Anne's, was laid in 1899. It remained incomplete for more than a century; even now it still awaits a steeple. Crisscrossing architectural genres from Romanesque to Victorian to modern, the huge structure is more attractive inside than out. In the nave, the ceiling soars above the black-and-white marble walls and stone floors, and elaborate stained-glass windows fill it with color. Carvings that represent life in Belfast top the ten pillars. The cathedral's most impressive features, though, are the delicate mosaic ceilings of the tympanum, and the baptistery constructed of thousands of pieces of glass.

Donegall St., Belfast, BT1 2HB. www.belfastcathedral.org. ⓒ **028/9032-8332.** Admission £2. Mon–Sat 9am–5:15pm, Sun 1–3pm. Closed during services (unless attending).

Belfast Zoo ★ ZOO   In a picturesque mountain park on the slopes of Cave Hill just outside of town and overlooking the city, this zoo was founded in 1920 as Bellevue Gardens and has been completely modernized in recent years. It emphasizes conservation and education, and focuses on breeding rare species, including Hawaiian geese, lowland gorillas, red lechwe (a kind of antelope), sea bears, Barbary lions, and golden lion tamarins. The Rainforest House is a tropical environment filled with birds and jungle creatures. Special tours and one-off events run all year. Most activity days are quite kid-oriented, although there are also some more grown-up events such as all-day photography competitions. Check the website for up-to-date listings.

Antrim Rd., Belfast, BT36 7PN. www.belfastzoo.co.uk. ⓒ **028/9077-6277.** Apr–Sept daily 10am–7pm (last admission 5pm, animal houses close 6pm); Oct–Mar daily 10am–4pm (last admission 2:30pm, animal houses close 3pm). Admission £11 adults; £5.50 seniors, students, and children; £30 families.

the art of conflict: BELFAST'S STREET MURALS

The huge street murals in West Belfast are painted by amateur artists, albeit immensely talented ones. Each mural tells a tale of history, strife, anger, or peace. The densest concentration is around the **Falls and Shankill roads.** During the Troubles, from the late 1960s to the mid-1990s, this area was the center of the conflict. That dark chapter officially ended with the Good Friday Agreement of 1998, but divisions between some Catholic and Protestant communities still run deep and raw.

The Falls Road is staunchly Catholic and Republican (those who want to see Ireland united as a single country). Shankill, just half a mile away, is resolutely Protestant and Loyalist (those who want Northern Ireland to remain part of the United Kingdom).

Although all are deeply political, there is a noticeable divide between the tones of the murals. Those on the Falls Road tend to be about solidarity with the downtrodden (and not just in Ireland—you'll see murals about war and oppression in other parts of the world, too). On the corner of Falls Road and Sevastopol Street is the surprisingly small Sinn Fein headquarters. At one end of the building is a mural of the late hunger-striker

Bobby Sands (1954–81), arguably the most famous political mural in Ireland.

By contrast, the Shankill murals are generally darker, featuring more violent and threatening imagery, although some of the worst were removed a few years ago.

Locals in all districts are very proud of their murals and are used to people visiting to take photos. They're safe to visit, but you should still exercise the usual caution you would in any rough city neighborhood. It's also advisable to avoid these parts of town on **parade days**—ostensibly celebratory events, these tend toward unpleasant displays of nationalism, erupting into street violence. The biggest, and most controversial, is the Protestant "Orange Order" parade on July 12. Any parades that are likely to cause trouble are well covered by the local media, though, so it's easy to know when one is coming up.

The best, safest, and certainly the most informative way to see the murals is to take a **Black Taxi Tour** (see above). The tours are a real Belfast highlight, and could hardly be more convenient—the drivers will pick you up at your hotel and drop you off anywhere you like in the city.

Black Taxi Tour ★★★ TOUR For many years, Belfast was best known for its most conflicted neighborhoods, where in the 1970s and '80s protest and violence occurred daily. For anyone born before 1990, the name Belfast is probably still synonymous with sectarianism, even though peace has (precariously) held on the Catholic Falls Road and its nearby parallel, the Protestant Shankill Road, for nearly 15 years. Today there's a growing industry around exploring these infamous districts, and Black Taxi Tour is by far the best one. The tours are conducted in London-style cabs that take you through the neighborhoods, past the barbed wire, towering fences, and partisan murals, as guides explain their significance. Drivers, who are all locals, are relaxed, patient, and unbiased, with a talent for explaining this complicated history to outsiders in an easy and engaging way. Tours aren't just limited to politics; the guides will also take you to see the *Titanic* shipyard and other parts of the city, if you wish. Just ask

JOINING THE national trust

Several of Ulster's best historic sites are managed by the **National Trust,** a not-for-profit organization that preserves thousands of buildings and areas of natural beauty across the U.K. (including Northern Ireland), keeping them accessible to the public. Taking out a yearly membership gives you unlimited free admission to all of them, which can work out cheaper if you plan to visit several. If you also happen to be visiting Britain on your trip, or within a year, it could be a wise investment.

The current membership costs are £55.50 for individuals, £92 for couples, £26 for children, and £60.50 to £97 for families. You can sign up for membership at any National Trust property, or join in advance online at **www.national trust.org.uk.**

Alternatively, American visitors can join the U.S. wing of the National Trust, the **Royal Oak Foundation.** Visit www. royal-oak.org or call ℂ **212/480-2889** for more information. Royal Oak members get the same benefits, plus money off lectures, tours, and other special events held in the U.S.

when you book. The standard tour lasts about 90 minutes, and guides will pick you up and drop you off anywhere in the city.

Belfast. www.belfasttours.com. ℂ**028/9064-2264.** £25 for up to 2 passengers, then £10 for each additional passenger, up to 6 people.

Belfast Botanic Gardens & Palm House ★ GARDEN   Dating from 1828, these gardens were established by the Belfast Botanic and Horticultural Society. Ten years later, they gained a glass house, or conservatory, designed by noted Belfast architect Charles Lanyon. Now known as the Palm House, this unique structure contains an excellent variety of tropical plants, including sugar cane, coffee, cinnamon, banana, aloe, ivory nut, rubber, bamboo, guava, and spindly birds of paradise. If the weather's fine, stroll in the outdoor rose gardens that date back to 1927. They occasionally hold festivals and other special events here; check local listings for details.

College Park, Botanic Ave., Belfast, BT7 1LP. ℂ**028/9031-4762.** Free admission. Palm House and Tropical Ravine: Apr–Sept Mon–Fri daily 1–5pm; Oct–Mar daily 1–4pm. Gardens: May–early Aug daily 7:30am–9pm; early–late Aug 7:30am–8:30pm; Sept 7:30am–7pm; Oct 7:30am–6pm; Nov 7:30am–4:30pm.

Cave Hill Country Park ★★ PARK   This park atop a 360m (1,181-ft.) basalt cliff offers panoramic views, walking trails, and archaeological and historical sights. The park gets its name from five small caves thought to have been Neolithic iron mines; several other ancient sites are scattered about the place, often unmarked. These include stone cairns, dolmens, and **McArt's Fort**—the remains of an ancient defensive hill fort in which Wolfe Tone and his fellow United Irishmen planned the 1798 rebellion. It's mostly gone now, but you can explore the ruins, which sit atop the park's most famous viewpoint. The **Cave Hill Visitor Centre,** on the second floor of Belfast Castle (see listing above), contains a diverting exhibition on the history of the park and the castle itself. You can also pick up maps of the park here. A great walk around the entire circuit of the park can be found on the website of Walk NI, a useful link set up to promote hiking in Northern Ireland. The route description, plus a handy map, can be downloaded from www.walkni.com/walks/79/cave-hill-country-park. It should be manageable for anyone of reasonable fitness, though it may be too challenging for children; ask for advice at the park visitor center before you set out.

Visitor Centre: Belfast Castle, off Antrim Rd., 6.5km (4 miles) north of city center, Belfast, BT15 5GR. www.belfastcity.gov.uk/parksandopenspaces. ℭ **028/9077-6925.** Free admission. Visitor Centre: Sun–Mon 9am–5:30pm; Tues–Sat 9am–10pm.

City Hall ★ ARCHITECTURE   This glorious explosion of granite, marble, and stained glass is testament to Belfast's grand industrial past. Built in classical Renaissance style in 1906, it has white Portland stone walls and a soft green copper dome. There are several statues on the grounds, including a grim-faced statue of Queen Victoria that stands out front, looking as if she wished she were anywhere else. Bronze figures around her represent the textile and shipbuilding industries that powered Belfast's success. There's also a memorial to the victims of the *Titanic* disaster. Inside the building, the elaborate entry hall is heavy with marble but lightened by stained glass and a rotunda with a painted ceiling. Somehow it all manages not to be tacky. There are often exhibitions upstairs, and to learn more about the building's history, take a free guided tour. Call or ask in the lobby for details.

Donegall Sq. North, Belfast, BT1 5GS. ℭ **028/9027-0456.** Free admission. Guided tours Mon–Fri 11am, 2pm, and 3pm, Sat 2pm and 3pm; otherwise by arrangement.

Coppermoon ★★ SHOP   A riotously creative little boutique, Coppermoon sells art and gorgeous little knickknacks. Plenty of local designers are represented, including makers of bags and accessories; funky, steampunk-style jewelry; glass and ceramics; and quirky pieces of homeware, from lampshades made of bottles to wittily embroidered pillows. They also create beautiful, individually designed cards.

3 Wellington St., Belfast, BT1 6HT. www.coppermoon.co.uk. ℭ **028/9023-5325.** Mon–Wed and Fri–Sat 9:30am–5:30pm; Thurs 9:30am–9pm; Sun 1–5pm.

Crown Liquor Saloon ★★★ HISTORIC PUB   Easily the most impressive Victorian pub in the city, and possibly the country, the Crown Liquor Saloon piles on the atmosphere as thick as fog. The old "gin palace," as pubs of this era are known, owes its elaborate appearance to Italian workers who came to Ireland in the late–19th century to work on churches but ended up finding work here. There is definitely something ecclesiastical about some of the finer features, from the stained glass in the windows to the pew-like "snugs," complete with elaborately carved doors designed to shield the more refined class of Victorian patrons from their fellow drinkers. The floors are intricately tiled and the ceiling is made of hammered copper. This place was considered so important to the iconography of Belfast that it was actually bought for the nation by the National Trust in the 1970s. This ensures its impeccable upkeep while it continues to run as a working pub.

46 Great Victoria St., Belfast, BT2 7BA. www.nicholsonspubs.co.uk/thecrownliquorsaloonbelfast. ℭ **028/9024-3187.** Mon–Wed 11:30am–11pm; Thurs–Sat 11:30am–midnight; Sun 12:30–10pm.

Grand Opera House ★★ PERFORMING ARTS   One of the main landmarks of Belfast's "Golden Mile," the Grand Opera House opened in 1895. The interior is full of late-Victorian detail, including an extraordinarily grand auditorium, complete with an elaborately painted frieze on the high ceiling. It hasn't always been well treated. It was severely damaged twice by IRA bombs, but a full restoration in the mid-2000s returned the place to its former glory. Today it continues to be a cornerstone of the Belfast live arts scene with a tremendous variety of shows, from touring plays, ballet, and opera to big-ticket musicals, concerts, and stand-up comedy. Ticket prices vary greatly, but expect to pay between £15 and £30 for most shows. Check the website for a detailed listing of what's on.

2-4 Great Victoria St., Belfast, BT2 7HR. www.goh.co.uk. ℭ **028/9024-1919.** Ticket prices vary.

Queen's University ★ ARCHITECTURE   Founded by Queen Victoria in 1845 to provide nondenominational higher education, this is Northern Ireland's most prestigious university. The main 19th-century Tudor revival building may remind you of England's Oxford, especially because its design was based on that of the Founder's Tower at Magdalen College. But that's hardly all there is to this university, which sprawls through 250 buildings and where 17,500 students are studying at any given time. The whole neighborhood around the university is a quiet, attractive place to wander, and University Square on the north side of campus is simply beautiful. At one end of the square is the Union Theological College, dating from 1853, which housed the Northern Ireland Parliament after the partition of Ireland in 1921 until its abolition in 1972. Access to parts of the campus may be restricted during exam times.

Queen's Welcome Centre, Queen's University, University Rd., Belfast, BT7 1NN. www.queens eventus.com/QueensWelcomeCentre. ℭ **028/9097-5252.** Free admission; tours (large groups only) £3.50 per person. Year-round Mon–Fri 9:30am–4:30pm; also Sat–Sun 11am–4pm during summer vacation.

St. George's Market ★ MARKET   This eclectic street market is one of the city's oldest attractions. The current iron-and-glass structure opened in 1896, although a market has been held on this spot for much longer. Friday is the **Variety Market:** 250 stalls of fresh produce, antiques, clothing, and bric-a-brac. There's also a lively fish market that supplies many of the local restaurants. On Saturday the **City Food and Craft Market** specializes in artisan foods with plenty of tempting fresh snacks on offer, plus a nice assortment of local crafts. The **Sunday Market** is a happy combination of the two, although the balance tends to be in favor of crafts.

May St. at Oxford St., Belfast, BT1 3NQ. ℭ **028/9043-5704.** Free admission. Fri 6am–2pm; Sat 9am–3pm; Sun 10am–4pm.

Titanic Belfast ★★★ MUSEUM   This ambitious museum, which opened in 2012 to great fanfare, tells the story of the *Titanic* in revelatory detail. Located next to the very site where the doomed vessel was constructed, the enormous, angular frontage, clad in 2,000 individual sheets of aluminum, juts out in four directions at the actual height of *Titanic*'s bow. The innovative design continues across the nine well-laid-out galleries covering everything from her construction to the triumphant launch, disastrous sinking, and the lasting cultural phenomenon that rose in her wake. A special ride takes you on a virtual tour of the shipyard to see how *Titanic*, and her sister ship, *Olympic*, were built. In a split-level gallery you can even "explore" the wreck yourself, via enormous high-definition screens and other interactive gizmos. Finally, the **Ocean Exploration Centre** takes the story into the 21st century with high-tech exhibits on the science of sea exploration, including a live link to an undersea probe. In truth, the content can sometimes feel stretched to fill the space, but it's all impressively done. Needless to say, there's an extremely well-stocked gift shop at the end. Crowds can swell at busy times, so it's advisable to book ahead.

1 Olympic Way, Belfast, BT3 9DP. www.titanicbelfast.com. ℭ **028/9076-6386.** £15.50 adults, £11 seniors Mon–Fri, £13 seniors Sat–Sun, £10 students Mon–Fri, £11 students Sat–Sun, £7.50 children 5–16, £39 families, children 4 and under free. Parking £1.50 per hr. for 1st hr., then £1 per hr. afterward. Apr and Jun–Aug daily 9am–7pm; Apr and Sept daily 9am–6pm; Oct–Mar daily 10am–5pm; last admission 1 hr. 40 min. before closing.

Titanic Boat Tour ★ TOUR   Many historic shipyard buildings were demolished in the early 2000s to make way for new development; a controversial move, but one that also opened up long-obscured views of the harbor from the river. This jaunty and informative boat trip takes you past many of them. Despite the name, there aren't that many *Titanic*-related sights left, but this is also a good introduction to Belfast's maritime past and a pleasant way to spend an hour. With typically dry Belfast wit, the crew's T-shirts read "She was alright when she left here." In summer the tour goes as far as Musgrave Channel, where there's a large breeding colony of seals. The departure point is on Donegall Quay, about 100 meters (330 ft.) to the left of the big fish sculpture.

The Obel, Donegall Quay, Belfast, BT3 3NG. www.laganboatcompany.com. ℂ **028/9024-0124.** £10 adults; £8 seniors, students, and children 6–16; £30 families; children 4 and under free. Tours daily 12:30, 2, and 3:30pm (no 3:30 tour in winter).

Titanic Dock and Pump House ★★ HISTORIC SITE   Another of Belfast's major ship-related attractions, this fascinating tour takes you around the dry docks at the old Harland and Wolff shipyard, where *Titanic* and *Olympic* were constructed from 1909–11. Designed to appeal to a general audience, not just enthusiasts, it's a great way to learn about what it was really like to work here at the turn of the last century, when Belfast was one of the world's greatest industrial cities. The enormous Edwardian pump house, which could drain a staggering 21 million gallons of water in just over an hour and a half, is worth the price of admission by itself. An audio-visual room includes some rare film footage of the *Titanic* in situ at the dock. Fully guided versions of the tour take place on weekends at 2pm; if you want to join one of these, tickets cost a couple of pounds extra. There's also a large visitor center with plenty of interesting exhibits, a gift shop, and a cafe.

Queen's Rd., Queen's Island, Belfast, BT3 9DT. www.titanicsdock.com ℂ **028/9073-7813.** Admission £5 adults, £4 seniors Mon–Fri, £4.50 seniors Sat–Sun, students £4, children 5–16 £3, £12 families, children 4 and under free. Mon–Thurs 10:30am–6pm, Fri 9:30am–5pm, Sat–Sun 10:30am–5pm.

Ulster Museum ★★★ MUSEUM   This is one of Belfast's best and most comprehensive museums. The collection is impressive, from dinosaur bones and prehistoric artifacts to art and other treasures from Ireland and around the world. Highlights include a collection of 16th to 18th-century Dutch and Italian paintings; a hoard of priceless 16th-century Spanish jewelry, recovered off the coast near Belfast in the 1960s; clothes, textiles, and ceramics from Asia and Africa; and items relating to the Ascendancy, the period of Protestant rule in Ireland that finally came to a head with the rebellion of 1798. There's also a particularly strong collection of objects from the Classical world; the **Life and Death in Ancient Egypt** exhibit has about 2,000 artifacts from Pharaonic times (including a mummy), and there are also items from ancient Mesopotamia, Rome, and Greece. There is a good program of special exhibitions, talks, and even the occasional concert; check the website to see what's on.

At the Botanic Gardens, Belfast, BT9 5AB. www.nmni.com. ℂ **028/9044-0000.** Free admission. Tues–Sun 10am–5pm. Closed Mon (except bank holidays).

W5 ★ CHILDREN'S MUSEUM   This fab hands-on science play center for kids is part of the Odyssey Complex, a huge indoor arena on Queen's Quay that's bursting with activities. Properly known as "Whowhatwhenwherewhy"—you can see why they abbreviate it to W5—it's a high-tech, interactive learning environment. Kids can take part in over 250 individual activities, all in the spirit of science-based fun. They can do everything from create animated cartoons, try to beat a lie detector test, and even

khaleesi DOES IT

The most popular TV show in the world is filmed in Northern Ireland, and the publicity that HBO's *Game of Thrones* has brought to the region has been a massive boon for tourism. Major filming locations have included **Castle Ward** (see listing above); **Cushendun** (p. 224) and **Ballintoy** (p. 223) on the Antrim Coast Drive; and the **Tollymore Forest Park** in County Down (p. 221).

Brit Movie Tours offer a bus tour of many of the most scenic places used in the show. The tour, which also covers a few extras like the **Giant's Causeway** (see p. 224), leaves from the City Tours office in Victoria Square, central Belfast, and returns roughly 8½ hours later. They run all year on Saturdays and Sundays, and also on Tuesdays and Thursdays from April to September. Departure time is always 10am. Tickets cost £35 adults, £20 children 11 and under, and £90 families. Private tours, for up to six people, can be booked for £400.

For details and booking, visit www.britmovietours.com or call ℂ **0844/247-1007** in Northern Ireland and Britain (ℂ **44/207-118-1007** in the rest of the world).

present the weather on TV. There are also plenty of special events and temporary exhibitions. The Odyssey also contains a cinema, game arcades, and a sports arena.

2 Queen's Quay, BT3 9QQ. www.w5online.co.uk. ℂ**028/9046-7700.** £8 adults, £6.50 seniors and students, £6 children, £22–£38.50 families. Mon–Fri 10am–5pm, Sat 10am–6pm, Sun noon–6pm; last admission 1 hr. before closing.

Out from Belfast

Further afield from Belfast, the Ards Peninsula, beginning about 16km (10 miles) east of the city, curls around the western shore of Strangford Lough. This bird sanctuary and wildlife reserve is a place of great natural beauty. It's also lined with historic buildings and ancient sites, from the austere **Castle Ward** and the elegant **Mount Stewart House,** to the mysterious, megalithic **Giant's Ring.** A couple of roads traverse the peninsula: the A2 (coast road) and the A20 (Lough road, the more scenic of the two). To the north of the city, **Carrickfergus Castle** is worth a stop for a dose of over-the-top Medievalism.

Castle Ward ★★ HISTORIC HOME   Castle Ward is "famed," as its National Trust caretakers put it, "for its mixture of architectural styles." Which rather undersells the bizarre clash of stylistic elements—neo-Gothic and Classical—that might suggest that a war between two very adamant architects broke out here during the design phase. Apparently, the eclectic appearance results from the much divided tastes of the owners. Lord Bangor, whose predilection was for the studied classicism of Palladian design, brought his preferences to bear on the front entrance. Lady Anne, who favored the contemporary Gothic look so popular during the late 1700s (when designs were drawn up), left her mark on the garden-facing wing. Whatever the real reason for the peculiar mismarriage, it has the effect of suggesting that two building projects were joined at the hip, since the segregated design splits the house right down the middle and runs as deep as the choice of mundane everyday items inside the house, too. Needless to say, Anne and Bernard's marriage did not last into eternity, but their home does provide insight into the extreme lengths, given enough cash, some of us go to make a point. On a good day, the grounds make for salubrious exploration, with a lake, tower houses, and children's play center—not a bad spot for a picnic, either. Castle Ward has achieved a degree of latter-day fame as one of the key locations for the HBO series *Game of Thrones*—albeit heavily disguised (see box below).

Park Rd., Strangford, Co. Down, BT30 7LS. www.nationaltrust.org.uk. © **028/4488-1204.** £7 adults, £3.50 children, £17 families. Grounds: Mar and Oct daily 10am–5pm; Apr–Sept daily 10am–8pm; Nov–Feb daily 10–4pm. House: Mar–Oct daily noon–5pm.

Carrickfergus Castle ★ CASTLE   This impressive Norman castle looms darkly over the entrance to Belfast Lough, where William of Orange landed in June 1690 en route to the Battle of the Boyne. The central part dates to the 12th century, the thick outer walls were completed 100 years later, and the gun ports are a relatively new addition at only 400 years old. The outside is more impressive than the inside, which has been largely dedicated to inspiring young imaginations. The use of waxwork figures (riding horses, threatening to shoot people over the walls) is a bit over the top, although sometimes actors in medieval costume add a touch of hammy fun. There's a visitor center and a small museum. In the summer, medieval banquets, a medieval fair, and a crafts market are held, all adding a touch of play and pageantry.

Marine Hwy., Carrickfergus, BT38 7BG. © **028/9335-1273.** Admission £5 adults, £3 seniors and children 4–16, children 3 and under free. Apr–Sept daily 10am–6pm; Oct–Mar daily 10am–4pm. Carrickfergus is on A2, 12 mi northeast of Belfast.

Castle Espie Wetland Centre ★ CASTLE   This marvelous wildlife center, named for a castle that has long since ceased to be, is home to a virtual UN of rare migratory geese, ducks, and swans. Some are so accustomed to visitors that they will eat grain from their hands, so children can have the disarming experience of meeting Hooper swans eye to eye. Guided trails are designed for children and families, and the center sponsors activities and events year-round. A favorite of bird-watchers in search of waterfowl, the center has thousands of pale-bellied brents in early winter. The book and gift shop is enticing, the kids' play area is excellent, and the restaurant serves good lunches and home-baked cakes.

78 Ballydrain Rd., Comber, BT23 6EA. www.wwt.org.uk/wetland-centres/castle-espie. © **028/9187-4146.** Admission £7.50 adults, £5.50 seniors and students, £3.50 children 4–16, £19 families, children 3 and under free. Mar–Apr and Sept–Oct daily 10am–5pm; May–Aug Mon–Fri 10am–5pm, Sat–Sun 10am–5:30pm; Nov–Feb daily 10am–4:30pm.

Castlewellan Forest Park ★★ PARK   Surrounding a fine trout lake and watched over by the impressive, mid-19th-century Castlewellan Castle (sadly closed to the public), this forest park just begs for picnics and outdoor activities. Woodland walks, a formal walled garden, and an interesting lakeside sculpture trail await. Anglers can fish for trout (brown and rainbow) in the lake. The **Peace Maze,** planted in 2000, is an enormous—and very difficult to conquer—hedge maze, and appropriately named, given that it's meant to represent the path to peace in Northern Ireland. The real draw is the National Arboretum, opened in 1740 and now ten times its original size. The largest of its three greenhouses features aquatic plants and a collection of free-flying tropical birds. The town of Castlewellan, elegantly laid out around two squares, is a short distance away, as is the ancient fort of Drumena Cashel (see below).

Forest Office: The Grange, Castlewellan Forest Park, Castlewellan, Co. Down, BT31 9BU. © **028/4377-8664.** Entry and parking: £4.50. Daily 10am–sunset.

Drumena Cashel ★ HISTORIC SITE   The walls of this irregularly shaped ancient stone-ring fort—a farmstead dating from the early Christian period—were partially rebuilt in the mid-1920s and measure 2.7m (9 ft.) to 3.6m (12 ft.) thick. The *souterrain* (underground stone tunnel) is T-shaped and was likely used in ancient times for cold storage. During the age of the Viking invasions, it likely provided a degree of protection for the local population. There were once thousands of such fortifications in Ireland, and this is one of the better-preserved examples in this region. Castlewellan is about 30 miles south of Belfast.

Signposted from A25, 3km (2 miles) southwest of Castlewellan, Co. Down. Free admission (open site).

Giant's Ring ★★ HISTORIC SITE   This massive and mysterious prehistoric earthwork, 180 metres (590 ft.) in diameter, has at its center a megalithic chamber with a single capstone. Ancient burial rings like this were thought to be protected by fairies and were left untouched, but this one is quite an exception. In the 19th century it was used as a racetrack, and the high embankment around it served as grandstands. Today, its dignity has been restored, and it is a place of wonder for the few tourists who make the journey.

Ballynahatty, Co. Down. 6km (3¾ miles) southwest of Belfast center, west off A24. Free admission (open site).

Grey Abbey ★ HISTORIC SITE   The impressive ruins of Grey Abbey sit amid a beautifully landscaped setting, perfect for a picnic. Founded in 1193 by the Cistercians, it contained one of the earliest Gothic churches in Ireland. Many Cistercian ruins were quite elaborate, but this one is surprisingly plain. Amid the ruined choirs there is a fragmented stone effigy of a knight in armor, possibly a likeness of John de Courcy, husband of the abbey's founder, Affreca of Cumbria. There's also a small visitor center. Grey Abbey is in the appropriately named Greyabbey, about 15 miles west of Belfast.

Greyabbey, Co. Down. No phone. Free admission. Apr and May Tues–Sun 10am–5pm; Jun–mid-Sept daily 10am–5pm; mid-Sept–Oct and Mar noon–4pm; Nov–Feb Sun only noon–4pm.

Legananny Dolmen ★ HISTORIC SITE   This renowned granite dolmen (Neolithic tomb) on the southern slope of Slieve Croob looks, in the words of archaeologist Peter Harbison, like "a coffin on stilts." This must be one of the most photographed dolmens in Ireland, and you must see it up close to fully appreciate the impressive size. The massive capstone seems weightlessly poised on its supporting uprights. The Dolmen is signposted about halfway between Dromara and Castelwellan on the lower slopes of Slieve Croob Mountain, about 25 miles south of Belfast.

Signposted off Leganny Rd. Leitrim, Co. Down, BT32 3QR. No phone. Free admission (open site).

Mount Stewart House, Garden and Temple of the Winds ★★ MANSION   Once the home of Lord Castlereagh, this 18th-century house sits on the eastern shore of Strangford Lough. Its lush gardens hold an impressive array of rare and unusual plants. Inside, the art collection is excellent, including the *Hambletonian* by George Stubbs and family portraits by Pompeo Batoni and Anton Raphael Mengs. The Temple of the Winds, a rare 18th-century banqueting house, is also on the estate, but it's open only on public holidays. There's also a handy cafe on-site. Admission to the house is by guided tour only. As of this writing, a major program of restoration is underway at the Mount Stewart, although access is still being allowed. It may be wise to call ahead just to check everything's open before you set out.

Portaferry Rd., Newtownards, Co. Down, BT22 2AD. www.nationaltrust.org.uk/mount-stewart. © 028/4278-8387. House and Lakeside Garden: £6.70 adults, £3.50 children, £17 families. House:

Early Mar–Oct daily 11am–5pm. Lakeside Garden: Early Nov–early Mar 10am–4pm; early Mar–Oct 10am–5pm. Last admission 1 hr. before closing.

Nendrum Monastic Site ★ HISTORIC SITE   Hidden away on an isolated island, this site dates from the 5th century. This site is much older than Grey Abbey across the water, and the remains of the ancient community founded by St. Mochaoi (St. Mahee) are fascinating. Foundations show the outline of ancient churches, a round tower, and beehive cells. There are concentric stone ramparts and a sundial, reconstructed from long-broken pieces. Its visitor center shows informative videos and has insightful exhibits. The road to Mahee Island crosses a causeway to Reagh Island and a bridge still protected by the 15th-century Mahee Castle.

Mahee Island, Ringneill Rd., Comber, Co. Down, BT23 6EP. *©***028/9054-3037.** Free admission. Mar and mid-Sept–Oct Tues–Sun noon–4pm; Apr–May Tues–Sun 10am–5pm; Jun–mid-Sept daily 10am–5pm; Nov–Feb Sun only noon–4pm.

Silent Valley Mountain Park ★★ PARK   Between 1904 and 1922, the 36km (22-mile) dry-stone Mourne Wall and dam was built to enclose Silent Valley, creating the Silent Valley Reservoir, the major source of water for County Down. The 36km (22-mile) **Mourne Wall Trek** follows the wall that threads together 15 of the range's main peaks. The steep path is more than most hikers want to take on, and certainly shouldn't be attempted in a single day. But it is a fine, long walk for experienced ramblers and offers wonderful views. More information about the route, including maps and a photo log of every stage, can be found at www.mournewall.co.uk. A good alternative is the more modest walk from the fishing port of Kilkeel to the Silent Valley and Lough Shannagh. An even less strenuous alternative is to drive to the Silent Valley Information Centre and take the shuttle bus to the top of nearby Ben Crom. It runs on weekends during May, June, and September, and daily in July and August.

Visitor Centre: Head Rd., Annalong, Newcastle, Co. Down, BT34 4HU. www.niwater.com/silent-valley. *©***028/9035-4716.** Admission £4.50 per car. May–Sept daily 10am–6:30pm; Oct–Apr daily 10am–4pm.

Tollymore Forest Park ★★ PARK   All that's left of the once-glorious Tollymore House is this delightful 480-hectare (1,186-acre) wildlife and forest park. The park offers a number of walks up into the north slopes of the Mourne Mountains or along the Shimna River (which is known for its exceptionally fine salmon). The Shimna walk has several beguiling little landmarks, including caves and grottos. The park is dotted with follies, such as faux-medieval castle gatehouses and other fanciful fakes. The forest is a nature preserve inhabited by a host of local wildlife like badgers, foxes, otters, and pine martens. And don't miss the trees for the forest—there are some exotic species such as the magnificent Himalayan cedars and a 30-metre tall (98-ft.) sequoia in the arboretum.

Off B180, 3.2km (2 miles) northwest of Newcastle, Tullybrannigan Rd., Newcastle, County Down. *©***028/4372-2428.** Free admission. Parking £4.50. Daily 10am–dusk.

Ulster Folk and Transport Museum ★★ MUSEUM   One of Northern Ireland's best living history museums, it's made up of buildings rescued from demolition and reconstructed, piece by piece. The majority of the buildings are from the 19th century; they include houses, schools, a chemist, a pub, and even a working farm. The level of detail is impressive—the shops are fully decked out as they would have been in Victorian times, complete with shelves overflowing with authentic bottles, jars, and items of clothing. Costumed guides add to the sense of fun. As you wander about you may encounter a Victorian housewife engaged in some day-to-day household drudgery or watch a village blacksmith working away in a forge using authentic methods from the period. There are frequent special events, such as craft demonstrations and classes, horse-drawn vehicle days, or wild-life hunts. The Transport Museum contains a wealth of historic vehicles, from old cars and small planes, to buses and trams.

Signposted off A2 (Bangor Rd.), Cultra, Hollywood, Co. Down, BT18 0EU. www.nmni.com/uftm. ℭ 028/9042-8428. Folk or Transport Museum: £8 adults, £6 seniors and students, £4.50 children 5–17, £16.50–£22 families, children 4 and under free. Combined ticket to both museums: £9.50 adults, £7 seniors and students, £5 children 5–17, £18.50–£24 families, children 4 and under free. Mar–Sept Tues–Sun 10am–5pm; Oct–Feb Tues–Fri 10am–4pm, Sat and Sun 11am–4pm. Closed Mon (except public holidays).

ANTRIM COAST

Allow enough time to properly explore the spectacular Antrim Coast drive. Although it's just 60 miles long, there is so much to admire along this scenic route that you'll want to take a full day or more to do it justice, with plenty of stops along the way. At the end of it all is the Giant's Causeway, one of the most impressive, and certainly one of the most unique, natural formations in the world. From here, it's a short hop to Derry (see p. 227), a handsome old city with a turbulent and colorful past.

Tourism Offices

On the Antrim Coast Drive there are small tourism offices in **Larne** (Narrow Gauge Road; ℭ **028/2826-0088**); **Cushendall** (25 Mill Street; ℭ **028/2177-1180**), and **Bally-castle** (7 Mary Street; ℭ **028/2076-2024**).

Exploring the Antrim Coast

The most extraordinary stretch of countryside in Northern Ireland, the evocatively named **Glens of Antrim,** are really nine green valleys stretching north and west from Belfast and curving around toward Donegal. The names of the glens are all based on local legends, and although the meanings are largely lost to the ages, the popular trans-lations are: **Glenarm** (glen of the army), **Glencloy** (glen of the hedges), **Glenariff** (ploughman's glen), **Glenballyeamon** (Edwardstown glen), **Glenaan** (glen of the rush lights), **Glencorp** (glen of the slaughter), **Glendun** (brown glen), **Glenshesk** (sedgy glen), and **Glentaisie** (Taisie's glen).

The area's attractions are formidable and include the awe-inspiring **Giant's Cause-way,** the picturesque **Carrick-A-Rede Rope Bridge,** and **Old Bushmills Distillery.**

Carnlough ★ The first major stop along the Antrim Coast Drive is this quiet vil-lage, known for its glassy harbor bobbing with sailboats. It's filled with interesting little shops and restaurants. Just outside Carnlough is a peaceful, yet little known, waterfall and beautiful spot called **Cranny Falls.** You can walk there on a marked trail from the waterfront. Start by crossing the white stone bridge; from there the route goes through some idyllic countryside, following the route of an abandoned railway, past a disused quarry, until it reaches the falls after about a mile. Along the way are occasional markers telling you more about the history of the area.

Carnlough, Co. Antrim (no tourism office).

Carrick-a-Rede Rope Bridge ★★★ Eight kilometers (5 miles) west of Bal-lycastle off the A2 road, this rope bridge spans a chasm 18 meters (59 ft.) wide and

THE antrim coast DRIVE

The drive along the Antrim coast road is one of the most memorable routes in Ireland, offering sweeping views of midnight-blue seas against gray unforgiving cliffs and deep green hillsides.

A good place to start the drive is in Carrickfergus, just north of Belfast. It stretches to **Portrush,** a few miles on from the spectacular **Giant's Causeway** (see p. 224). The whole route is about 113km (70 miles), though you can skip some sections if you don't want to spend the whole day in the car. The journey is manageable in a couple of hours, but allow much longer if you can, because it's the sort of drive you want to savor. The main highlights of the drive each get their own listings in the next few pages, but here's an overview of what the route has to offer.

Once you join the coast road itself, about 26km (16 miles) or so north of Carrickfergus, the first town is **Glenarm,** decked out with castle walls and a barbican gate. In **Carnlough** (see p. 222), a quiet seaside village, you can climb the white stone bridge and walk along a path for about a mile to the Cranny Falls waterfall.

Keep going north along the coast from there and the road passes through the National Trust village of **Cushendun** (see p. 224), which is known for its tea shops and whitewashed cottages. Along the way the coastal drive meanders under bridges and stone arches, passing crescent bays, sandy beaches, harbors, and huge rock formations. The ocean gleams beside you as you curve along its craggy shoreline, and the light creates intense colors. In the spring and autumn, you can often have the road all to yourself.

Later, for the most spectacular views, turn off the main coastal road at Cushendun onto the **Torr Head Scenic Drive** (p. 225). Just note that this narrow, rugged, cliff-side road is vertigo-inducing. It climbs in seemingly perilous fashion to the tops of hills that are bigger than you might think, and on a clear day, you can see all the way to the Mull of Kintyre in Scotland.

In the late spring and summer, you can take a ferry from the bustling beach town of **Ballycastle** to **Rathlin Island,** where seals and nesting birds make their homes at the **Kebble National Reserve.**

The heart-stopping **Carrick-a-Rede Rope Bridge** (p. 222) allows the brave to cross on foot over to a small island just off the coast. Those not willing to wobble their way across—no matter how good the views—can press straight on to the little town of **Ballintoy,** a picture postcard waiting to happen, and filled with charming stone cottages and flowery gardens.

Ballintoy is stretched out at the edge of **Whitepark Bay,** a wide, crystalline curve of sandy beach at the foot of rocky hills surrounded by green farms. On a sunny day, you might find it hard to go farther.

The last major stop along the way is the eerily lunar **Giant's Causeway** (p. 224), one of the world's true natural wonders. And after all that driving, don't you think you've earned yourself a tipple at the **Old Bushmills Distillery** (p. 225)?

24 meters (79 ft.) above the sea between the mainland and a small island. Local fishermen put up the bridge each spring to allow access to the island's salmon fishery, but visitors can use it for a thrilling, and very wobbly, walk and the chance to call out to each other, "Don't look down!" (By the way, that is *excellent* advice.) If you are acrophobic, stay clear; if you don't know whether you are, this is not the place to find out.

Note: The 19km (12-mile) coastal cliff path from the Giant's Causeway to the rope bridge is always open and is worth the exhaustion.

119A Whitepark Rd., Ballintoy, Co. Antrim, BT54 6LS. www.nationaltrust.org.uk/carrick-a-rede. © **028/2076-9839.** Admission £5.70 adults, £3 children, £14 families. Mar–May and Sept–Oct daily 9:30am–6pm; Jun–Aug daily 9:30am–7:30pm; Nov–Dec daily 9:30am–3:30pm.

Cushendun ★ Another 15 miles north of Carnlough, around the headland, the A2 road passes through the tiny, picturesque village of Cushendun. The place is so pretty that the National Trust bought most of it in the 1950s to preserve it from overdevelopment. The seafront is lined with an elegant sweep of perfect white, Cornish-style cottages, and the quaint tea shops do a bustling trade. The Glendun River winds its way through the village, crossed by a lovely old stone bridge, while down on the beach are atmospheric sea caves. Just north of the village, in a field overlooking the coast, are the scant remains of **Curra Castle.** Cushendun is a good place to stop and take pictures before heading on down the main A2 road—or, if you want the most amazing views, the Torr Head Scenic Drive (see p. 225), which hugs perilously to the coast.

Cushendun, Co. Antrim (no tourism office).

Dunluce Castle ★★ It may not be the biggest castle nor the best preserved, but the views from the precariously positioned Dunluce Castle are stellar; the dramatic setting affords views of Portrush and, across the water, Donegal's Inishowen Head. Owned by the MacDonnells of Antrim, it's assumed that there's been a fort here since early-Christian times; certainly, the precarious cliff-hugging position indicates its suitability as a defensive structure, but most of what is now visible and available for you to investigate was built in the 16th and 17th centuries, the oldest parts being the round towers and curtain walls. Although the castle was attacked by Elizabethan cannons back in 1584, the most dramatic event in Dunluce's history happened one evening in 1639 when—much to the horror of the lady of the house, Catherine Manner, wife of Randal MacDonnell, the 1st Earl of Antrim—the sea-facing wall of the kitchen simply dropped into the sea, taking several servants to their doom. A real city girl who in any case hated the sound of the sea, Ms. Manner took this as her opportunity to move out of the castle and so inspired hubby Randal to relocate to Glenarm, where the Antrim Earls have been ever since. In other parts of the castle, you'll come across quite discernibly different stages of architectural development, with partially visible bartizans (pepper-pot turrets) characteristic of Scottish design, medieval, Renaissance and Jacobean elements each marking different sets of home improvement carried out by a short-lived succession of owners. One enticing footnote: A recent archaeological dig here uncovered the remains of a town that was previously thought completely destroyed during a rebellion in 1641. Only a tiny fraction of what is now thought to exist has so far been excavated.

87 Dunluce Rd., Bushmills, Co. Antrim, BT57 8UY. © **028/2073-1938.** £5 adults, £3 seniors and children 4–16, £13 families. Mar and Oct–Nov daily 10am–5pm; Apr–Sept daily 10am–6pm; Dec–Jan daily 10am–4pm; last admission 30 min. before closing.

Giant's Causeway ★★★ A UNESCO World Heritage Site, this natural rock formation is extraordinary. Sitting at the foot of steep cliffs and stretching out into the sea, it is a natural formation of thousands of tightly packed basalt columns. The tops of the columns form flat stepping-stones, all of which are perfectly hexagonal. They measure about 30cm (12 in.) in diameter; some are very short, others are as tall as 12 meters (39 ft.). Scientists believe they were formed 60 or 70 million years ago by volcanic eruptions and cooling lava. The ancients, on the other hand, believed the rock formation to be the work of giants. To reach the causeway, you walk from the parking area down a steep path for nearly 1.6km (1 mile), past amphitheaters of stone columns and formations with fanciful names like Honeycomb, Wishing Well, Giant's Granny, King and His Nobles, and Lover's Leap. If you wish, you can then climb up a wooden staircase to Benbane Head to take in the views, and then walk back along the cliff top. There is a regular shuttle service down from the visitor center for those who can't face the hike. *Note:* The underground visitor center has a cafe, shop, interpretive center, and hugely expensive parking. However, the Causeway is a free, open site, so if you can find safe and legal parking, there's nothing to stop you from just walking straight down.

44 Causeway Rd., Bushmills, Co. Antrim, BT57 8SU. www.nationaltrust.org.uk/giants-causeway. © **028/2073-1855.** Visitor center and parking: £8.50 adults, £4.50 children, £21 families. Visitor center: Mar and Oct 9am–6pm; Apr–Jun and Sept 9am–7pm; Jul–Aug 9am–9pm; Nov–Jan 9am–5pm.

The Old Bushmills Distillery ★★ Licensed to distill spirits in 1608 but with historical references dating from as far back as 1276, this ancient distillery is endlessly popular. Visitors can tour the working sections and watch the whiskey-making process, starting with fresh water from the adjacent River Bush and continuing through distillation, fermentation, and bottling. At the end of the tour, you can sample the wares in the Potstill Bar, where you can learn more about the history of the distillery. Tours last about 25 minutes. The Bushmills coffee shop serves tea, coffee, homemade snacks, and lunch. *Tip:* Try to visit during the week for the full experience. Though tours do take place on weekends, the distillery itself is only in operation from Monday to Friday.

Main St., Bushmills, Co. Antrim, BT57 8XH. www.bushmills.com. © **028/2073-3272.** £7.50 adults, £6 seniors and students, £3.50 children 8–17, £20 families. No children under 8 on tour. Apr–Oct tours offered about every 20 min. throughout the day Mar–Oct Mon–Sat 9:15am–4:45pm, Sun noon–4:45pm (last tour 4pm); Nov–Feb Mon–Sat 10am–4:45pm, Sun noon–4:45pm (last tour 3.30pm).

Torr Head Scenic Drive ★★ This diversion is spectacular, but it's not for those with a fear of heights or narrow dirt roads; nor is it a good idea in bad weather. But on a sunny, dry day, the brave can follow signs from Cushendun (see p. 224), up a steep hill at the edge of town onto the **Torr Head Scenic Drive.** After a precipitous climb, the road narrows further and inches its way along in rugged fashion at the edge of the cliff overlooking the sea. There are places to park along the way and take in the sweeping views. On a clear day, you can see all the way to the Mull of Kintyre in Scotland. Arguably the best views of all are to be had at Murlough Bay (follow the signs).

Torr Rd., heading north out of Cushendun, Co. Antrim.

Where to Stay on the Antrim Coast

Causeway Smithy ★★ A short hop from the Giant's Causeway (you can just see it in the distance, across rolling green fields), this warm and friendly B&B is a fab find. The guest rooms are stylish, with polished wood floors and modern-print wallpaper. Big bay windows look out over the verdant countryside and flood the rooms with light during the day. Each of the three rooms is located in a separate annex, and you have your own key, so there's more of a feeling of freedom and privacy than one might usually find from countryside B&Bs. The tasty breakfasts are served in a little guest lounge. There's no restaurant, but owner Denise is full of recommendations about where to go in the evenings.

270 Whitepark Rd., Bushmills, Co. Antrim, BT57 8SN. www.causewaysmithybnb.com. © **075/1506-6975.** 2 units. £100. Free parking. Rates include breakfast. **Amenities:** Wi-Fi (free).

Londonderry Arms Hotel ★ Anyone looking for a brush with history while bedding down around the Glens of Antrim should look into the Londonderry Arms. If the heaps of memorabilia tracing this former coaching inn's pedigree don't captivate you, you can always turn to hotel manager, Maureen Morrow, for an unabridged account of the Arms and its special place in Carnlough's development. Built in 1848 by the Marchioness of Londonderry (what a mouthful), many people stay just because Churchill once owned the place (he was the Marchioness's great-grandson). It's believed he stayed in what is now room 114, one of the pricier executive suites; nearby room 116 is larger, however, and has a lovelier view (on a clear day, it's Scotland you will spy from your window). Many of the standard rooms tend to be in the back of the hotel or in a new section; they're generally comfortable but less impressive, and while you'll pay less, you'll miss the front-facing views. You can make up for the lack of in-room glamour by making full use of the smart public rooms with their strong nod to Old World ambience (and if you're gob-smacked by the great big moose head mounted on one wall, don't miss seeing "the hunting room"). The restaurant is a good bet here, too, with bar food served when the more considered lunch and dinner menu isn't available; ingredients are sourced from local suppliers.

20 Harbour Rd., Carnlough, Co. Antrim, BT44 0EU. www.glensofantrim.com. ✆ **028/2888-5255.** 35 units. £85–£135. Limited free parking (on street). Breakfast included. **Amenities:** Restaurant, bar, room service.

Lurig View ★ The atmosphere at this sweet little B&B in Glenariff is akin to that of a family home. Or it would be if we all had parents as nice as Rose Ward and her husband, Chris. They're as friendly as can be and happy to help with planning itineraries, making dinner reservations, and so on. Bedrooms are very cute, decorated with paintings of flowers chosen to match the accent colors of the room, which makes for an inventive touch. Breakfast is served outside if the weather's good. If you really must, there's a lounge with a TV that guests can use, but a better choice is to get out and explore. Glenariff is a pretty little town and one of the most popular destinations along the Antrim coast. There's a forest park within about 10 minutes' drive, and the beach is a short walk from the front door.

38 Glen Rd., Glenariff, Ballymena, Co. Antrim, BT44 0RF. www.lurigview.co.uk. ✆ **028/2177-1618.** 3 units. £60. Free parking. Breakfast included. **Amenities:** Wi-Fi (free).

The Meadows ★ There's a lovely view of the sea from this jovial guesthouse on the main Antrim coast road. You can even see Scotland on a (very) clear and sunny day. Bedrooms are basic but cozy, and the bathrooms are modern and well-equipped. Most are doubles, but for families or groups, there's one room that sleeps four and another that's equipped for those with mobility problems. The hearty, tasty Ulster fry breakfasts are great fuel for a long drive ahead. Anne Carey is a thoughtful and friendly host, adept at making her guests feel welcome. She also accepts the euro, as well as British pounds—a helpful touch for those travelling on both sides of the border.

79 Coast Rd., Cushendall, Ballymena, Co. Antrim, BT44 0RX. www.themeadowscushendall.com. ✆ **028/2177-2020.** 6 units. £60. Free parking. Breakfast included. **Amenities:** Wi-Fi (free).

Whitepark House ★★ This fantastic little place is just a couple of miles from the Carrick-a-Rede rope bridge (see p. 222). It was built in the mid-1700s and still retains a traditional air. Beds are wrought-iron framed; one is a four-poster, while the others have canopies. Heavy silk fabrics lift the design of the room. Views overlooking the sea offer a spectacular vista to wake up to in the morning (the garden-view rooms are almost as nice). As for the hosts, Bob and Siobhan Isles are genuinely warm people; the fact that they've won awards for their hospitality comes as no surprise whatsoever. Breakfasts are delicious, and the full Ulster fry is the specialty, of course, but Bob also takes care of his vegetarian guests (he is one himself) with non-meaty options.

150 Whitepark Rd., Ballintoy, Co. Antrim, BT54 6NH. www.whiteparkhouse.com. © **028/2073-1482.** 3 units. £120. Free parking. Breakfast included. Children allowed, but must have own room (no discount). **Amenities:** Wi-Fi (free).

Where to Eat on the Antrim Coast

Red Door Tea Room ★★ CAFE   This sweet little cottage tearoom is cozy and welcoming inside, with a turf-burning stove and the day's menu chalked on blackboards behind the counter. But you'll want to sit outside if the weather allows, because the view from the garden over lush green fields to Ballintoy Harbour is stunning. They serve tempting, fresh cakes and desserts, so dig into the delicious Victoria sponge cake (two layers, separated by jam and cream). Also on the menu: simple light lunches (salads, soups, bagels, sandwiches, or even a plate of tasty fresh fish). It all adds up to a welcome rest stop along the Antrim coast road.

Ballintoy Harbour, Ballintoy, Co. Antrim, BT54 6NA. © **028/2076-9048.** £4–£12. Easter week and Jun–Sept daily 11am–5pm; week after Easter–May weekends only 11am–5pm. Closed Oct–Mar.

Smuggler's Inn ★ IRISH/INTERNATIONAL   A convenient lunch spot right across from the Giant's Causeway, the Smuggler's Inn serves traditional pub lunches. There are a few sandwiches and light snack options, or you can go for the works like hefty burgers, fish and chips, or Cajun chicken goujons (finger-shaped pieces of meat, breaded and deep-fried). There's also a separate children's menu. In the evening it's much the same kind of thing, but pushed up a notch in terms of choice (steaks join the menu, as do the occasional dish with a bit more ambition, such as roast duck with fruity red cabbage and a sherry reduction). Like several places around here, euros are accepted as well as pounds. The Smuggler's Inn also has rooms available for between £60 and £90 per night, depending on the season.

306 Whitepark Rd, Giants Causeway, Bushmills, Co. Antrim, BT57 8SL. www.smugglersinnireland. com. © **028/2073-1577.** £9–£17. Food served daily noon–2:30pm and 4–9pm.

Thyme & Co. ★ MODERN IRISH   Another nifty little cafe on the Antrim coast drive, Thyme & Co. serves delicious, healthful lunches. The ingredients are locally sourced and the short menu is thoughtfully put together. Dine on fish cakes made from salmon and smoked haddock (something of a house specialty) or a tasty pie or quiche. The dining room is a pleasant space, and the staff is always friendly and cheerful. On Fridays and Saturdays in summer they stay open into the evenings, when they serve thin-crust pizzas. They do takeout, too.

5 Quay Rd., Ballycastle, Co. Antrim, BT54 6BJ. www.thymeandco.co.uk. © **028/2076-9851.** £4–£10. Pizzas £6–£10. Tues–Sat 8:30am–4:30pm; Sun 10am–3:30pm. Closed Mon.

DERRY

Northern Ireland's second city is a vibrant place, surrounded by 17th-century walls; you can climb the steps to the top and walk the ramparts all the way around the town center. Although they were the focus of attacks and sieges for centuries, the 5-foot-thick fortifications are solid and unbroken to this day. Historians believe the city was modeled on the French Renaissance town of Vitry-Le-Francois, which in turn was based on a Roman military camp, with two main streets forming a central cross and

VISITING NORTHERN IRELAND: f.a.q.

What's the border crossing like?
There is no marked land border between the Republic of Ireland and Northern Ireland. The only immediate difference you are likely to notice is that the road signs change.

Will I need a passport?
You don't need a passport or a separate visa when crossing between the Republic of Ireland and Northern Ireland.

Is driving in Northern Ireland the same?
Broadly speaking, yes, but with one major difference: Road signs in Northern Ireland show *miles,* not kilometers. Signs around the border usually show both. Don't forget to check that your travel insurance and any car-rental agreements are equally valid in Northern Ireland.

Does Northern Ireland use the euro?
No. The currency in Northern Ireland is the **British pound (sterling).** In practice, euros are accepted in some border areas, major tourist attractions, and hotels; however, you will almost always be given change in pounds. ATMs are the easiest and cheapest way to get currency.

What are those letters and numbers at the end of Northern Irish addresses?
They're British-style postcodes (zip codes). Postcodes are only just being introduced in the Republic, but every address in Northern Ireland has one. This is actually a big advantage if you're driving, as it makes GPS navigation much easier. Where possible we've included postcodes for all the listings in this chapter.

What about cellphone calls in each country?
Your mobile phone company will treat Northern Ireland as the U.K., so inform them in advance if you think you'll be crossing the border. This might avoid higher international roaming charges.

ending in four city gates. It's made for walking, combining a medieval center with sprawling Georgian and Victorian neighborhoods.

Tourism Office

The **Derry Tourist Information Centre** can be found at 44 Foyle Street (www.derry visitor.com; ✆ **028/7126-7284**).

Where to Stay in Derry

The Saddler's House and the Merchant's House ★★ Two charming buildings, full of character, with one pair of owners, these lovely B&Bs are among the best accommodations in Derry. Choose from the elegant Merchant's House, which was built in the mid–19th century (one of relatively few town houses from the period left in the town), or the Saddler's House, a slightly simpler, late-Victorian building. Both have been beautifully maintained and renovated with design-magazine interiors and antiques galore. Breakfast is served in whichever house you choose. The same owners also have three self-catering places in Derry, including a small terraced cottage opposite the cathedral; an apartment in the old pump house, within the walled part of the city; and a 1950s-style apartment. *Tip:* The Merchant's House family room sleeps up to five with its own kitchen for just £100 to £135 per night.

36 Great James St., Derry, BT48 7DB. www.thesaddlershouse.com. ✆ **028/7126-9691.** 7 units. £60–£80. Limited free parking (on street); otherwise, paid street parking nearby. Rates include breakfast. **Amenities:** Wi-Fi.

Troy Hall ★★ A lavish Victorian mansion close to the Derry city center, Troy Hall was built in 1897, complete with the Gothic flourishes that were so popular in the period. Turrets give the red brick exterior an almost fairytale look, while the sweeping back lawn is a mere remnant of what was once a huge estate. The building suffered terribly over the years until the current owners restored it to its now pristine condition. The spacious guest rooms are individually designed but share a country-house-style chic, furnished with handmade wood or wrought-iron beds and occasional antique pieces. Family rooms sleep up to five. Excellent breakfasts are served in the equally well-restored dining room, also known as the Turret. Central Derry is about 5 minutes by car or cab, and there's a bus stop nearby, too.

9 Troy Park, Culmore Rd., Derry, BT48 7RL. www.troyhall.co.uk. ✆ **078/8436-1669.** 3 units. £80. Free parking. Rates include breakfast. **Amenities:** Wi-Fi (free).

Where to Eat in Derry

Badger's ★ IRISH A friendly, proper local pub, right in the center of Derry, Badger's serves hearty, traditional grub—stews, fish and chips, steak and Guinness pie, burgers, and the like, plus a few lighter options such as hot sandwiches and wraps. Plates are generous, and of course, you can wash it all down with a pint of the black stuff. The dining room is satisfyingly unreconstructed with plenty of polished wood and low-hanging lamps. No matter what the time of day, there always seem to be a few locals propping up the bar, which helps keep the atmosphere authentic.

16-18 Orchard St., Derry, BT48 6EG. ✆ **028/7136-0763.** £5–£12. Mon–Sat 11:30am–1am; Sun 11:30am–midnight. (Food served Thurs noon–7pm; Fri–Sat noon–9pm; Sun noon–4pm.) No children after 9pm.

Brown's Restaurant and Champagne Lounge ★★ BRASSERIE One of Derry's best restaurants, Brown's serves excellent Irish food using plenty of local and regional ingredients. Menus change frequently, but start with the local seafood tasting plate if it's on the menu—the turf-smoked salmon is particularly delicious. For main courses they have chargrilled beef served with celeriac and truffle puree, and sea bass filet with fennel, samphire, and citrus butter. The menu occasionally takes an unexpected turn. Moroccan-style goat with couscous and apricot puree, anyone? But there's something to please everyone, and it's all beautifully prepared and presented. There's a six-course tasting menu available for £40 (£65 with wines) and a three-course early-bird special for £20.

1 Bonds Hill, Derry, BT47 6DW. www.brownsrestaurant.com. ✆ **028/7134-5180.** £19–£24. Tues–Fri noon–23pm and 5–9:30pm; Sat 5–9:30pm; Sun noon–3:30pm.

Primrose Café ★★ CAFE This cheerful cafe is nicely old-fashioned without being remotely tired. Drop in for a bowl of delicious soup, fresh sandwiches, or a tasty pie (served with a side of excellent chips). Or you could just have a plate of homemade scones and some tea, served the proper way with a teapot and fine china. Service is skillful and prices are reasonable—just what you want from a casual lunch on the go.

15 Carlisle Rd., Derry, BT48 6JJ. ✆ **028/7126-4622.** Lunch £3–£8. Mon–Sat 8am–5pm; Sun 11am–3pm.

Exploring Derry

The Bogside Murals ★★ MURALS Just outside the walled city center, the Bogside was developed in the 19th and early–20th centuries as a home to Catholic workers. In the late 1960s, civil rights protests became regular events here, and the

DERRY OR LONDONDERRY: what's in a name?

The short answer is: quite a lot.

Depending on which side of the border you're on, Northern Ireland's second city is called two different things. Road signs and maps in the Republic say **Derry;** in Northern Ireland they point to **Londonderry.**

This stubborn dispute dates to the Plantation of Ulster in the 1600s, when English settlers were given land in Ireland as an attempt to entrench Protestant rule. A new city was founded by the City of London trade guilds and named Londonderry in their honor. Nationalists have always objected to the term, preferring Derry, an Anglicization of *Daire Calgaich,* the name of the much older settlement that once stood on the same site.

During the Troubles, the dispute was a cause celebre. Many attempts have been made to change the name, including several unsuccessful court cases. Loyalists fiercely defend the name. But having a city with two names poses a knotty problem for residents and visitors alike—what to call it? The best advice is just to be tactful. If you're drinking in a pub with a big Irish tricolor on the side, it's probably best to use Derry; but if they're flying the Union Jack, opt for Londonderry. Of the two, Derry is probably the more commonly used in town, and certainly throughout the Republic, so we've chosen to call it Derry in this book.

Fed up with effectively being forced to make a political statement whenever they talk about their own city, residents have long since tried to find an acceptable solution to the Derry/Londonderry dilemma. In the '90s, local radio DJ Gerry Anderson suggested the wry compromise "Stroke City." (American readers: Stroke is a slash in the U.K.) Quick-witted locals swiftly nicknamed the DJ "Gerry/Londongerry."

To see further evidence of how far back this titular dispute goes, just look no further than a United States road atlas. Near Manchester, New Hampshire, is a small old town called Derry. In the early–19th century there was a dispute over its name, so a group of residents set up a new town just to the south called—you guessed it—Londonderry.

residents declared their neighborhood as "Free Derry," independent of local and British government. The situation came to a head on January 30th, 1972, later to be known as "Bloody Sunday," when British troops opened fire on a peaceful demonstration, killing 14. (The soldiers said they'd been fired upon first; eventually, in 2010, after a 12-year inquiry, the British government finally accepted this to be untrue and apologized.) Most of the Bogside has been redeveloped, but the Free Derry corner remains near the house painted with the mural reading "You Are Now Entering Free Derry." Since the 1990s, a group of local artists known as the **Bogside Artists** has painted further murals around the district, similar to those on the Falls Road in Belfast. Though some are overtly political in nature, many depict simple yet powerful messages of peace. Effectively this has turned parts of the Bogside into a free art museum, and together the murals have become known as the **People's Gallery.**

The Bogside, Derry.

Cathedral of St. Columb ★ CHURCH   Within the city walls near the Bishop's Gate, this cathedral, built by the Church of Ireland between 1628 and 1633, is a prime example of the so-called "Planters Gothic" style of architecture. It was the first cathedral built in Europe after the Reformation, although several sections were added afterward, including the impressive spire and stained-glass windows depicting scenes from the siege of 1688 and 1689. The chapter house contains a display of city relics such as the four massive original padlocks for the city gates. On the porch, a small stone inscribed *"In Templo Verus Deus Est Vereo Colendus"* ("The true God is in His temple and is to be truly worshipped") is part of the original church built on this site in 1164. There's an old mortar shell on the porch as well. It was fired into the churchyard during the great siege; in its hollow core it held proposed terms of surrender. The flags around the chancel window were captured during the siege.

London St., Derry, BT48 6RQ. www.stcolumbscathedral.org. (*✆*) **028/7126-7313.** Requested donation £2 adults; £1.50 seniors, students, and children. Mar–Oct Mon–Sat 9am–5pm; Nov–Feb Mon–Sat 9am–1pm and 2–4pm; also Sun at service times, year-round.

Centre for Contemporary Art ★ ARTS CENTER Drop in here to see new and touring works by contemporary artists from Ireland and further afield. Themed seasons include visual art, film screenings, performances, and public debates. The center builds strong international links, too, and often hosts residencies for artists from across the globe. Recent seasons have included a retrospective of a pivotal, early-20th-century Dublin workers' strike as a springboard for cultural debate, art inspired by the Derry city landscape, and creative responses to revolution and unrest in Egypt. It's all serious and fascinating stuff for grown-up minds. Admission to the center and most events is free, but there may be a charge for some.

10-12 Artillery St., Derry, BT48 6RG. www.cca-derry-londonderry.org. (*✆*) **028/7137-3538.** Free admission. Tues–Sat noon–6pm. Closed Sun and Mon.

Guildhall ★ ARCHITECTURE Just outside the city walls, between Shipquay Gate and the River Foyle, this Tudor Gothic-style building looks much like its counterpart in London. The site's original structure was built in 1890, but it was rebuilt after a fire in 1908 and again after a series of sectarian bombings in 1972. The hall is distinguished by its huge, four-faced clock (designed to resemble Big Ben) and its 23 stained-glass windows, made by Ulster craftsmen, which illustrate almost every episode of note in the city's history. The hall is used as a civic center for concerts, plays, and exhibitions. One nice bit of historical trivia: The Guildhall clock is designed not to strike between midnight and sunrise. This is because at the time it was finished in 1893, there was an expensive hotel nearby, and the management protested that a clock striking every hour through the night would disturb their sleeping guests.

Shipquay Place, Derry, BT48 6DQ. (*✆*) **028/7137-7335.** Free admission. Mon–Fri 9am–5pm; Sat–Sun by appointment. Free guided tours Jul–Aug; inquire at reception.

The Tower Museum ★★ MUSEUM This engaging museum chronicles the history of Derry from the earliest times to the 21st century. It's located in **O'Doherty Tower,** a reconstructed medieval fortress originally built in the early–17th century (rather wonderfully to pay off a tax debt, rather than for any specific defensive purpose) before it was reconstructed later on. The **Story of Derry** exhibition presents a chronology of life in the city from the first Monastic settlers through the Plantation era, up to the turbulent 20th century, when the city was a focus of the civil rights movement driven by the Troubles. The main attraction, however, is the large, multi-floor exhibition devoted to an historic shipwreck that happened off the coast of Derry in the 16th century. **An Armada Shipwreck** tells the story of *La Trinidad Valencera,* part of the massive Spanish Armada that attempted to invade England in 1588. The ship was

CLIMBING THE walls

One of the best ways to explore Derry is via its old stonewalls. Climb the stairs to the top and you can circle the entire walled city in about 30 minutes. Steps off of the parapets are frequent, so you'll never get stuck up there. If you start at the **Diamond,** as the square in the center of the walled section is called, and walk down Butcher Street, you can climb the steps at **Butcher's Gate,** a security checkpoint between the Bogside and the city during the Troubles. Walk to the right across **Castle Gate,** which was built in 1865, and on to **Magazine Gate,** which was once near a powder magazine. Shortly afterward you'll pass **O'Doherty's Tower,** which houses the worthwhile Tower Museum. From there you can see the brick walls of the **Guildhall** (see listing above).

Farther along, you'll pass **Shipquay Gate,** once located very near the port, back when the waters passed closer to the town center. The walls turn uphill from there, past the Millennium Forum concert hall, and up to **Ferryquay Gate.** Here in 1688, local apprentice boys, anticipating an attack, barred the gate against attacking forces, thus saving the town.

Next you'll pass **Bishop's Gate,** where a tall brick tower just outside the gate is all that remains of the **Old Gaol** (jail). The rebel Wolfe Tone was imprisoned here after the unsuccessful uprising in 1798. Farther along, the **Double Bastion** holds a military tower with elaborate equipment used to keep an eye on the Bogside—it's usually splashed by paint hurled at it by Republicans. From there you can easily access the serene churchyard of **Cathedral of St. Columb** (see listing above). From the next stretch of wall, you have a good view over the political murals of the Bogside down the hill.

A bit farther along the wall, an empty plinth stands where once there was a statue of Rev. George Walker, a governor of the city during the siege of 1699. It was blown up by the IRA in 1973. The small chapel nearby is the **Chapel of St. Augustine** (1872), and the building across the street from it with metal grates over the windows is the **Apprentice Boys' Memorial Hall.** Walk but a short way farther, and you're back to Butcher's Gate

separated from the main fleet and sank during a storm. Four hundred years later the wreck was salvaged, together with an extraordinary hoard of treasure including clothes, shoes, pottery, cannons, goblets, and other items that revealed tantalizing glimpses of life on board.

Union Hall Place, Derry, BT48 6LU. www.derrycity.gov.uk/museums/tower-museum. ⓒ **028/7137-2411.** Admission £4.20 adults; £2.70 seniors, students, and children; £9.50 families. Apr–Oct Mon–Wed and Fri–Sat 10am–6pm; Thurs 10am–8pm; Sun noon–4pm; Nov–Mar Tues–Sat 10am–5pm.

PLANNING YOUR TRIP TO IRELAND

C hances are you've been looking forward to your trip to Ireland for some time. You've probably set aside a significant amount of hard-earned cash, taken time off from work, school, or other commitments, and now want to make the most of your holiday. To accomplish that, you'll need to plan carefully. The aim of this chapter is to provide you with the information you need, and to answer any questions you might have on lots of topics.

13

GETTING THERE

By Plane

The Republic of Ireland has three major international airports. They are, in order of size, **Dublin (DUB)** (www.dublinairport.com; ℂ **1/814-1111**), **Cork (ORK)** (www.cork-airport.com; ℂ **021/413131**), and **Shannon** (www.shannonairport.com; ℂ **061/712000**). Northern Ireland's main airport is **Belfast International Airport (BFS)** (www.belfastairport.com; ℂ **028/9448-4848**).

The Republic of Ireland has seven smaller regional airports, all of which offer service to Dublin and several that receive some (very limited) European traffic. They are Donegal, Kerry, Knock, Sligo, and Waterford. In Northern Ireland, the secondary airports are Belfast City Airport and Derry City Airport. Airline service to these smaller airports changes frequently, so be sure to consult your preferred airline or travel agent as soon as you begin to sketch your itinerary.

By Ferry

If you're traveling to Ireland from Britain or the Continent, traveling by ferry is a good alternative to flying. Several car and passenger ferries offer reasonably comfortable furnishings, cabin berths (for longer crossings), restaurants, duty-free shopping, and lounges.

Prices fluctuate seasonally and depend on your route, your time of travel, and whether you are on foot or in a car. It's best to check with your travel agent for up-to-date details, but just to give you an idea, the lowest one-way adult fare in high season on the cruise ferry from Holyhead to Dublin starts at around £30. A car usually costs about £80 including one adult passenger, £30 per extra adults, £15 per extra child.

Irish Ferries (www.irishferries.ie; ℭ **0818/300-400** in the Republic of Ireland, or ℭ **353/818-300-400** in Northern Ireland/U.K.) operates from Holyhead, Wales, to Dublin, and to Rosslare from Pembroke, Wales, to Rosslare, County Wexford. They also sail from Cherbourg and Rosscoff in France.

Stena Line (www.stenaline.com; ℭ **01/204-7777**) sails from Holyhead to Dun Laoghaire, 13km (8 miles) south of Dublin; from Fishguard, Wales, to Rosslare; and from Cairnryan, Scotland, and Liverpool, England, to Belfast, Northern Ireland.

P&O Irish Sea Ferries (www.poferries.com; ℭ **0871/664-2121** in Britain, ℭ **01/407-3434** in Ireland, or ℭ **352/3420-808-294** in the rest of the world) operates from Liverpool to Dublin and from Cairnryan, Scotland, to Larne, County Antrim, Northern Ireland.

GETTING AROUND
By Car

The biggest decision most people make when it comes to getting around Ireland—outside the major cities—is whether or not to rent car. Trains are fine for getting between big towns, but they tend not to go to charming little villages; and the great houses and castles are usually miles from any major town. Buses out in the country are slow and service to places off the beaten track can be infrequent.

If you're not confident driving in a foreign country—and remember, on the *left-hand side of the road*—then fine! You'll have a wonderful trip. Where there's a will there's a way; if you're *really* determined to see that ancient dolmen on a remote hilltop, miles from any town, you'll get there. It will just be more challenging. The sacrifice you'll make not renting a car is simply loss of freedom.

In the summer, weekly rental rates on a manual-transmission compact vehicle begin at around €160 and ascend steeply. Rates are much cheaper out of season.

Unless your stay in Ireland extends beyond 6 months, your own valid driver's license (provided you've had it for at least 6 months) is all you need to drive in Ireland. Rules and restrictions for car rental vary slightly and correspond roughly to those in other European nations and the U.S., with two important distinctions: Most rental-car agencies in the Republic won't rent to you (1) if you're 24 and under or 75 and over (there's no upper age limit in the North), or (2) if your license has been valid for less than a year.

DRIVING LAWS, TIPS & WARNINGS

Highway safety has become a critical issue in Ireland during the past several years. The number of highway fatalities is high for such a small nation—Ireland regularly comes out near the bottom of European league tables for accident rates.

In an effort to rein in the Irish drivers, the Republic now uses a penalty "points" system similar to that in the U.K. and the U.S. While visitors won't have points added to their licenses, they may still be penalized with fines if they speed or commit driving infractions.

All distances and speed limits on road signs in the Republic of Ireland are in kilometers, while in Northern Ireland they are in miles. Take care if you're driving around the borderlands—the border is unmarked, so you can cross over from one side to the other without knowing it. It's easy to get confused and speed accidentally.

If you're not used to driving in rural areas on the left-hand side of the road, take precautions. Try to avoid driving after dark, and stay off the road when driving

road rules IN A NUTSHELL

1. Drive on the left side of the road.

2. Road signs are in kilometers, except in Northern Ireland, where they are in miles.

3. On motorways, the left lane is the traveling lane. The right lane is for passing.

4. Everyone must wear a seat belt by law. Children must be in age-appropriate child seats.

5. Children 11 and under are not allowed to sit in the front seat.

6. When entering a roundabout (traffic circle), yield to traffic coming from the right.

7. The speed limits are 50kmph (31 mph) in urban areas; 80kmph (50 mph) on regional and local roads, sometimes referred to as non-national roads; 100kmph (62 mph) on national roads, including divided highways (called dual carriageways); and 120kmph (75 mph) on freeways (called motorways).

conditions are compromised by rain, fog, or heavy traffic. Getting used to left-side driving, left-handed stick shift, narrow roads, and a new landscape are enough for the driver alone to manage, so it's helpful if you can have somebody along to navigate. You can also rent a GPS navigation device with your car. Most major rental firms offer them.

Roundabouts (what Americans call traffic circles or rotaries) are found on most major roads and take a little getting used to. Remember to always yield to traffic coming from the right as you approach a roundabout and follow the traffic to the left, signaling before you exit the circle.

One signal that could be misleading to U.S. drivers is a flashing amber light at a pedestrian traffic light. This almost always follows a red light, and it means yield to pedestrians but proceed when the crossing is clear.

The Republic has relatively few types of roads. Motorways (M) are major highways, the equivalent of Interstates in the U.S. National (N) roads link major cities on the island. Though these are the equivalent highways in North America, they are rarely more than two lanes in each direction (and are sometimes as small as one American-sized lane). Most pass directly through towns, making cross-country trips longer than you'd expect. Regional (R) roads have one lane of traffic traveling in each direction and generally link smaller cities and towns. Last are the rural or unclassified roads, often the most scenic back roads. These can be poorly signposted, very narrow, and a bit rough, but they usually travel through beautiful countryside locations.

Both the Republic and Northern Ireland have severe laws against drunk driving. The legal limit for both is 35 micrograms of alcohol per 100 milliliters of breath. What that equates to varies by person, but even one pint of beer can be enough to put you over the limit. The general rule is: Do not drink and drive.

RENTING A CAR

Try to make car-rental arrangements well in advance of your departure. Ireland is a small country, and in high season it can virtually run out of rental cars—but long before it does, it runs out of affordable rental cars. Major international car-rental firms are represented at airports and cities throughout Ireland and Northern Ireland; specific locations and contact numbers are given in the "Fast Facts" section of each chapter.

If you rent with a credit card that claims to provide free protection, be sure to call your card's customer service line to make certain there are no restrictions on that coverage in Ireland. Not all cards do offer insurance protection for car rentals in Ireland.

By law, you must be between the ages of 25 and 74 to rent a car in Ireland. The only documentation you should need is your valid driver's license and a photographic ID, such as a passport, plus a printout of your reservation if you have one.

By Train

Iarnród Éireann (Irish Rail) (www.irishrail.ie; © **1850/366222** or 01/836-6222) operates the train services in Ireland. Train travel is generally the fastest way to get around the country. Most lines radiate from Dublin to other principal cities and towns. From Dublin, the journey time to Cork is about 2½ hours; to Belfast, just over 2 hours; to Galway, just under 2½ hours; to Killarney, 3¼ hours; to Sligo, 3 hours; and to Waterford, about 2¼ hours.

In addition to the Irish Rail service between Dublin and Belfast, **Translink** (www.nirailways.co.uk; © **028/9066-6630**) operates routes from Belfast that include Coleraine and Derry, in addition to virtually all 21 localities in Northern Ireland.

One useful piece of lingo: When buying any sort of travel tickets—air, ferry, train or bus—a "single" means one-way, a "return" is round-trip.

By Bus

Bus Éireann (www.buseireann.ie; © **01/836-6111**) operates an extensive system of express bus service, as well as local service, to nearly every town in Ireland. The Bus Éireann website provides timetables and fares for bus service throughout the country. Similarly, **Translink** provides detailed information on services within Northern Ireland (www.translink.co.uk; © **028/9066-6630**). Bus travel in both countries is affordable, reliable, and comfortable—but also slow.

By Plane

Ireland is such a small country that there is very little point in flying from one end to the other. In any case, the options for internal flights seem to get more limited every year, partly because of improved roads and faster rail journey times. **Aer Lingus Regional** (www.aerarann.com; © **081/836-5000**), a joint operation between the national carrier and the smaller **Aer Arann,** still runs a couple of flights daily between Dublin and Kerry. The British budget airline **Flybe** (www.flybe.com; © **0044/139-268-3152**) has one or two daily flights between Dublin and Donegal.

WHEN TO GO

A visit to Ireland in the summer is very different from a trip in the winter. Apart from climatic considerations, there are the issues of cost, closures, and crowds. Generally speaking, in summer, airfares, car-rental rates, and hotel prices are highest and crowds at their most intense. But the days are long (6am sunrises and 10pm sunsets), the weather is warm, and every sightseeing attraction and B&B is open. In winter, you can get rock-bottom prices on airfare and hotels. But it will rain and the wind will blow, and many rural sights and a fair proportion of the rural B&Bs and restaurants will be closed.

All things considered, we think the best time to visit is in spring and fall when the weather falls in between seasons, but you get lower-than-high-season prices and the crowds have yet to descend.

Weather

Rain is the one constant in Irish weather, although a bit of sunshine is usually just around the corner. The best of times and the worst of times are often only hours, or even minutes, apart. It can be chilly in Ireland at any time of year, so think *layers* when you pack.

Winters can be brutal, as the wind blows in off the Atlantic with numbing constancy, and strong gales are common. But deep snow is rare and temperatures rarely drop much below freezing. In fact, Ireland is a fairly temperate place: January and February bring frosts but seldom snow, and July and August are very warm but rarely hot. The Irish consider any temperature over 68°F (20°C) to be "roasting" and below 34°F (1°C) as bone-chilling. For a complete online guide to Irish weather, consult **www.ireland.com/weather.**

Average Monthly Temperatures in Dublin

	JAN	FEB	MAR	APR	MAY	JUNE	JULY	AUG	SEPT	OCT	NOV	DEC
Temp (°F)	36–46	37–48	37–49	38–52	42–57	46–62	51–66	50–65	48–62	44–56	39 49	38–47
Temp (°C)	2–8	3–9	3–9	3–11	6–14	8–17	11–19	10–18	9–17	7–13	4–9	3–8

HOLIDAYS

The Republic observes the following national holidays: New Year's Day (Jan 1); St. Patrick's Day (Mar 17); Easter Monday (variable); May Day (May 1); first Mondays in June and August (summer bank holidays); last Monday in October (autumn bank holiday); Christmas (Dec 25); and St. Stephen's Day (Dec 26). Good Friday (the Friday before Easter) is mostly observed but is not statutory.

In the North, the schedule of holidays is the same as in the Republic, with some exceptions: The North's summer bank holidays fall on the last Monday of May and August; the Battle of the Boyne is celebrated on Orangeman's Day (July 12); and Boxing Day (Dec 26) follows Christmas.

In both Ireland and Northern Ireland, holidays that fall on weekends are celebrated the following Monday.

SPECIAL INTEREST TRIPS & TOURS

Organized Tours

There seems to be a limitless array of organized tours in Ireland, from Ghost Tours of Dublin to trips to the Aran Islands from Galway to horseback rides through the Burren. Some of the best of the best are noted here.

Dublin Bus (www.dublinsightseeing.ie; ℂ **01/703-3028**) runs a good range of tours in Dublin and the southeast. They include a North Coast and Castle Tour, a South Coast and Gardens tour, as well as the extremely popular Ghost Bus. Most tours cost about €30.

Irish City Tours (www.irishcitytours.com; ℂ **01/898-0700**) run hop-on, hop-off tours of Dublin and Belfast in addition to several day trips from Dublin. The destinations covered include **Powerscourt** (p. 87), the **Cliffs of Moher** (p. 160), and the **Giant's Causeway** (p. 224). Prices range from about €30 to €65.

A number of smaller tour companies are run by locals who lead excellent excursions to various regions. **Mary Gibbons Tours** (www.newgrangetours.com;

© **01/283-9973**) leads absorbing, in-depth tours from Dublin to Newgrange and the Hill of Tara. And in Belfast, don't miss the extraordinary **Black Taxi Tours** (www. belfasttours.com; *©* **028/9064-2264**) that take you through the areas where the Troubles had the most impact and explain it all in compassionate, firsthand terms. See p. 213 for details.

Package Tours

Package tours are simply a way to buy the airfare, accommodations, and other elements of your trip (such as car rentals, airport transfers, and even activities) at the same time and often at discounted prices.

One good source for package deals of all kinds is the airlines themselves. Most major airlines offer air/land packages, with surprisingly cheap hotel deals. Several big online travel agencies—such as **Expedia** (www.expedia.com), **Travelocity** (www. travelocity.com), **Orbitz** (www.orbitz.com), and **Lastminute** (www.lastminute. com)—also do a brisk business in packages.

Fully escorted tours are where a travel company takes care of absolutely everything, including airfare, hotels, meals, tours, admission costs, and local transportation. Although we hope this book will help you to plan your trip independently and safely, many travelers still prefer the convenience and peace of mind that a fully escorted tour offers. They are particularly good for people with limited mobility. On the downside, you'll have little opportunity for serendipitous interactions with locals. The tours can be jam-packed with activities, leaving little room for individual sightseeing, whim, or adventure. Plus they often focus on heavily trafficked sites, so you miss out on many lesser-known gems.

One highly recommended Irish company is **C.I.E. Tours** (www.cietours.com; *©* **020/8638-0715**). They offer fully escorted tours, help organize self-guided tours, and will even arrange individual, chauffeur-driven tours. Another, **Hidden Ireland Tours** (www.hiddenirelandtours.com; *©* **087/221-4002**), specializes in more off-the-beaten-path tours of Kerry, Galway, and Donegal.

A good company for travelers from the U.S. and Canada is **Authentic Ireland** (www.authenticireland.com; *©* **888/771-8350** or 065/293-3088). In addition to escorted, self-guided, and private tours, their range covers themed tours such as castle and golfing vacations.

Those wanting to combine their trip with some serious learning opportunities might be interested in the **International Summer School** program at the National University of Ireland, Galway (www.nuigalway.ie/international-summer-school; *©* 091/495-442).

OUTDOOR ACTIVITIES A TO Z

ADVENTURE CENTERS All manner of land- and water-based activities can be undertaken at the **Killary Adventure Company** in Leenane, Co. Galway (www. killary.com; *©* **095/43411**). From bungee jumping, hill walking, and clay-pigeon shooting to kayaking, windsurfing, waterskiing, and gorge walking, there's pretty much nothing you can't do. Also recommended is the **Atlantic Adventure Centre** in Lecanvey near Westport (www.atlanticadventurecentre.com; *©* **098/64806**). They specialize in water-based fun like canoeing and kayaking that's carried out at the blue flag beaches of Old Head, Bertra, and Carramore.

BIRD WATCHING One of the best sources of information is the **Irish Birding** home page (www.irishbirding.com) featuring links on birding events, sites, and news.

Another excellent resource is **Birdwatch Ireland** (www.birdwatchireland.ie), an organization devoted to bird conservation in the Republic of Ireland. An equivalent organization in Northern Ireland is the **Royal Society for the Protection of Birds** (www.rspb.org.uk/nireland).

CYCLING If you're booking from the United States, consider **Backroads** (www. backroads.com; ✆ **800/GO-ACTIVE** [462-2848] or ✆ 510/527-1555) and **VBT** (www.vbt.com; ✆ **800/BIKE-TOUR** [245-3868]). Both are well-regarded companies offering all-inclusive bicycle trips in Ireland. Included are bikes, gear, luggage transportation via a support van, tasty food, and accommodations in local inns and hotels of character—everything bundled into one price. If you want your cycling trip to be orchestrated and outfitted by affable local experts, consider **Irish Cycling Safaris** (www.cyclingsafaris.com; ✆ **01/260-0749**).

DIVING The **Irish Underwater Council (CFT,** or **Comhairle Fo-Thuinn;** www. diving.ie; ✆ **01/284-4601**) is an association of more than 70 Irish diving clubs. Its website lists information on diving and snorkeling, dive centers, and dive hotels (no pun intended) throughout the Republic and publishes the *CFT Guide to Dive Sites* and other information on exploring the Emerald Isle's blue waters. The **UK Diving** website, www.ukdiving.co.uk, features information on diving in the North, including an excellent wreck database you can access either through a conventional listing or by pinpointing on a map. Irish dive centers and schools include **Discover Scuba** (www. discoverscuba.ie; ✆ **086/382-2165**); **Baltimore Diving Centre,** Baltimore, County Cork (www.baltimorediving.com; ✆ **028/20300**); and **Scubadive West,** Renvyle, County Galway (www.scubadivewest.com; ✆ **095/43922**).

FISHING Many top-tier hotels in the countryside have exclusive access to lakes and ponds and will rent boats, gear, and *ghillies* (fishing guides) to their guests. Over a dozen such hotels have gotten together to form the **Great Fishing Houses of Ireland** (www.irelandfishing.com). Their website also lists fishing schools.

GOLF A couple of U.S. tour operators specialize in travel package golf tours to Ireland. Among them are **Golf International** (www.golfinternational.com; ✆ **800/833-1389** or 212/986-9176 in the U.S.); and **Wide World of Golf** (www.wideworldofgolf. com; ✆ **800/214-4653**).

HORSEBACK RIDING **Equestrian Holidays Ireland** (www.ehi.ie) is a collection of riding centers, each registered with the Association of Irish Riding Establishments, offering a wide variety of accommodations and holiday riding experiences. EHI properties include **Killarney Riding Stables** (Ballydowney, Co. Kerry; www.killarney-riding-stables.com; ✆ **064/663-1686**) and **Connemara Coast Trails** (Loughrea, Co. Galway; www.connemara-trails.com; ✆ **091/843-968**).

KAYAKING For a rich source of information about kayaking in Ireland, visit the **Irish Canoe Union** website (www.canoe.ie). Courses and day trips for all levels of experience are available from **Deep Blue Sea Kayaking** (www.deepblueseakayaking. com; ✆ **086/820-5627**) and **Shearwater Sea Kayaking** (www.shearwaterseakayaking.ie; ✆ **086/836-8736** for Sean Price or **087/988-5658** for Eileen Murphy).

SAILING Sailing schools hold courses for sailors at all levels of experience and sometimes offer day sailing as well. Ireland also has scores of yacht and sailing clubs along the coast and lakes. The best sources for information are Discover Ireland (www.discoverireland.ie) and the **Irish Sailing Association** (www.sailing.ie; ✆ **01/280-0239**).

WALKING   An excellent online resource with plenty of recommended walks is **www.gowalkingireland.com.** Before leaving home, you can order maps and guidebooks, including details of available accommodations en route, from **East West Mapping** (www.eastwestmapping.ie; 𝄐 **053/937-7835**). For a full walking holiday package in the southwest, contact **SouthWest Walks Ireland** (www.southwestwalksireland.com; 𝄐 **066/718-6181**). North American readers can also consult **Backroads** (www.backroads.com; 𝄐 **800/GO-ACTIVE** [462-2848]).

WINDSURFING   Try the following centers for equipment rental and lessons: the **Surfdock Centre** (Grand Canal Dock Yard, Ringsend, Dublin, Co. Dublin; www.surfdock.ie; 𝄐 **01/668-3945**); the **Dunmore East Adventure Centre** (Dunmore East, Co. Waterford; www.dunmoreadventure.com; 𝄐 **051/383-783**); **Oysterhaven Windsurfing Centre** (Oysterhaven, Kinsale, Co. Cork; www.oysterhaven.com; 𝄐 **021/477-0738**); and **Craigavon Watersports** (1 Lake Rd., Co. Armagh; www.craigavonactivity.org; 𝄐 **028/3834-2669**).

RESPONSIBLE TRAVEL

Responsible tourism is conscientious travel. It means being careful with the environments you explore and respecting the communities you visit. Two overlapping components of responsible travel are **ecotourism** and **ethical tourism.** The **International Ecotourism Society (TIES)** defines ecotourism as responsible travel to natural areas that conserves the environment and improves the well-being of local people. TIES suggests that ecotourists follow these principles:

o Minimize environmental impact.
o Build environmental and cultural awareness and respect.
o Provide positive experiences for both visitors and hosts.
o Provide direct financial benefits for conservation and for local people.
o Raise sensitivity to host countries' political, environmental, and social climates.
o Support international human rights and labor agreements.

You can find some eco-friendly travel tips and statistics, as well as touring companies and associations—listed by destination under "Travel Choice"—at the **TIES** website, **www.ecotourism.org**).

In the U.K., **Tourism Concern** (www.tourismconcern.org.uk) works to reduce social and environmental problems connected to tourism.

Volunteer travel has become increasingly popular among those who want to venture beyond the standard group-tour experience to learn languages, interact with locals, and make a positive difference while on vacation. Volunteer travel usually doesn't require special skills—just the willingness to work hard—and programs vary in length from a few days to a number of weeks. Some programs provide free housing and food, but many require volunteers to pay for travel expenses, which can add up quickly. For general info on volunteer travel, visit **www.volunteerabroad.org** and **www.idealist.org.**

FAST FACTS: IRELAND

Area Codes   Area codes in Ireland range from one number (the Dublin area code is "1") to three. Area codes are included in all listings in this guide. Within Ireland, you dial 0 before the area code. Outside of Ireland, however, you do not dial 0 before the area code.

Business Hours **Banks** are generally open 10am to 4pm Monday to Wednesday and Friday and 10am to 5pm on Thursday. Post offices (also known as An Post) are generally open from 9am to 5:30pm Monday to Friday and 9am to 1:30pm on Saturday. Some take an hour for lunch from 1 to 2pm, and small or rural branches may close on Saturday. **Museums and sights** are generally open 10am to 5pm Tuesday to Saturday and 2 to 5pm on Sunday. **Shops** generally open 9am to 6pm Monday to Saturday with late opening on Thursday until 7 or 8pm. Some shops in larger towns and cities will also open on Sundays (typically from late morning to late afternoon). Major shops, such as department stores, often stay open much later than other businesses.

Car Rental See "Getting Around: By Car" earlier in this chapter and the individual listings under "Fast Facts" in the other chapters in this book.

Disabled Travelers For disabled travelers, Ireland is a mixed bag. Its modern buildings and cities are generally accessible, but many of its buildings are historic, and those often lack wheelchair access. Trains can be accessed by wheelchairs but only with assistance. If you plan to travel by train in Ireland, be sure to check out Iarnród Éireann's website (www.irishrail.ie), which

includes services for travelers with disabilities. A detailed guide can be found online at **www.irishrail.ie/ travel-information/ disabled-access.**

If you're conducting research prior to your trip, one of the best Irish-based online resources is **www. disability.ie.**

For advice on travel to Northern Ireland, contact **Disability Action** (www. disabilityaction.org; ✆ **028/9029-7880**). The Northern Ireland Tourist Board also publishes a helpful annual *Information Guide to Accessible Accommodation*, available from any of its offices worldwide.

Finding accessible lodging can be tricky in Ireland. Many of the buildings here are hundreds of years old, and older hotels, small guesthouses, and landmark buildings still have steps outside and in. The rule of thumb should be: Never assume that a B&B, hotel, or restaurant has accessible facilities; ask about your requirements before booking. Where there are serious mobility issues with a property, we've tried to mention them in this book.

Doctors Health care in Ireland is comparable to that in other European nations. In the Irish system, private doctors and hospitals provide care and patients purchase healthcare insurance. See the individual listings under "Fast Facts" in the other chapters of this book.

Electricity The Irish electric system operates on 220 volts with a large plug bearing three rectangular prongs. The Northern Irish system operates on 250 volts with a similar plug. To use standard American 110-volt appliances, you'll need both a transformer and a plug adapter. Most new laptops have built-in transformers, but some do not, so beware.

Embassies & Consulates The **American Embassy** is at 42 Elgin Rd., Ballsbridge, Dublin 4 (dublin.usembassy. gov; ✆ **01/668-8777**); the **Canadian Embassy** is at 7–8 Wilton Terrace, Third Floor, Dublin 2 (www. canadainternational.gc.ca/ ireland-irlande; ✆ **01/234-4000**); the **British Embassy** is at 29 Merrion Rd., Dublin 2 (www.gov.uk/government/ world/organisations/british-embassy-dublin; ✆ **01/205-3700**); and the **Australian Embassy** is at Fitzwilton House, Seventh Floor, Wilton Terrace, Dublin 2 (www.ireland.embassy.gov. au; ✆ **01/664-5300**). In addition, there is an **American Consulate** at Danesfort House, 223 Stranmillis Rd., Belfast BT9 5GR (belfast.usconsulate. gov; ✆ **028/9038-6100**).

Emergencies For the **Garda (police),** fire, ambulance, or other emergencies, dial ✆ **999.**

Internet & Wi-Fi Wi-Fi is widespread in Irish hotels and B&Bs, even in rural areas. It's not universal, however; in this book we always note in the listings if Wi-Fi is available. Most B&Bs and smaller hotels provide it free, but larger hotels sometimes charge for access.

Language Ireland has two official languages: English and Gaelic (which is also known as Irish). All native Irish can speak English. Gaelic is growing in popularity, and there is a strong national movement to preserve and expand the language. Areas of the country where Gaelic is protected and promoted are known as the **Gaeltacht** and include Donegal, Galway, and parts of Kerry. In these regions signs are in Gaelic only (no English translation is provided). As Gaelic is a complex and ancient language that you will not be able to figure out on your own, don't hesitate to ask for help (in English) if you get lost—despite the government's best efforts, everybody in the Gaeltacht regions speaks English.

LGBT Travelers Ireland has come a long way since homosexuality was legalized in 1993 (1982 in the North), but gay and lesbian visitors should be aware that this is still a conservative country. Cities like Dublin and Galway are more liberal in their attitudes (particularly among the younger generation), and discrimination on the basis of sexuality is illegal throughout Ireland. Nonetheless, it's advisable to proceed with caution when travelling in rural areas. Recommended

websites for gay and lesbian travelers include **Gay Ireland** (www.gay-ireland. com) and **Outhouse** (www. outhouse.ie).

Lost Property If your passport is lost or stolen, contact your country's embassy immediately. Be sure to tell all of your credit card companies the minute you discover that your wallet is gone and file a report at the nearest police station.

Mail In Ireland, mailboxes are painted green with the word POST on top. In Northern Ireland, they usually look the same but are painted red with a royal coat of arms symbol. From the Republic, an airmail letter or postcard to any other part of the world, not exceeding 50 grams, costs €.90. From Northern Ireland to Europe, airmail letters not exceeding 20 grams cost £.97; to the rest of the world it's £1.28.

Money The Republic of Ireland uses the single European currency known as the **euro** (€). Euro notes come in denominations of €5, €10, €20, €50, €100, €200, and €500. The euro is divided into 100 cents; coins come in denominations of €2, €1, 50¢, 20¢, 10¢, 5¢, 2¢, and 1¢. As part of the United Kingdom, Northern Ireland uses the British **pound sterling** (£). The British pound is not accepted in the Republic, and the euro is not accepted in the North—if you're traveling in both parts of Ireland you'll need some of both

currencies, although shops on the border tend to accept both, as do some of the bigger tourist attractions in the North. For those traveling between Great Britain and Northern Ireland, although the pounds issued in Northern Ireland are legal tender in Great Britain and vice versa, the paper money actually *looks* different, and you may find that cabdrivers and small business owners in the North won't accept bills issued in Great Britain. In that case, you can change the money into locally issued versions at any large central bank, free of charge.

The British currency used in Northern Ireland has notes in denominations of £5, £10, £20, £50, and £100. Coins are issued in £2, £1, 50p, 20p, 10p, 5p, 2p, and 1p denominations.

Note for all international travelers: The values of most currencies have been fluctuating a great deal lately, so it is best to begin checking exchange rates well in advance of your visit to get a feel for where they will stand for your trip.

The easiest and best way to get cash away from home is from an ATM (automated teller machine), sometimes referred to as a "cash machine" or a "cashpoint." The **Cirrus** and **PLUS** ATM networks span the globe; look at the back of your bankcard to see which network you're on. Be sure you know your personal identification number (PIN) and daily withdrawal limit before you depart.

Passports See "Embassies & Consulates" above for who to contact if you lose your passport while traveling in Ireland.

Pharmacies Drugstores are called "chemists" and are found in every city, town, and most villages of any size. See the individual listings under "Fast Facts" in the other chapters of this book.

Police In the Republic of Ireland, a law enforcement officer is called a **Garda,** a member of the *Garda Síochána* ("Guardian of the Peace"); in the plural, it's **Gardaí** (pronounced *Gar-dee*) or simply "the Guards." Dial ⓒ **999** to reach the Gardaí in an emergency. Except for special detachments, Irish police are unarmed and wear dark blue uniforms. In Northern Ireland you can also reach the police by dialing ⓒ **999.**

Safety By U.S. standards, Ireland is very safe, but, particularly in the cities, it's not safe enough to warrant carelessness. Be wary of the usual tourists' plagues: pickpockets, purse snatchers, and car thieves. Most advice is standard for travel anywhere. Do not leave cars unlocked or cameras and other expensive equipment unattended. Ask at your hotel which areas are safe and which are not. Take a taxi back to your hotel if you're out after about 11pm.

In Northern Ireland, safety has to be a somewhat greater concern, due

to the long-running political tensions there. Violence is no longer commonplace; however, occasional flare-ups do happen, especially during the Orange marching season in the late summer. Still, visitors rarely have problems with this since they are simply not the targets of it. See chapter 12 for more information.

Senior Travel Seniors are sometimes called "O.A.P.'s" in Ireland (it rather unfortunately stands for "Old Age Pensioners"). People over the age of 60 often qualify for reduced admission to museums and other attractions. Always ask about an O.A.P. discount if special rates are not posted. Discover Ireland (www.discoverireland.ie) can offer advice on how to find the best discounts.

Smoking Ireland and Northern Ireland both have broad antismoking laws that ban smoking in all public places, including bars, restaurants, and hotel lobbies. However, most restaurants and pubs have covered outdoor smoking areas.

Taxes As in many European countries, sales tax is VAT (value-added tax) and is often already included in the price quoted to you or shown on price tags. In the Republic, VAT rates vary—for hotels, restaurants, and car rentals, it is 13.5%; for souvenirs and gifts, it is 23%. In Northern Ireland, the VAT is 20% across the board. VAT charged on services such as hotel stays, meals, car

rentals, and entertainment cannot be refunded to visitors, but the VAT on products such as souvenirs is refundable.

Telephones In the Republic, the telephone system is known as Eircom; in Northern Ireland, it's BT (British Telecom). Every effort has been made to ensure that the numbers and information in this guide are accurate at the time of writing. **Overseas calls** from Ireland can be quite costly, whether you use a local phone card or your own calling card.

To call Ireland from home:

1. **Dial the international access code:** 011 from the U.S., 00 from the U.K., 0011 from Australia, or 0170 from New Zealand.

2. **Dial the country code:** 353 for the Republic, 44 for the North.

3. **Dial the local number,** remembering to omit the initial 0, which is for use only within Ireland (for example, to call the County Kerry number 066/12345 from the United States, you'd dial 011-353-66/12345).

To make international calls: First dial 00 and then the country code (U.S. or Canada 1, U.K. 44, Australia 61, New Zealand 64). Next you dial the area code and local number. For example, to call the U.S. number 212/000-0000 you'd dial ⓒ 00-1-212/000-0000. The toll-free international access code for AT&T is ⓒ 1-800-550-000; for Sprint, it's

C 1-800-552001; and for MCI, it's *C* 1-800-551-001.

To make local calls: To dial a local number within an area code, drop the initial 0. To dial a number within Ireland but in a different area code, use the initial 0. As in many parts of the world, phone booths are slowly disappearing; however, you will still find them. Calls from a phone booth usually require coin payment, but at some you need a calling card (in the Republic) or phone card (in the North). Both are prepaid computerized cards that you insert into the phone instead of coins. They can be purchased in post offices, grocery stores, and shops (such as newsstands).

Time   Ireland follows Greenwich Mean Time (1 hr. earlier than Central European Time) from November to March, and British Summer Time (the same as Central European Time) from April to October. Ireland is 5 hours ahead of the eastern United States. Ireland's latitude makes for longer days and shorter nights in the summer and the reverse in the winter. In June, the sun doesn't fully set until around 11pm, but in December, it is dark by 4pm.

Tipping   For taxi drivers, hairdressers, and other providers of service, tip an average of 10 to 15%. For restaurants, the policy is usually printed on the menu—either a gratuity of 10 to 15% is automatically added to your bill, or it's left up to you. As a rule, bartenders do not expect a tip, except when table service is provided.

Toilets   Public toilets are usually simply called "toilets" or are marked with international symbols. In the Republic of Ireland, some of the older ones carry the Gaelic words FIR (men) and MNA (women). Check out malls and shopping centers for some of the newest and best-kept bathrooms in the country. Free restrooms are available to customers of sightseeing attractions, museums, hotels, restaurants, pubs, shops, and theaters. Many of the newer gas stations (called "petrol stations" in Ireland) have public toilets, and a few even have baby-changing facilities.

Visas   Citizens of the United States, Canada, Australia, and New Zealand entering the Republic of Ireland or Northern Ireland for a stay of up to 3 months do not need a visa, but a valid **passport** is required.

For citizens of the United Kingdom, when traveling on flights originating in Britain, the same rules apply as they would for travel to any other member state of the European Union (E.U.).

Water   Tap water throughout the island of Ireland is generally safe. However, some areas in the west of Ireland have been battling with out-of-date water-purification systems. Always carry a large bottle of water with you.

Wi-Fi   See "Internet & Wi-Fi" above.

Women Travelers
Women should expect few if any problems traveling in Ireland. Women are accepted traveling alone or in groups in virtually every environment, and long gone are the days when women were expected to order half-pints of beer in pubs, while men were allowed to order the bigger, more cost-effective pints of ale. In fact, the only time you're likely to attract any attention at all is if you eat alone in a restaurant at night—a sight that is still relatively uncommon in Ireland outside of the major cities. Even then, you won't be hassled.

If you drink in a pub on your own, though, expect all kinds of attention, as a woman drinking alone is still considered to be on the market—even if she's reading a book, talking on her cellphone to her fiancé, or doing a crossword puzzle. So be prepared to fend them off. Irish men almost always respond well to polite rejection, though.

In cities, as ever, take a cab home at night and follow all the usual advice of caution you get when you travel anywhere. Essentially, don't do anything in Ireland that you wouldn't do at home.

Index

General Index